The Art of Micro Design

This book is due for return on or before the last date shown below.

24. NOV 87.		
16. FEB 88.		
13. NOV. 1990		
~~26. NOV. 1990~~		
9 DEC 1991		
10 DEC 1993		
08 DEC 1992		

Don Gresswell Ltd., London, N.21 Cat. No. 1207

The Art of Micro Design

A. A. Berk, BSc, PhD

Newnes Technical Books

Newnes Technical Books
is an imprint of the Butterworth Group
which has principal offices in
London, Boston, Durban, Singapore, Sydney, Toronto, Wellington

First published 1984

British Library Cataloguing in Publication Data
Berk, A. A.
The art of micro design.
1. Microprocessors 2. Logic design
I. Title
621.3819'58'35 TK7895.M5

ISBN 0-408-01403-2

Library of Congress Cataloguing in Publication Data
Berk, A. A.
The art of micro design.
Bibliography: p.
Includes index.
1. Microprocessors—Design and construction.
I. Title.
TK7895.M5B45 1984 001.64 83-19405
ISBN 0-408-01403-2

Typeset by Butler & Tanner Ltd, Frome and London
Printed and bound by Thomson Litho Ltd, East Kilbride, Scotland

Preface

The aim of this book is to supply practical and theoretical assistance to those engineers and enthusiasts who wish to gain a knowledge of microprocessor system design. The book covers all the essential areas of 8-bit microprocessor systems and their peripheral circuits, and considers three typical MPUs in some detail. Very little actual electronics is required, and the topics are described in sufficient depth to allow the reader to begin immediate design. The book is set out in a heuristic manner, to allow the reader to build his knowledge by stages. Much reference and sample material is included, to allow an understanding of the text without the need for external reference. However, the material is described in a manner which allows the serious designer to transfer to manufacturers' data sheets without the usual 'jargon shock' which this can entail.

The text has been designed to be as up-to-date as possible in this remarkable era of almost daily advances in the technology. There are many chips and devices in wide use today which have been superseded by the latest advances. This book tends to describe these latest advances, rather than the presently more common devices. There are two reasons for this: the first is lack of space; the second is that anyone just starting, or simply updating their knowledge, should not be considering an obsolete alternative.

Engineers are faced, in real life, with the problem of controlling (in the broadest sense) 'outside world' activities by designing black boxes with a number of specified characteristics. In times gone by, they would solve such problems by invoking a complex net of gears, cogs and cams. Indeed, the majority of the wealth of our Western civilisation arises from the ingenious mechanical engineering of the last hundred years. However, this method of controlling the environment has given way to a subservience to electronic devices.

The specific path for the design of a controlling machine depends, of course, upon the medium chosen for its fulfilment: for instance, whether to employ mechanics entirely, hydraulics combined with pneumatic logic, transistors and stepper motors, etc. A mechanical approach would start with an engineering drawing phase, followed perhaps by some experimentation and finally a prototype. An electronic approach could start with a logic diagram, followed by a circuit which would fulfil the logic, some experimentation and a prototype.

This book is concerned with the matter of building on the reader's understanding of basic electronic logic to provide him or her with the necessary data to conceive of a design path for the above problems using microprocessors. The general path is similar to the above examples, but the advantages of using state-of-the-art devices is exemplified by considering the following.

Imagine that a large and complex manufacturing machine, with dozens of limit switches and solenoid operated valves, requires a sequential controller. There are several activities in the sequencing of the machine's operations which must overlap in real time, and in addition an operator's front panel must be updated and read for operator input continuously. This problem can be, and indeed traditionally is, solved using relays. Any engineer knows the simplicity of using relays; there is no feedback from the items being controlled, and several channels can be switched simultaneously. The problem lies in two main areas—initial design, which may be convoluted and involved as well as being a compromise, and reliability. This leaves aside the problem of speed, which, surprisingly, is often unimportant. Of course, anything which can be done with relays can be designed instead with transistors and latterly with logic integrated circuits. Imagine now that a 'super design-aid' exists. It accepts the entire problem as a set of commands, and displays it in simulation, by some means. As you discover flaws in the logic, it allows you to modify and redesign at will—instantly. When you are satisfied, it ejects a couple of ICs from a slot in its front panel. You plug these into a standard printed circuit board, and the controller, with all its complexity, is complete and ready to go.

A major aim of this book is to provide the reader with information upon the design of standardised hardware which, by using a development system, may be turned into any type of electronic controller, from one controlling a washing machine to the more complex ones of the personal and business computers now flooding the market. The microprocessor provides the most general type of control, and can drive large computing installations vying with the largest mainframe computers.

As to the level of knowledge necessary for an understanding of the book, a familiarity with the function of the simpler logic gates and devices is assumed. In addition, from time to time, some general electronic theory is referred to; however, very little is needed, and none is so central that the text is incomprehensible without it. One important building block for an understanding of all that follows is a familiarity with binary and hexadecimal notation. However, this is covered in an appendix, and can be assimilated at will if required. Timing diagrams are presented when required, and no attempt is made to simplify any of the concepts involved to the point where the reader is given insufficient information to use the concepts introduced in his own designs.

Finally, I am indebted to numerous people who have encouraged me over the years, and I should like to mention two in particular. First, Mr J.B. Berk BA, my father, whose deep understanding of science and engineering has led me to appreciate technology in general. In addition, he has my gratitude for his painstaking technical reading of the text, and many excellent suggestions for its improvement. Second, I should like to extend my thanks to Mrs E.A. Berk BSc, MSc, PGCE, my wife, for her continuous encouragement and her kind perseverance with my illustrations, which she redrew in order to make them legible for the publisher's draughtsmen.

A.A.B.

Contents

1

Basic microprocessor systems

This chapter introduces the heart of the microcomputer and its 'system' attributes. The major blocks in an MPU system are described, along with important items of jargon which the reader will encounter continually while examining MPUs and their associated peripherals. The concepts of bus structure, input and output, and MPU internal registers are also introduced. One of the most central ideas in an understanding of how an MPU works is the reset function; this gives an idea of the way in which a system is started from scratch. Finally, addressing is treated in detail to allow the reader to consider the necessary steps for designing a system.

Note that throughout the text a logic 0 is at zero volts, and a logic 1 is at +5 volts. In addition, when electronic lines are used to enable blocks of logic, if the 'enabled' state is achieved by setting the line to a zero the line is said to be 'active low', and is shown on the diagrams by placing a bar over the labels for the lines.

Introduction

The term microprocessor unit (MPU) refers to an integrated circuit (IC). This IC is normally in the position of controlling a system of ICs and other peripheral devices. It is usual to refer to the system as a 'microcomputer'. These terms are broad and often used differently, as would be expected in an embryonic subject where jargon arises naturally from common usage. The trend today is to pack more and more on the IC chip, and there is now a plethora of complete systems containing MPU, memory and even I/O (input/output lines) on a single chip. These chips are not referred to as MPUs, but rather as 'single-chip microcomputers'. Some would further distinguish a subset of microcomputers called controllers, i.e. microcomputers dedicated to a given control function of a specific machine or system. In addition, some use the term 'computer' for large micro installations, probably to allay any implication of small size and capability. However, it is more and more becoming recognized that a system or network of fast micros is considerably more attractive than a single mini or mainframe installation. The connotation of inferiority will, no doubt, drop away with time.

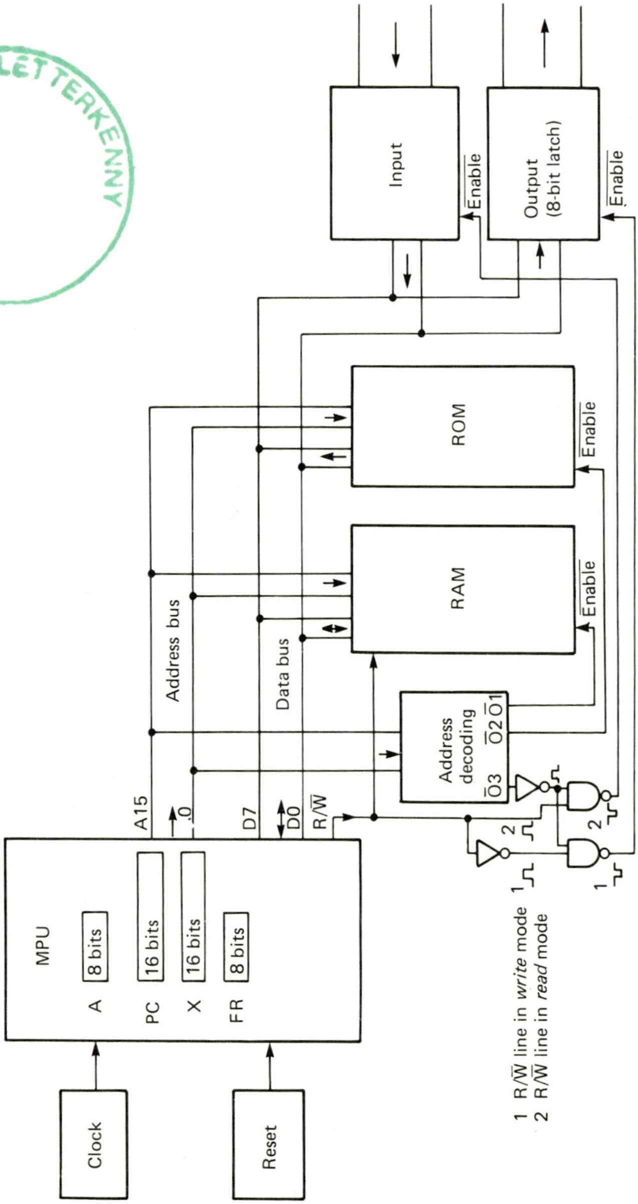

Fig. 1.1 A simple MPU system

Three typical MPUs are described in technical detail in Appendix 4, and this should be scanned very briefly at this point to give the reader a mental picture of the device which is central to the descriptions within this book. The concepts and terms found in that appendix will become more and more familiar as the text progresses. However, a quick look at the appendix will serve to illustrate that, no matter how complex the matters under discussion may turn out to be, when all is said and done an MPU is nothing more than a small package with a number of electrical wires attached to it!

A basic microcomputer system

The example, given in the preface, of an ideal design method using a 'super design-aid' exemplifies one of the primary *raisons d'être* of the MPU concept. The idea is to dispense with the necessity of large grids of logic devices such as transistors or ICs, and collect together all the common attributes of a control system under the auspices of just one chip (IC). The obvious danger is that this super-controller will contain so many functions, in order to encompass the entire field, that very few are used in any one area. This appears to be wasteful. However, the major lesson of the past decade is that the opposite is true. Much time and money is saved by providing the human designer with a few extremely powerful devices which have the potential to be adapted to perform any class of 'miracle'. The waste of functions on the chip becomes irrelevant. The designer only has to learn how to use a few devices, and theoretically he can bring out just those attributes needed for each application.

The MPU is a device having nothing more than the capacity for following instructions. It is capable, once started, of scanning through areas of electronic memory, where a set of instructions is stored as bit patterns, and executing these instructions one by one.

The above statement begs a large number of questions, some of which can be explained with reference to Figure 1.1. This is a sketch of a basic MPU system incorporating eight essential elements. These are listed below with some explanation, followed by a certain amount of important functional detail.

MPU

The MPU is at the centre of the system, and is shown with some internal memory, termed 'registers'. The A and FR registers have eight bits of storage each, and the X register has sixteen, as has the

PC. These registers are entirely internal to the MPU, and the instructions which it executes operate on these registers. In fact, the exact state of the MPU at any time can be considered as nothing more than the exact state of the registers. If the MPU is to be interrupted to perform some other task for a time, the registers only have to be stored verbatim before the interruption, and reinstated after, and the MPU continues as if nothing had happened. Of course the outside world, via the input and output (I/O) sections, will have changed, being affected by the changing state of the whole system.

Clock

The 'clock' is simply a square-wave oscillator. Its frequency determines the speed with which the processing occurs. However, one should not fall into the trap of comparing the speeds of different MPUs by the frequency of their clocks. The Zilog Z80 MPU, running at a frequency of 2 MHz, processes instructions at a comparable speed to a Motorola M6800 running at 1 MHz. This is based upon the fact that typically the Z80 requires at least four of its clock cycles to perform an instruction, while the 6800 only requires two. Some MPUs require more than one square-wave clock, but this type of requirement is dying out with more sophisticated designs.

Reset

The 'reset' block is a piece of circuitry which pulls the 'reset' pin of the MPU to a reset level (typically 'zero') whenever the processor is to be restarted from scratch in its attempts to execute a set of steps. When a reset is issued, the processor performs a given set of operations automatically. The system designer is meant to use this fact to ensure that the program he wishes the MPU to execute is duly started. This will be referred to a little later. For the moment, think of the reset block as simply a pushbutton which connects the reset pin of the MPU to ground when it is pressed. Otherwise the pin is held at logic 1 (+5 volt maximum).

RAM

The block labelled 'RAM' stands for random access memory. The name implies, historically, not just that the memory locations within that block are accessible in a random sequence, but also that this block contains memory which is both readable and changeable. The term RAM, in industry standard usage, also implies that the memory is 'volatile'—i.e. switching off power to the RAM chips causes them to lose their contents. Upon power-on, a random selection of bits normally resides within the memory.

ROM

The other memory block is labelled 'ROM'—a term treated in full later. The letters stand for read only memory. The implication is that this type of memory cannot be altered within a system during normal processing. A program must be stored on this type of chip under certain special conditions, normally using a specialised piece of hardware for the purpose. ROM can also be manufactured with a program formed onto the chip. ROM is generally used to store the non-volatile element of a program, which is thus immediately available for execution upon power-up.

Input

The 'input' block is used to allow the system, and the MPU in particular, to read the state of a set of lines which arise from 'outside world' events. As the binary state of these lines changes, the MPU can fetch the bits and make decisions upon their values. These lines may be used to sense the state of any form of event, from the closure of simple switches to the analogue value of a parameter such as temperature or pressure via analogue-to-digital converters. A certain degree of voltage level changing may be needed, however, before arriving at the MPU system's input block.

Output

The 'output' block is shown here as a set of latches. The MPU can set the binary value of each latched line. By this means it would be capable of providing control over anything from a set of switches to the value of a continuous parameter such as the phase angle at which a triac should switch on—via a digital-to-analogue converter.

Address decoding

The final block is of primary importance to the system designer, and in this age when all but the most complex ICs have plug-compatibility, it is perhaps this section which exercises the designer's most critical powers. To the programmer, a system is primarily a set of memory locations and an instrument for instruction execution. It is up to the 'address decoding' block to decide the exact address at which each location of memory and I/O resides. The method by which an address is specified, and exactly how memory is addressed, will be introduced shortly. Suffice it to say, as shown in the diagram, that each block of memory or I/O has an 'enable pin' (assumed to be active low, and hence labelled with a bar). The address decoding block converts the address information output by the MPU into enabling signals for each block.

Before the concepts introduced above can be brought together to describe their exact functioning, it is essential to introduce a further element of Figure 1.1, namely the 'bus' structure which connects all the blocks together.

The buses

As mentioned above, MPU systems are designed from chips which plug together in an almost standardised manner. However, the 40 pins on a typical IC package provide no small number of connections, and as these conveniently group together into bundles of functionally alike lines, it is convenient to speak of such groups as 'buses'. Thus the typically 16 lines of address, labelled A0, A1, ... A15, form the 'address bus'. Similarly, the eight lines carrying data to and from the MPU (D0, D1, ... D7) are collected together under the term 'data bus'. Notice how the labelling of these lines starts at 0. The number of lines in the data bus for any given MPU is an important parameter in the general classification of MPUs; e.g. an MPU with eight such lines is called an 'eight-bit processor'. This is an important number as it determines, as will be seen, the quantity of information which the MPU may transfer at any time to or from devices external to the MPU.

The MPU's lines not included above normally form a rather loosely grouped bundle called the 'control bus'. The control bus in Figure 1.1 consists of just one line called the 'read/write (R/W) line'. The state of this line determines the direction of data flow along the data bus. Since the MPU is controlling the system, it is clear that this signal is issued as an output line from the MPU to the rest of the system. To imply the physical states of the line, the line is labelled to show that a logic 1 on the line denotes a read into the MPU along the data bus, and a logic 0 denotes a write from the MPU to some memory location. This latter state is indicated by placing a bar over the 'W' of the label R/W. If you stick firmly to this type of convention from the beginning, reading complex circuit diagrams is made considerably easier.

As an example of the use of buses, consider the RAM introduced above. Data is stored in the RAM as a pattern of bits when four conditions occur simultaneously. First, the correct data must be presented to its data bus. Second, the address at which this data is to be stored within the RAM chip must be presented to its address lines. Third, its R/W line must be at a logic 0 (writing). To effect the storage, when these three conditions are coincident, the fourth condition is to bring the enable pin of the RAM chip down to 0. Only a short pulse is required while the other conditions are present, provided they have been present long enough to settle to their final values. The exact timings which are necessary can be determined from manufacturer's data. The exact order in which these conditions are presented varies from application to application: for instance, most microprocessors will present the address on the address bus before any other conditions are considered—order of presentation and timings are considered in detail later.

The RAM's data, stored at a given address, may be returned along its data bus when that address is re-presented to the address lines; in addition, the chip must be enabled and the R/W line must be high. The chip's data bus is thus a two-way highway, with direction decided by R/W.

As can be seen from the diagram, all the blocks are physically connected to one or more of the buses. This means that data, for instance, issued by the MPU appears at several devices at once. As for the RAM above, it is up to the MPU to place the correct bit pattern on the address bus, to alert the receiving device, at the same time as the data. The address decoding block notices which area the address refers to, and sets that block's enable low. It is then up to that block to decode the rest of the address bus's pattern to ensure that exactly one location is contacted. At the same time, as above, the R/W line signals the data direction.

A problem arises in that there is more than one integrated circuit connected to each data bus line, and many of these are capable of outputting *to* that line. The majority of ICs do not react favourably when outputs are connected together! Logic ICs always have definite logic levels (+5 volts or ground) on their outputs, and connecting them together normally causes some damage. Bus orientation therefore necessitated the invention of a method of switching the outputs of devices into a third state. While in this third state, an output must 'float' and not interfere in any way with logic levels which may be present there by virtue of system interconnection. Such devices are termed 'tri-state', and when their outputs are disabled (i.e. in this third state) they may be considered to be unplugged. It is this particular innovation which allows simple plug-compatibility between many different chips.

It is via the enable pins shown in Figure 1.1 that the third state is entered. When a device's enable pin is at a logic 1, the device is apparently unplugged from the system. As the MPU is the bus master, it never needs to enter the third state. All data which is placed on the data bus is either issued by the MPU, or is meant for the MPU. Most MPUs, however, have a control line which, when activated, will send the bus lines tri-state to allow other devices to take over the buses.

Input and output

The I/O lines in this system are configured as simple memory locations. When a set of data is sent to the 'output block' with its address placed on the address bus, the decoding enables it, and the data bits on the eight data lines are loaded into the eight-bit latch upon the falling edge of the signal on the enable line. Despite the fact that the data bus continues to change, the latch 'freezes' the state of the data bus at the instant of the falling edge, and presents that state on the output lines. It is up to the MPU to ensure that the data is present a short time, at least, before the block's enable line becomes active. The eight data bits appearing on the output pins of the latch may be used to switch on a pattern of lights, relays, triacs, etc., perhaps via transistor buffers.

The address decoding for this process, shown in Figure 1.1, has two components. One is the address decoding block itself, the other is a set of logic gates which allows the R/W line to perform the final distinction between enabling input or output. This can provide economies in decoding. In fact, the R/W line may be fed into the address decoding block itself, and separate enabling lines could issue to each I/O block. The gates are drawn with the usual convention for NAND and inverter gates. The waveforms are drawn for their active states. When 03 is low, one of the two NAND gates may be activated to produce a low on its output depending upon the state of the R/W line. Thus a 'read' by the processor to that location will automatically be routed through to the input block; similarly, a write goes to the output.

When the enable on the input block goes low, the states of the lines into that block are passed through to the data bus to allow the MPU to sample those lines directly. When the process of transfer is concluded, the input block goes back to the third state.

By the above processes, the MPU simply sits at the end of a bunch of wires called buses, and shuffles ones and zeros to and from the buses.

The MPU registers

It was necessary, for an understanding of the MPU, to introduce the above concepts. The way in which the MPU uses the data gained from, and sent to, the rest of the system can now be explained.

To return to a previous comment, the MPU's state at any time can be described entirely by the state of its registers. It will come as no surprise, therefore, to learn that the data on the data bus, and the address on the address bus, pass through these registers. In fact, when one first meets a new MPU, it is wise to begin by looking at the structure of its registers. It is here that the character of the instructions which it is able to execute may be discovered. The more powerful these instructions, the easier it is to make the MPU perform sophisticated or specialised tasks. Some MPUs have a very large number of registers, allowing for storage of many intermediate variables. An example of this is the RCA 1802. This MPU has a number of interesting attributes which make it very easy to use in small control systems. For instance, it has 32 eight-bit registers for the storage of variables, among other things. On the other hand, some MPUs have complex sets of registers dedicated to allowing certain logical and arithmetic tasks to be performed on eight- or 16-bit words with great ease. The Z80 is an example, and will be described at length.

The MPU shown in Figure 1.1 has four characteristic registers:

A register

It is through this register that the majority of data passes to and from the buses. In addition, 'A' is used as an accumulator—the results of all arithmetic and logical calculations appear in this register after execution.

PC register

PC is the register which holds the program counter. As its name implies, this register holds the current address at which the next instruction is to be found. The PC requires 16 bits, as the address bus has 16 lines, allowing for 2^{16} different bit patterns or addresses to be uniquely specified. This allows, therefore, in a typical system, 65 536 (64K) different locations to be accessed. Each location affects eight data lines, and hence each location contains one byte (eight bits) of information. As the program of instructions is executed, the PC contents are placed on the address bus by the MPU, along with a 'read' state on the R/W line in order to fetch the next instruction. The PC is then incremented automatically. Each instruction fetched in this way is placed in a further register within the MPU before being acted upon. However, this register is not accessible to the user, and hence is not shown specifically. Each instruction may consist of more than one byte, and thus the MPU may have to fetch, perhaps, three bytes of data to assemble a complete instruction before execution is performed. When the first byte of an instruction is fetched, the MPU partially decodes it to determine whether any further bytes are needed for its completion. The fetching and executing of an instruction is an important concept, and the cycles associated with this process are considered in detail in Chapter 2.

X register

This register, commonly called an index register, is typical of many currently available MPUs, and is normally used as a pointer (index) to the current location being accessed in a table of values stored in memory. There are many other uses for the X register, which contains 16 bits in order to store a complete address.

FR register

This final register is the flag register. The byte of data stored contains a number of flags (one-bit indicators) which provide such information as whether or not the result of the previous instruction yielded zero, or whether an overflow has occurred in the addition of two numbers.

It should be clear from the above that data, I/O states and instructions have rather a lot in common. They are all simply sets of bits held together in eight-bit bytes. They are all fetched into the MPU's registers in exactly the same way, and along the same buses. It is up to the MPU to ensure that these three classes of information are not confused. Instructions, for instance, are pointed to by the PC in a sequential manner, and they will remain separate as long as the programmer does not instruct the MPU to execute the contents of, say, an I/O location. However, there is no electronic reason why the latter event should not occur, and indeed one can conceive of ingenious uses of such an idea. The whole matter is in the hands of the programmer—part of the great power of the MPU.

During the execution of a program, therefore, the contents of the program counter are placed on the address bus, R/W is set to 1, data is collected and treated as part of an instruction, and the process is repeated until a complete instruction has been fetched. This is then executed, which may involve setting the accumulator (A) to some value. The next step is to fetch and execute the next instruction. This may involve sending the contents of the A register to the I/O latch, and thus switching on some solenoids or motors. The next set of instructions could involve reading the state of the input lines to view the results of the output instruction in the external devices under control. By this means, a simple closed-loop controller can be produced.

As can be seen, an MPU is a comparatively intelligent device, capable of a number of complex decision processes. These processes are themselves controlled by a program which is stored on the MPU during its manufacture. This is termed the *microprogram*, and it controls and initiates all the processes of the MPU. The microprogram is in continuous execution from the moment the power supply is switched on to the MPU. The exact workings of the microprogram are hidden from the user of the chip, except in so far as it affects the accessible registers and the electronic states of the pins on the MPU. A description of the microprograms of the MPUs introduced here is beyond the scope of this work, and only the external effects associated with the MPU will be referred to.

The final problems to be broached are: how to start the process of execution of a program written by a programmer and stored in memory, how the MPU is told where the program resides, and how the system is started from scratch. These are described in the next section.

Reset

The reset block in Figure 1.1 has been described earlier. It is through the reset pin on the MPU that processing is started. A 'reset' is said to occur when the reset pin on the MPU is brought to a low level, and then returned to its normal high state. There are many different responses to a reset, and these depend upon how the designer of the MPU in question has designed his chip. A typical reset response is described below.

When power is switched on to a system, by the very nature of electronic devices it must be assumed that the components of the system may be in any random state. This may not be entirely true in practice, but the law of averages argues strongly that this be the only safe assumption. The reset function was incorporated to allow for this precursor. Different MPUs provide different attitudes to the reset condition, and three different actions are described for MPUs introduced in Chapter 2. Here the simple response described is the one used by the Z80.

Within the microprogram of the MPU is included a small section which waits for a reset. When this occurs, all function ceases and the program counter is set to a specific stated address called the *reset address*. This has the effect of causing the MPU to begin execution of any program stored at the reset address. It is up to the system designer to ensure that the hardware is set up with this reset program resident within the system at the appropriate address. A simple method of achieving this is to ensure that there is some ROM in the system with the program starting at the reset address. If the reset address is 0000, for instance, then the ROM's address map must include the location 0000. The first instructions of a reset program would include such commands as a reset to the output latch to ensure that the devices being controlled do not suddenly switch on for no apparent reason when power is applied to the MPU. The reset block of Figure 1.1 may be automatic upon power-up, or simply implemented by a pushbutton from the MPU's reset pin to 0 volts. Upon power-up, the user would simply press the button, and the system would start. In addition, if the MPU were to enter an infinite loop by accident during normal operation, it would be perfectly normal to press the reset button. Reset may be activated at any time while the MPU is processing.

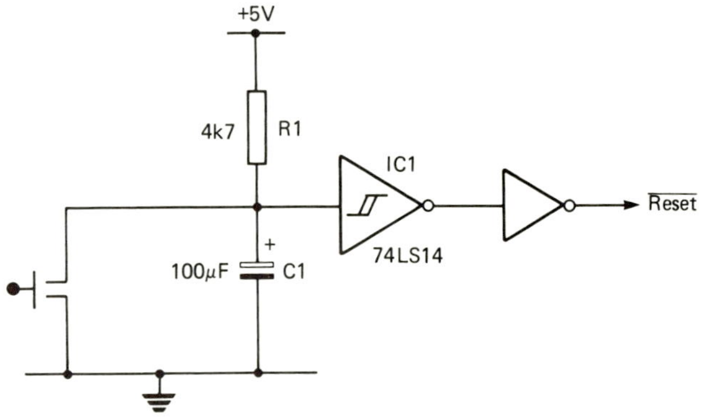

Fig.1.2 A simple reset circuit

In order to ensure that power-on does not leave the MPU, and its system, in an undefined state, it is normal to arrange a 'power-on reset' circuit. One such set-up is shown in Figure 1.2. When power is switched on, initially, C1 is discharged and the input to the Schmitt trigger (IC1) is low. This holds RESET low until C1 charges up, through R1, to a level which switches the Schmitt to its other state. It is at this point that the processor performs its dedicated reset function. The C–R constant should be chosen to ensure that power has come fully up and settled before the MPU is allowed to begin its reset sequence. The values shown seem to perform very well with standard regulated power supplies. A press button is incorporated to allow an operator to discharge the capacitor and effect a reset by hand.

Address maps and decoding design

For a full understanding of this section, a knowledge of the information presented in Appendix 1 on hexadecimal and binary notation is required.

The design of the address map for a system depends largely upon the size of the system and the number of different blocks which must be accommodated. For a small system providing the automatic control of a few parameters on a mechanical device, the minimal amount of address decoding should be chosen to keep the cost and complexity to a minimum. In a system meant to form a complete computing facility with everything from manufacturing planning to data and word processing, the address decoding will be fairly involved to take full advan-

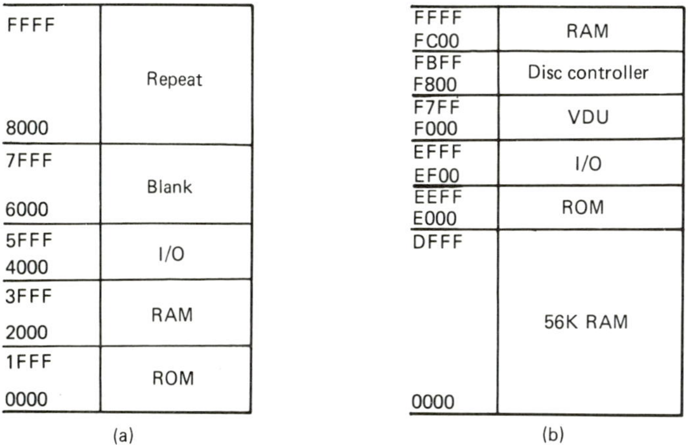

Fig. 1.3 Address maps: (a) simple controller, (b) complete computer system

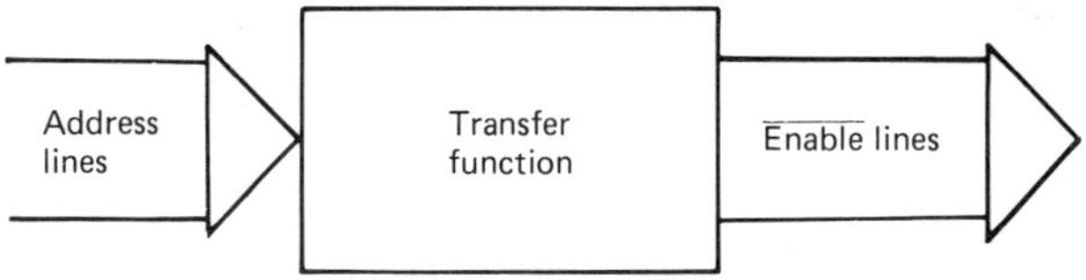

Fig. 1.4 Address decoding

tage of every memory location possible. Two address maps are given as examples of these two extremes along with a solution to the design problems; see Figure 1.3. The address decoding described assumes that the system is a single-board system in both cases. In fact, the larger system may well reside on a number of boards, and the address decoding will thus be distributed over these boards. The principles described, however, apply equally well.

Figure 1.3(a) shows a possible map for the simple controller, and 1.3(b) shows the larger system, with a large number of peripheral devices, each of which must be uniquely addressed.

To understand the type of hardware which is used to provide the necessary enable lines for a number of blocks, consider Figure 1.4. This condenses the problem into its basic form. The patterns of bits on the address bus are converted by a static transfer function into zeros (conventionally) on a number of enable lines—one for each device to be addressed. This transfer function may be realised in a number of ways. Figure 1.5 shows a simple element in such a transfer function. Here, the pattern '1110' (E in hex) on the upper four address lines (in the address bus) places '1111' on the inputs of a NAND gate, which thus gives a zero on its output as an enabling command. Any address having this pattern (E in hex) of bits in its most significant hex digit, therefore, enables this line. Thus, for example, the addresses E056 or EA7F on the address bus would cause this result. Simple logic gates are often used in minimal systems to provide address decoding. However, with faster and faster processor speeds, it is essential to choose a

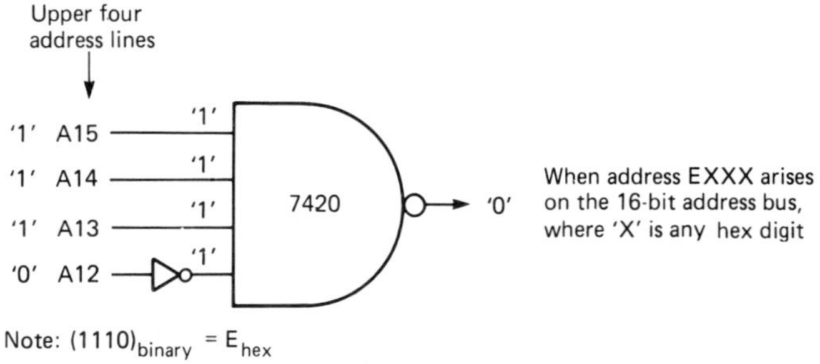

Note: $(1110)_{binary} = E_{hex}$

Fig. 1.5 Enabling for devices at addresses E000–EFFF

logic family which is fast enough to provide the enabling pulse in time. TTL and LSTTL technology are fast enough for all the commonly used MPUs at present. CMOS is often too slow, unless the MPU is being clocked slowly, as may well be the case in a small controller.

To determine the logic required, the number of blocks to be enabled must be decided upon. Figure 1.6 expands the controller of Figure 1.3(a) to show an example of a possible set-up. Figure 1.3(a) included a block labelled 'repeat' starting at 8000. To understand this, note that Figure 1.6 does not use A15 for its decoding. The addresses 0000 and 8000 only differ in the state of A15—0 for 0000 and 1 for 8000.

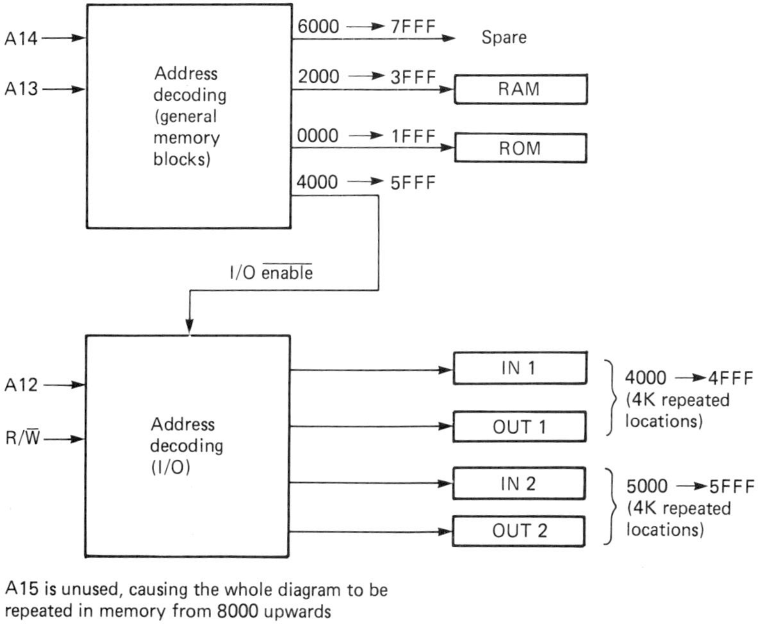

Fig. 1.6 The controller's blocks in detail

Since only A14 to A0 are used for the memory map, reads from 0000 and 8000 are indistinguishable to the electronics, and they will contact exactly the same memory device, and the same location within that device. Similarly, 0001 and 8001 are identical, and so on—in fact, adding 8000 (in hex arithmetic) to any of the lower addresses gives the identical upper address location. The repeat block, therefore, is simply a block of addresses where the programmer could contact exactly the same devices in the same order as if he were to restrict himself to the lower blocks. There is no reason why he should restrict his reading and writing to addresses below 8000, but it is much neater and easier for him to do so, and nothing is lost. The reason for repeating in this manner is to save chips and complexity—it is simpler and cheaper to leave address lines unused than to incorporate logic for their decoding, if only a small quantity of memory is needed anyway.

To decode Figure 1.6, A14, A13, A12 and R/W are chosen to be input into the transfer function, and seven separate devices (probably actual chips) are decoded, each of which may need to be fed portions of the address bus for decoding within these chips. The addresses 6000–7FFF are left spare for any further devices which may be needed. A picture is drawn to imply that a typical solution to this problem could use two separate decoding elements. One of these produces the four memory blocks of Figure 1.3(a), and the other refines one of these (namely I/O) into a further four lines. This would accommodate, for instance, two input and two output chips of the type shown in Figure 1.1. This set-up is chosen as there are single chips which will perform the entire transfer function shown, converting four address-type lines into eight enables. Such a chip is the 74139, for instance, which is a dual 2-to-4 line decoder. Each of the four possible bit patterns on the two input lines produces a zero on just one of the four output lines.

The question arises as to how to choose the correct address lines for the decoding logic. Here, as before, the R/W line is used to distinguish between input and output in the I/O section. In choosing the map of Figure 1.3(a), it was decided that a single ROM of 8K was required, and that this would be the largest single chip requiring decoding. It was also decided that it was not necessary to decode fully all the possible memory of the MPU. Three blocks were required, and the rest of the map could simply be left unused, or be allowed to contain repeats of the basic blocks. Thus, as mentioned above, A15 may be left unused. A crucial point to assimilate is that despite the fact that there are two different addresses at which any piece of data appears to reside (e.g. 0000 and 8000), there are no two locations which may be accessed by a single address. If the electronics were mistakenly arranged so that a single address could contact two separate locations, it would be possible, when enabled, for these locations to place their contents on the data bus simultaneously, and cause an electronic contention which would make the information incomprehensible.

In Figure 1.6, IN1 and OUT1 occupy a single address location, and are distinguished by the state of R/W—a 1 on this line activates IN1, and a 0 activates OUT1. In order to distinguish between the two I/O locations (IN1/OUT1 and IN2/OUT2), A12 alone is decoded. A given I/O pair is selected for each state of this line. This implies that the 12 address lines A11, A10, . . . A0 are irrelevant for this decoding. Thus each I/O pair occupies $2^{12} = 4096$ (4K) repeated locations.

In order to select an I/O address, Figures 1.6 and 1.3(a) show that the current address must be in the range of 4000–5FFF (a total of 8K addresses). A12 distinguishes between 4 and 5 in the most significant hex digit of the address, and hence each of the I/O pairs occupies 4K repeated bytes at the addresses indicated in Figure 1.6.

The considerations discussed above are typical system design problems with which the hardware engineer quickly becomes conversant. A primary design task for any micro system should be to decide upon its memory map.

The system considered here assumes a single block of RAM, 8K in size. This is rather impractical, as RAM chips are normally less than 8K each. It is probable that some further RAM decoding will be necessary to enable each of the two or more RAM chips normally required if 8K is to be included. If little memory is required, a single chip can be connected to the RAM enable, and a certain amount of repetition will again occur.

The above provides, therefore, the chip-level address decoding for the system. Within each chip, there is a complex variety of decoding to ensure that just one location is accessed by each address bus pattern. Thus, for instance, the ROM chip itself is connected to the 13 address lines A12–A0. These provide the $2^{13} = 8192$ (8K) locations within the chip itself.

For a 2K byte RAM chip, therefore, the lower 11 address lines must be fed to the chip—i.e. A10–A0. If this is the only RAM in the system, A11 and A12 do not need to participate in the RAM enable decoding. This implies that they are irrelevant, and the four bit patterns on these lines yield four copies of the RAM locations as follows: 2000–27FF, 2800–2FFF, etc. Note that if any other 11 of the lines A12–A0 are connected to the RAM instead of the lower ones, the same number of locations would be decoded within the RAM, because $2^{11} = 2K$. However, the locations would not be contiguous, which causes problems in software. The same statement holds for the ROM.

A further method of realising the hardware of address decoding is to use a chip which is programmed for the exact transfer function from n lines to m in general. ROMs will perform this type of function admirably, but once again speed is critical, and only certain types of ROM may be used. This will be explained later.

Before describing the problem of Figure 1.3(b), one last note is applicable. In the case considered above, the basic decoding hardware chosen started with the fact that 8K was the largest single block in the system. This was chosen as the starting point for partitioning memory into 8K blocks, each block perhaps containing many copies of smaller memory blocks (chips). This was necessary for the particular decoding chip used in Figure 1.6. If 4K blocks had been chosen, it would have meant that two enable lines would have been valid within the ROM's 8K. This would have meant that the two lines would need to have been 'ANDED' together so that a zero on either would produce a zero on the ROM's enable pin. This is not particularly economical in that it requires an extra gate—or two if inverted logic is being used. To alleviate these problems, 'open collector' logic gates should be used, as their outputs can be connected together. Figure 1.7 shows this

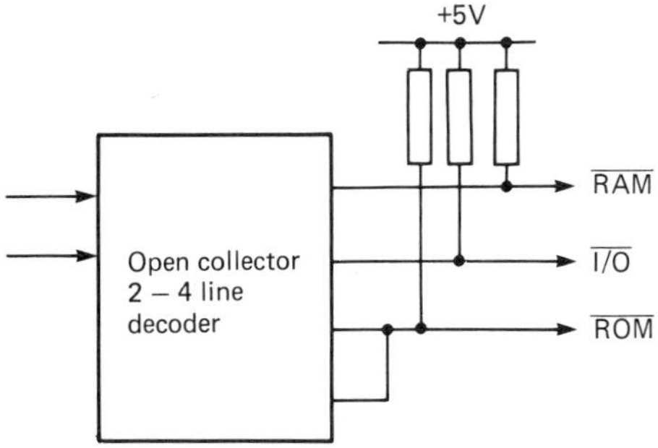

Fig. 1.7 Open-collector decoder chip

arrangement. The outputs of such a chip are simply the collectors of the output transistors, which implies that an external load resistor is required. The outputs are 'low going', and thus when one of the ROM enables becomes valid, it pulls the ROM line low. By this means, a balance can be found between block size and the size of each individual chip. The 74156 and 74159 are excellent examples of such chips, and should be studied in detail for this type of application. In addition, it is normally possible to purchase ROMs for address decoding with open collector outputs—this provides one of the simplest and most cost-effective methods of producing complex decoding requirements. In addition, programmable ROMs (PROMs), containing a specified bit pattern, can normally be supplied by the distributor. The bit pattern should be specified by the system's designer and supplied to the distributor as a 'truth table'.

Figure 1.8 shows a possible expansion for the address map of the complete computer system of Figure 1.3(b). This is a fairly complex map of addresses, and would be rather involved if implemented using standard logic chips. For this reason, Figure 1.9 shows a very neat two-chip solution to the address decoding block of Figure 1.8, incorporating two ROMs. These ROMs would, in fact, probably be PROMs in low-volume or prototype situations, and bipolar chips would be needed for their speed. Typical transfer speeds would then be of the order of 20 ns. In a system where the MPU clock speed requires access to memory in less than 400 ns for reliability, non-bipolar programmable ROMs cannot be used. In addition, in large systems, address buses are often supplied via buffers to the decoding and memory sections. These buffers introduce their own delays, and further press the need for fast decoding chips.

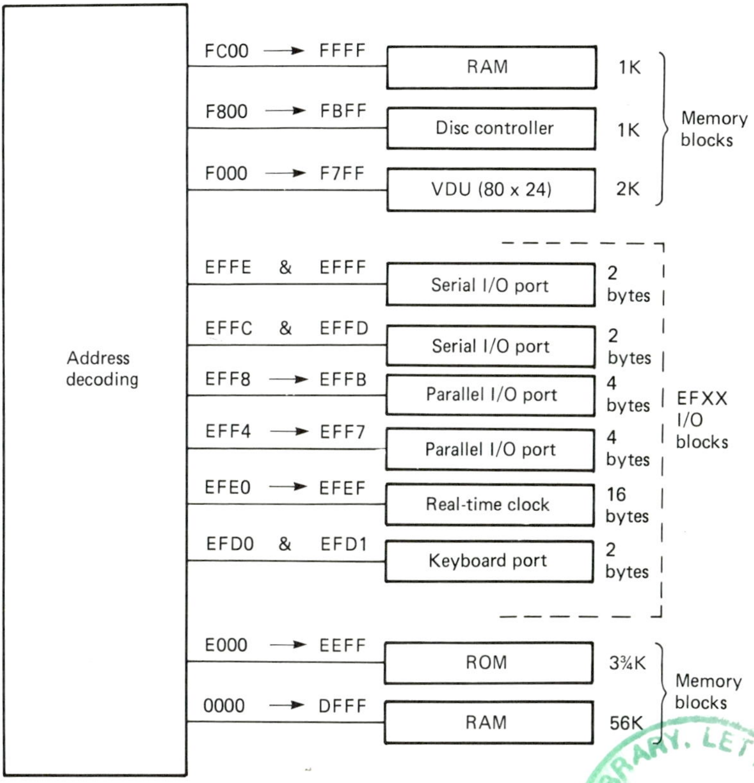

Fig. 1.8 Computer system address map

The blocks resident within the system of Figure 1.8 have been loosely split into a memory group and an I/O group. However, this distinction is irrelevant to the electronics, as each device is nothing more than a set of memory locations. One PROM decodes the top eight addresses, and the second PROM simply expands one small part of the address map—namely, the 256 bytes from EF00 to EFFF shown in Figure 1.9. This also requires eight addresses for input, as $2^8 = 256$.

Each block in the system is addressed uniquely (there are no repeats) as the PROM can be programmed to set any of its output lines low for any specific set of addresses. In addition, just as for the 2K RAM chip which needed 11 address bits, each block in the system must also be fed a number of address lines. The number of address lines (m) required for a block of locations which is a power of 2 is given by: number of locations $= 2^m$. For example, the 1K RAM block on B5 of the upper PROM would have $m = 10$.

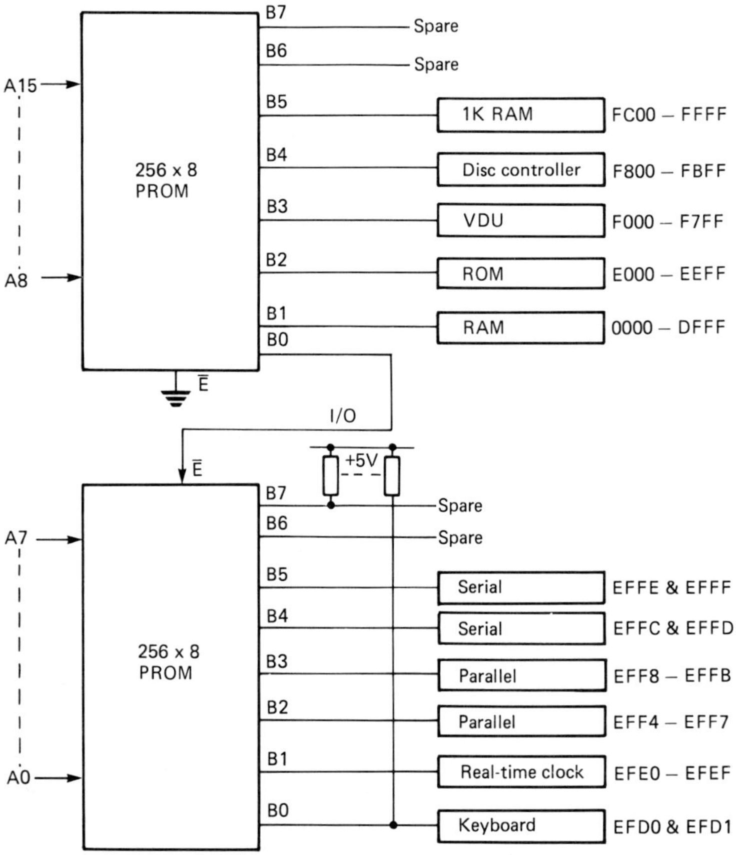

Fig. 1.9 Address decoding using two PROM chips

In order to calculate the truth table required for such PROMs, consider the information in the upper PROM to decode the visual display unit (VDU), for instance. The VDU occupies 2K bytes of system memory from F000 to F7FF, and is connected to bit 3 of the PROM. The supplier of the PROM is not interested in the exact system lines which are to be connected to his chip; he names the pins as shown in Figure 1.10, and simply numbers the 256 PROM address locations from 00 to FF. Figure 1.9 shows A8–A15 of the system connected to the PROM's address lines A0–A7. The VDU occupies F000–F7FF in the system, i.e. the binary patterns F0, F1, ... F7

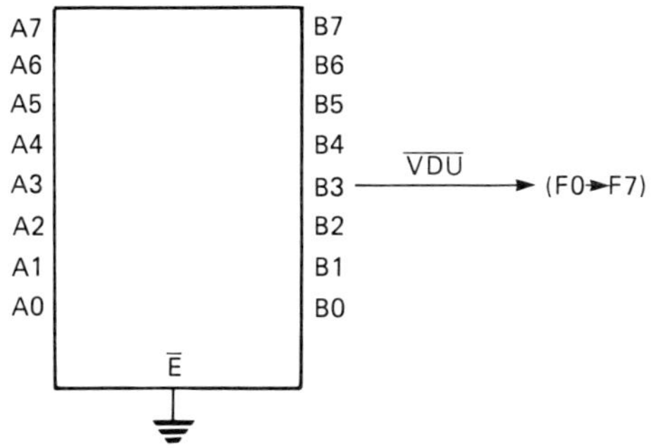

Fig. 1.10 PROM decoder

appear on the upper address bus lines, and each such occurrence must enable the VDU. Thus the VDU must be enabled whenever the PROM receives a bit pattern within this range along its address bus. These locations should be filled with a pattern which sets 1s on all outputs except for B3, which requires a 0 to enable the VDU. Thus the binary pattern

B7	.	.	.	B3	.	.	B0	
1	1	1	1	0	1	1	1	(F7)

is stored in each of the locations F0 to F7. This is the type of information which a PROM programmer must be given.

Figure 1.10 also indicates that PROMs, like any bus-oriented devices, have an enable pin. This is particularly useful, here, for connecting the devices in series. This enable pin, however, causes one problem, as can be seen in Figure 1.9. When the lower PROM is not enabled by the upper PROM, there will be a 1 on the E pin. This puts the lower PROM into its tri-state mode. The enables of the I/O devices on the lower PROM then receive no definite electronic state, and must be pulled up to 1 by the resistors shown to prevent noise on those lines predominating and causing false enables. The upper PROM is enabled all the time, and thus puts definite 1s and 0s on its output pins all the time.

One disadvantage of the PROM approach, however, is that general patching of the blocks to allow them to occupy different locations is often more difficult to provide for the user. A new PROM must be specified if the address map is to be changed. However, here it is seen that some spare lines are available, to allow other devices to be attached at specific locations, or to allow existing blocks to be moved. A better system for patchability, if there is enough memory space left in the system to allow blocks to be moved, is shown in Figure 1.11. Here, an open-collector 4-to-16 line decoder, the 74159, is shown connected to the upper four address lines. Each of the outputs provides a 4K block of decoding, with address regions shown. An address pattern on the address bus within a given 4K block causes a zero on the appropriate output line of the decoder. If two of these lines are connected together, for instance, then any address within the 8K of memory produced by the union of the two regions will give a zero from the join. This allows memory blocks of sizes larger than 4K to be

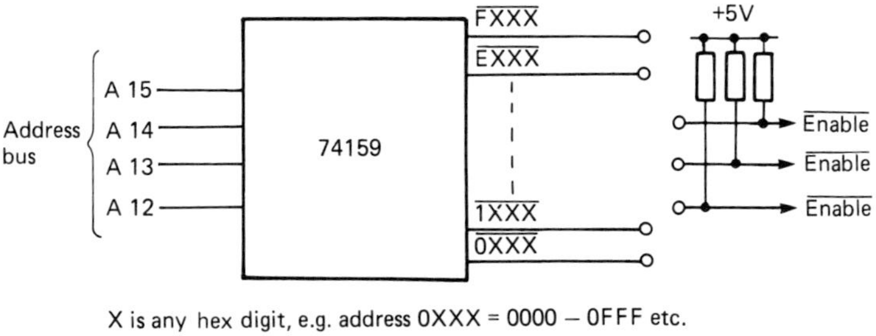

Fig. 1.11 4 to 16 line open-collector decoder

decoded by the 74159. In addition, the open-collector IC must have load resistors connected to its outputs when in use—these are best connected as shown, to keep the resistor count to a minimum.

This completes the section on address decoding. The general principles introduced in this section are continually referred to throughout the following text. It should be clear to the reader that this forms the first and most basic activity for the designer. In addition, as mentioned before, with chips becoming more and more plug-compatible, this area may be the only serious activity which is truly left for the designer to decide.

The next chapter builds upon the principles introduced here, and describes in some detail the software of the MPU itself, as well as the detailed method by which instructions are fetched from memory into the MPU, and then executed. In addition, an example of a control-type system is given.

2

Machine code and the fetch and execute cycle

This chapter introduces the elements of machine code—the programming language of the MPU, and how the instructions are fetched and executed. To aid the comparison between three important eight-bit MPUs, introduced in the next chapter, the simple processor of Chapter 1 will be endowed with a few basic machine-code instructions which it can execute. These instructions will form a subset of those introduced later for the real machines. The exact manner by which these instructions can be used to control external devices is also demonstrated by examples.

An important concept introduced here is the processor timing diagram. This is used as the basis for an explanation of the workings of the processor, as well as a method of designing system electronics. With these concepts firmly established, a fuller understanding of the MPU is best obtained by consideration of some real processors in detail.

A simple machine code set

Figure 2.1 shows the register set introduced in Chapter 1, plus a set of machine-code instructions which the MPU can decode and act upon. A program consists of a string of bit patterns which the MPU fetches from memory, decodes as instructions, and executes. The bit patterns corresponding to the instructions in Figure 2.1 are itemised in the '*opcode*' (third and fourth) columns—both as binary digits and corresponding hex equivalents. In future, only the hex will be used.

Before describing how the program elements are stored in and fetched from memory, the actual instructions themselves will be explained. Reference should be made to the section in the last chapter dealing with the registers.

The first column in Figure 2.1 is the description of each instruction. The notation (M) implies the contents of the location in memory whose address is M. The bracket notation will be used continuously from now on to denote 'the contents of'. Thus, if the data 3A is stored at location 103F then (103F) equals 3A. The n and d are eight-bit numbers: n is used to mean a piece of data, and d is used for an added displacement to the X register. Thus, 'load A with n' means 'place the eight-bit number called n in the register A'. Also, 'X + d' is a 16-bit number made up by adding the eight-bit number 'd' to the lower eight-bits of the 16-bit number contained in the X register (with a carry from the lower eight bits if necessary). When the register notation A, X, FR or PC is used, it usually denotes the contents, and thus brackets are omitted—use will be quite clear from the context.

The second column in Figure 2.1 is for the mnemonics associated with each instruction. These are simply shortened forms of the instruction descriptions; among other things, they make any text referring to the set less cumbersome. In addition, there are special programs called 'assemblers' which will accept a string of mnemonics as data and convert them into corresponding machine-code bit patterns automatically. Thus the programmer need not remember the machine code for an instruction, but rather the more easily learned mnemonic. The hex bit pattern for an instruction is termed an 'opcode', short for 'operation code'. To further assist the use of the instruction tables,

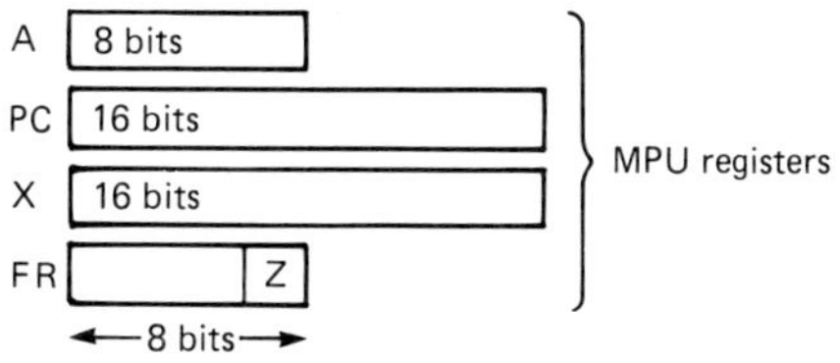

Instruction	Mnemonic	Opcode Bit pattern	Hex	No. of bytes	Action
Load A from M	LDA, M	00111010	3A	3	A ← (M)
Load A with n	LDAI	00111110	3E	2	A ← n
Load A from X + d	LDAX	10100110	A6	2	A ← (X + d)
Store A at M	STA, M	00110010	32	3	A → (M)
Store A at X + d	STAX	10100111	A7	2	A → (X + d)
Add A and (M)	ADD, M	10111011	BB	3	A ← (M) + A
Subtract (M) from A	SUB, M	10110000	B0	3	A ← A − (M)
Add A and n	ADDI	10001011	8B	2	A ← A + n
Subtract n from A	SUBI	10000000	80	2	A ← A − n
Increment A	INCA	00111100	3C	1	A ← A + 1
Increment X	INCX	00001000	08	1	X ← X + 1
Jump to location M	JMP	11000011	C3	3	PC ← M
Jump to M if zero	JPZ	11001010	CA	3	PC ← M if Z = 1

Fig. 2.1 Table of instructions for a simple MPU

most manufacturers include a column of instruction length in bytes as part of their data. This is included here, and will be referred to below. In addition, a column showing the action of each instruction is also normally given.

While reading the following explanation of the instruction set of the MPU used here, the reader should be conscious of the way in which the registers of the MPU are at the heart of all the activities of the processor. As explained before, the state of the MPU at any time, from a programming point of view, is defined completely by the registers. This point should be kept in mind throughout the following.

The instructions are described in the order in which they appear in Figure 2.1. The following descriptions are general and an example given shortly will make their use clear.

LDA, M

When the MPU fetches this instruction from memory, it decodes it as a command to fetch a data byte (M) from memory location M, and copy this data byte, called the 'operand', into the A register without affecting the contents of M (i.e. A's contents are replaced by (M)). The opcode for the LDA instruction is 3A, but the address 'M' must also form part of the instruction, in order to tell the MPU where the data byte is to be found. The 16 bits of address M appear as the second and third bytes of the instruction, making it a three-byte instruction, a fact that the microprogram of the MPU recognises from the actual opcode. As the instruction itself includes the full address of the operand as a *16-bit number*, it is called an 'extended addressing mode' instruction. There are many other ways of expressing the address of the operand, in memory, as will be seen, and each of these ways is called an 'addressing mode'. Sometimes the operand of the instruction is not called up via its actual address; the next instruction provides such an example.

LDAI

This instruction loads A from the second byte of the instruction itself. Thus, this is a two-byte instruction, the first byte of which is '3E', and the second byte 'n' is the actual piece of data to be loaded into A. Since the loading occurs immediately upon fetching the whole instruction, without reference to memory again, this is called an 'immediate addressing mode' instruction.

LDAX

The X register, being a 16-bit register, may also hold an address. Most MPUs allow such a register to be used to provide the address of the operand. This mode, therefore, is called 'indexed addressing'. It is particularly useful for the fetching of items held in a table. As can be seen from the LDAX instruction, A is loaded with the byte found in the location with address 'X + d', where X is the 16-bit number in the X register, and d is an eight-bit displacement, or offset. If d represents a positive eight-bit number, X must contain the first address location of the table, and only 256 items may be placed in the table. This will be the assumption for the MPU here.

Thus the LDA-type instruction has three different addressing modes to supply the address of the byte to be loaded into A. Most MPUs allow many different addressing modes for each basic instruction type, as will be seen later.

STA, M

Having operated on A's value, this may need to be stored, perhaps for future use, or even for immediate printing on paper. Either way, a 'store' instruction would be required—the one here allows A to be stored at any address M. This is a three-byte instruction, using the extended addressing mode once again.

STAX

Again, the X register may be used to decide where the byte in A is to be stored (indexed addressing); and here, as for LDAX, two bytes are used, with the displacement forming the second byte. If the results of a set of calculations are to be stored in a data table, this is the type of instruction which may be used. The advantages are that each such store instruction only requires two bytes in the program instead of three, but more importantly, each store may be effected by incrementing X (see a later instruction) without actually having to calculate the address of each subsequent member of the table.

ADD, M and SUB, M

These are extended-mode instructions, and A always forms one of the two required operands for the process. In addition, A always contains the result. These instructions, therefore, destroy the contents of A. The exact mode used for this binary arithmetic depends upon the MPU being considered. Most MPUs offer a carry flag in the FR register, which is a one-bit indicator set to a 1 if the addition overflows, as in the following example:

$$\begin{array}{rl} & 10011010 \\ + & \underline{11001001} \\ = & \underline{01100011}\ \text{carry } 1 \end{array}$$

(See Appendix 1 on binary and hex if necessary.)

Subtraction also has bits in the FR register dedicated to its use. This group of instructions is among the most complex and varied offered by the MPU.

ADDI and SUBI

These instructions act like the previous two but they are the immediate-mode equivalents, where the number to be subtracted from or added to A is held in the second byte of the instruction.

INCA and INCX

These instructions introduce a further addressing mode, called 'inherent' or 'implied' mode. The instructions do not operate on data stored in addressable memory. They are one-byte instructions whose data resides at locations, usually within the MPU itself, which are implied by or are inherent within the opcode itself. Here, the A or X register is incremented by 1.

JMP

In order to allow the MPU to run a program containing repeated loops, or branches to and from separate modules of code, most MPUs are quite rich in instructions which cause a change in the order in which the program is executed. These are called 'jump' or 'branch' instructions. Only two are described here. The one in this section is an unequivocal jump to an address, the 16 bits of which are contained in the instruction—i.e. extended mode. When this opcode is fetched, the MPU fetches the next two bytes and loads the PC register with this

16-bit address. This causes program execution to jump to that location for the next instruction to be fetched.

JPZ

This instruction is an example of a very important group of instructions which any MPU will offer. In order to allow the MPU to make decisions dependent upon the outcome, say, of a calculation, that outcome is allowed to force the MPU to perform a jump. Thus here, if the outcome of the last operation was a zero, the jump is performed. Otherwise, execution continues by fetching the next instruction in memory. In order to tie this down further, let us suppose that any instruction which affects the A register in any way also affects one of the bits of the FR register. This is called the 'zero flag', and is shown in Figure 2.1 as the least significant bit of FR. Each active bit of FR is given a letter; this particular bit is called 'Z'. If a load instruction, for instance, sets A to 00, then Z will be set to 1, and this will occur every time that the A register is set to 00 by any means. Note that, in general, flags are active high. Similarly, if the program causes a subtract on two equal numbers, Z will be set (i.e. to 1). It will be further assumed that Z will not be reset again until the next instruction comes along which resets A to 00. Thus Z will not be affected by a jump or a STAX instruction, for instance.

The JPZ instruction therefore performs the jump only if Z is 1 when JPZ is fetched for execution.

This set of instructions is not meant to form an exhaustively complete set, but rather implies an introduction to a surprisingly wide number of concepts, and certainly sufficient for the workings of the MPUs given as examples later. The next section shows how some of these basic instructions may be combined to form a program, and later how the program is started, fetched and executed electronically from power-up.

Some simple programming

This section is not meant to act as an introduction to programming, and any attempt to learn methods of program writing should be referred to another text. The programming described here, and throughout, is meant purely to supplement the electronics. To that end, the following example introduces concepts which will help with an understanding of the design, for instance, of control systems.

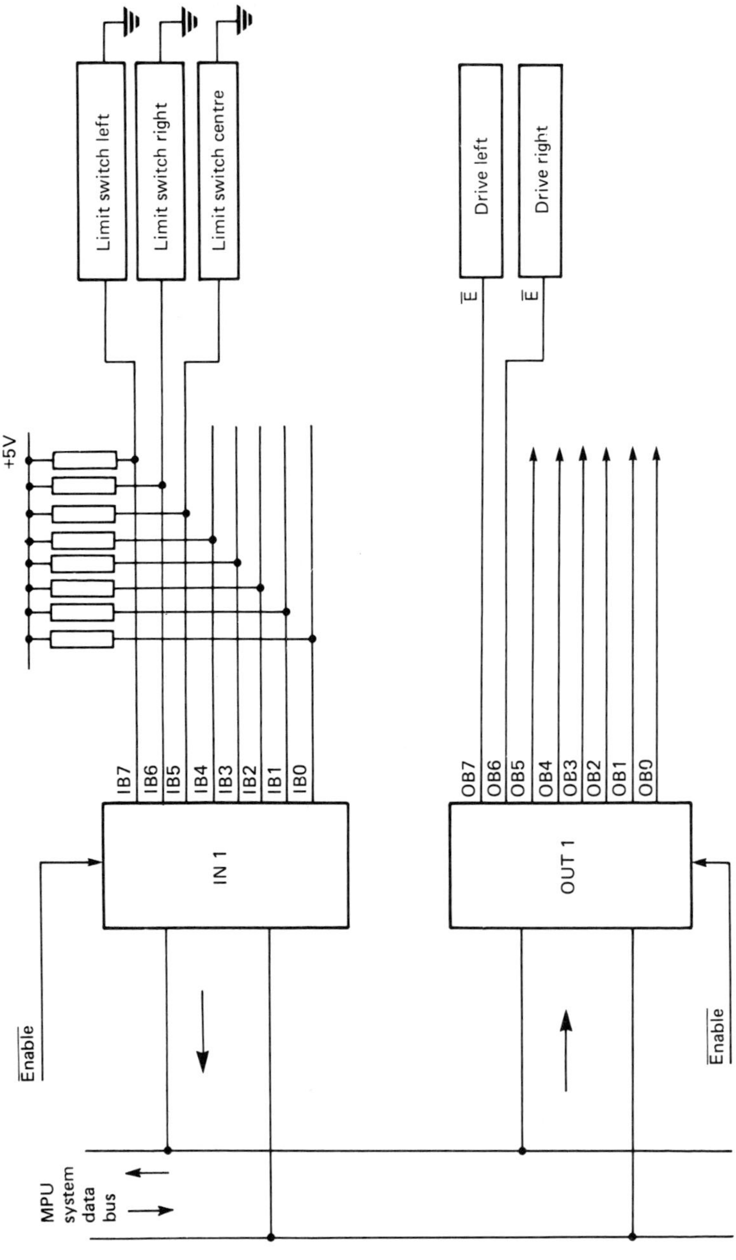

Fig. 2.2 Example—application I/O interface logic

Referring back to Figure 1.6, a simple control loop can be written using the instructions introduced so far for this sytem. In order to provide such an example, consider IN1 and OUT1 expanded further, as shown in Figure 2.2. The eight bits of input are labelled IB0 to IB7, and output as OB0 to OB7. The system being controlled consists, perhaps, of a plate which is attached to an actuator which is subject to continual stress. The job of the control system is to 'centre' the plate if knocked off. To this end it is able to drive the plate 'left' or 'right', and sense when the plate is centred, or at its extreme left or right limit. The bits of the IN1 and OUT1 bytes in memory which correspond to these activities are shown. Pull-up resistors on the input bits ensure that, when the switches are open, ones are sent to IN1. In addition, drives are switched on by applying a zero to the appropriate bits of OUT1. Figure 1.6 shows that any location from 4000 to 4FFF may be used to contact IN1 or OUT1, and that IN and OUT are distinguished by reading or writing from any one of these locations. From now on, only the location 4000 will be used. Figure 2.3 shows the system as a bit map of 4000. MSB stands for most significant bit, and LSB for least significant bit.

To drive the plate left, the number 01XXXXXX should be stored at location 4000, where 'X' is anything. From now on, for simplicity, X will be taken as 1, thus drive left is accomplished by storing 7F at 4000. To sense whether the plate is at its centre, 4000 must be loaded into the A register, and the number checked to see if it is equal to 11011111 which is equal to DF. The assumption is made that only one of the three sensors is active at any time—and often none of them is active. It is now possible to discuss the type of programming (software) which might be used in this application.

To define the problem more closely, it is always advantageous to draw a flowchart of the situation. At this point, the actual program-

Reading from 4000

MSB							LSB
Limit switch left	Limit switch right	Limit switch centre	1	1	1	1	1

Writing to 4000

MSB							LSB
Drive left	Drive right	X	X	X	X	X	X

X = don't care
All bits active low

Fig. 2.3 Example—I/O bit map for hardware

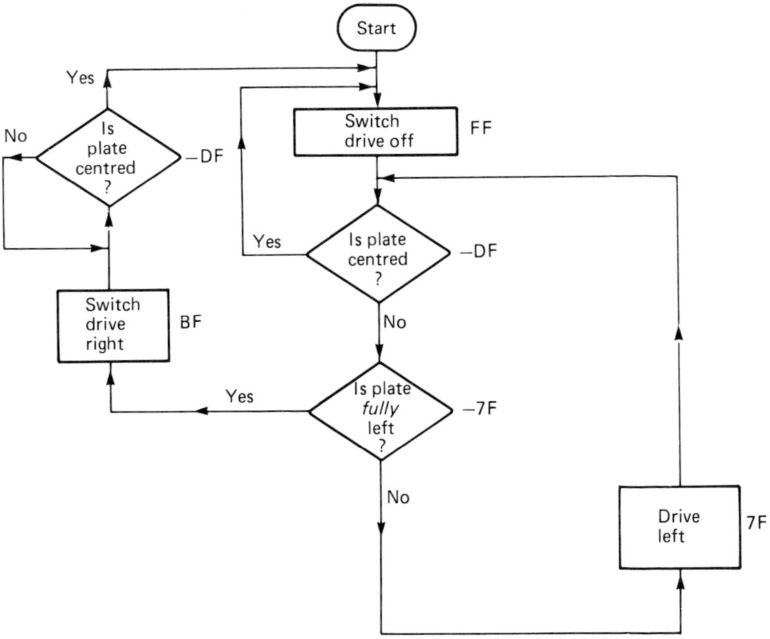

Fig. 2.4 Example—overall flowchart

ming language in which the program is to be written is not important; the flowchart of Figure 2.4 is independent of the code, and simply puts the situation down in a visually easy-to-read form. The convention used is as follows. Boxes which enter or leave this routine are rectangular with curved sides, boxes which contain statements of actions are rectangular, and boxes containing questions from which more than one exit is possible are shaped like diamonds with the possible different answers to the questions written on the exit branches. Arrows direct the running of the routine.

This routine may only be entered at the start box. The drive is reset to off for neatness at the beginning. The centre limit switch is checked first; if the plate is centred, no action is necessary, and the routine leaves the first diamond by the 'yes' branch. This loop is continued until the external stress takes the plate off centre. As soon as this occurs, the plate left sensor is checked; if it is active, the plate must have been pushed fully to the left, and the drive is thus set on driving to the right to centre the plate. The centre sensor is then checked again and again until active; only then is the drive switched off. The plate is not controlled again until the external stress drives it off centre. If the plate is not centred, and the left sensor is not active, the routine falls through to the bottom of the flowchart. In this case, on the first run through the routine the computer does not know whether the plate is left or right of centre, and it must make a guess. It drives left, and checks the centre sensor. If its guess was correct, the centre is eventually reached, and the loop continues as above. If its guess was wrong, the left position will eventually be met, the 'plate left?' question will be answered with a 'yes', and the loop will send the plate back to the centre as before.

The success of this routine depends very largely upon the mechanical set-up chosen for the actuators. However, this is irrelevant for the concepts being introduced here. In general, it is in this type of system that software and hardware meet—the most successful systems are those in which both software and hardware are considered side-by-side.

To turn this routine into a program using the instructions introduced in the previous section, certain procedures must be invented to perform functions such as checking the centre sensor, and turning on 'drive right'. All the necessary modules are now described with reference to the flowchart box by box, and to Figure 2.2.

Start

The routine is either entered from another piece of programming, such as a 'set-up' procedure, or started immediately upon power-up or reset.

Drive off

The drive is switched off by setting bits 6 and 7 of OUT1 to 1s—i.e. the data FF is stored at location 4000. This forms the first few bytes of the program. There is no instruction in our simple processor for loading any memory location directly using extended addressing. The process of sending data to a memory location must occur indirectly. Therefore A must be loaded with FF, and then stored at 4000.

Is plate centred?

To check to see whether the plate is centred, (4000) must be loaded into the A register, and some method of discovering whether bit 5 is low must be found. If bit 5 is low, a jump back to the start of the program must be made. There is only one conditional jump instruction available here (JPZ) and somehow this must be utilised. The zero flag is used to form the decision. To see how this is done, recall that only one sensor may be active at any time. The centre sensor, we have seen, is active when (4000) equals DF. Thus subtracting DF from the number in A will produce zero if and only if the sensor is active. The code therefore contains an instruction to load A from 4000, a subtraction of DF and a 'jump if zero' back to the start. If the result is not zero, the program continues to the next box.

Is the plate left?

This is similar to the last box, but the number 7F is subtracted from A, and the 'jump if zero' instruction sends the program into a piece of code to drive right if successful. Otherwise, action continues with the box below.

Drive left

As mentioned above, 7F stored at 4000 will send the drive left.

Drive right

The value BF stored at 4000 accomplishes this control.

As can be seen, the right limit switch is not used in this application, but the reader will find it a useful exercise to derive some other flowcharts using both sensors to achieve the same end. Another useful exercise would be to consider the difference it would make to the programming and the system if two sensors were capable of being active at the same time.

The next step is to 'code' the flowchart in Figure 2.4 into a program

Address	Hex	Mnemonic	Comments
0000	3E	LDAI FF	Load A immediately
0001	FF		with FF.
0002	32		Store A at 4000 to
0003	40	STA, 4000	turn drive off.
0004	00		
0005			
0006			
0007			

Fig. 2.5 Example—first few program instructions

containing actual machine code instructions. To achieve this, a memory map of the system must be consulted. Figure 1.6 provides such a map. The program must start at 0000, all variables used throughout the program must be contained between 2000 and 3FFF, and the I/O is confined here to 4000. Figure 2.5 indicates a method of documenting the program to show how the program is built up and how it works. The first few bytes are shown as discussed above. Figure 2.1 should be referred to constantly to choose the correct opcodes. The table in Figure 2.5 shows the address of each byte so that when a jump to some part of the program is required, its address is obvious from the program listing. However, this does not require the address of each piece of data to be apparent, and a more compact form of the listing is shown in Figure 2.6. It is worthwhile leaving plenty of space over to

Address	Hex	Mnemonic	Comments
0000	3E FF	LDAI FF	Load A with FF.
0002	32 4000	STA, 4000	Store A at 4000 to switch drive off.

Fig. 2.6 Example—a neater instruction presentation

the left for arrows which will indicate the flow of the program when it is built up a little more. Note that the address shown to the left on each line is the address of the first byte on that line only.

To write the rest of the program, the flowchart is consulted and copied into code using the information given in the sections above. This gives a piece of code, the first part of which is shown in Figure 2.7 and described in detail in the following.

To check the centre sensor, address 0005 contains a load instruction to fetch the contents of 4000. This takes up three bytes, and 0008 performs an immediate-mode subtraction with DF to see if bit 5 is zero. If it is, the subtraction gives zero in A, and Z is set. This forces the JPZ instruction in the next line of code to force the MPU back up to address 0000. This is shown by the arrow. Before continuing, the

	Address	Hex	Mnemonic	Comments
→	0000	3E FF	LDAI FF	Load A with FF.
IF Z = 1	0002	32 40 00	STA, 4000	Store A at 4000 to switch drive off.
	0005	3A 40 00	LDA, 4000	Check centre sensor by loading A with (4000) and subtracting DF. If zero, plate is centred, so jump back to to start, otherwise continue.
	0008	80 DF	SUBI DF	
	000A	CA 00 00	JPZ	

Fig. 2.7 Example—drive off and check centre sensor

reader should try to build up the rest of the code using the above section as a start.

The rest of the program is shown in Figure 2.8. The code illustrated follows the flowchart exactly. The reader should follow the program and chart through, reading the comprehensive comments in Figure 2.8.

The use of careful documentation in programming cannot be

Address	Hex	Mnemonic	Comments
0000	3E FF	LDAI FF	Drive off.
0002	32 40 00	STA, 4000	
0005	3A 40 00	LDA, 4000	Start again if
0008	80 DF	SUBI DF	plate centred.
000A	CA 00 00	JPZ, 0000	
000D	3A 40 00	LDA, 4000	Check plate
0010	80 7F	SUBI 7F	left.
0012	3E 7F	LDAI 7F	If not, switch drive
0014	32 40 00	STA, 4000	left and jump to check
0017	C3 00 05	JMP, 0005	if plate centred again.
001A	3E BF	LDAI, BF	If plate is left, switch
001C	32 40 00	STA, 4000	drive right.
001F	3A 40 00	LDA, 4000	Check if centred, and
0022	80 DF	SUBI DF	continue this until
0024	CA 00 00	JPZ, 0000	true, then jump to
0027	C3 00 1F	JMP, 001F	start.

Fig. 2.8 Example—complete program listing

stressed sufficiently. The simplest piece of code can be the cause of complete bafflement, even to the originator, after a few days. Imagine being confronted by:

3E FF 32 40 00 3A 40 00 80 DF CA 00 00 3A 40 00 80 7F 3E 7F 32 40 00 C3 00 05 3E BF 32 40 00 3A 40 00 80 DF CA 00 00 C3 00 1F

which is the program in Figure 2.8 as it would appear when examining the contents of 0000–0029 after the program has been written and stored.

Running the program

By the process described in the last section, a program, consisting of 42 bytes of binary data, has been written on paper. The next question is how to load the program into the controller, and start the program running.

The first step is to include the program within the hardware of the system as a sequence of bytes of data. To do this, and to ensure that the program is not lost when the system is switched off, the program must be stored on ROM of some type. This is best done, initially, on an erasable programmable ROM—an EPROM—which allows adjustments to the program if necessary. The program can be stored on a typical EPROM using a device called an 'EPROM programmer'. Later on in the book, a programmer is described for a common form of EPROM. For the moment, suffice it to say that the program could be typed into an EPROM programmer, and stored on an EPROM starting at its lowest address. This EPROM could then be plugged into the controller of Figure 1.6, if its ROM slot were pin-compatible with the EPROM. The address decoding is set up to start the EPROM at 0000, and thus the system would contain the program from 0000 to 0029, as is required by the program itself to allow the jump instructions to work correctly.

Figure 1.2 described a simple reset circuit; assuming that all the hardware was complete, switching on the power would cause the MPU to start processing from 0000, and the program would be in progress.

In order to test a program as simple as this, all that is needed is a number of switches and LEDs (light emitting diodes). Press-button switches could be connected to simulate the limit switches, and LEDs for the drives. By this means, the switches could be operated to ensure that the program runs correctly. The next step would be to connect it to the actual hardware.

The sequence of events described here can work quite well for a very simple program and proven hardware. The problem comes when the application is complex and the hardware is in development at the same time. For this contingency, the professional approach would be to use a development system of some kind.

Development systems

A development system is nothing more than a computer with I/O configured in the same way as the target system under development. This computer would normally have the same MPU as the target system, though this is by no means necessary, as the system may have a simulator or emulator for the target MPU. Figure 2.9 sketches a plan for the development of a microprocessor system. It assumes the availability of a computer of the size of that shown in Figure 1.8. It

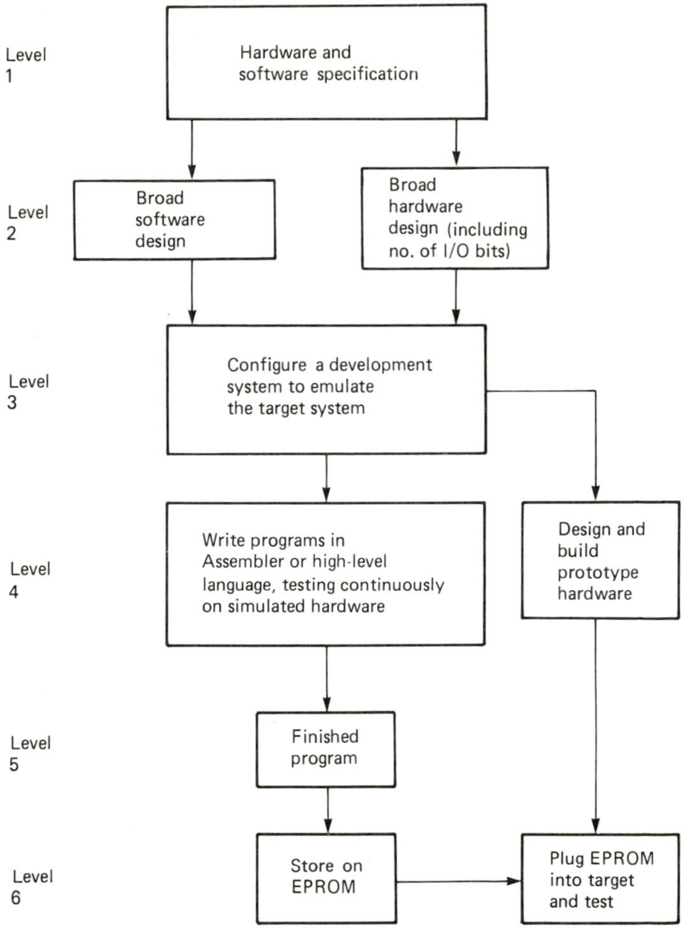

Fig. 2.9 Project management chart

also assumes, for simplicity, that the I/O can be patched to be the same as that of the target system. It is also useful if the system can allow the program to be run at the correct memory locations, and eventually be run in EPROM at those locations; though initially, the program would be tested in RAM to allow ease of change. After levels 1 and 2 in Figure 2.9 have been agreed, level 3 is able to be actioned and the target system hardware is fixed. Level 4 involves two design and prototype activities, one software and the other hardware. The software can continue without the actual final hardware because the development system has a simulation of the final system to use for testing throughout the programming process. The hardware can continue in parallel because the specification has been agreed, and the I/O structure is therefore fixed—both activities in this level need the address decoding to be decided in detail. Levels 5 and 6 bring the process of producing the first prototype to a conclusion. Naturally, this is the start of a testing phase when it may be necessary to rethink and redesign from the first level downwards. However, if the system is well defined, and the target hardware well known, the process should be mostly complete by the time level 6 is reached. There are many different approaches to development; the one shown here is basic but adequate, as well as being very economical.

The software packages available for developing further software are very varied. Two major types of software package may be mentioned here—the assembler and the compiler. An assembler, as mentioned before, is a program which allows the operator to write his programs in mnemonics. The assembler program takes the mnemonic-based code as source data to be converted into machine code for the MPU. A compiler is a similar program which takes a high-level language such as BASIC or FORTRAN and converts that to machine code. The advantages of the latter is that writing programs in high-level languages is much easier than writing in lower-level languages such as mnemonic code. BASIC, for instance, contains a very large number of English words. Learning BASIC is a very simple business. The disadvantages are firstly, that the machine code thus produced is very inefficient in terms of memory storage, and secondly that BASIC is quite far removed from the actual hardware where bits and bytes have an electronic meaning. However, the incredible increase in throughput of programming which can result from the use of a high-level language is most worthwhile. In addition, compilers are becoming more and more able to produce efficient code, as well as allowing more and more low-level commands and linking in to machine-code routines.

It should also be noted that there are many new languages to choose from, such as Pascal and FORTH—a number of these new languages are specifically structured for particular types of program task.

The 'super design-aid' described in the preface is in fact a reality, and for some time this has been the path by which electronic systems are produced.

Fetch and execute

This section describes how the MPU takes in opcodes electronically, and how the buses are used.

Time for an MPU is not a continuous quantity; it is discrete and split into time slices, or clock cycles. All the activities of the MPU are synchronous with this clock. For some MPUs, it is possible to define the exact activity of the buses by the state of the clock. For others, only a broad outline of the bus states can be inferred from the logical state of the clock. The MPU considered here is of the 'fixed-cycle type', and is described below.

The term 'fetch and execute cycle' is applied to the sequence of events whereby an opcode and its data are fetched from memory, and the instruction thus fetched is executed. Different instructions require different numbers of clock cycles for their execution, and hence the specific form of the fetch and execute cycle differs from operation to operation. To describe the sequence most efficiently, a timing diagram is used, as illustrated in Figure 2.10. This diagram shows an example

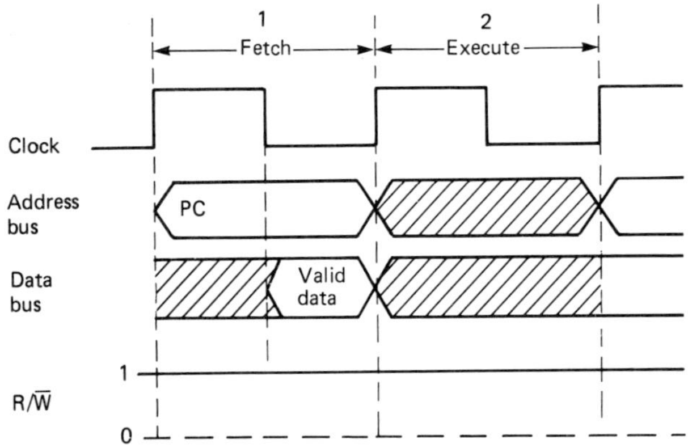

Fig. 2.10 Fetch and execute cycle

of a fetch and execute. The clock, against which all events occur, is shown at the top. Each rising edge starts a new event. To illustrate the activities of the address bus and the data bus, rather than showing a picture of the logical state of each line in each bus, an entire bit pattern is indicated. Areas of cross-hatch are times during which the actual pattern is irrelevant. It can be seen that on the rising edge of cycle no. 1, the program counter contents are output along the address bus. It takes time for the complete pattern to be established, and this is indicated by sloping lines building up to a complete pattern on the address bus. The read/write line is constantly in the read (high) state, and it thus is logical to infer that the memory location being addressed through the address decoding would be active and outputting its data to the data bus. Exactly when this process begins depends upon several factors:

(a) The exact time at which the memory device receives a complete pattern of bits along the address bus.
(b) The exact time that the delays within the address decoding logic take to enable the memory device.
(c) The transfer delay within the memory before data is available at its output buffers.

This is not a complete list, but it serves to illustrate that the MPU cannot be expected to decide exactly when the data it finds presented on the data bus is valid. For this reason, it ignores all input until the second half of the current clock cycle. Assuming that the clock is not too fast for the peripheral electronics, it will be sure that the data present on the data bus is the information it was requesting. Typical speeds found would be of the order of 1 megahertz. At 1 MHz, the first half of the cycle would last for 500 nanoseconds. The weakest point in the chain of events is normally the transfer time for the memory chips being addressed. While the other processes would normally take approximately 20 to 50 ns, the memory would be expected to take between 200 and 450 ns. The actual stated characteristics of the memory itself are important in MPU system design, and the timing diagram illustrated here is the normal method for discovering and showing timing problems. The exact time at which the MPU samples the data on the data bus is normally determined by an edge of the clock. This depends upon the actual MPU being used, and will be left until MPU examples are given.

The second cycle, no. 2, is devoted, here, to the internal execution of the instruction fetched. This instruction could be an inherent mode, single-byte instruction, and would thus require no further data to be fetched for its completion. In this second cycle, any information can be present upon the address and data buses, and as long as the R/W line is high, neither the memory nor the MPU is affected. The MPU is inactive externally, and with R/W high, no modification of any memory location can be effected.

This MPU is a constant-cycle processor in the sense that the first half of the cycle is devoted to establishing the address and control bus states, and the data bus is not used until the second half. During an execution cycle, the data bus is free during both halves of the cycle, and thus it is true to say that the data bus is free for other use during the first half of each clock cycle. This allows a number of different techniques to be used by external devices for the utilisation of the data bus in a manner which is totally transparent to the MPU and thus to the programming.

It is essential for the MPU system designer to obtain a thorough knowledge of the timing diagram characteristics of the chosen MPU.

From this, the actual peripheral device chips may be chosen. It is rarely necessary to use just those chips within the actual family of the MPU itself, most bus-oriented devices will fit onto the majority of MPUs with perhaps a minimum of interfacing. The detailed data for the chips being used should always be consulted fully.

The next two chapters give the software and hardware of three MPUs as examples to develop the ideas introduced so far.

3

Three typical MPUs: software

This chapter describes the software architecture of some actual examples of MPUs. It cannot be emphasised enough how important it is for the engineer to understand at least the basis for the programming of these devices. It is generally agreed, in this field, that the only way to succeed is by an understanding of the way in which hardware (the electronics) and software (the programming) weld together within a system. In the environment of the large mainframe computer, the practicality of being an expert both in hardware and software was difficult to envisage. However, this necessity is forced upon the MPU system designer from the very beginning, due to the very accessibility of the MPU and its straightforward application.

The three MPUs described here are the Z80 (originally manufactured by Zilog), the 6800 (originally from Motorola) and the RCA 1802. The first two are in very wide use indeed, and are good examples, therefore, of the commonest type of machine available. Between the two of them, they give examples of most of the types of hardware and software architectures found on the majority of processors in existence. The third MPU is an example of a CMOS processor with a number of extremely interesting characteristics, making it an excellent contrast to the other two. The 1802 is specifically designed for application to control systems, and gives a good example of those characteristics which an MPU manufacturer is able to offer if he sets out to design specifically for control. It should not be forgotten that the early processors were designed to provide easily produced controllers—the full gamut of personal and industrial computers is regarded by some as nothing more than a spin-off!

This chapter is meant to form the basis for the reader's knowledge of the type of software architecture available on MPUs in general. To this end it has the form of an introduction to three main topics for each of the three processors presented. These are:

(a) The register set provided on each MPU, followed by a discussion of the important concept of the stack, and a general description of interrupts.
(b) The addressing modes available.
(c) The machine code instruction set.

An important aim of the chapter is to equip the reader with enough comparative information to allow an appreciation of any MPU with which he may come into contact. By assimilating the information given here, a critical appraisal of any new MPU should be possible. In addition, this chapter is written in a form which will transfer immediately to the jargon and setting out of the manufacturer's data on all of the MPUs presented here. It should be possible for the reader to pick up any data on these machines and understand it sufficiently to allow him to use it immediately for design. The next chapter completes the introduction by presenting electronic data to the same depth.

This book is not meant to form a substitute for the great quantity of data which is included in manufacturers' data sheets and manuals. Before any design is attempted, the manufacturer's data on any chip being used must be obtained and studied. It is also worth pointing out that MPUs are often multi-sourced. Several manufacturers make the 6800 chips, for instance, and all of these companies publish data and manuals on the device. The chips are all interchangeable, but the manuals are often written in widely differing styles. The particular presentation of one manufacturer may suit a given reader more easily than another.

The Z80 register set

This processor is upward compatible with the Intel 8080 processor, providing a more easily interfaced MPU with a number of distinct advantages over the 8080. The Z80, for instance, has a simpler clock requirement. Figure 3.1 shows the register set of the Z80. Some of these registers have been introduced in the previous chapters in principle. The A register and PC are as described before, and IX and IY are similar to the X register. The F register is shown in further detail at the foot of the figure, and its bits are as follows:

'Z' is the zero flag as described on page 29. Any operation which zeros the A register will set Z to a 1 to allow later instructions to take note that this condition has occurred.

Cross-hatching denotes an unused bit, the state of which must at all times be considered as indeterminate.

'C', 'S', 'P/V', 'N' and 'H' are used to flag the conditions which are encountered during arithmetic and logical operations on the accumulator. They may be used by the programmer in a number of ways. One important use is in the conditional branch, and jump instructions.

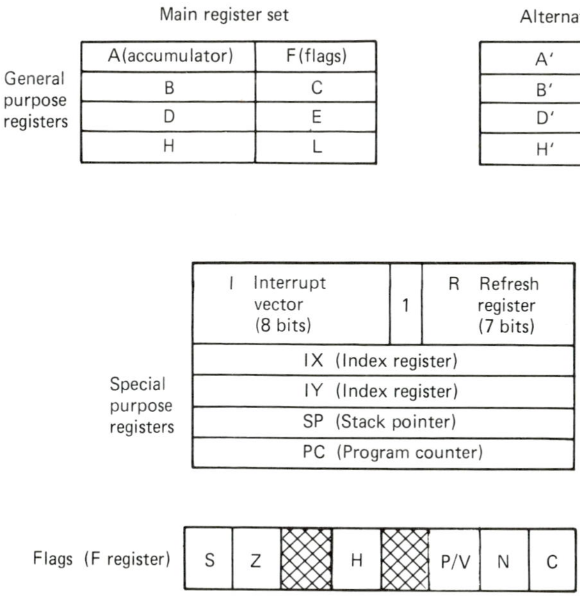

Fig. 3.1 The Z80 register set

An example of this was given in Chapter 2, where the JPZ instruction was used to change the order of execution depending upon whether or not the A register had just been set to zero. These are not described in full detail here, as they are more properly encountered in a text on software, and require a deep understanding of binary arithmetic. A brief description follows to allow a comparison with the other two processors in this chapter.

'C' signals that a carry has occurred during the last operation. For instance, if the eight-bit numbers FF and 01 were added together in A, the result would be too large to be held in A, which is only eight bits in length; the actual answer should be 1 0000 0000—this is held as 00 (hex) in A, and the upper bit is held in C as a 1. In this way, arithmetic requiring greater precision than eight bits can be performed by linking together eight-bit operations.

'S' is the sign of the binary number in A if signed arithmetic is being performed. This type of arithmetic is used to solve the tricky problem of representing negative numbers within a computer. Under this regime, S would have the same value as the most significant bit of A—if this bit is 1, the number is negative. Binary arithmetic of this type is not described further here, and the reader is advised to refer to a standard computer text.

The 'P/V' flag holds either the parity of the A register's value (after logical operations) or the overflow status after certain operations are performed for which the 8-bit nature of the operands is insufficient for their accuracy.

'N' and 'H' are used for BCD arithmetic.

The general-purpose registers B, C, D, E, H, L are used by the MPU for the storage of data during program execution; they can either be used separately as eight-bit registers, or, as indicated in the diagram, as 16-bit register pairs. In addition, there is a further 'alternate' register set, identical to the first which may be exchanged with the first by a couple of single-byte instructions—one exchanges AF with A′F′, and the other exchanges the sets of general purpose registers.

The I register is used in the application of interrupts, and is described in the interrupt section below. The R register is used for the easy addition of a particular type of RAM chip (dynamic memory) and is simply incremented each time an opcode fetch is performed. The resulting number is output onto the address bus at a given time, and used by the external memory logic to keep this type of memory refreshed to prevent loss of data. This is described in full detail in Chapter 5.

The stack and the stack pointer (SP) are explained in detail below.

The Z80 stack and interrupts

There is a group of instructions, as will be seen shortly, that require a series of memory locations called a stack. This set of locations is resident in the normal read/write memory (RAM), and the current location being used by the program is pointed to by the 16-bit register SP; it is completely under the programmer's control.

The stack is a set of memory locations acted upon by the stack instructions without the programmer's having to be concerned with an exact knowledge of their memory addresses. The MPU automatically takes care of the actual addresses, under the instructions' control, via the SP register. SP is automatically incremented and decremented as necessary. This allows the programmer to concentrate on the actual activity in hand more easily and pass onto the MPU some of the tedious 'housekeeping' associated with a complex program. An excellent use of this type of instruction is for intermediate variable storage during a calculation. As many stacks as required may be implemented, and each is contacted simply by loading SP with an address.

Not all MPUs have a formal stack, but its existence makes a number of important operations very simple and flexible.

All MPUs have some form of interrupt logic, normally one or more pins on their package which when brought to an active level (usually low) will stop execution of the current program at the end of the current instruction, and allow the MPU to 'vector off' to an 'interrupt routine'. This requires some method of at least storing the current PC value to ensure that when the interrupt routine is finished, the current program can be continued as if nothing had happened.

In this manner, a background process may be proceeding completely transparently to the normal operation of the program—apart from slowing it down. A useful example of this would be for a timer function. The MPU could be controlling a complex process whereby certain members of the sequence must be performed according to time. If the MPU were being interrupted continually, say every tenth of a second, the interrupt routine could simply increment the contents of a set of memory locations (with appropriate carries) and return to the main program. To tell the time, for correct sequencing, the program would simply read these locations. The interrupt routine would be keeping it up to date every tenth of a second, without the main program even realising it. By this means a fairly accurate clock is implemented and updated transparently entirely by software. Such an interrupt routine might take of the order of 50 microseconds—that is, every 0.1 of a second the process 'wastes' 0.00005 of a second. This, therefore, accounts for just 0.05% of the MPU's time—a most acceptable overhead in any regime.

The question arises, however, as to what to do with the current state of the MPU registers so that they are retrievable without loss when the interrupt routine finishes. This is where the stack is used. On some MPUs, the complete register set is stored in a series of memory locations starting at the current address in the stack pointer. This ensures that if the interrupt routine uses any of these registers, their contents can be reinstated without loss at the end. It is up to the programmer, as part of the set-up routine at the beginning of the program, to ensure that a suitable portion of RAM is set aside for this purpose. The stack is a 'first in last out' (FILO) stack, and this process is called 'stacking the registers' or 'pushing the registers onto the stack'. The Z80, however, stacks just one piece of data—the PC contents—allowing a return to the main program after an interrupt. The other registers must be protected by the interrupt routine itself. Here again the stack can be of use, but there is another method for the Z80 which simply entails exchanging the current registers for the alternate set. The alternate set may then be used by the interrupt routine and exchanged back without loss just before returning to the main program. The actual instructions used for these processes will be described shortly.

The stack is also useful for intermediate storage of data. There are special one- or two-byte 'push' and 'pop' instructions which simply put the contents of any given 16-bit register or pair of eight-bit registers onto or off the stack. Again, it is stored in FILO format. This is illustrated in Figure 3.2. Here, the last two stack instructions were 'push IX' and 'push AF'. The sequence of events is as follows. The MPU fetches the instruction to push IX. It then decrements the stack pointer which was currently at SP in the figure. The high byte of IX

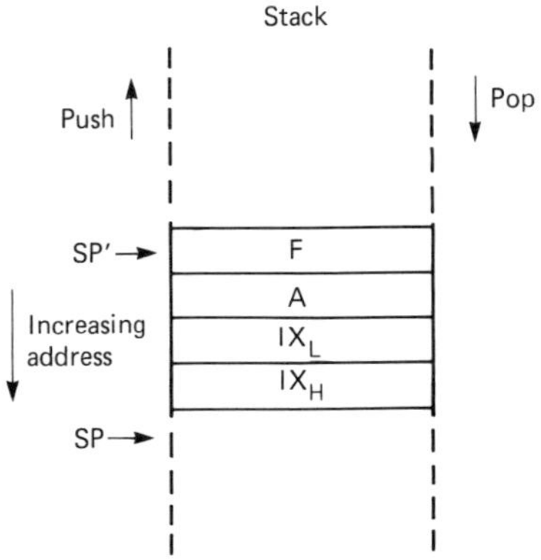

Fig. 3.2 The stack

is then stored at that location, SP is decremented again and the low byte stored. The next stack instruction is 'push AF' and the same events occur leaving SP pointing to a location (SP′) which contains the contents of F.

To retrieve the data, the pop instructions are executed in the reverse order.

Thus, as mentioned above, the stack allows very simple instructions to save registers and data without requiring the programmer to choose the specific memory locations in use. Once the stack is set up, it takes care of itself as long as it contains enough memory for the program's use.

The next two sections provide comparison information on the 6800 and 1802 processors.

The 6800 register set

The 6800 was first manufactured by Motorola, and is now available in a number of forms. The 6802 version is easier to use than the original 6800, and all electrical information in this text refers to the 6802. However, from a programming point of view, they are identical.

The register set of the 6800 is considerably simpler than that of the

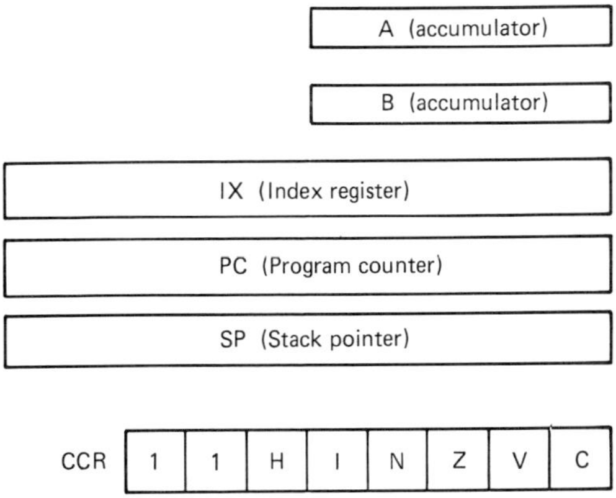

Fig. 3.3 The 6800 register set

Z80, as Figure 3.3 illustrates. This serves to show that a very large number of registers is not necessary for sophistication of processing power.

The 6800 has two accumulators, labelled A and B, which are nearly identical in use, with A taking precedence in some cases. There is no alternate set of registers, and only one index register IX. This latter fact is, perhaps, one of the 6800's drawbacks when compared with the Z80. The PC and SP are as described above. The F register is, here, termed the 'condition code register' (CCR), and has a similar use to that of the Z80. One advantage of the 6800 CCR is that it is affected by a larger number of operations than that of the Z80. It is not just accumulator operations which affect it. For instance, if an increment of IX causes it to change from FFFF to 0000 (hex) then Z is set to 1. The general action of the CCR bits is described below:

'H' is a 'half carry' which is set under some operations when the lower four bits of the accumulator carry into the upper four bits.

'I' is an interrupt mask bit and is described under interrupts.

'N' is set when the previous operation gives a negative number—it is thus similar to 'S' in the Z80 F register.

'Z' is the same as for the Z80, but is set more generally as mentioned above.

'V' is overflow as for the Z80.

'C' is carry as for the Z80.

The general structure of the 6800, therefore, is very similar to the Z80, and many of the techniques learned for one carry easily to the other.

The Z80 postdated the 6800, and includes a number of features which are absent in the latter. Motorola's answer to this, and a number of other criticisms, was to bring out what many would call the ultimate eight-bit MPU—the 6809. It is, in many ways, more like a minicomputer CPU without the advantages of a minicomputer's width of data bus. This limits its use in the minicomputer's traditional role of complex data processing tasks, which are more amenable to the 16-bit and 32-bit approach. However, the world of hardware control is excellently suited to the eight-bit approach with its simpler hardware needs and ease of programming. Indeed, there are many applications which would benefit from an even simpler approach using a one-bit processor. The fewer data bits, the simpler are the problems of interconnection, and the cheaper is a basic system. These are important considerations at the very widespread lower end of the control spectrum. The reader will find that the majority of principles introduced within the three examples presented here transfer easily to the 16-bit and higher MPUs.

The 6800 stack and interrupts

The 6800 stack is exactly as for the Z80, multiple stacks are possible, and all revolves around SP. One important difference exists in the data stored on the stack during interrupts. When a 6800 is interrupted, it stacks all its registers immediately following completion of the current instruction, before vectoring to the interrupt routine. This means that every time an interrupt occurs, a large amount of data is pushed onto the stack. If there are interrupts within interrupts, a few levels of such activity will fill a comparatively large amount of memory. However, this means that retrieving the exact position of the processor before the interrupt is simple and unequivocal.

To return from an interrupt, the last instruction of an interrupt routine must be an 'RTI' instruction. This simply 'pulls' the last seven bytes off the stack and puts them back into the registers in the following order: CCR, A, B, IX (high byte), IX (low byte), PC (high byte), PC (low byte)—the stack pointer is not stacked. This is, of course, opposite to the order in which these bytes are stacked during an interrupt. Note how the PC is pulled off the stack last. Loading the PC causes program execution to jump immediately to the address contained in PC. As with any MPU which pushes data before an interrupt, and pulls it after, it is important that the interrupt routine should leave the state of the stack unaltered during its execution. If the interrupt routine pushes anything onto the stack for intermediate storage, it must be pulled off again before RTI is executed—otherwise that data will be loaded into the registers erroneously.

The 1802 registers

The 1802 is manufactured by RCA, and combines a number of unique characteristics with many that are in common with the above two processors. The 1802 is a CMOS processor, and when combined with entirely CMOS logic and peripheral circuits it provides a controller which is easily supplied from battery power. In addition, the 1802 has a number of I/O lines which are directly manipulated by dedicated machine code instructions. The disadvantages of the processor are its very simple machine-code set, and relatively slow operation. However, its advantages for control circuits are manifold and this processor should always be considered in very simple low power applications. It also gives an interesting contrast to the other two MPUs introduced in this book, and thus allows another standpoint.

Figure 3.4 illustrates the 1802 register set. The set revolves around a block of 32 bytes arranged in pairs to give 16 address registers if desired. The notation used by RCA is shown, and implies that the sixteen 16-bit registers R(0), R(1), ..., R(F) are split into separate

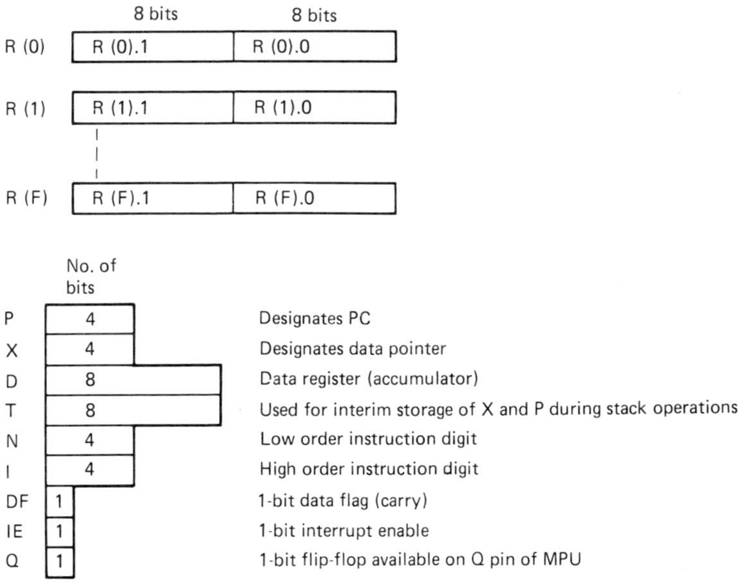

Fig. 3.4 The 1802 register set

bytes, with the upper byte of each denoted by a '·1' and the lower by '·0'. Thus the lower half of the sixth R register is denoted by R(5)·0. One of these 16-bit registers is designated as the PC, and one as a type of index register—the 'data pointer'. There are 16 possible choices for the PC, for instance, and thus a four-bit number (stored in P) labels all possible choices. Thus if the PC were currently the eleventh R register, R(10), then P would equal 1010 or 'A' in hex. Similarly X points to the 1802 equivalent of the index register. The 1802 may thus be said to have more index registers and program counters than both the preceding MPUs together. However, this does not automatically imbue the 1802 with any great sophistication.

'D' is the accumulator of the 1802.

'T' is used to store the X and P registers during stack operations, as described below.

'N' and 'I' will become clear later, but for reference, they together store the last instruction fetched.

'DF' is the carry flag just as for the 6800 and the Z80.

'IE' is the interrupt enable, and will be seen to be similar to those of the other two MPUs.

'Q' provides a very interesting departure from the other two MPUs: it is a register which may be manipulated by machine-code instructions, but its state appears as a 1 or 0 at the Q pin of the MPU. It may thus be used to set, directly, an external device with the proper buffering.

The 1802 stack and interrupts

These operations are very rudimentary on the 1802, but nevertheless provide the same advantages as for the 6800 and the Z80.

There is no dedicated SP, and no push and pop instructions; these have to be simulated by other means. The first three R registers have special meanings. After a reset, P is set to 0, which means that R(0) is the PC, and care must be taken not to interfere with this register unless P is changed to force another R register to take over as the PC. Similarly, when an interrupt is encountered R(1) and R(2) have special meanings. Firstly, some attempt must be made to store the current status of the MPU before servicing the interrupt. This is done by storing X and P in the T register. Thus the actual addresses stored in the program counter and index register are not themselves stored, just the pointers to those registers. It is very important, therefore, that these R registers are not corrupted during the interrupt. To vector out to the interrupt routine itself, the value '1' is placed in P and '2' in X. Thus the address at which the interrupt routine resides needs to be stored in R(1) previously. Note how the current PC itself is not manipulated, just the P register which points to it. The R register which holds the current PC just waits to be used again after the interrupt. There is an instruction to save the T register on a stack and then restore it later. This finally restores X and P to allow re-entry to the original program. In general, while programming the 1802, the programmer finds himself setting up appropriate R registers before events occur; manipulation of the 4-bit pointers is then all that is needed to effect a result.

An 1802 stack must be set up using one of the R registers and the X register. To save anything on the stack, it must first be loaded into the D register. Next, storage of the D register is effected to an address which is held in one of the R registers—namely the one pointed to by X. During pushing and popping, the stack pointer often has to be decremented and incremented by the programmer.

It is fair to comment that the stack operations of the 1802 are rather cumbersome and program-intensive, though the advantages of the concept of a stack still remain in principle.

The next three sections compare the instruction sets of the three MPUs. In order to learn the detailed programming of any of these processors, the manufacturer's manuals should be consulted—see the Bibliography.

The instructions and addressing modes introduced in Chapter 2 provide an introduction to most of the concepts required for an understanding of all three of the MPUs presented here. It is a worthwhile exercise to review that chapter before proceeding as the material presented there is referred to continually in the following.

The Z80 addressing modes

The addressing modes of Chapter 2 are included in those provided for the Z80. The full set is described below.

Immediate and immediate extended modes

These are as for the previous definition of the immediate mode, but these two labels distinguish between the cases where the data following the opcode is one byte or two bytes long. For instance, if the opcode is a load immediate of the A register, this only requires one data byte as the A register is only one byte long. This would, thus, be an immediate mode instruction. If the opcode was an immediate load of the IX register, however, the mode would be immediate extended. As a point of interest, the Z80 uses a two-byte opcode (DD 21 in fact) for this instruction, and hence the instruction takes up four bytes within a program.

All extended instructions in the Z80 store the 16-bit data in the instruction in low-byte-first format. That is, of the two bytes required, the low order byte is stored first. For instance, the instruction to load IX with the data E4B6 would be stored in memory as:

DD 21 B6 E4

This can cause confusion when reading Z80 code, and should be remembered throughout.

Modified page zero

'Page zero' is the name given to the first 256 bytes within the address map—i.e. locations 0000–00FF.

The type of instructions which use modified page zero addressing are sometimes called 'restarts'. Many MPUs allow certain dedicated locations in their memory maps to hold unique types of data. The Z80 allows some locations near to 0000 to hold the addresses of commonly called routines. The restart instructions jump to these special locations with single-byte opcodes. The result is that the programmer may set these locations up as he wishes, and very economically call the associated routines within the program.

Relative mode

This mode introduces a very important and common form of MPU jump instruction. The form of such an instruction is normally two bytes. The first byte identifies the type of jump, i.e. the conditions under which the jump should be performed, and the second defines the address to which the jump should be made. An address, of course, normally requires two bytes for its definition, but in this case only a displacement from the instruction's address itself is given in the second byte—the MPU calculates the absolute address to which it should jump automatically. The form of the second byte is called a 'signed two's complement offset'. To see how this works, an example is given below. Consider the instruction:

01A3: 28 13

The first four digits are the address at which the 28 instruction is resident. The data 13 is thus resident at 01A4. The 28 instruction is a relative jump on zero to an address calculated from 13. This jump will only be executed if the Z flag is 1. To calculate the address to which the MPU will jump if Z = 1, consider the fetch and execute which the MPU performs when it reaches the address 01A3 in its execution. The PC = 01A3, and the MPU fetches 28, and increments PC to 01A4. On decoding this opcode, it knows that there is a further byte to fetch before proceeding; this is fetched and held in a temporary register while it checks the Z bit of the F register; and PC is incremented to 01A5. If Z = 1, the jump must be performed. 13 is taken as the displacement from the present PC, which thus yields the hex number 01A5 + 13 = 01B8. This is the address to which the jump is performed. The address byte is in 'signed two's complement' form here because any offset from 00 to 7F is treated as above—that is, any eight-bit number with its most significant bit (MSB) set to zero. If the MSB is a 1, however, the offset is negative and a jump 'backwards' or lower down in the memory map is implied. To see this, consider the condition that the second byte of this instruction is 00. By applying the above principles, you should satisfy yourself that, no matter what Z equals, the program simply continues executing from 01A5. If, however, the address byte is FF, the definition of the relative jump is that 01 is subtracted from PC to find the next program byte (if Z = 1). That is, the program jumps to 01A4—a fairly dangerous condition as this location holds the byte FF, which is not meant to be an instruction! It is up to the programmer to ensure that any address byte used in an instruction refers to a logical and valid place in the memory map. If the byte is FE, the address to which the jump is performed is PC − 2, i.e. 01A3, and the jump is repeated over and over again until Z = 1—a rather difficult condition to encounter unless the MPU is interrupted, A is zeroed, and the program re-entered. The address calculation proceeds in this fashion for all the numbers from FF to 80, which is the maximum length of 'backward' jump possible by this means.

The signed two's complement numbers introduced here, therefore, form a set which is centred, in a certain sense, around 00. Thus FF is equivalent to −1, FE to −2, etc. down to 80 (−128 in decimal), with 01, 02, etc., the positive integers up to and including 7F (127 in decimal). The power of this type of instruction is that the resulting program does not mention absolute addresses *for the purpose of jumps*. Hence, the program may be relocated anywhere in memory. Such code is termed '*relocatable*', but may contain specific reference to absolute locations *for the purposes of storage of variables*. As long as these locations are kept free, the code may be relocated and run consistently as a self-contained unit anywhere in memory.

One use of this concept is in the development of control software. It is normal, as previously mentioned, to employ a powerful and large development system to write the software for a controller, which is then loaded onto EPROM and plugged into the target hardware. To develop the code, the resulting program must not vie with the development system's software (often called the operating system), which is normally quite large and complex. It is sometimes useful to develop a number of relocatable software modules resident anywhere where there is some free memory. These may then be strung together, loaded onto EPROM and plugged into the target system at just the right locations for the reset function to start the controller correctly. However, though such matters are beyond the scope of this book, we may say at this point that it is not always expedient to develop software in this manner, and the majority of development systems have some very powerful software to allow non-relocatable programs under development to be relocated at will.

Extended addressing

This mode, as before, allows an instruction to hold the full address, to which it refers immediately after the opcode or codes. Again, the 16-bit address is held low byte first.

Indexed addressing

As described in Chapter 2, the form of this type of instruction is an opcode followed by a displacement. In the Z80, the displacement is a two's complement signed number. Thus the index register may be loaded with the address of the start of a table, and all references to that table's contents may be made using indexed addressing. All the common types of instruction allow this mode to be used. The index register's contents are not changed by the use of these instructions. The use of this type of memory addressing is so common that the Z80 is provided with two index registers.

Register addressing

This mode refers to instructions which operate on registers implied by the setting of certain bits within the opcode. An example would be the instruction to load one of the main eight-bit registers from any other. The opcode of this instruction is 01rs (in binary), where r and s are three-bit numbers each of which refers to one of the seven registers B, C, D, E, H, L, A in the following order:

register	*r or s*
B	000
C	001
D	010
E	011
H	100
L	101
A	111

where r is the recipient register. Note that F is not included in this regime.

As an example, to load the contents of H into C, the instruction would consist of one byte: 01001100 = 4C.

Implied addressing

This type of instruction automatically implies one of the registers and none other may be substituted. For instance, all the arithmetic and logical instructions leave their results in the accumulator (A register). The A register is thus implied automatically and unequivocally by this type of instruction. For example, the 'add immediate' instruction does not need to say which register will contain the result, the A register is automatically implied.

The 'inherent mode' introduced in Chapter 2 is included in this and the previous Z80 addressing modes.

Bit addressing

The Z80 has a number of powerful and very useful instructions to manipulate the individual bits of a register or memory location. The actual bit to be manipulated is coded into 3 bits of the opcode itself. For example, the two-byte opcode: CB C7 sets the least significant bit of the A register to a 1. The fact that it is the A register, and the least significant bit, is coded into the actual value of the second of these two bytes. The C7 is split up as follows:

11 abc def

where 11 is constant, abc are three bits to identify the bit being set, and def are the three bits which identify which register is being operated upon. This logical structure for the opcode of certain instructions is a common feature of the Z80 and the 1802, but is hardly used on the 6800.

Register indirect addressing

This is one of the most useful and common modes for the specification of an address within an instruction. Broadly speaking, the instruction acts upon the contents of a memory location whose address is contained in one of the 16-bit register pairs. This is the same as indexed addressing apart from the provision of a displacement in the latter case.

An example of this type of instruction would be to store the contents of the A register in the memory location whose address is contained in the pair HL. Thus HL acts simply as a pointer to this memory location. Sometimes, 16 bits of data are fetched or acted upon in memory. In such a case, the HL register pair, for instance, would point to the lower byte of the two to be acted upon. The MPU knows that it must increment the address and act on the next byte found as being the higher order byte of the 16-bit number required.

It is important to realise that it is common for an instruction to use two different addressing modes at the same time. For instance, when the A register is loaded from a memory location, the source of the data may be found by indexed addressing from the IY register, whereas the destination is found by register or implied addressing.

This description of the addressing modes which the Z80 uses has been given in some depth as it provides examples of many of the most common forms of addressing encountered on eight-bit MPUs presently in production. It is important to point out, also, that the sophistication of an MPU in a software sense may be discovered by an examination of two main attributes. These are the addressing modes and the registers. When one encounters a given MPU for the first time it is well worth looking at these with some care.

The 6800 addressing modes

The 6800 is very similar to the Z80. It has fewer distinguishable addressing modes, and all opcodes are one byte in length. This means that there is a possible maximum of 256 different instructions. In fact, only 197 of these are recognised and performed. There are 72 different instruction types, and it is the different addressing modes which make up the 197. For comparison, the Z80 uses two-byte opcodes, and hence has a possible maximum of 65 536 different instructions. However, 158 different instruction types are provided, and this is made up to several hundred with the use of different addressing modes.

The six addressing modes of the 6800 are described below.

Inherent

As in Chapter 2, this mode is used when the opcode itself contains enough information for the MPU to determine the source and destination of the instruction.

Immediate

This is exactly as described above. The 6800 data does not distinguish between immediate and immediate extended as does the Z80, despite the fact that both exist on the 6800.

Extended

This is the same as for the Z80.

Relative

This is as for the Z80.

Indexed

Again as for the Z80, but remember that the 6800 only has one index register, the X register.

Direct

Unlike the Z80, the 6800 is capable of using the zero page in memory in a special and highly economical manner. The Z80 has only very few instructions which are tied down to page zero. The 6800, on the other hand, devotes this entire addressing mode exclusively to the addresses 0000 to 00FF. These addresses may be labelled by a single byte, and thus direct mode instructions are only two bytes in length. The first byte defines the instruction to be executed, and the second the address to which it refers in the range 00 to FF, with the two leading zeros of the 16-bit address understood. The fact that there are only two bytes to be fetched means that the instructions are faster and more economical in memory usage. Most of the common instructions of the 6800 may be used in this mode. The important point for the designer is that if such instructions are to be used, a certain amount of RAM must be placed in the zero page. An ideal example of the use of the zero page, therefore, would be for the storage of variables. Under such a regime, for example, fast economical instructions would refer to the zero page during the execution of calculations or use of data tables.

This completes the description of the 6800 addressing modes. As can be seen, the majority of Z80 modes are present in a slightly different form. The two main modes which are missing on the 6800 are register indirect and bit addressing. In addition, the 6800 has no apparent logic as to the way in which the opcode is made up. The reason for this lies partly in the difference between the register structures of the two machines.

It is fair to comment that, though the Z80 appears more sophisticated in a number of ways, the 6800 has the advantage of greater speed for many of the tasks of which the two processors are capable. Both MPUs are available in a number of clock frequencies, and for the same clock frequency the 6800 can be much faster. However, as will be seen, the enhanced machine-code set enjoyed by the Z80 makes complex programming tasks somewhat easier.

The 1802 addressing modes

The 1802 is rather different from the two preceding processors, as has already been pointed out. Many of the instructions are just one byte in length. One exception to this is the immediate mode group, which are two bytes long. This implies that no immediate loads of 16 bits at a time are possible—this would require at least three bytes, and on the Z80 sometimes four. Referring to Figure 3.4, the 16-bit register pairs must therefore be loaded eight bits at a time by successive instructions.

The way in which the opcodes of the various instructions arise is often very logical, as with the Z80. In fact, the opcode, when it is fetched, is stored in the IN register pair, as mentioned in Figure 3.4, with the high-order hex digit in I, and the low-order in N. In the description of the 1802 instruction set, the opcodes are normally split into the I part and the N part. The I portion normally designates the instruction type, and the N portion defines which of the 16 registers the opcode refers to. For example, if I = 1 the instruction is an increment register instruction. N denotes the register to be incremented. Thus the opcode 13 would cause register R(3) to be incremented as a 16-bit register.

Note from Figure 3.4 that the R registers are split into two bytes and labelled with ·0 or ·1 depending upon their order within the 16-bits.

The four addressing modes available are as follows.

Register addressing

In this mode, the instruction's operand is the contents of the R register pointed to by the N portion of the opcode. An example of this was given above.

Register indirect

This is the main mode for addressing operands on the 1802. In this mode, an address in memory is held in one of the R registers—namely the one pointed to by the N portion of the opcode. Thus, to operate on a location in main memory, the address of that location must first be loaded, a byte at a time, into one of the R registers. The I portion of the instruction's opcode then defines the action to be taken on that memory location, and the N portion points to the R register which holds its address. The 1802 instruction set therefore forces a rather cumbersome type of programming upon the user.

Immediate

This is the normal type of immediate mode, as has been referred to above.

Stack

This defines the 1802's method of implementing its stack. In stack addressing, a given R register is used to store the stack pointer. R(X) is commonly used, and, in the case of interrupts, the MPU uses R(2) for this purpose. It is fairly normal, therefore, for an 1802 program to use R(2) throughout for its stack. Once the stack is set up, it is easy to use, and pushing and popping are performed by instructions which are otherwise utilised to store data at normal memory addresses. This type of manipulation by the programmer is an example of stack addressing in general.

This completes the description of the addressing modes found on the three processors described as examples in this chapter. It is important for the reader to notice the general similarities between these MPUs at this level. This similarity implies that once one knows one or two MPUs it is normally easy to pick up the details of any others. Comparing three examples should give some basis for a classification of MPUs in general, particularly with a view to discovering which characteristics to look for when a new machine is presented. To complete this from a software point of view, the next three sections give an overview of the types of machine-code instructions which the three MPUs offer. As previously, any new concepts which are needed for an understanding of these sections are treated in detail in the Z80 case. Transferring to the other two MPUs is then an easy matter, and reference is made to the Z80 case as necessary.

The Z80 instruction set

It will be useful, during the following, to keep Figure 3.1 close at hand, as constant reference is made to the Z80 register set.

The data on the Z80 classifies the instruction set into the following groups:

Eight-bit load: for transferring single bytes.
16-bit load: for transferring two bytes at a time, including push and pop.
Exchanges: for swopping 16-bit registers.
Block transfer and block move: for dealing with memory blocks.
Eight-bit arithmetic and logic: single-byte operations including increments and decrements.
General-purpose AF operations.
16-bit arithmetic: 16-bit add, subtract, increment and decrement.
Rotates and shifts: shifts of the bits in eight-bit registers and memory locations.
Bit manipulation: for setting, testing, or resetting individual bits in eight-bit registers or memory locations.
Jump call and return: for changing the order of execution of programs.
Restart: calls to special routines starting at page zero locations.

Input and output: for manipulating I/O locations.
Miscellaneous CPU control: a few special instructions including interrupt handling.

The above groups are now treated in detail to complete the description of the Z80 software structure. At the same time, the last important concepts of machine code can be introduced, to provide a comparison for all eight-bit MPUs.

Eight-bit load group

This group of instructions is quite large and comprehensive. 'Any eight-bit register' in the following implies one from the set A, B, C, D, E, H, L. Note that the flag register (F) is absent. As a note on the jargon, the term 'load' normally means data coming in, the term 'store' means data going out. For example, 'loading A' implies that the A register is to be set to some value, while 'store A' means that the byte in A is to be copied into some other location—always leaving A unchanged.

This group deals with the important business of transferring data to and from the registers and memory locations. Any program will use the process of storing and retrieving variables and the easier this function is made by the manufacturer, the more economical and simple the programming becomes. The Z80 is quite rich in this area, as can be seen below.

Any eight-bit register may be loaded from any memory location using indexed addressing. An example would be the loading of H from the fourth entry in a table of values using IY. We could set IY to the table's first location, and the instruction would contain an indexed load of H with an offset of 03—remember that the labelling always starts at zero.

It is also possible to load any eight-bit register from any other such register with a single-byte instruction.

Any eight-bit register may also be loaded using immediate addressing, whereby the data to be loaded appears in the instruction itself.

Register addressing via the HL pair is also available. Here, as in indexed addressing, the HL register contains the 16-bit address at which the data to be retrieved is resident. This data may, thus, be transferred to any eight-bit register via HL. However, BC and DE may not be used in this way except to load the A register. The A register has some other unique characteristics; it may be loaded from or stored into I or R. It is also the only register which may be loaded by extended addressing, that is with the data byte held in a location whose 16-bit address is contained in the instruction.

The other class of instruction in this group allows data to be stored out to memory. Any eight-bit register can be stored to memory using the address held in HL, via register indirect mode—here again, HL holds a special place among the 16-bit register pairs. Indexing addressing may also be used to store any of the above registers. Here, the fourth entry in a table may be set from a register instead of copied into it as in the above example.

Once again, the A register has some special attributes. It may be stored via register indirect mode using BC and DE, and it may be stored to memory using extended addressing. The latter is a very useful feature which would be welcome on the other registers both for storing and loading.

16-bit load group

This group is more limited, in conformity with the eight-bit nature of the MPU.

Extended addressing may be used to load or store the contents of BC, DE, HL, SP, IX, IY. The extended address in the instruction points to the memory location holding the low byte of the pair being loaded or stored. That is, if DE is to be loaded, the extended address in the instruction holds the address of the byte to be loaded into E; the MPU automatically increments that address to fetch D's byte. In addition, the extended address itself is stored in the program with its low-order byte first.

Extended immediate may also be used to load any of the above 16-bit registers. Here, the actual data to be loaded into the register is held in the instruction—low byte first. This convention of two-byte storage is different, for instance, from the 6800, where the bytes are stored the other way around—with the high byte first.

Although SP may only be stored by one instruction (extended addressing, as mentioned above) its contents may be derived by several methods: extended addressing and extended immediate above, or by copying the contents of HL, IX or IY into SP. Note that the contents of the other 16-bit registers are copied from one to another, byte by byte, by use of the eight-bit loads. Note also that the index registers cannot be loaded to and from other registers—they always have to go via pairs of memory locations.

The pop and push instructions are included here too. Any of the pairs AF, BC, DE, HL, IX, IY may be pushed onto or popped from the stack. The stack locations therefore allow the index registers to be loaded to and from any other 16-bit pair.

Exchanges

There are six instructions in this group. Two of these are one-byte instructions to exchange the registers with their alternates. AF may be exchanged with A′F′ using one instruction, and BC, DE, and HL exchanged with their alternates, all at once, using another. HL and DE may be exchanged with each other. The final three instructions allow the first two bytes of the stack to be exchanged with HL or IX or IY.

Block transfer and search

These operations allow blocks of data of any size in memory to be moved around the memory map. Data blocks may also be searched for the occurrence of a given data byte. The registers HL, DE, BC and A are used in the following ways:

for block moves:	HL	the source location
	DE	the destination
	BC	a decrementing counter
for searches:	HL	the current location
	BC	a decrementing counter
	A	the search byte

The registers above have to be set up by the program before the instruction is encountered. As 16-bit registers are used, the full 64K of memory is at the disposal of these powerful instructions. As the moves proceed, BC is decremented until it reaches zero, and HL and DE are incremented or decremented depending upon the actual instruction chosen—i.e. moves may be effected from the top of a block of memory downwards, or from the bottom upwards. During searches the same holds, a block may be searched in either direction. The comparison between the byte being searched for and the byte being pointed to by HL is stored as an effect on the flag register. This may then be used to action a particular type of jump, and hence record the success or failure of the search.

The only disadvantage of these instructions lies in the Z80's special ability to provide a refresh signal for dynamic memory (see Chapter 5). If this control line is being used in the system, this type of memory loses its contents if the refresh line stops its activity for a given length of time. The refresh line pulses for each opcode fetch, and there is only one of these for each block instruction, no matter how large the block. This means that if the block is large, the memory may lose its contents.

This has to be borne in mind by the programmer in certain Z80 computer systems.

Eight-bit arithmetic and logic

These operations allow arithmetic and logical operations to be performed with the result always placed in A. Operands for all the following operations may be in any of the usual eight-bit registers, or pointed to by HL, indexed via IX or IY, or stored in the instruction in immediate mode.

The operations available are addition and subtraction (with or without carry), AND, OR, XOR, compare, increment and decrement. The comparison occurs between an operand stored as above, and the A register. The result of the compare, which is a subtraction, is stored in the F register by the state of the flags, but does not affect the contents of A; this operation is, therefore, non-destructive. The increment and decrement do not leave their results in A, unless A is incremented or decremented, and the operand is not available by immediate mode as this has no meaning.

These instructions are the normal operations one finds on eight-bit machines. Though not exhaustive as a set, they form the basis for any type of arithmetic and logical process which is required.

General-purpose AF operations

There are five instructions in this group. The decimal adjust instruction allows BCD (binary coded decimal) arithmetic to be performed with ease. The A register may be complemented or negated. Finally, the carry flag may be complemented or set to 1. These operations aid the use of the last section in various logical and arithmetic calculations.

16-bit arithmetic

It is not normal to find many 16-bit operations on an eight-bit MPU, though the following are essential. Normally they have to be constructed by stringing together eight-bit operations. The Z80, however, allows a few of these instructions to be performed without this necessity. The 16-bit operations are useful when dealing with addresses as well as for ease of higher precision arithmetic.

Only add (with or without carry), subtract with carry, and increment and decrement are available. These may be performed between various of the 16-bit registers, with HL taking on the role of accumulator in an analogue of A for the eight-bit operations. The IX and IY registers are also able to participate as destinations in the add operation. Any of the 16-bit registers may be incremented or decremented.

Rotates and shifts

This introduces a new form of instruction. The bits of any eight-bit register, or of any memory location, may be acted upon by these instructions. Broadly speaking, these instructions treat the byte being acted upon as a shift register. The bits may be shifted along the byte left or right in various ways. Consider the byte A7 in the D register:

D: 10100111

A right shift of this byte would cause all the bits to move one place right. However, the question arises as to what is shifted into the leftmost position. Several possibilities exist on the Z80; a 0 can be shifted into the left place, and the bit shifted out of the rightmost position can be shifted into the carry flag—the carry's previous value being discarded. Thus:

D: 01010011 carry: 1

In another case, the carry's previous value could be shifted into the left bit instead of zero, and the rightmost bit shifted into the carry position. If carry were 1 before such an instruction, the situation after would be:

D: 11010011 carry: 1

This is called a 'rotate through carry'.

The Z80 offers a rich variety of such operations, but the detail of their use and operation is beyond the scope of this book. Suffice to say that these operations are useful for a large number of complex arithmetic and logical tasks. Again, such tasks may be constructed in other ways from the basic set of operations, but the existence of such instructions aids programming considerably.

On other MPUs, this type of instruction would also be useful for the manipulation of individual bits within a byte. However, the Z80 includes a number of direct bit-manipulation operations which make this unnecessary.

Bit manipulation

Any bit in the eight-bit registers, or any memory location via HL or indexing, may be set, reset, or tested by a Z80 instruction. The Z bit in F is set to 1 if the test instruction finds a zero in the bit under test. This, once again, is the normal method for providing a test facility. If the test succeeds, a conditional jump will cause the program to jump to a routine which is only entered if the test finds a zero. This is the way in which the program takes notice of the result.

Manipulation of the individual bits is extremely useful in control applications. As seen in Chapter 2, bits can be designated as controls for switching on machines or for reading the states of sensors.

Jump call and return

The concept of a jump, conditional or otherwise, has already been introduced. This section now introduces a special kind of jump which forms the basis of much of modern programming structure—namely the 'call' instruction. It exists in one form or another for most machines and programming languages. It allows separate modules of software, known as 'subroutines', to be written independently and simply called upon to be executed as often as, and wherever, required. The essence of this type of construction is the 'return' instruction. Calling a subroutine is very similar to interrupting. The call may be made at any point in the program. It is important, as with the interrupt, for the main program to be re-entered at the correct place after the subroutine has finished. This requires the programmer or the MPU to store the current PC contents before the subroutine is entered. As for interrupts, the stack is the easiest place for this data. The Z80 MPU does this automatically upon executing the call instruction. The final instruction in a subroutine must be a return, whereupon the MPU pops the stored PC off the stack and hence returns to the main program as before. The main difference from interrupts is that the programmer is not usually so interested in preserving the registers: indeed, the subroutine may well pass its results to the main program through the registers. This difference is a direct result of the fact that interrupts may occur at any time, asynchronously with the program's execution. Calls, however, are arranged by the programmer, and it is thus possible for him to allow for their execution at known places within the program, and plan for the result with some special code placed after the call.

As with interrupt routines, it is of paramount importance, if the stack is used, to ensure that the state of the SP on entry to the routine is preserved by the time the return is made—otherwise, the wrong data may be popped off the stack into PC. Calls, like jumps, may be made conditionally upon the state of the bits in the F register. Indeed, on the Z80, even returns may be made conditionally on these bits. The conditional states under which jumps, calls and returns may be made on the Z80 are:

> Carry, non-carry, zero, non-zero, odd parity, even parity, negative sign, positive sign, unconditional.

The jumps and calls above are all made by immediate extended mode. This requires the two-byte address to be stored as part of the instruction itself. However, instructions also exist to allow relative-mode jumps unconditionally or conditionally upon the first four of the above list. This type of instruction contains a signed two's complement number in its second byte to allow a jump relative to the current PC position—this type of relocatable instruction, therefore, only requires two bytes.

There are one or two other instructions in this set. Unconditional jumps may be made to any location by indexed addressing or to the address contained in HL. The important 'decrement and jump if non-zero' or 'DJNZ' instruction is also included here. This is a relative jump only, and is executed only if the B register is non-zero; in addition, the contents of B are decremented. Thus, a loop may be set up in the program by loading B with the number of times the loop is to be performed; each time the jump is executed, B is checked, decremented and the jump performed until B is zero.

The return from interrupt instructions are also included in this set, and are described in detail later.

Restart

This group of instructions has been introduced before. They are, in fact, one-byte calls to any one of eight memory locations in page zero. They can be used for economical usage of memory by frequently called subroutines.

Input/output

This section introduces another important concept offered by some MPUs: a separate memory map for I/O operations which does not use the normal memory locations. In the example in Chapter 2, ordinary memory locations were used for I/O addressing. This is a perfectly valid method of causing I/O to be performed. However, there are advantages in keeping I/O separate from memory, not least of which is that the development system normally needs as much addressable memory as it can have for the storage of operating systems, assemblers, development programs, etc. If a separate map can be used outside program and variable memory, the development system can utilise its memory to the full, while fully and efficiently emulating the finished target controller system.

In order to have another memory map, it is necessary to provide another address line of some type. The Z80 provides this line in the form of its I/O request line or 'IORQ'. The line goes active (low) each time the MPU performs an I/O instruction. At the same time, the lower eight address lines of the address bus contain a valid I/O address—a bit pattern which must be used by some dedicated address decoding to alert the I/O device being contacted. This implies that the Z80's I/O map only contains 256 locations (of eight bits each). These locations are termed '*ports*'. In addition, the R/W line is used to signal a read from an I/O port, or a write, just as for memory. The system designer must decide on the utilisation of the I/O port map just as for the memory map. The only difference is that the I/O decoding is only active when IORQ is low—it is also necessary, of course, for the memory decoding to be inactive while the I/O map is in use.

The instructions for I/O operations are termed 'INs' and 'OUTs'. The A register may be loaded directly from an I/O port by the immediate mode IN instruction (DB)—the port from which the data is to be loaded appears as the second byte of the instruction. This is a very efficient method of reading the state of 'the outside world'. Similarly, the immediate OUT instruction (D3) sets any port to the state of the value held in A. In addition, any eight-bit register may be loaded from or stored to any port by an IN or OUT using register indirect addressing via the C register. Here, C must be set up to the port address before the instruction can be executed.

There are also some block input and output commands which allow a block of ports to be set from, or read into, a table in memory.

The flexibility of this I/O structure is most useful for control software. However, it must be catered for carefully in the hardware. The Z80 does not contain any special pins which may be set or reset by machine-code instructions specifically. The 1802, however, as will be seen, does have this attribute. The software of the 1802 is considerably less sophisticated than that of the Z80, and it is important, when considering design, to balance the straightforward nature of the 1802 hardware with the ease of software use of an MPU such as the Z80.

Miscellaneous CPU control

This group contains seven instructions, five of which have to do with interrupts and will be explained in the interrupt section of Chapter 4. These are the interrupt mask set and reset, and the three interrupt mode selections.

The other two instructions are useful one-byte operations. The first is the NOP or 'no operation' code. This literally does nothing when it is executed other than allowing the PC to increment as normal to fetch the next instruction. It can be used for a variety of purposes. It is useful as a time waster in a program where the processing is too fast for some operation, perhaps in I/O, to be performed. The other use is as a filler in machine-code programming. Other instructions can always be inserted in place of a block of NOPs at a later date.

The other instruction in this group is the 'HALT' instruction. This causes the MPU to halt operation and execute NOPs until an interrupt is received. NMI or INT (if enabled) will bring the MPU out of this state. As the MPU is executing NOPs, there is no danger of the refresh ceasing, and hence dynamic RAM is unaffected. The MPU has a HALT pin which it resets to low during this condition, thus signalling to external hardware if necessary.

The 6800 instruction set

The 6800 instruction set has many of the main groups of instructions of the Z80, with a few notable exceptions. There are no I/O instructions—all I/O ports are treated indistinguishably from memory. The example in Chapter 2 of machine control is the 6800's method of treating the outside world. There is no great overhead in this approach, but it must be borne in mind in system design. There are also no block instructions or bit-manipulation instructions. All bit manipulations either occur via logic operations or using rotates and shifts through the carry flag. Also, many of the different versions of each instruction are absent, owing to the very much smaller register set. The storage of instructions can be more efficient, in terms of the amount of memory needed on the 6800, for two reasons. First, all opcodes are single bytes; secondly, page zero is treated differently by the direct addressing mode (refer to the 6800 addressing mode section). Such increases in the efficiency of memory storage imply faster fetching and faster processing.

To retain compatibility with manufacturers' data on the 6800, the classification of the instructions in the following is different from that presented above. In addition, heavy reference is made throughout to the Z80 case to prevent needless repetition. The different headings are:

Accumulator and memory instructions: all the eight-bit load, store, arithmetic and logical instructions.
Index register and stack: all the 16-bit operations.
Jump and branch: includes all jumps and calls.
Condition code register: the 6800 can operate directly on the CCR (equivalent to F register).

The reader should re-familiarise himself with the 6800 addressing modes and register set before proceeding.

Accumulator and memory instructions

The 6800 has two accumulators and most of the eight-bit instructions can operate on or provide their results in either A or B.

A and B can be added together (result in A), or any byte can be added to A or B by an immediate mode instruction. The contents of any memory location can be added to A or B by direct, indexed or extended mode addressing. The same is true for add with carry, subtract (with or without carry), compare (non-destructive, Z is set), AND, XOR and OR. The accumulators may also be compared with each other, non-destructively.

A and B may also be set to any values by immediate mode instructions, as well as being loaded or stored by direct, indexed and extended mode operations.

The rotates and shifts of the Z80 are available on A and B, with one or two exceptions, using the carry flag in the CCR.

Push and pull are the equivalent of push and pop on the Z80, but may only be performed on A and B.

A and B can be incremented, decremented, cleared to zero, complemented and tested for zero or minus. The same operations may be performed directly on any memory location via indexed or extended mode instructions.

A and B can also be transferred, i.e.copied into each other—but not exchanged.

The final two types of instruction in this group are the decimal adjust, for BCD arithmetic which can only be performed on A, and the bit-test instruction which can be performed on A or B using an operand derived by any of the memory addressing modes. The action is to AND A or B with the operand non-destructively. This instruction does not affect either the register or the operand involved; it purely acts on the CCR. Bit V is cleared and Z and N are set according to the outcome; the other bits are unaffected. This instruction allows any bit to be tested, for instance, by setting the operand to a byte all of whose bits are set to zero except for the bit to be tested. This ensures a zero result unless the given bit is equal to 1 in the accumulator. Such operations are useful for checking input lines.

This concludes the largest section of 6800 codes. As can be seen, the operations are offered in a manner which is considerably more straightforward than for the Z80. This makes programming correspondingly easier to contemplate. However, some powerful instructions are missing, and these must be simulated from those above. This is not normally a problem, and commonly used ones are written as subroutines by the programmer. The arithmetic and logical structure is very similar to the Z80 for eight-bit operations. However, if much 16-bit manipulation is to be effected, the Z80 is more amenable as can be seen from the following.

Index register and stack

The 16-bit operations here often require two bytes to be fetched or stored in memory. Unlike Z80, these are always arranged high byte first.

The X register may be compared with any pair of bytes held in memory either by immediate mode or by any of the other modes, including indexed addressing. This is non-destructive, as usual, and only affects the CCR. The operation is fully 16-bit in nature, and the N bit, for instance, is set if the 16th bit of the result is 1.

The X and SP may be incremented and decremented, as well as being loaded and stored using all the modes. In addition, SP may be loaded with the X register minus 1, and X may be loaded with the SP plus 1.

This completes the 16-bit operations of the 6800.

Jump and branch

The 6800 uses the term 'branch' to mean jumps using relative addressing. There are very few 'jumps' (extended addressing) on the 6800. The usual unconditional jump is included using extended and indexed addressing, as well as in branch form, using relative addressing. In addition, unconditional jump to subroutine and branch to subroutine exist—neither of them exists in a conditional form.

The most important group is that of the conditional branches. This is the set of instructions provided by the 6800 for making decisions. Branches may be made conditionally upon the following:

> Carry clear or set, zero or non-zero, greater than zero, less than zero, greater than or equal to zero, less than or equal to zero, V set or clear, if higher, if lower or same, if minus, if plus.

Some of these are subtle conditions which are included for completeness but not explained further. Suffice to say that the conditions are quite comprehensive from an arithmetic and logical point of view.

The NOP instruction is included here, and is similar to that of the Z80.

Return from subroutine is the same as for the Z80, but return from interrupt is quite different, as is seen in the explanation of interrupts.

There are two further instructions in the set. One is called the 'software interrupt'. This acts in the same way as an interrupt, including stacking all the registers. The vector for this instruction is stored at the top of memory with the NMI and IRQ interrupt vectors (see the interrupt section). The other instruction is the wait for interrupt; this is similar to the Z80 with some important differences. The registers are stacked as for an interrupt, execution ceases, and the buses are put into the tri-state mode until the interrupt arrives along IRQ—which must be enabled. At that point, the interrupt proceeds normally, except that the registers are not stacked again.

One of the most striking points about this section is the fact that calls to subroutines are not capable of being made conditional. However, conditional calls can be constructed from a string of other instructions, but this is less convenient than on the Z80, where a single instruction is provided for the purpose. The omission of extended conditional jumps can also be a disadvantage.

Condition code register instructions

A and the CCR may be loaded from each other for direct setting of the flags. In addition, C, I and V may be set or reset by machine-code instructions.

This completes the instruction set of the 6800. Though the set is simpler than the Z80 it provides a very sophisticated structure well fitted to all tasks from simple controllers to large computer systems. Indeed it is sometimes argued that the complexity of the Z80 is a disadvantage, providing too many possible methods of attaining a given end. The 6800 is often said to combine sufficient sophistication with ease of use.

The 1802 instruction set

Once again, the manufacturer's data is adhered to in the following classification of the instruction set. The 1802 addressing modes and Figure 3.4 should be referred to throughout. The instruction groups are as follows:

Memory reference: D (the accumulator) is stored or loaded.
Register operations: R register manipulation.
Logic operations: operations on D including shifts.
Arithmetic operations: arithmetic on D.
Short branches: conditional jumps within the current 256-byte page only.
Long branches: to any memory location.
Skips: conditional jumps over the next instruction.
Control: miscellaneous instructions.
Input/output byte transfer: dedicated I/O instructions.

A more detailed description of the above follows.

Memory reference

Recall from page 60 how the opcode, when it is fetched by the processor, is stored in two halves in the I, N register pair. Very often, instructions operate on that R register pointed to by the N (or lower) part of the instruction; the R register thus indicated is written 'R(N)'. There are seven memory reference instructions, and a number of these use N in this manner. For instance, D may be loaded from a memory location whose address is contained in R(N). This instruction also comes in a form called 'load and advance'; in this case the address stored in R(N) is incremented each time it is used, thereby allowing a data table to be operated upon. The same pair of instructions may also be used via X instead of N, thus requiring X to have been set up accordingly. The usual immediate mode load of D is included here, as are the only two store instructions available to the 1802. Both store D, one uses N and the other uses X to find the R register containing the recipient's address. Thus no extended store or load of D is possible—all such instructions must go via addresses already set up in an R register. The store via X also automatically decrements the address in R(X).

Register operations

This set includes increment and decrement of R(N), and increment of R(X); there is no decrement R(X). Also included are the important GET and PUT instructions which allow the low and high bytes of R(N) to be loaded into D or loaded from D. There is no extended instruction of this type, and thus no R register may be loaded immediately from the instruction itself. These register contents are only available a byte at a time through a D—a severe restriction in terms of efficient programming.

Logic operations

A restricted but adequate set of operations exist, with the usual OR, XOR, AND and various shifts being included. The usual immediate mode is used as well as via X where any memory location pointed to by R(X) may contain an operand. The result is always left in D. The DF register is all that is available in terms of flags.

Arithmetic operations

Various add and subtract instructions exist, both immediate and via X. Again, the DF register is all that is available in terms of flags.

Short branch

Memory can be considered to be split into pages of 256 bytes each starting at 0000–00FF and ending with FF00–FFFF. Note how all locations within a given page have the same high-order byte. This set of instructions allows a conditional or unconditional jump to a location on the 256-byte page within which the short branch instruction is stored. The instruction is two bytes in length, with the second byte specifying the address within the page. This set is therefore analogous to the relative mode instructions of the 6800 and Z80, with the proviso that the offset is not interpreted in the same way. A number of conditions are allowed, depending upon the value of D and DF.

In addition to the above, a set of special branches are available which typify the control nature of the 1802. They take into account all the states of the Q flag and the four 'EF' or external flag pins on the MPU. Branches may thus be made conditional upon, for instance, EF=1 or Q=0. It is this type of facility which sets the 1802 apart from the previous MPUs, and explains its advantage for control in a minimal system. The 1802, with appropriate voltage level buffers, may therefore control one simple servo with Q, and sense four lines of input, through the EF lines, with no further logic packages of an I/O nature. Q may even be used to communicate serially to another computer system if required.

Long branch

These are equivalent to the extended-mode jumps of the previous MPUs, with the two bytes of address stored in the instruction: high byte first as for the 6800. Conditions include zero and non-zero for D, DF and Q, as well as the usual unconditional jump.

Skip

This introduces another type of jump popular with a number of machines. In general, jumps of the various types introduced so far provide a method of causing a given routine to be jumped to for execution if a condition is fulfilled. Another philosophy for such decisions is the skip. Here an instruction, which may be a jump to a given routine, is placed immediately after the skip. If the skip's condition is fulfilled, the program skips over the next instruction. If the skip is not fulfilled, the next instruction is executed. This is simply another method of allowing the programmer to process a given piece of code depending upon the outcome of some type of decision process. One of the skip instructions on the 1802 is called a short skip; here an unconditional skip is performed over a single-byte instruction. The other skips are all long skips over two bytes. Conditions are: D, DF, Q zero or non-zero, and IE = 1.

Control

This set allows the programmer to set P or X from N—i.e. with one-byte instructions. Q may be set or reset. T can be stored out to memory via X. NOP and IDLE, which are similar to the Z80 NOP, are included here, with IDLE waiting for a DMA (explained later) or an interrupt.

This set also includes the three stack-handling instructions which are very rudimentary compared to the Z80 and 6800, but allow a stack to be implemented with subroutines. The 1802 is conceptually complex to use in this mode as the majority of work taken over by the MPU in the Z80 and 6800 cases must be performed by the programmer piecemeal on the 1802.

Input/output byte transfer

This section again shows off the 1802's application to control. A little external circuitry is required (discussed later), whereupon the data bus becomes one of seven eight-bit I/O ports. Three pins of the 1802, called the N lines, provide a bit pattern to alert external circuitry as to which of the seven I/O ports is being addressed, and the data bus contains the byte to be transferred to or from that port. The fourteen instructions in this section allow R(X) to point to a byte in memory which is to be stored to (output) or loaded from (input) any of these seven I/O ports.

This completes the description of the 1802's instruction set. The major point to note is that the 1802 is especially suited for simple and/or low-power control systems. With a good development system at the disposal of the designer, the machine-code set should not be a disadvantage in terms of available functions. This is simply because software packages resident in the development system should assist the programmer to simulate all the necessary higher functions which have to be constructed piecemeal during programming. An example of this is in the use of subroutines. Considerably more work is required to implement subroutines on the 1802 than is necessary on the 6800 and Z80. Such exercises are quite mechanical and repetitive, and should be offered automatically on the development system's operating system or within its assembler. However, a penalty is paid in terms of memory utilisation and speed of processing. These disadvantages are normally irrelevant in the simplest control examples, and will be found to be balanced by the great simplicity of the 1802's external hardware.

The next chapter describes the hardware attributes of the Z80, 6800 and 1802. Timing diagrams give the exact state of the buses, on a cycle-by-cycle basis, for an appreciation of the way in which these processors work.

4

Three typical MPUs: hardware

This chapter describes the detailed way in which the Z80, 6800 and 1802 function in a hardware sense. That is, the cycle-by-cycle operations of the MPU lines are explained with appropriate timing diagrams of the type introduced in Figure 2.10. This data is provided in a form which introduces concepts used throughout the field of microprocessors. Once again, the manufacturers' data is followed to allow an easy transfer to the data sheets when actual design is approached. The emphasis is on general concepts which transfer to all other 8-bit MPUs on the market. Enough detail is presented to ensure an understanding of the peripherals and design ideas given in later chapters.

The basic Z80 machine cycles

As in Figure 2.10, the Z80 fetch and execute occurs according to the transitions of its clock. However, it is not of the fixed-cycle type of MPU and there is no definite bus state for any given state of the clock.

The clock states are shown at the top of Figure 4.1. This diagram uses the standard Z80 term for clock cycles, namely 'T-states'. To understand the following, continual reference must be made to Appendix 4, which shows the Z80 pin-out diagram. That appendix also shows typical times for the three standard cycles of a Z80A running at 4 MHz.

The clock is labelled with a Greek phi, and a number of other lines are shown which will be explained below. The address bus is labelled A0–A15, and the data bus D0–D7. All the other lines are control bus lines specific to the Z80. The timing diagram of Figure 4.1 constitutes a partial definition of these lines—partial because this diagram is only valid for one type of MPU activity, and the lines shown act differently under other circumstances.

Figure 4.1 shows those lines which are always valid or active during the fetch and execute cycle. The first two T-states just fetch the op-code stored at the memory location pointed to by PC. The bit pattern stored in the PC appears on the address bus during the first half of T1.

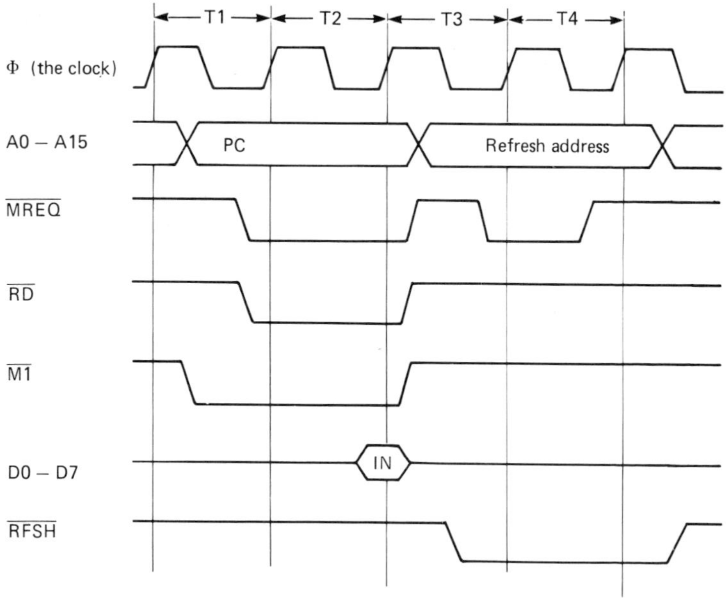

Fig. 4.1 Fetch and execute—the Z80 M1 cycle

The Z80 equivalent to the R/W line of the simple MPU introduced in Chapter 1 is a set of four lines; RD, WR, MREQ and IORQ, all of which are active low. The action of two of these lines is shown in Figure 4.1.

The first two T-states of Figure 4.1 are straightforward and very similar to Figure 2.10. After PC has been placed on the address bus, half a clock cycle passes before anything further occurs. After the falling edge of T1, MREQ and RD become active to signal a 'Read from memory'. WR and IORQ are inactive and not shown. The data coming back from memory is not assumed to be valid until the end of the second half of T2. This gives the memory and decoding logic time to present valid data to the data bus, and time for these electronic states to settle. In addition to the control lines above, two new types of control line are introduced in Figure 4.1. These are M1 and RFSH. The type of cycle described here (an opcode fetch) is called an M1 cycle, and the M1 line signals this fact. This may be used by external logic in a number of ways, and will be referred to later. The other control line shown is the refresh line. During T3 and T4, the contents of the 7-bit refresh register (R) are placed on the lower 7 bits of the address bus (A0–A6) with A7 set to 1. At the same time, RFSH becomes active to signal the presence of a refresh address. MREQ becomes active during this time too. These signals are used by some systems to keep dynamic memory refreshed, as described in the next chapter. While T3 and T4 are proceeding, the time is used by the MPU for the execute part of the fetch and execute. For more complex instructions, more T-states are required for the execute section, and thus a fetch and execute could take longer than four cycles.

To indicate the type of time scale involved in these processes, let us assume that the version of the Z80 being considered is the Z80A, which is designed to operate at 4 MHZ. That is, a T-state is 250 ns in length. Typically for the Z80A, the address bus contents become valid less than 110 ns after the rising edge of T1, and MREQ and RD are active some 90 ns after the falling edge of T1. The contents of the data bus are sampled by the MPU on the rising edge of T3, and must be stable 50 ns before this. Thus the memory has from 90 ns after T1 falls to 50 ns before T3 rises to present its data to the MPU. The delay is

$$375-90-50=235 \text{ ns}$$

This is called the memory access time. It is relatively short here, but is within the capabilities of many memory chips. The problem comes with the delays in address decoding and any driver chips which may be interposed between memory and MPU. As will be seen, it is in bus-oriented systems containing a number of different boards plugged into a motherboard that the problem occurs. Another source of delay is the fact that all waveforms take time to rise and fall. These rise and fall times should be included in the above speed calculations by an adjustment of about 20 ns (giving, here, 215 ns as the access time). However, this time is dependent upon such factors as the capacitance which the lines have to drive, and the physical length of the conductors used to carry these signals.

The next important type of cycle is the memory read or write cycle. This is illustrated in Figure 4.2. The memory read cycle is called an M2 cycle, and write is an M3. As an example, those 8-bit loads which affect memory would require an M1 followed by an M2 or an M3.

Note that the address bus becomes valid, and RD and MREQ become active, at the same time as for M1. However, RD is active for longer, and the data is not expected until later. Thus the opcode fetch is more time-exacting than M2 or M3 type reads.

The write cycle is different from the read in that the data is sent out by the MPU. The sequence is that data is presented well before the memory is enabled for writing by WR, and then remains on the data bus well after the write has been performed. This allows WR to be used as an R/W line just as in Chapter 1. It is a constant 1 during a read just as R/W, and it pulses low, for a write, while the data is present on the data bus.

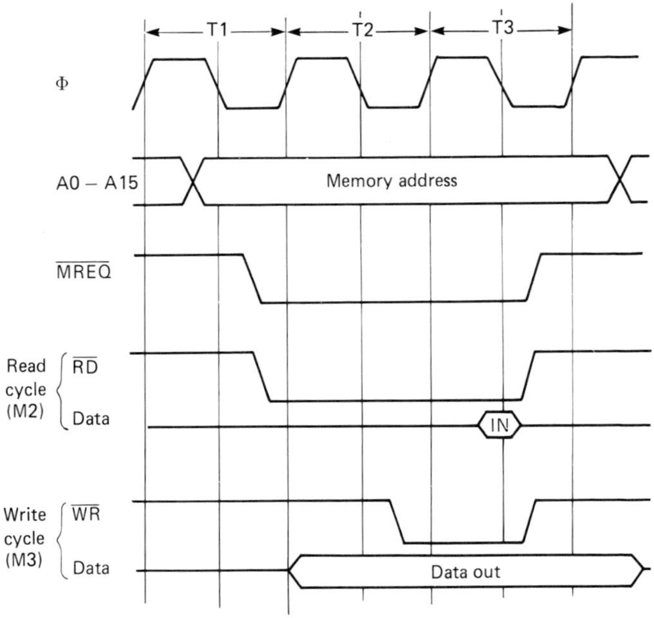

Fig. 4.2 Z80 memory read and write

Normally, memory chips are capable of accepting data during a write many times faster than they can issue data during a read. The type of time-scale to be expected is of the order of 50 ns after enable and R/W are active. This implies that, for memory, reading, and in fact specifically the reading of an opcode, is the most time-critical activity, and all timing within the design should reflect this factor.

Z80 wait states

In order to deal with slow memory, or other external circuits which cannot respond quickly enough to a request for data by the MPU, the Z80 has a line which may be used to force it to wait for any number of clock cycles. If a low is present on the WAIT line during the falling edge of T2, the MPU freezes the states of all its bus lines for a complete clock cycle, during which it again samples the WAIT line, and waits again if low. This is illustrated for an M1 cycle in Figure 4.3. T1 and T2 are the same as before, except that the data is not expected until the end of the wait period. The WAIT line is low when T2 falls, and thus a wait state (TW) is inserted during which everything freezes.

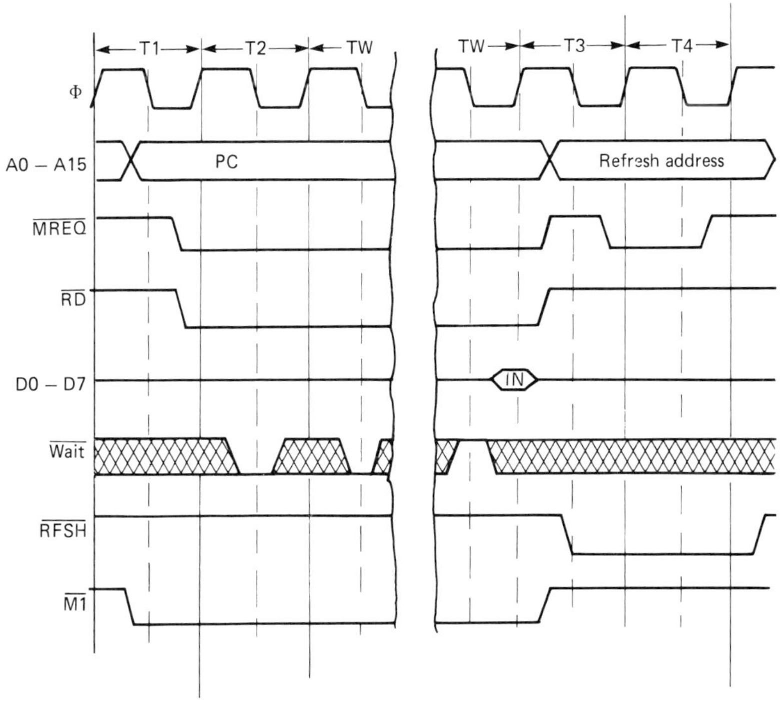

Fig. 4.3 Z80 M1 cycle with wait states

The WAIT line may be low indefinitely, each wait state sampling WAIT to decide whether the TWs should end. If WAIT is high on the falling edge of a TW, the data is expected at the end of that cycle, and T3 and T4 continue as normal. Note that the RFSH is also frozen, preventing dynamic memory from being refreshed during a wait.

The same type of activity occurs for M2 and M3 cycles. For M2 (read), data is not expected until the falling edge of T3 after the last TW, and for M3 (write), all lines, including the data bus, are frozen in their active states during TWs.

The advantage of this system is that slow memory can be arranged, with a small section of extra logic on the address decoding, to feed an automatic wait state to the processor every time it is accessed to ensure that it has time to respond. An example of such logic will be given later. In addition, some MPU cycles, as will be seen, include an automatic wait state as part of their normal activity to ensure correct timing.

Input/output cycles

The concept of the I/O map was introduced on page 69. To see how this may be catered for, Figure 4.4 sketches the address maps of the Z80, some logic to separate I/O from memory, and the timing diagrams of the input and output instruction cycles.

The main memory-map devices and address decoding are fed 16 bits of address, while the I/O map is only given the lower eight, the upper eight bits being irrelevant for the 256 I/O ports available. Thus four hex digits are required for the main memory addresses, while two are enough for I/O. The 'main memory map' block in the diagram is meant to represent the memory chips, along with their address decoding blocks, which require the control bus and the address bus for their logic. Similarly, the 'I/O map' block for the I/O lines and their decoding logic. Only one of these maps is active at any time, and the MPU distinguishes between them by its IORQ line, shown being fed directly to the I/O block, and inverted to the memory block. IORQ is inactive (high) for all the memory cycles described so far, and only becomes low in the cycles following the fetch of an I/O instruction. The cycle illustrated in Figure 4.4, therefore, could follow a cycle such as that of Figure 4.2 containing the fetch of an I/O instruction opcode.

As for the preceding instructions, the address becomes valid during the first half of T1. Note, however, that the Z80 only uses the lower eight bits of address for this type of task, providing 256 different I/O ports. Each I/O port transfers data to the entire data bus, and hence is eight bits wide. This allows $256 \times 8 = 2K$ I/O bits to be accessed.

The IORQ line becomes active during the first half of T2, and this can cause racing problems if a wait is to be sampled on the falling edge of T2. The Z80 therefore inserts its own wait state before T3 regardless of the state of WAIT in T2. This allows time for the IORQ state to be decoded by external circuitry, and supply a WAIT if required. The WAIT line is then sampled on the falling edge of this first TW, and waits are inserted exactly as before for as long as each TW finds WAIT in the low state. The read from an I/O port does not expect the data back along the data bus until the middle of T3, as for memory read, but note that RD becomes active later than before—during the first half of T2, rather than the second half of T1. This is no restriction, however, owing to the extra wait state which automatically occurs. External circuitry therefore has more time to reply with data than memory has during a read cycle. WR and the output data are also available for more time than is the case for memory, owing to the extra wait state.

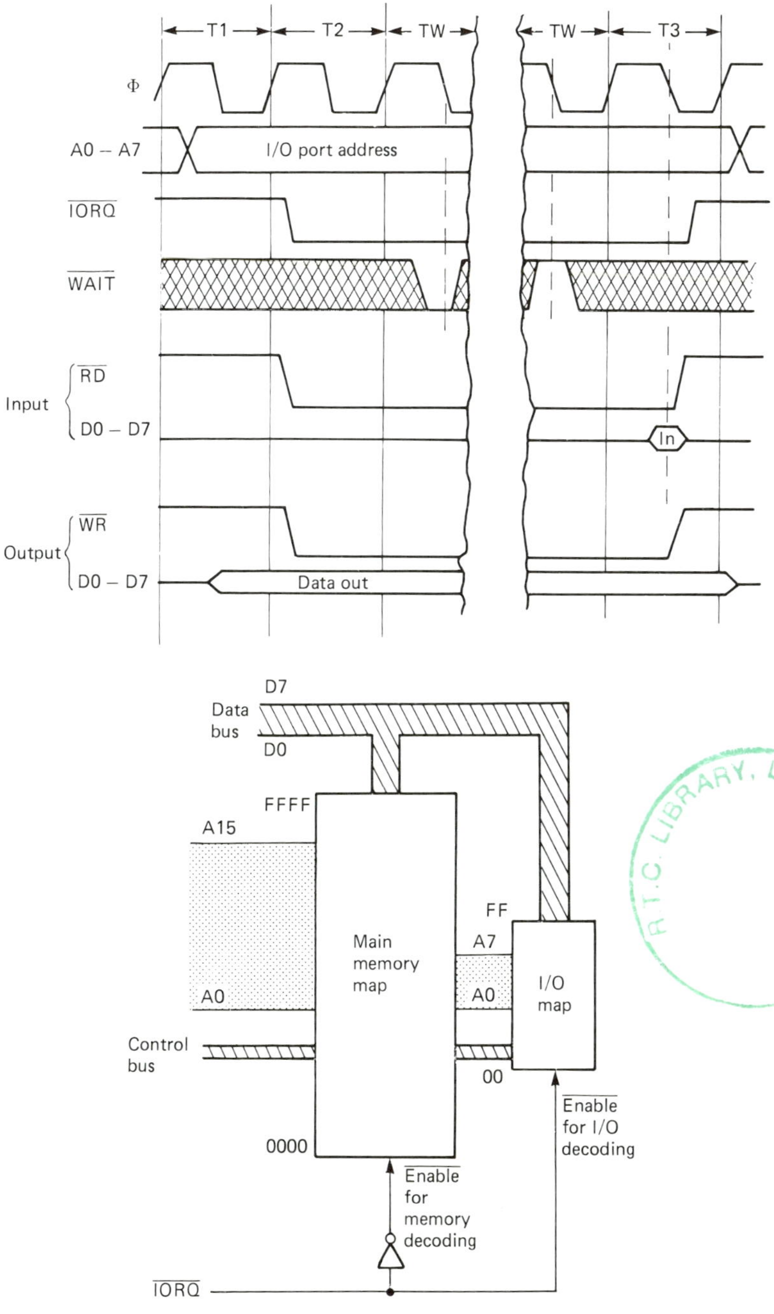

Fig. 4.4 Z80 I/O cycle addressing and timing

Other control lines and cycles

All but three of the Z80 lines have now been introduced. The three remaining cycles are HALT, BUSRQ and BUSAK. There are several other types of cycle to be described, and these are introduced in this section.

HALT is an (active low) line on the Z80 which signals that the HALT instruction has just been fetched. This instruction is used to ready the Z80 for an interrupt—either NMI or INT if enabled. The HALT line may be used, therefore, by external circuitry to enable a device which is capable of producing interrupts. While the MPU is halted, NOPs are executed—i.e. ordinary M1 cycles are performed to keep the memory refreshed, but the opcode thus fetched is ignored. The interrupt lines are sampled on the rising edge of T4, and HALT is removed during the second half of that T4 if an interrupt is present. The next cycle would be an interrupt cycle, described in the next section.

BUSRQ is an input line used to cause the MPU to go tri-state and thus release the buses for use by other devices. As for interrupts, when the BUSRQ line is taken low, the current instruction is completed before any action is taken. BUSAK is an MPU output line which signals that the current instruction has finished and the buses are tri-state. BUSRQ is only sampled on the rising edge of the last T-state of any instruction. The buses float, with the BUSAK line low, from the first half of the next clock cycle, and continue to do so, ignoring interrupts, until the rising edge of a subsequent clock cycle samples a high state on BUSRQ. BUSAK is then set high in the second half of that cycle, and the buses returned to normal at the start of the next cycle. Refresh is also stopped during this type of cycle. A typical use of this type of operation would be for a direct memory access. By this means, external devices may fill memory with data, or retrieve data from memory, directly, using the buses without the advent of the MPU. Very fast memory access may thus be affected. Another use of the BUSRQ line would be for multi-processor applications over a common set of buses.

Z80 interrupts

The use of interrupts, and hence use of the stack, is of fundamental importance in control-type systems. This aspect of the MPU's activity, therefore, is described in full detail below for the Z80. From the comprehensive description given here, any MPU's interrupt should be able to be grasped, as the Z80 has one of the most complex such structures.

The Z80 has two interrupt pins 'INT' and 'NMI'. INT is maskable—that is to say, there is an interrupt mask flip-flop within the MPU which, when set to 1, forces the MPU to ignore the INT line. The mask is set or reset by machine-code instructions. NMI (non-maskable interrupt) would be used for important interrupt signals, such as emergency signals, which are unequivocal.

The sequence of events which occurs when an INT interrupt is received is as follows:

(a) The current instruction is completed fully before any action is taken. This ensures an orderly and well-defined exit from the program.
(b) If the mask flip-flop is set, the program continues and the interrupt is ignored.
(c) If the mask is not set, the current PC is placed on the stack, and the interrupt mask set to prevent further interrupts. If the programmer wishes interrupts to continue to be serviced, the interrupt routine must contain an 'EI' instruction to enable interrupts again.
(d) The PC is then loaded with an address called the interrupt vector. In some MPUs this vector is fixed; in the Z80 there are three modes of interrupt vector production, and these are described later. This causes the program execution to jump to the interrupt routine starting at the interrupt vector address.
(e) If the routine uses the registers, the current ones must be stored as described on page 47 before the routine can proceed.
(f) At the end of the routine, an orderly return to the interrupted program must begin. Firstly, the registers are retrieved. The final instruction of the routine must be a 'RETI' instruction, for which the opcode is ED 4D. Its action is to pop the last two bytes off the stack and load them into the PC. This causes the program to resume as before, unless the stack has been used and not properly restored during the interrupt routine. This is completely under the control of the programmer, and it is up to him to 'housekeep' in a satisfactory manner.

NMI is different from INT in the following ways:

(a) It cannot be masked, and is thus edge-triggered to prevent an NMI from continually interrupting itself if held at an active level for too long.
(b) It always vectors to the location 0066—it is up to the hardware designer and/or the programmer to ensure that this location contains memory with the start of the interrupt routine or a jump instruction to that routine.

(c) Although the NMI masks the INT to prevent INT interrupts, it also saves the state of the interrupt mask and restores it again when the routine is exited. The NMI does this to prevent the main program from losing its INT mask status because of an NMI. The mask is restored (set or unset as appropriate) when the final instruction of the NMI routine is a 'RETN'—this instruction also restores PC as in (f) above, and replaces the RETI instruction.

The way in which the INT derives its interrupt vector is quite complex, and depends upon the mode which is set up by a machine code instruction before the interrupt is received—usually at the start of the program. These modes are described later. First, however, the timing diagrams are described to allow the hardware designer to design the necessary logic to incorporate interrupts into his systems.

On the falling edge of the NMI line, a latch is set internally within the MPU to ensure that the NMI is not missed if it disappears too quickly. In addition, the NMI remaining low does not affect the subsequent resetting of the latch—NMI is thus an edge-triggered line. Figure 4.5. illustrates the MPU response to the NMI having been set. The latch is sampled on the rising edge of the last T-state of the current M cycle. If low, a special type of M1 cycle is performed not dissimilar to the normal M1 cycle, including refresh. The PC contents are placed on the address bus, and, since MREQ and RD are active as usual, data will be forthcoming from the next memory location. However, this data is ignored, and instead the PC is saved on the stack (after T5 in Figure 4.5), and then the MPU jumps to location 0066, where a suitable interrupt service routine must be stored. NMI cannot be masked by software, and it is normal to use NMI for important processes which require an instant response when they demand attention. Note that BUSRQ masks all interrupts including NMI.

The response to an INT interrupt is more complex, and the line is level active. This implies that if the INT goes low and back to high before it can be sampled, it will be missed. The sampling occurs, as for NMI, at the rising edge of the last T-state of any M cycle. Figure 4.6 illustrates the INT response. Again, this is a type of M1 cycle. However, the RD line is not active, IORQ takes over instead. M1 and IORQ are low simultaneously, with RD and MREQ both high. This condition is unique, and thus may be used by external logic to signal the presence of an INT cycle. This is very important, as INT may derive its jump vector from external hardware. The three modes by which the interrupt vector is supplied are described shortly. To give the external devices time to supply this information, two automatic wait states are inserted by the MPU as shown after T2. The vector is

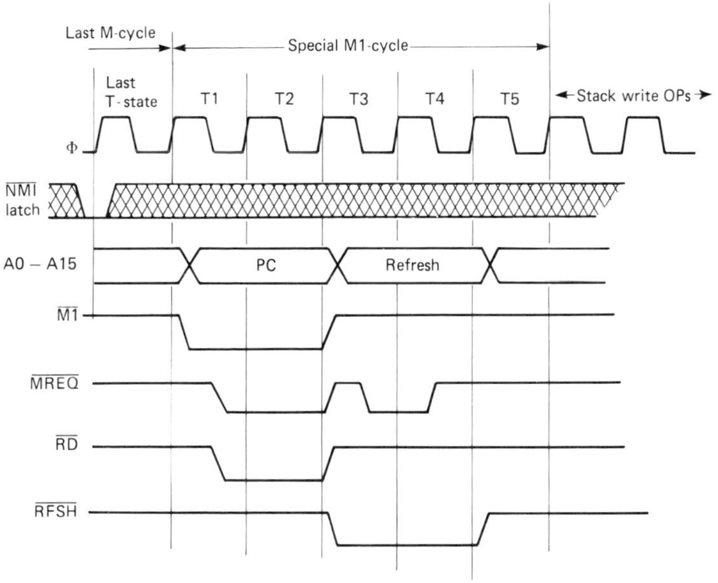

Fig. 4.5 Z80 NMI response cycle

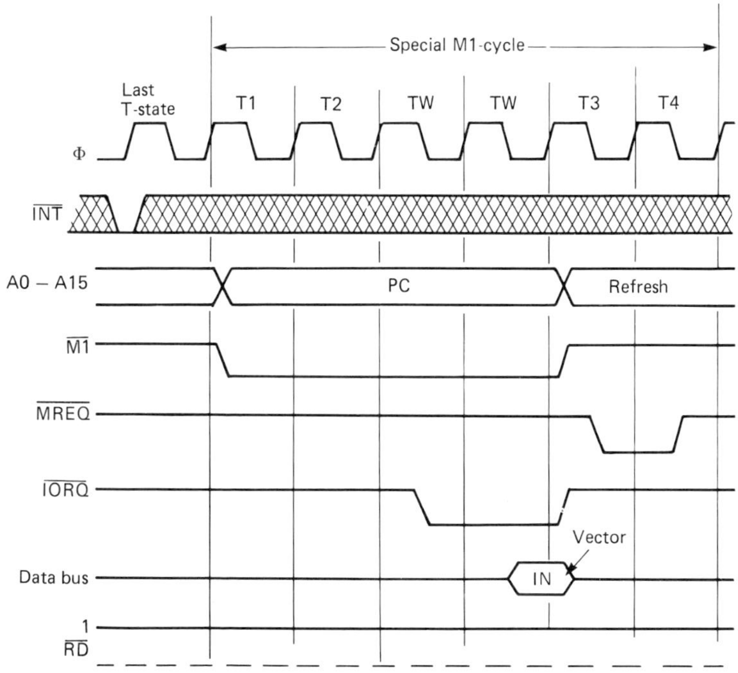

Fig. 4.6 Z80 INT response cycle

expected to be supplied in the form of an eight-bit offset along the data bus, and must be presented for sampling on the rising edge of T3. If the WAIT line is low during the falling edge of the second automatic TW, further WAIT states are inserted as usual, and the rising edge of T3 thus delayed. Note that a normal refresh does occur during T3 and T4.

The next activity after the T4 state shown in Figure 4.6 is to stack the PC and jump to the interrupt routine.

Sample logic will be described later for the utilisation of the signals referred to above, but the ways in which the INT may accept an interrupt vector are now described.

There are three modes by which the MPU may derive an INT vector, and each mode is entered by a machine-code instruction.

Mode 0

This mode is entered by the 'IM0' instruction (opcode ED 46). After this instruction, any INT will cause the MPU to fetch its next instruction, via the data bus, from the external hardware—usually the interrupting device. How the designer causes the hardware to feed this instruction to the MPU is not described here. Suffice it to say that family chips exist to perform the task, using the signals described above, and the design of special hardware is not difficult. The next two modes are more important for the Z80.

Mode 1

'IM1' causes INT to vector to address 0038, just as NMI vectors to 0066.

Mode 2

'IM2' causes this powerful mode of interrupt vectoring to be implemented. To use this mode, the register I (see Figure 3.1) must be loaded using the eight-bit load instruction to load I from A. It should be borne in mind, however, that upon a reset, the I register is set to 00.

Figure 4.7 illustrates the way in which the interrupt vector is derived in this mode. The programmer sets up a table of 16-bit addresses, somewhere in memory, which are the start addresses of a number of

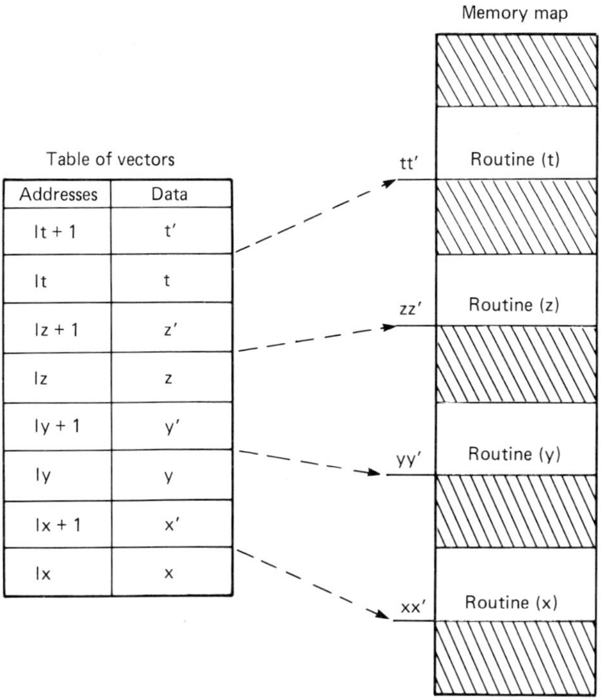

Fig. 4.7 Z80 mode 2 INT vectoring

interrupt service routines, each one devoted to a particular interrupting device. A large number of different devices may be capable of causing an INT in any given system, and it may be necessary to treat each interrupt differently. The 16-bit addresses in the table, tt', zz', yy' and xx', thus point to routine (t), routine (z), etc. The addresses at which these two-byte vectors are stored are It and It+1, Iz and Iz+1, etc., where I, the most significant byte of these latter addresses, is found in the I register, and the least significant byte is supplied by the interrupting device. A possible hardware configuration which can cause this to occur will be given in a later chapter.

The sequence of events in this mode for deriving the interrupt vector is as follows:

(a) When the interrupt is serviced, as shown in Figure 4.6, the data bus must contain an eight-bit word which the MPU can fetch, at the start of T3, to make up the lower byte of an address with the I register in the upper byte. The byte x, y, z or t is thus supplied by the interrupting device. PC is stacked at this point.

(b) The address, Iy for instance, is used by the MPU as a basis for fetching a further address contained in Iy and Iy + 1 – i.e. a 16-bit address is fetched—yy′ in this example. This is placed in the PC register, and the interrupt routine, routine (y), is thus started.

Interrupts are very important in control systems, and they should be borne in mind whenever external devices must call the attention of the MPU. In general, there are two methods by which the state of external sensors etc. may be communicated to the MPU. Either the MPU 'polls' these inputs, cycling around the lines continually reading their state whenever there is time, or the external lines are allowed to call attention to themselves by the interrupt lines. The former method may miss some of the states; the latter may cause a hopeless tangle of interrupts upon interrupts. Each method has its advantages, and they are described later.

The 6800 family

The 6800 family of MPUs has a number of similar chips with differing hardware attributes. One version of the 6800 has RAM and ROM on chip, another has I/O lines included. The hardware of the 6802 and 6808 versions is typical, and the software is identical to the original 6800. The following describes the 6802 version, which requires a very simple clock—in fact a crystal may be connected directly to the MPU—and has 128 bytes of RAM on chip. The 6808 version is similar but has no internal RAM. The processor is of the fixed-cycle type, and is very similar to the MPU described in Chapter 2. Appendix 4 gives the pin-out and brief pin description. As with the Z80, there are several control lines apart from the reset pin, crystal clock pins, and address and data buses. These are described in detail below, along with timing diagrams for the MPU's cycles, which are more straightforward than the Z80.

There are several versions of the 6802, with 1 MHz, 1.5 MHz (the 'A' version) and 2 MHz ('B' version) cycle times. However, the crystals for these frequencies tend to be cumbersome, so the 6802's internal clock generator includes a divide-by-four circuit to allow smaller, higher-frequency crystals to be used; the highest is 8 MHz. An external clock is also allowed; under these circumstances pin 38 (XTAL) is grounded and the clock fed into pin 39 (EXTAL). This allows the processor to be synchronised with external hardware if required.

The original 6800 differs from the 6802/8 versions in that it requires two non-overlapping clocks at the machine-cycle frequency which must be generated by a special clock generator. It also has no RAM on chip, and in exchange offers a few more control lines for such activities as tri-state control of its buses for multi-processor applications, and special lines to allow DMA cycles to be effected. The 6802, however, is easier to use for control type applications where the minimum of external circuitry is required.

The basic 6802 machine cycles

Figure 4.8 illustrates the basic 6802 read and write cycles. The 6802 does not distinguish between opcode fetches and normal memory reads. In addition, there is no separate I/O map, and hence a number of the Z80 timing diagrams are collapsed into this single diagram for the 6802.

The E pin of the 6802 sends out a machine-cycle clock (crystal clock divided by four) to signal to external circuitry the state of the cycle at any time. VMA is a signal which may be used to alert I/O, memory etc. to the fact that the address bus contains a valid memory address. The VMA signal (active high) is set to the inactive level when machine code instructions are being executed internally to the MPU. However, R/W is also high at these times to prevent a miswrite to memory. A misread from memory, during internal execution, would be irrelevant as the MPU disregards it anyway. VMA is particularly necessary for memory enabling when the HALT condition is to be utilised to the full (see below). VMA is required for certain 6800 family peripheral devices, and is useful in the correct enabling of I/O devices.

Typical times for Figure 4.8 depend upon the version of the 6802

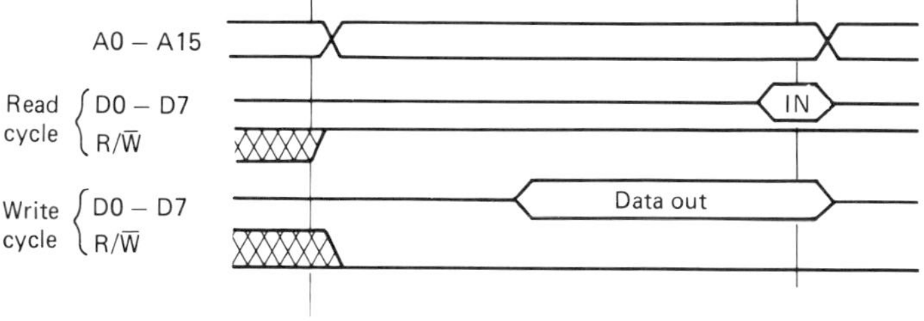

Fig. 4.8 6802 read and write cycles

chosen. For the fastest (B) version, the machine cycle would take 250 ns per half-cycle. The address bus, VMA and R/W lines are all valid approximately 150 ns (maximum) into the first half-cycle. For a read into the MPU, valid data is expected back along the data bus 40 ns before the end of the second half-cycle. This allows access time of up to

$$500-150-40=310\text{ ns}$$

for external memory and I/O devices without the necessity of halting the processor in any way. This allows a little more time than the Z80A, but is still quite fast, and any external and general buffering logic will add further delays, which implies that the memory devices themselves will have to be very fast in their response. In addition, once again, this calculation does not allow for waveform rise and fall times.

The write cycle is similar but the data from the MPU appears on the data bus 160 ns (maximum) after the rising edge of E—writing is rarely a problem with memories, as they will normally accept data within a time of the order of 50 ns. Therefore, the conditions given here are more than adequate.

It is essential that the basic times associated with these cycles are noted when designing a system. It is easy to construct systems which are logically correct but fail to use or supply data in the correct time frame for normal running.

Figure 4.9 illustrates a typical small 6802 system. The internal RAM is not enabled, and HALT and MR are not in use. VMA is used along with E to correctly control a block of 6800 family I/O devices, and the ROM can be assumed to be resident at the top of memory, so that at switch-on the MPU jumps to a location within the ROM which is pointed to by bytes stored in its top two locations. The interrupt lines are available for use, and also have vectors stored in ROM. To ensure proper control of the enabling logic for all memory locations, VMA is also fed to the address decoding logic—this may be considered to be good engineering practice.

A fetch and execute for the 6800 family takes a minimum of two clock cycles, the first of which is a normal memory read cycle as shown in Figure 4.8. An example of such an instruction would be an immediate load of A. The first cycle would be the opcode fetch, and the second a further memory read cycle to take in the operand and load it directly into A. This instruction is simple enough to require no further execute cycles. Some instructions require extra time to perform the execution in addition to the necessary read and write cycles associated with their data. For instance, the DEX instruction, to decrement the X-register takes four cycles. The first is the normal opcode fetch, and the next three are required for internal execution of

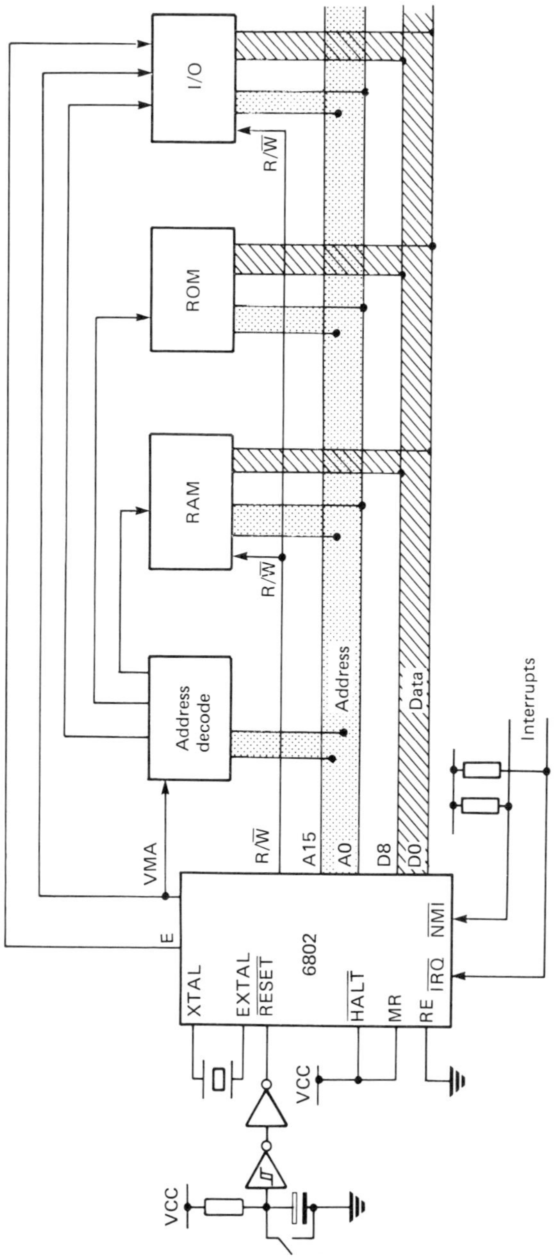

Fig. 4.9 Typical 6802 system

the code. VMA is valid for the first two cycles and falls low for the last two.

As mentioned above, this MPU has some characteristics in common with the MPU described in Chapter 2. The 6800 family is of the constant-cycle type in that the first half of each cycle does not use the data bus. If E and VMA are ANDed together, they form a signal whose low state may be used to inform external circuitry as to when the data bus is free for external use. As long as these external activities never overlap with (E AND VMA) in the high state, the MPU is totally unaware of their existence. The address bus, however, is not tri-state, and if this is to be used externally, a set of buffers must be used to switch them away from the MPU at this time. It is fair to point out, however, that such a practice with the address bus pushes the timing constraints on memory access even more finely, as the address would be fed to the memory for even less time than is the case normally. Again, external circuitry can be designed to allay this problem, but is beyond the scope of the present work. If external devices must use all the buses, the designer is probably better advised to use the 6800 itself.

The basic 6800 family control lines are very straightforward. R/W is the only line provided for determining the direction of data flow, and is described in Chapter 2. The only signal provided to alert memory and I/O of an impending data transfer is VMA. This is in sharp contrast to the Z80 which has a number of control lines to signal a large number of different conditions of the MPU. The 6800 does not have a method of refreshing dynamic memory; in common with all other MPUs, this activity must be performed by special logic.

The other control lines of the 6802 are as follows:

HALT When this pin on the MPU is taken low, activity halts at the end of the current instruction, VMA goes low, and the 'BA' pin goes high. In addition, the address bus contains the address of the next instruction. This pin is useful for single-stepping the MPU, whereby instructions are performed one at a time by the press of a button. This is a very powerful method of debugging machine-code programs.

BA This pin signals that either a HALT condition has been entered or that a software wait instruction has been executed. In the first case, BA returns to its inactive state (low) when HALT disappears. In the second, BA returns after an interrupt. This pin, rather like BUSAK on the Z80, is fed to external circuitry to confirm that the MPU has entered the halt as requested. This may take some time if the MPU is in the middle of a long instruction, and the external activity, using the halt, should not be allowed to start until BA does go high.

RESET, IRQ and NMI These are reset and interrupt pins which will be described in detail later.

RE and VCC standby RE (RAM enable) enables the internal 128 bytes of RAM if there is no external memory at these locations. The internal RAM is fully decoded to be at locations 0000–007F. This RAM is very useful in minimal systems—the stack and some variables may be situated here if the RAM usage is small. This saves an extra RAM chip with all its associated connections. The VCC standby pin is used to supply the first 32 bytes of this RAM from an external power source to allow this to be backed up independently of the rest of the power requirements. This power source must be capable of supplying about 8mA, and may be used, for instance, to allow important variables and constants to be saved during system power-down.

The 6802 MR control line

The MR (memory ready) line is very important in system design. It allows slow external devices to force the MPU into the 6802 version of the Z80's wait state. If this facility were not offered on an MPU, then slow devices would need to be caterd for by slowing the entire MPU down, with an attendant loss of overall speed.

The effect of a low signal on the MR pin is to stretch the high state of the E signal shown in Figure 4.8 by an integral number of half-E periods. That is, the High-state time of E may be multipled by two, three, four, etc. The 6800 family cannot be slowed below 100 kHz, as the internal register memory is dynamic, and will lose its data if not continually refreshed by the presence of the clock. Thus the maximum allowed stretch of the E signal is 10 microseconds.

The timing of MR is critical, and Figure 4.10 illustrates how MR should be treated, as well as its effect. For a given cycle to be stretched, the 6802 requires the request for an E stretch to be made during that machine cycle, but a minimum time period (tPCS) before the impending falling edge of E at the end of the cycle. The value of tPCS is a little less than the clock period of the crystal clock. This clock, if generated from an external source, may be used to synchronise a stretch request of a given cycle with the timing of E. However, this should not be necessary. When the address of a slow device is placed on the address bus, with VMA active, the address decoding logic must be arranged to select the device and to send a 0 along to the MR line, at least tCPS before E falls. The same is true for the stretch to end. During the stretch, all the lines shown are frozen, and the data is not expected by the MPU until just before E falls, as normal. E is stretched, as shown, by half-machine-cycles until MR rises. If MR rises in a given half-cycle before the set-up time starts, then that will be the last stretched cycle. If not, a further cycle of stretch is executed.

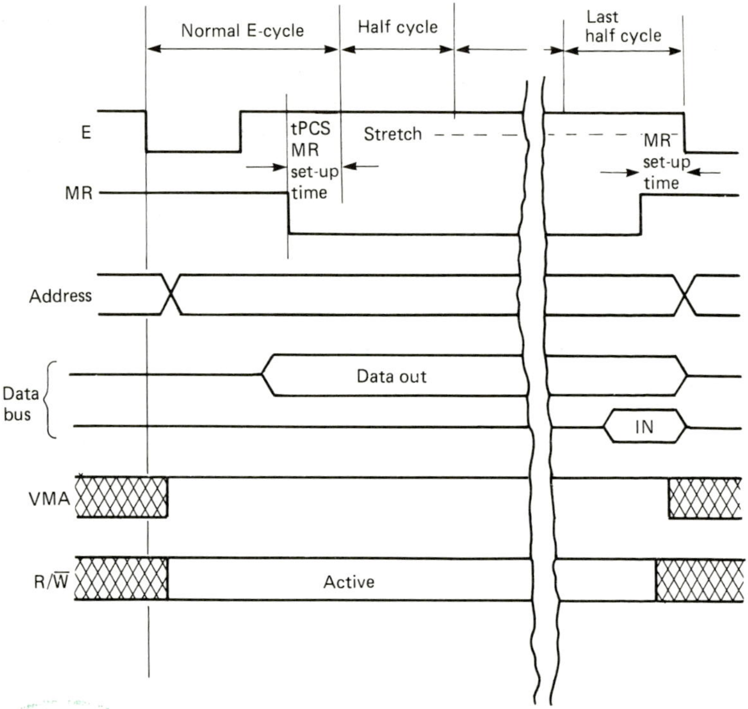

Fig. 4.10 6802 memory-ready cycles

This stretching can also be used by dynamic memory refresh logic to freeze the processor every so often to perform a refresh without the fear of missing a memory request from the MPU.

If the slow device is only slow at *supplying* data to the data bus, and not in *taking in* data, the R/W line could be gated into the MR logic to cause the MR to occur only when R/W is high. This would allow the MPU to work a little faster, if required, than would otherwise be the case.

The 6800 family reset

The reset on the 6800 is more involved than that of the Z80. Figure 4.11 shows the timing of the reset cycle. Logic as in Figure 1.2 is quite adequate for the reset pin on the 6800.

The reset line must remain low for at least eight machine cycles before going high, and if a reset is performed at any time during normal operations, it must be held low for at least three cycles—these times are necessary to allow the MPU to re-initialise itself. While reset is low, the address bus contains the address FFFE, and VMA, R/W (and BA) are all low. In addition, interrupts are not accepted until after the reset sequence defined by Figure 4.11. If reset rises tPCS before E falls, then that cycle will be the first of the reset sequence. If the time is less than this necessary set-up time, the rising edge of reset is ignored for a further cycle.

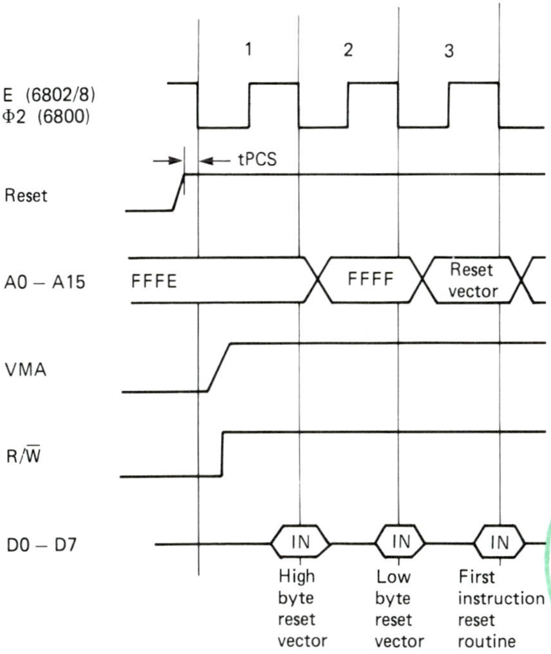

Fig. 4.11 6800 reset timing

The 6800 reset sequence causes the two bytes of a 16-bit address called the 'reset vector' to be fetched one byte at a time. The high-order address byte is assumed, by the MPU, to be resident at location FFFE, and the low byte at FFFF. The address bytes must be arranged to be resident at those locations by the hardware designer—either by locating some ROM at the top of memory, or by the method shown in Figure 4.12. Here the tri-state buffers (such as the 74LS244) with their outputs on the data bus have inputs set to 1 and 0 voltage levels to give bit patterns equal to the two bytes of the reset vector. Their enables are address-decoded at FFFE and FFFF. When the enable of such a device is taken low, the bit pattern set up on the input is allowed through to the output. When the enable is high, the outputs are tri-state to prevent these buffers from interfering with the normal operation of the data bus. Figure 4.12 also provides a general method of arranging hardware to place a given bit pattern on the data bus when required.

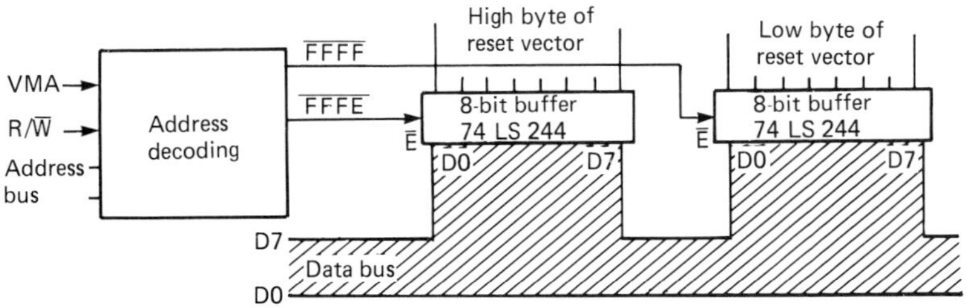

Fig. 4.12 A hardware reset vector

To fetch this reset address, the MPU performs two normal read cycles, one for each byte, as shown in Figure 4.11. The MPU loads these bytes into the PC. The third cycle of this sequence puts the reset vector in the PC onto the address bus and uses it to fetch the first instruction of the reset routine. At this point, the NMI will be serviced if present, but the interrupt mask is set, preventing an IRQ from occurring until a subsequent instruction resets it.

It is thus possible for the reset routine to be stored anywhere in memory, being pointed to by the reset vector, which is stored at the top of memory. It is not uncommon to find that a system will have a ROM decoded to sit at the top of memory, containing the reset vector in its top two locations, and vectoring to some location in that ROM.

6800 interrupts

The general form of 6800 family interrupts has already been introduced. They are considerably simpler than for the Z80, and are vectored to in a similar way to the above description of the reset.

The address to which the MPU vectors on receiving an NMI is held at FFFC and FFFD, and for an IRQ at FFF8 and FFF9. IRQ is the 6800 equivalent of the Z80's INT, in that it is maskable. The I bit of the CCR is the mask, and, as for the Z80, enables IRQ if equal to a zero.

As mentioned on page 74, there is a further type of interrupt, similar to the above, but resulting from a software instruction called SWI, or software interrupt. It is similar to the others, and takes its vector from FFFA and FFFB.

All 6800 registers are saved on the stack upon an interrupt, and may be retrieved by a single instruction.

Figure 4.13 illustrates the interrupt service timing. Note that, as for the Z80, NMI is edge-triggered, IRQ is level-triggered, and the mask is set upon an IRQ and must be physically reset by the routine if required. In addition, the interrupt is not serviced at the end of the current instruction unless it has occurred greater than the requisite

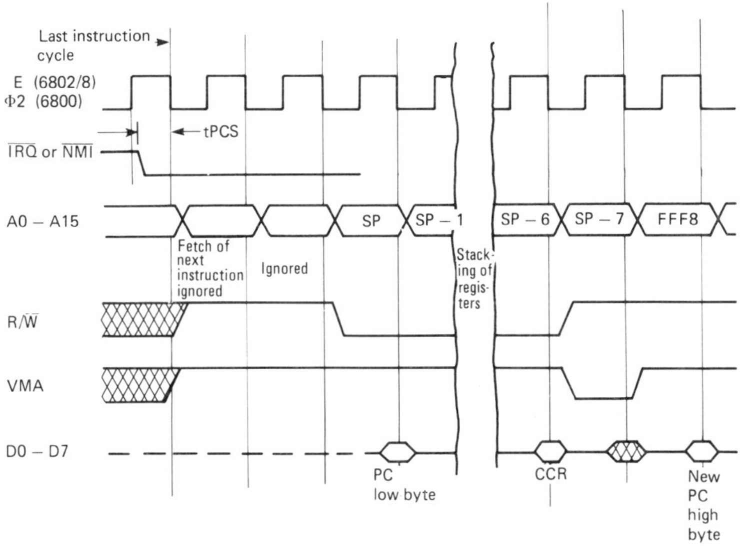

Fig. 4.13 6800 interrupt timing

time (tPCS) before the end of the final cycle of that instruction. Two read cycles are then performed, the data from which is ignored; these cycles are for internal MPU initialisations. In the next cycle, the R/W line falls and the low byte of the current PC is stored to the stack, followed by all the stacked data: cycle by cycle. This ends with the CCR being stored, followed by a cycle in which R/W is high and VMA is low. The interrupt vector, shown here as for the IRQ, is fetched and the MPU jumps to the vectored location as for reset. This process, as can be seen, takes a comparatively long time by normal instruction standards. However, if a wait instruction is executed by the MPU, the registers are stacked and the MPU waits for an interrupt, which can then be serviced very quickly as the stacking is already done.

The above indicates that the 6800 family is very much easier to use than the Z80, having considerably fewer control lines, while providing a similar degree of power for control and general computer activities. However, a few more external logic circuits would be required to completely match the Z80. As a contrast to these two competitively matched MPUs, the 1802 is described below.

The 1802

Again, to follow this section, Appendix 4 giving the pin-outs and brief description of the 1802's lines should be consulted.

The 1802 has a large number of useful control lines for observing the exact state of the MPU at any time. It is also capable of being controlled very closely by the state of certain input lines. SC0 and SC1 inform external circuitry of the type of cycle being performed, WAIT and CLEAR cause the MPU's mode of operation to be changed radically, and TPA and TPB signal the state of the MPU within its cycle for various purposes. The 1802 is also capable of allowing direct memory access (DMA) cycles to be performed, whereby memory may be written to or read directly by devices external to the MPU system without passing through the 1802's registers. Normally an extra DMA controller chip would be required in the system to take over, and control, the buses while the MPU goes tri-state. The 1802, however, is capable of acting as this DMA controller with a minimum of external logic.

To categorise the machine cycles of the 1802, Figure 4.14 gives a table of the states of SC0 and SC1 during different types of cycle, and details WAIT and CLEAR for different 1802 functions. This table must be referred to constantly for an understanding of the following. It should also be noted that there is no reset pin on the 1802.

	State code	
State type	SC1	SC0
S 0 [FETCH]	0	0
S 1 [EXECUTE]	0	1
S 2 [DMA]	1	0
S 3 [INTERRUPT]	1	1

$\overline{\text{Clear}}$	$\overline{\text{Wait}}$	Mode
0	0	Load
0	1	Reset
1	0	Pause
1	1	Run

Fig. 4.14 1802 state codes and control modes

The 1802 is a completely static device: its clock has a *maximum* stated frequency, but no minimum. The MPU may therefore be clocked by hand, using a debounced switch if required. Indeed, this provides a very simple way of observing the activity of the 1802 while executing a program. The SC0 and SC1 pins should be considered as 1802 versions of the Z80's M1, IORQ etc., which are used extensively to signal the type of operation being performed from cycle to cycle.

The 1802 has an eight-bit data bus and an eight-bit address bus. The MPU can address a full 64K of memory, but the two bytes necessary for this capacity are multiplexed sequentially onto the address bus one byte at a time. Also, the 1802 is a CMOS processor with all that that entails. For instance, all inputs should be tied high or low when not in use, and the MPU will run at a higher maximum clock frequency if the power supply is raised above 5 volts. To this end, the 1802 has two power supply pins, labelled VCC and VDD, which are isolated from each other and from the input/output lines. The 1802 may therefore be operated at its maximum voltage on VDD, and hence at a higher speed if required, while still remaining compatible with TTL devices, as long as VCC is kept down to +5 volts. If entirely CMOS devices are employed within the MPU system, VCC, and the CMOS logic power supply, can be raised to 10 volts, and the whole system may be run even faster. While operating, the 1802 will be found to consume a current of the order of 1 mA, depending upon the speed of its clock.

The majority of 1802 lines have been referred to previously. The others are as follows.

CLOCK and XTAL These are as for the 6802, with CLOCK equivalent to EXTAL. The maximum frequency of the crystal or clock at 5 volt working is 2.5 MHz, which can be boosted to 3.1 MHz if VDD alone is raised to 10 volts, and further to 5 MHz if both VCC and VDD are at 10 volts. However, 16 clock cycles, minimum, are required for an instruction to be fetched and executed, which takes over 3 microseconds at 5 MHz. This brings the 1802 below the previous MPUs in speed.

MRD and MWR These are the equivalent of RD and WR on the Z80.

INTERRUPT This is the only interrupt offered by the 1802, and is maskable.

DMAIN and DMAOUT These will be explained fully shortly.

TPA and TPB These are clock lines to alert external circuitry of the correct times for certain activities. For instance, they are used to demultiplex the full 16 bits of address.

To perform any activity using the 1802, the first lines to be set up are the mode control lines: WAIT and CLEAR. To see how the 1802 functions, let us assume that a system has been constructed with a ROM containing a program decoded to start at address 0000. The objective is to reset the 1802 and run the program. Referring to Figure 4.14, this is achieved by holding WAIT high, and taking CLEAR low, i.e. taking the 1802 into the RESET condition. CLEAR should be held low for a time and then be taken high. This enters the run condition, which starts the 1802 executing from 0000. Thus, in such a system, the CLEAR acts like the normal RESET pin, and may have an R–C network attached to it as in Figure 1.2.

The 1802 machine cycles

All machine-code instructions take eight cycles of the clock for a fetch (S0 cycle) followed by one or two eight-cycle executes (S1 cycles). The memory read cycle, which must be used for the fetch, is illustrated in Figure 4.15, along with a memory write cycle which may be required in an execute.

The state of the address bus is signalled by the TPA line, whose falling edge should be used to latch the high address byte. Figure 4.16 shows a typical system configuration for the 1802; I/O is treated later. Figure 4.15 shows that the falling edge on TPA may be used, by the eight-bit latch of Figure 4.16, to strobe the high-order address bits

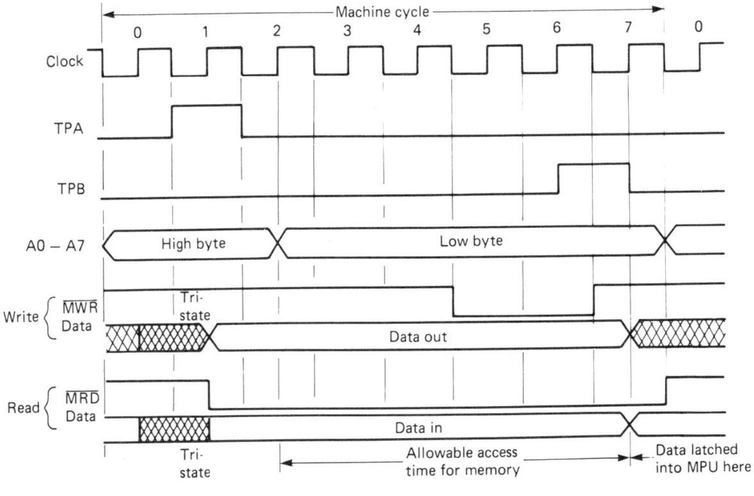

Fig. 4.15 1802 read and write cycles

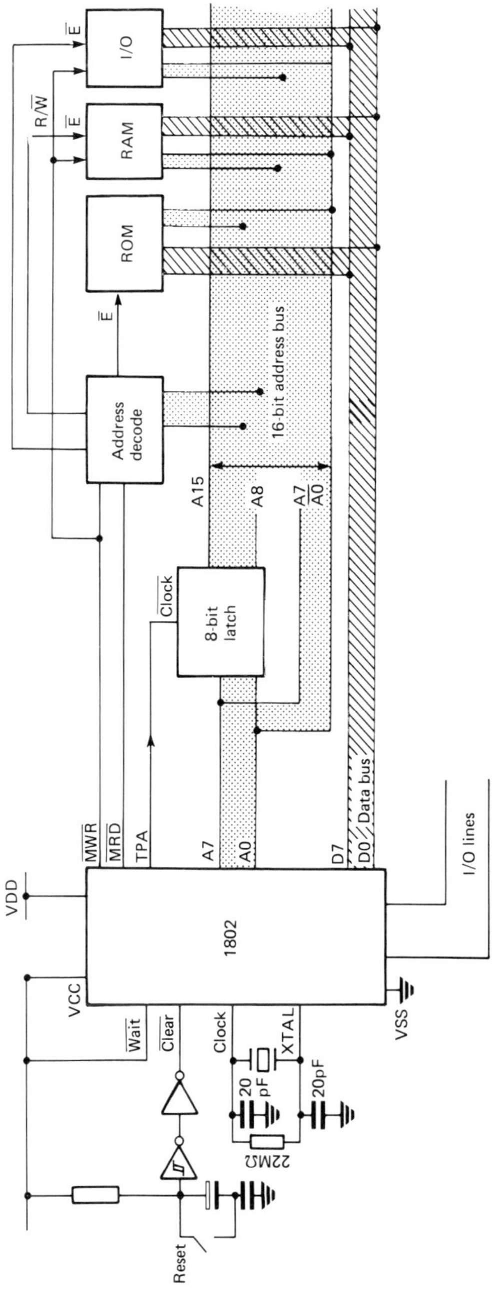

Fig. 4.16 A typical 1802 system

through to the outputs of the latch, where they remain until the next falling edge on TPA. This establishes the upper eight bits of address. The lower eight bits appear half a clock cycle later, and are fed straight through to the lower eight address lines of the address bus. It is only at this point that the address can be assumed to be fully established on the address bus.

The memory address decoding block should only be enabled when either MRD or MWR is low; at other times, non-memory functions are in progress. As can be seen, just after the rising edge of the third clock cycle, MRD is active, and the full address is resident on the 16 bit address bus of Figure 4.16. Thus a memory read has five clock cycles from this point before the data must be valid for sampling by the MPU. At the maximum frequency of 5 MHz, this allows 1000 ns for the transfer—more than enough for typical modern memory chips. The write cycle, similarly, provides the data well within the time limit required for the data to appear at the memory. Note how the MWR line is used as a R/W signal to the RAM.

All machine-code instructions require a single S0, or fetch cycle, which is nothing more than the read cycle of Figure 4.15. Most instructions only require one further cycle—an S1, or execute. This cycle is a variation on the read or write cycle depending upon the instruction. During S1, any further operand is fetched and the instruction executed. Some instructions require two S1 cycles, during which some of these fetch a third byte required for the instruction's execution. The instructions requiring a second S1 are the long skips and long branches, and the NOP instruction. These instructions therefore need 24 clock cycles for their complete fetch and execution.

Pause, load and DMA

Referring to Figure 4.14, the pause mode may be entered by setting CLEAR high and WAIT low. In this mode, the clock continues to run, but execution is halted at the next falling edge of the clock. All outputs are frozen, and DMA (see later) and interrupts are ignored. This state is useful as an analogue of the 6802's MR feature, or the Z80's WAIT. The address decoding to slow external devices can be arranged to stop the processor until the device is ready to accept or supply its data.

Figure 4.15 shows that the data bus is always tri-state at the falling edge of the first cycle. If some logic is constructed to set the MPU into the pause state at this time, the data bus will be available for multiprocessor, or any other use, during the pause.

In addition, sensing the start of a fetch by the state of SC0 and SC1 allows the processor to be single-stepped, instruction by instruction, for debugging.

Again referring to Figure 4.14, the load mode of the 1802 is unique. It allows one to build a system without requiring any resident ROM or programming. This is quite impossible on the Z80 and 6800, as neither of these MPUs has the *inherent* ability for loading a program into RAM, from an external source, for execution upon reset. This can always be arranged, but a form of DMA would be required. The 1802 has DMA logic for exactly this purpose on chip. Figure 4.17 shows the timing and type of circuit which may be used for this facility.

The timing diagram shows the load cycle being entered from the reset state, i.e. CLEAR and WAIT are first taken to 0 and 1 respec-

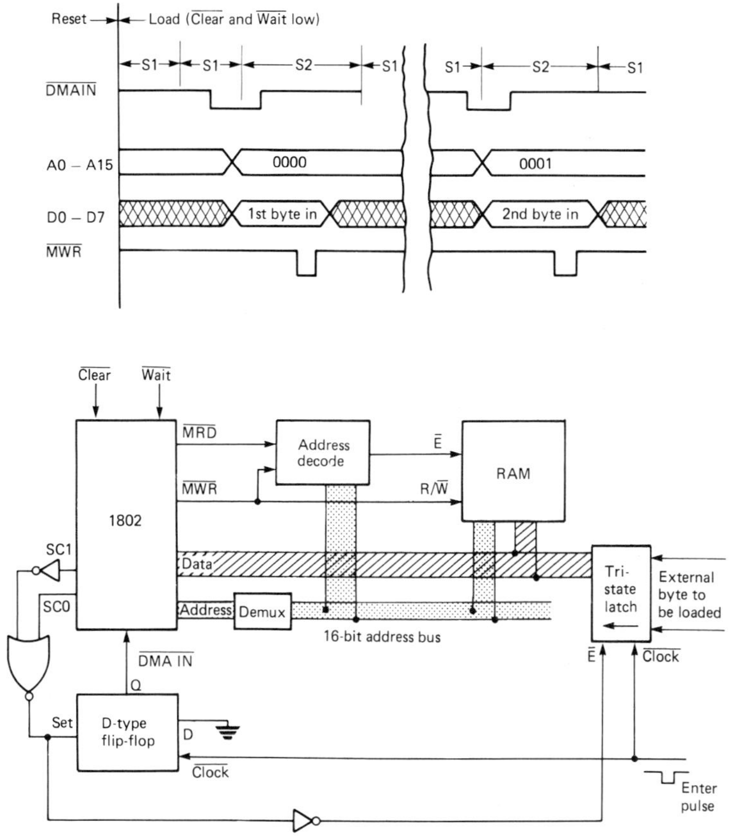

Fig. 4.17 1802 load facility

tively, then both set low. During the load mode, unless anything happens, the MPU executes S1-type cycles with MRD and MWR both high, and TPA low. TPB performs as normal. This is often termed an 'idle' state. The reset causes the register R(0) to contain 0000. During the DMA cycles, R(0) increments and appears on the address bus to allow the externally supplied byte to be loaded sequentially into memory, using the address bus to address the correct destination for each byte presented. DMA does not have to be entered from a reset; thus R(0) can be set to any value, by machine code, and the DMA then entered. This allows any block of memory locations to be loaded directly.

The DMAIN line is connected to the Q output of a D-type flip-flop. On the falling of the enter line, the 0 on the D input is transferred to DMAIN, and the processor enters an S2 cycle at the end of the current S1. This causes SC0 and SC1 to take on the values 0 and 1 respectively. If DMAIN is allowed to remain low, the subsequent DMA load is repeated continuously as the address bus is incremented—this is very useful for filling large blocks of memory at high speed from an external source. In this case, however, memory is to be loaded one byte at a time as the enter line is pulsed low. Thus, as soon as S2 is entered, the DMAIN line must return high, to prevent further loads until requested. This is achieved by using the SC lines to set the Q output of the D-type flip-flop to a 1 as soon as they signal the S2. When enter is pulsed, it is important for an external byte to be present on the input of the tri-state latch, as this is clocked into the latch at this point, but not allowed through the device yet—the outputs remain tri-state. When S2 begins, the active low enable of the latch is brought to a 0, and the byte stored in the latch is allowed onto the data bus. The DMA cycle which follows consists of setting the address bus to 0000 and pulsing MWR low to strobe the external byte into memory location 0000. S1-idle cycles then resume until the process is repeated, when R(0) is set to 0001.

The external byte for this process might be set up from a keyboard, a tape recorder, or any other source. The S1 states may be used to inform the external device that the system is ready for another byte. This type of feedback is referred to as 'handshaking', and there are several ways to achieve this in the DMA mode on the 1802.

The DMAOUT line may be used in a similar manner, with MRD, to cause data to be transferred from memory to external devices.

It is possible, by using the correct control lines, to arrange for DMA transfers to occur one byte per machine cycle. At the maximum speed, this allows 625K bytes to be transferred per second.

There have been two successful microcomputer kits brought onto the market using this highly cost-effective method of arranging a complete system. These were the Cosmac Elf from Netronics (USA), and the EDUKIT—designed by the author and manufactured by Modus Systems Ltd. Neither of these devices is available today. The advantage of the 1802 was that a very simple but effective teaching tool could be constructed from the 1802, a little RAM (the full 16 address bits were not demultiplexed), and some simple logic gates, without the need for any ROM or software. The user simply used LOAD to strobe his program in straight from a hex keyboard, and then set the switches to the run mode. Such systems can bring all the important concepts of MPUs to the user, with the added advantage of very down-to-earth experience. The weld between hardware and software, in the field of MPUs, can be made particularly apparent.

1802 I/O using EF and Q

It is in the field of simple control systems that the 1802 is most effective. The various I/O lines have already been introduced, and these are described fully below.

The Q line is the simplest: machine-code instructions set or reset it, and the cycles associated with this action are the fetch (S0) which is a normal read cycle to fetch the opcode, followed by a non-memory S1, which is characterised by the MRD and MWR lines both being high, with the data bus tri-state. The Q line can be fed to a transistor, and thus be used to control a single device.

The four EF lines are used to force decisions to be made for short branches, as described in the last chapter. This type of instruction requires two cycles for its execution, an S0 and an S1 as usual. Both cycles, however, are read cycles, as the MPU must fetch an eight-bit address for the short branch involved, as well as the opcode. The branch is either taken, or not, depending upon the state of a given EF line, and the PC is thus appropriately set up during the S1.

The EF lines may, of course, be connected to a set of sense switches, an analogue signal via an A-D converter or any other outside world event, with very little logic necessary. If the signals to be sensed are more numerous than can be coped with by four lines, another method of I/O must be used, which involves some extra logic. This is described shortly. First, however, let us consider the problem of causing a switch to be turned on when a temperature falls below some value, off when above, and left in the previous state if at that temperature. The temperature is assumed to be sensed accurately enough with four bits of A-D conversion. Figure 4.18 shows the hardware and software for such a device. The program is easily small enough to fit into a 256-

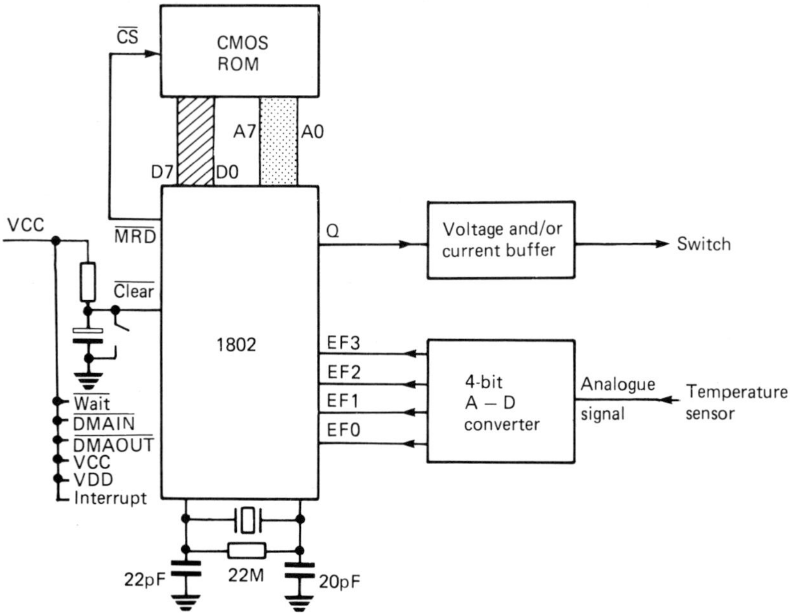

Assumed threshold temperature to set Q:

EF3	EF2	EF1	EF0
0	1	1	0

If temperature above this,
Q must be reset (to 0);
if below, Q to be set;
if equal, Q to be left.

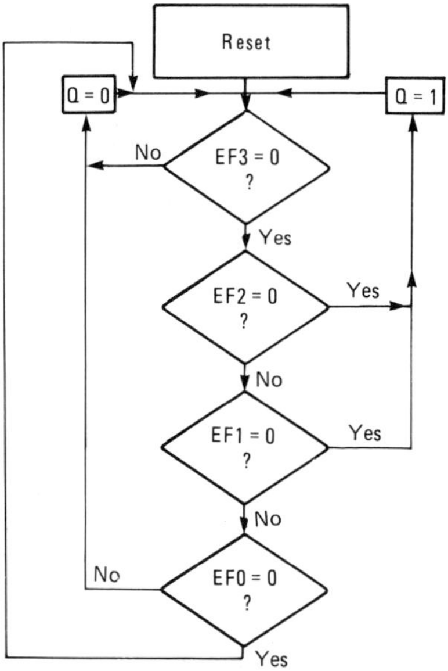

Fig. 4.18 1802 as a temperature-controlled switch

byte CMOS ROM or EPROM, and requires no RAM. Thus, the lower seven bits of address are sufficient, and inspection of the read timing diagram in Figure 4.15 shows that the MPU takes in an opcode at the end of the machine cycle when the lower address bits are valid and MRD is valid. Thus MRD may be used to enable the EPROM directly, saving any need for extra decoding logic. All unused inputs are tied high. A simple reset circuit with a reset button in case of failure may be used as shown.

The whole circuit can be powered from a battery, if required, from 4 volts to 10 volts. The A-D converter and the switch and buffer on Q could be powered separately if they require too much current.

The software for the continuous loop shown consists of short branches on the zero page, and the set and reset Q instructions. The reader should follow the logic through and ensure that the conditions laid down are satisfied.

This application is probably very slow compared to the speed of the processor, and the great power of an MPU in this type of context is that it can be performing many other tasks at the same time, by breaking into the loop using interrupts, for instance. The controller could be controlling a central heating system according to any manner of complex program set up on a keypad by the user. At the same time, it could be executing night-time or day-time control depending upon the input from a clock, and perhaps acting as a clocking-in system for a factory. The possibilities are bounded only by the degree of problem which can be found. Speed is less of a problem, as it is always possible to use several low-cost controllers—each controlling a subset of the tasks required.

Control of a more complex nature than that shown in Figure 4.18 can be effected using the N lines on the 1802, and this is described below.

1802 I/O using the N lines

These three lines on the 1802 are used by I/O instructions to output the state of the lower three bits of the N register. N0–N2 are normally 0, therefore only seven active bit patterns exist on these lines (001–111). The upper bit of the N register is used to set the MRD line for an I/O instruction. This state defines whether the data transfer is input or output, *with a high state being an input.* The N lines are outputs only, and they signal data transfers along the data bus from memory to an external device or vice versa. If this facility is not required, the N lines can simply be used as three machine-code-settable output lines, which, with the Q line, means that the 1802 has four output lines and four input lines on its package with no extra logic being required.

Figure 4.19 illustrates the use of the N lines while transferring data along the data bus. Before the instruction can be used, the X register must be set to point to an R register containing the address of the memory location whose contents are to be output along the data bus, or input from the data bus. The contents of the memory location are written M(R(X)) in standard 1802 terms. This means the contents of the memory location pointed to by R(X). This hierarchy of registers pointing to registers pointing to memory is typical of the 1802's rather cumbersome software structure. The input instruction has the opcode 6N, where N is any number from 9 to F. That is, the top bit of N is a 1, which appears on the MRD line during the execute of the input instruction. At the same time, the lower three bits appear on the N lines to select the required I/O port. The code for an output is 6N, where N is a number from 1 to 7. Again, the 0 in the upper bit of N appears on MRD, and the lower bits on the N lines. Note that the pattern N = X000 for any bit X is excluded as N0, N1 and N2 are normally 0, whether executing an I/O or not.

The input or output instruction is fetched as normal, using a read cycle and S0. Figure 4.19 shows the S1 execution, during which one of the I/O ports in the lower diagram is decoded and enabled for a transfer of eight bits of data along the data bus and into memory location M(R(X)). This location is enabled by the address decoding, and placed in the write state by MWR at the correct time. The enabling logic shown routes the correct port's data through to the system according to the N lines.

The output from M(R(X)) is similar, but the memory's data must be clocked into the correct port when it appears valid on the data bus. The precise time for this is distinguished by TPB being high. To construct such a clock signal, the logic must be sure that an output cycle is being performed, which requires one of the N lines to be high, and MRD to be low. The TPB signal then forms the strobe. The logic shown can be made up using just one IC package.

The input enabling logic could just be a tri-state buffer into the data bus from each outside port. A given buffer is enabled onto the data bus when the N pattern is appropriate, MRD is high and MWR is low. For output, an eight-bit latch clocked by data strobe would suffice. The rising edge of data strobe latches in the data for external presentation, and the falling edge of data strobe informs the external world that a byte of output is present.

By these means the 1802, like the Z80, has a separate I/O map, but containing only seven locations. Of course, the 1802, like any other MPU, can just as well treat I/O in the manner of the 6800—that is, as part of the normal memory map.

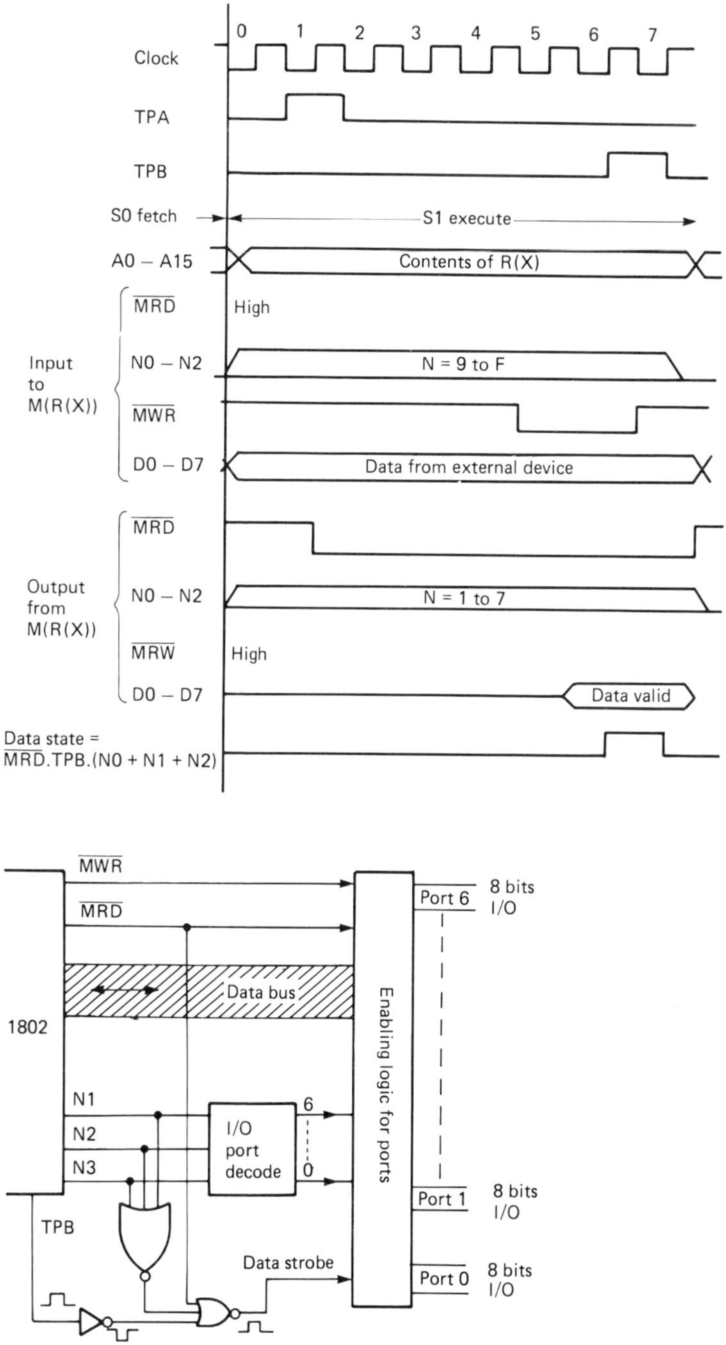

Fig. 4.19 1802 N lines for I/O

1802 interrupts

The single interrupt line is sampled only between the rising edge of TPA and the rising edge of TPB. The cycle which follows is an S3 non-memory cycle, with SC0 and SC1 as shown in Figure 4.14. It is broadly speaking similar to the read and write cycles of Figure 4.15, but MRD and MWR are high. The interrupt action takes just one machine cycle. The action is to set the interrupt mask to prevent further interrupts unless reset by the program. X and P are stored in T, which must be saved by the interrupt routine if further interrupts are to be allowed before a return to the main program. X is set to 2 and P is set to 1. R(X) may be used as a type of stack pointer by the interrupt routine, and thus R(1) must already have been set to an appropriate value if required. The action of setting P to 2 immediately causes the register R(2) to become the PC, and the next instruction after the S3 cycle is fetched from M(R(2)). That is, R(2) must already have been set to point to the start of the interrupt routine.

There are several special instructions dedicated to the use of interrupts; though rather cumbersome, interrupts are perfectly capable of serving the usual types of purpose on the 1802.

The S100 bus system

Up to now, all MPU systems have been broadly assumed to occupy a single board. That is, just one set of buses have interconnected the chips by simple electrical connection, and just one block of address decoding, perhaps with a number of parts, was sufficient. For large systems, it is often worthwhile distributing the different blocks of the system around a number of separate printed circuit boards (PCBs) plugged into edge-sockets, or connectors, on a common 'motherboard' of bus lines providing the interconnection throughout the system. The separate boards may be: memory board(s), processor board(s), I/O board(s), etc. Some advantages of such an approach are listed below.

(a) Power requirements can be supplied along the motherboard bus in the form of high-power raw (unregulated) DC, the regulation being performed on-board. This distributes the heat, for instance, produced in regulation, around the system. In addition, a regulator to supply a large number of boards would be rather cumbersome and expensive, and would have to be vastly overrated to ensure full regulation at full capacity.

(b) Maintenance is easier, and trouble-shooting in the field can be confined to simple board-swopping—repair being undertaken back at the laboratory. Such maintenance can be undertaken by the user, and the faulty board sent through the post for repair.

(c) It is normal to 'buffer' all signals—that is, pass them through special driver chips onto the motherboard, and receive them back on each board through Schmitt-trigger line-receivers. This prevents the MPU, for instance, from being asked to drive all the devices in a large system. The practice produces a high degree of noise isolation from board to board.

(d) The system may be started small, and built up by the addition of further boards, as and when required. In addition, fewer systems may be necessary for some applications. A few motherboard and power-supply 'crates' may be purchased, with a large number of boards of various different types, and any type of machine assembled by plugging boards into the 'crate', as required.

There are other advantages, and some disadvantages. For instance, the bus drivers and receivers have a finite delay time for the transmission of their signals—this can cause memory devices on the limit to be pushed over to the slow side in supplying data. In addition, multiboard systems are inherently more expensive than single boards. The power supply unit (PSU) can also be reduced considerably for a single board—firstly because there are fewer chips (no buffers, for instance), and secondly because the PSU can be rated down to fit the system exactly. There are many other arguments, and some of these will be made clear later.

Many different manufacturers have seized upon the advantages of designing for a bus, and many different buses exist. The only one described here is the S100 bus which was originally defined by MITS, for an 8080-based system, and subsequently used by IMSAI with some changes. Its first definition in an international sense was by the IEEE in 1979, which included an upgrade to allow its use for 16-bit systems. It is an early bus, and has the advantage of being 'set into the mythology' as it were. Many companies are manufacturing S100 boards, but it is not true to say that all boards adhere strictly to the standard. The important point about the S100 bus, for the reader of this book, is that it provides a good example of a standard bus. Whether it is an example of a good bus, however, is a matter for continued debate.

Any standard motherboard-based bus has two main areas of definition. These are the exact labelling of the bus lines, and the timing diagrams of the signals which must be present on these lines at any given instant in any given type of cycle. Appendix 3 on the S100 bus gives the labelling of the 100 bus lines, and, for completeness, a brief description of each line. An exact description of all the bus lines is beyond the scope of this book, and the reader should consult the bibliography for further reference. However, descriptions of some lines are given below. The S100 bus is physically 100 lines, normally printed in parallel on a PCB, connecting the 100 pins of double-50-way PCB edge-connector sockets, which are soldered onto the motherboard. There is often some bus termination on the motherboard at one or both ends of the bus. The exact mechanical dimensions of the edge-connector socket, as well as the edge-connector which is printed and gold-plated on the PCB, are defined. Similarly, the exact dimensions of the S100 boards themselves are defined. The motherboard may be of any size up to a maximum of 22 device sockets, and allows a maximum path length of 25 inches; this keeps transmission-line effects to a minimum.

The bus is quite suitable for multi-processor, DMA and 16-bit applications, using the full number of control lines. The description here just centres around those lines needed for eight-bit single-processor systems.

Figure 4.20 gives a schematic for a three-board system. The processor board is termed the *bus master*, as it controls the working of the whole system via a set of S100 control lines which it generates or monitors constantly. This is done in the block labelled 'S100 control line logic' on the processor board. Each board sends all its lines out to and picks up all its lines from the S100 bus through tri-state line-drivers and line-receivers. A typical device would be the 74LS244. These are referred to simply as 'buffers' from now on. The use of this word does not imply any memory on these chips.

The address bus of the processor board is also fed directly through buffers onto the address lines of the S100 bus. The S100 bus has no bidirectional 8-bit data bus, it has separate buses for data in (DI) and data out (DO), with respect to the processor board. These buses have to be formed by passing the MPU data bus through two eight-bit buffers. One set is enabled for all write operations (DO), and the other for reads (DI).

The memory and I/O boards must recombine these data buses for their own bidirectional data buses, by a reverse process. The address decoding is performed as required on the boards from the buffered control and address lines.

The PSU block feeds high-current, low-impedance power lines to the boards. Each board must contain regulators for the power levels it requires, and adequate decoupling components.

The ends of the bus are shown terminated, but for very short buses the terminations can be left out, and in reality should never need to be placed at both ends. The type of termination preferred by the

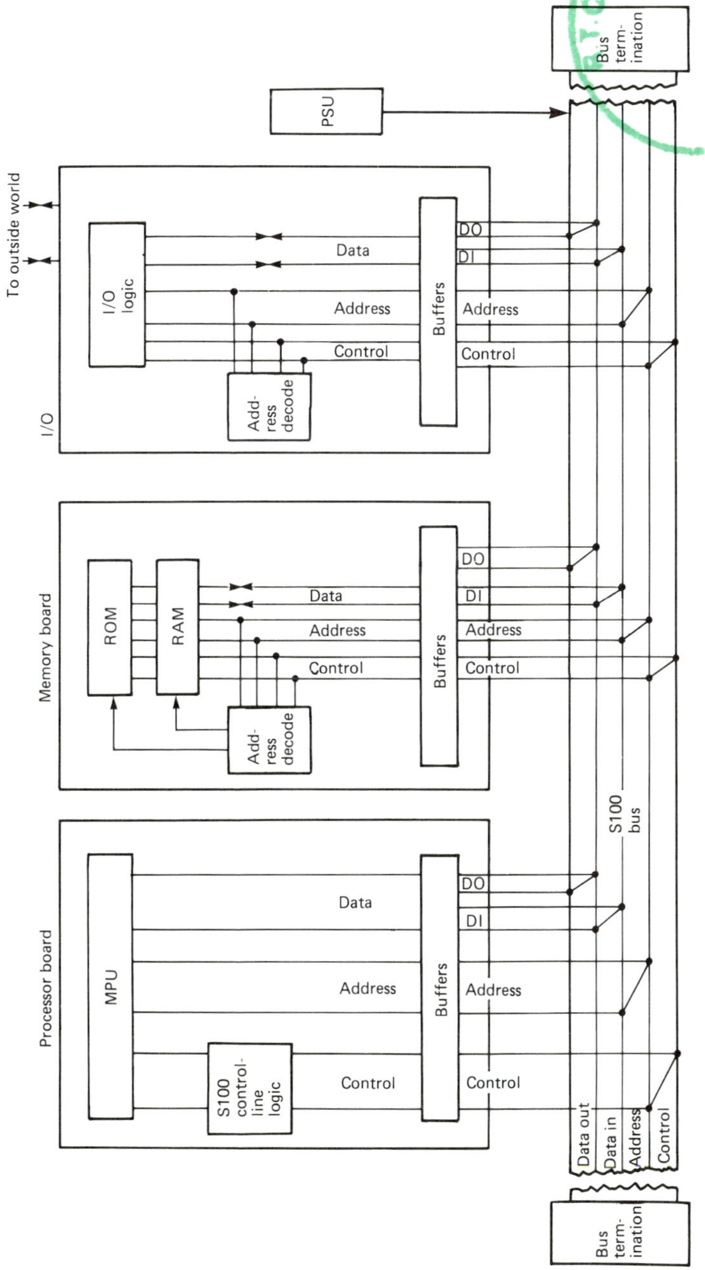

Fig. 4.20 An S100 bus system

author is shown in Figure 4.21. Here, a + 5 volt regulator from one of the S100 power supply lines is included on the motherboard, and the signal lines are terminated by a potential divider as shown. The most efficient form of such termination uses registor packs, which may be obtained containing pairs of resistors as shown.

The S100 bus, therefore, is just an extension of the MPU bus with some extra properties as will be seen. Which MPU produces the defined S100 lines is irrelevant as long as they conform to their electronic definitions. Thus the processor board may be based on the Z80, the 6800, the 1802, etc., or, with the use of some of the lines in the new extended definition of the bus, any 16-bit processor. The S100 bus, however, most easily adapts to the 8080 or the Z80, as this was the origin of many of the lines. Most of the lines described below appeal to the Z80's properties as described earlier in this chapter.

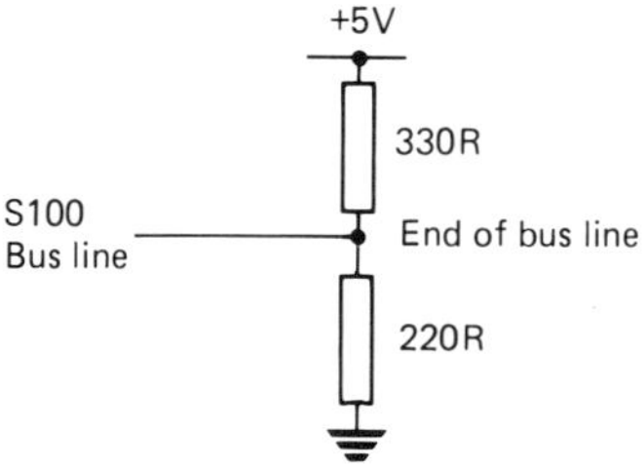

Fig. 4.21 Bus termination

Figure 4.22 shows possible enabling logic and buffering for the S100 data bus from a Z80 processor board. The bidirectional Z80 data bus is converted into data-in and data-out buses in the following manner. The Z80 data bus is shown connected to two buffers, pointing in opposite directions, and having active low enables. The DO side is enabled by an inverter with its input held high unless line 23 of the S100 bus goes low. This line may be used by other processor boards for gaining control of the data bus, and is called 'data out disable' (DODSBL). In simple systems this line is unused, and hence must be pulled to a definite state—a 4k7 resistor will not upset the bus termination. The DI side is only enabled for two conditions. An active level on RD will enable it, i.e. for any type of read, including I/O. An interrupt cycle, which may require an interrupt vector along the data bus, will also enable the DI buffer. To see this latter condition, refer to Figure 4.6. Here it is clear that when M1 and IORQ are both low, the MPU expects such a vector. This combination of states of M1 and IORQ is unique to this type of cycle, and in fact one of the S100 bus lines is defined in this manner—sINTA, shown on Figure 4.22. This is only to be set high when the MPU is requesting data back following an interrupt. Similarly, another of the S100 lines, pDBIN, is simply

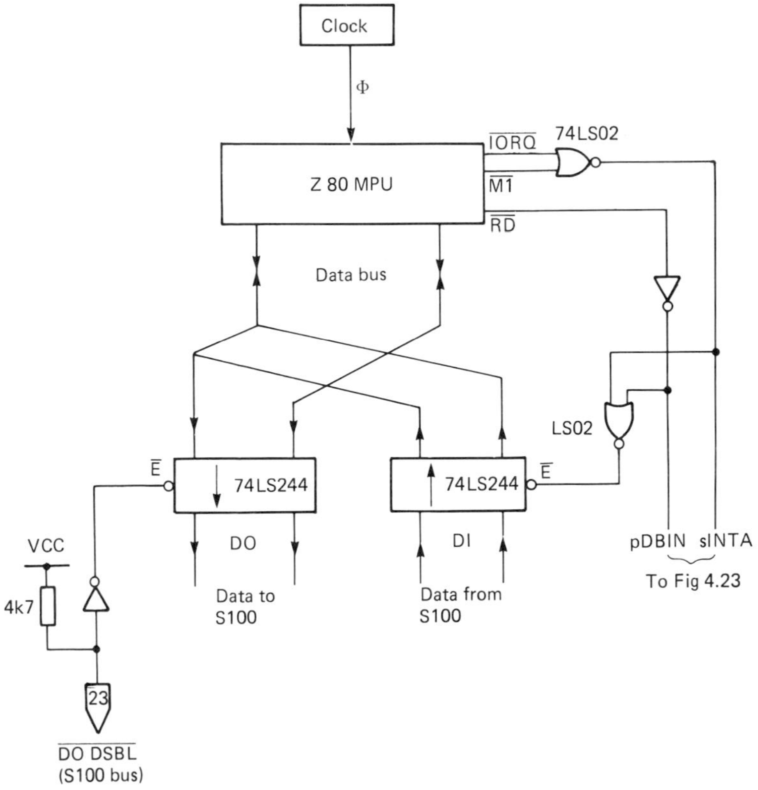

Fig. 4.22 Data bus enabling on a processor board (bus master)

the RD line for the system, and may be derived directly as shown—it is active high.

The address bus of the S100 bus is just the MPU address bus through buffers which may be disabled for other processor boards in an analogous manner to the above. Old S100 boards used to contain logic to repeat the states of the lower eight address lines onto the upper lines during an I/O instruction, when only the lower lines of the Z80 are active. This is no longer recommended, as it interferes with the new extended version of S100 whereby the I/O instruction can use all 16 address lines, as is the case for some MPUs. This address bus may be extended to 24 bits if required, and the data bus may be redefined in a specific manner as a single 16-bit bidirectional bus instead of two eight-bit single-way buses.

This introduces some of the most important parts of the S100 bus;

the logic of Figure 4.23 shows the most important control lines. This figure may be used in conjunction with the Z80 cycle diagrams at the start of this chapter to provide the reader with an electronic description of the bus. As usual, a bar over any line denotes that it is active low.

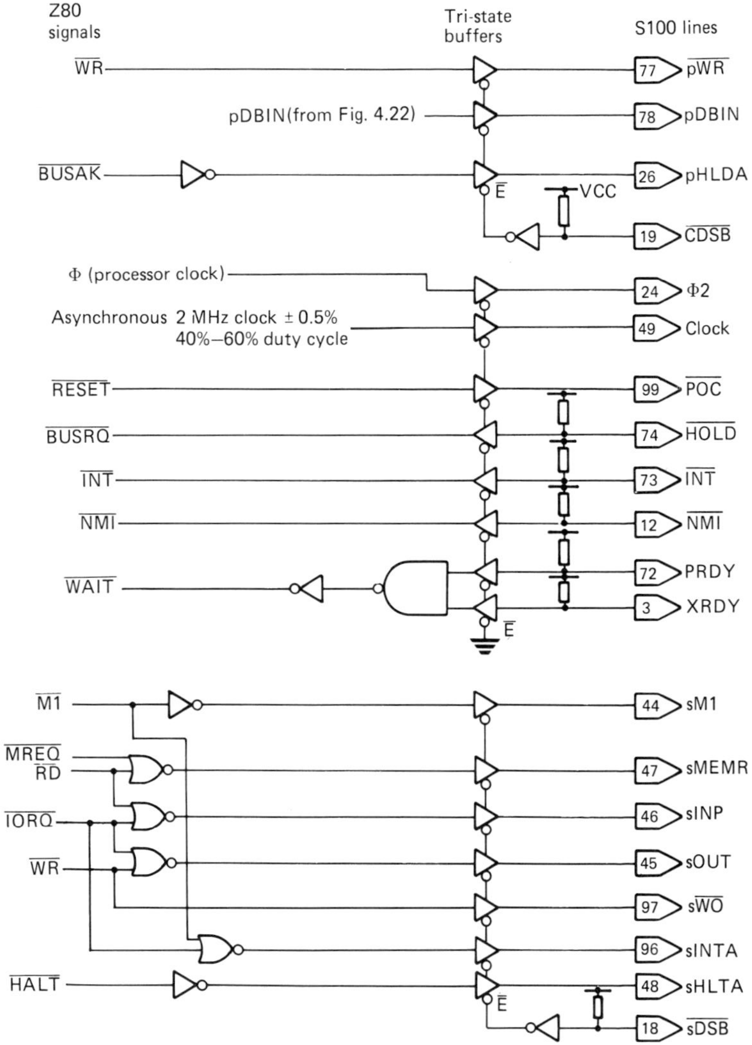

Fig. 4.23 Logic for generating S100 control lines

The control lines of Figure 4.23 are split into three groups. The top group all start with a lower-case p. These lines are outputs to the bus from the processor board. They pass through buffers which are disabled by the S100 line called CDSB. Any other board in the system may take this line low and thus disable these control lines in order to take over the system. The lower group of control lines in the figure start with a lower-case s. They are disabled by the SDSB line in the same way. The middle group are usually left enabled all the time.

The top group contains read and write lines, and a line to inform external boards that the processor is ready to give up the buses. The middle group of lines contains the reset pulse, the processor clock, and a 2 MHz clock which is not synchronised with processor activity. Inputs include the hold request, interrupts and two lines which may cause the MPU to enter a wait state.

The lower group of lines gives the MPU status at any instant. M1 is available to signal an opcode fetch. Read and write lines devoted to I/O are given, along with the sMEMR line which is active during a memory reference cycle of any kind. The WR line appears on the S100 bus as the sWO line. The line sINTA has been discussed above, and sHLTA signals that the MPU is halted.

This completes the description of the S100 bus, which will be used later in the book when specific peripherals are described.

Conclusion

The three MPUs here provide sufficient contrast to allow the reader to pick up data on any processor and feel familiar with the information presented. This applies to 16-bit and higher processors too. They are all bus-oriented, and have similar reliance on a clock and a reset. Even processors of a very different nature, such as the Fairchild F8 (which is a three-chip MPU) and the 2900 (which is a bit-slice processor made up of many chips), are easier to understand once the more common MPUs are fully mastered.

As in any field, mastering the jargon and the basic elements of the technology is half the battle. Most of the necessary material for an understanding of MPUs has been presented in the first four chapters of this book. The following chapters build on this basis to introduce peripherals and circuitry external to the MPU. This includes the necessary man-machine and machine-man interfaces which allow the working of the MPU to control the rest of the world.

5

Memory devices

This chapter describes in detail the various types of microcomputer memory which exist. The emphasis is on semiconductor memory, and ICs are described which are presently available. The previous chapters have introduced the concept of memory, and the ideas will be used throughout the following.

The chapter describes memory cells for static and dynamic RAM chips, along with design data for the use of typical examples of each type. A dynamic RAM system is described in detail for the Z80 processor. Read-only memory is described, along with a method of programming a common type of chip.

Magnetic media are also included in this chapter, but only as far as the basic principles. The basic principles of bubble memory are introduced as an example of a future advance in the field.

Introduction

Memory capacity is probably the most restrictive element within present-day computers. Processors are very sophisticated, and capable of highly complex activities. I/O devices are capable of providing almost any degree of interface to the outside world. Memory chips, however, are still not of sufficient capacity for even the most prosaic of storage requirements. Consider, for instance, the problem of providing a computer which is capable of accepting a complete paperback book through the telephone lines from some central store. The average book would probably have 60 000 to 70 000 words, or around 330 000 characters (letters and spaces) each of which takes up one byte of storage. This is a serious amount of memory for the RAM of a computer—the book would probably have to be stored on a cassette tape or magnetic disk and its pages called up one at a time from the tape or disk. This means that a sizeable computer system, with a fairly large power supply, would be required for the complete set-up. However, the I/O, MPU, keyboard and visual display would fit, with its power supply (a small battery), into a size about equal to a small paperback—the restriction is purely one of memory.

If low-power memory were available, with sufficient packing density, the above paperback-sized computer could be used to store several books, a personal diary and notepad, hours of music, dozens of timed messages, and anything else required with no cumbersome external memory devices such as disks or cassette tapes. The reason why memory devices are so far behind the state of the other computer components is simply that the storage of data in the quantities described above requires a tremendous number of devices on a chip. There is an upper limit to the number of devices which it is possible to fabricate on a single chip, if only by virtue of the manufacturing yield which present technology can achieve. The more complex a chip becomes, the more likely that it will be manufactured with one or more non-functional elements within the matrix. Unless redundancy can be built in, even a single non-functional element can cause the whole device to be scrapped. The practical upper limit achieved at the time of writing is of the order of 450 000 elements on a single chip. If these were all memory elements, ignoring all the other elements needed on a memory chip, and if each one were capable of storing one bit, this would still not yield enough memory for a single book, let alone the program to allow the user to read it. Even 450 000 bits of read/write memory (RAM) on a chip is still some time off; today we are using 64K bit RAMs as standard. Eight of these chips would be needed to achieve the single-paperback capacity. In addition, these chips are not of sufficiently low power to be able to be used for long periods on a battery.

As can be seen from the above example, we are still a long way from satisfying the demand for memory using RAM chips. The reason why RAM chips are of such low density is best understood by examining their internal characteristics. Some examples of memory structures are described below.

RAM

Semiconductor random-access memory (RAM) has taken the place of the original type of computer memory known as 'core memory'. The latter depended upon the magnetic properties of small rings of ferrite material. Despite the fact that this type of memory had the useful property of retaining its data while the power was switched off, core memory has been largely replaced with semiconductor RAM due to the higher packing density it is possible to achieve on a chip. As mentioned above, typical maximum densities of RAM memory now in common use are 64K bits. This would be implemented on a 16-pin package, with access times of 200 ns, or less.

RAM chips fall into two main classes: *static* and *dynamic*. Static RAM chips may be filled with data and ignored until that data is required again. The only requirement is that the power be retained. Dynamic memory, on the other hand, has to be 'refreshed' continually to 'remind' it of its data. Modern chips make this task of refreshing memory fairly straightforward, but provision has to be made for this activity in system design. In general, static memory has a much lower packing density than dynamic memory, hence the widespread use of the latter. The reason for this difference in packing density will become clear from the physical make-up of the two types of memory device.

Static RAM

Figure 5.1 shows a sketch of the basic static RAM element. This is a flip-flop, with six elements (transistors). The transistors shown are metal-oxide semiconductor field-effect transistors (MOSFETs). The

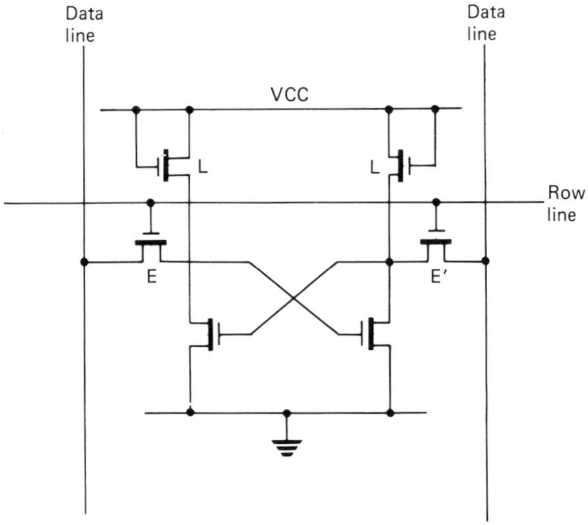

Fig. 5.1 The static RAM cell

load resistors (L) of the cross-coupled transistors are formed by MOSFETs, biased to be in the 'on' state, and designed to have the required resistance value in that state. These cells of six transistors are arranged in the rows and columns of a matrix, and any given cell is enabled by setting its row line to a 1, which switches on the MOSFETs labelled E and E′, and then enabling the read or write logic at the end of the data lines in that column. Note that many cells will be connected to a given row line, and when that row line is taken high they will all place

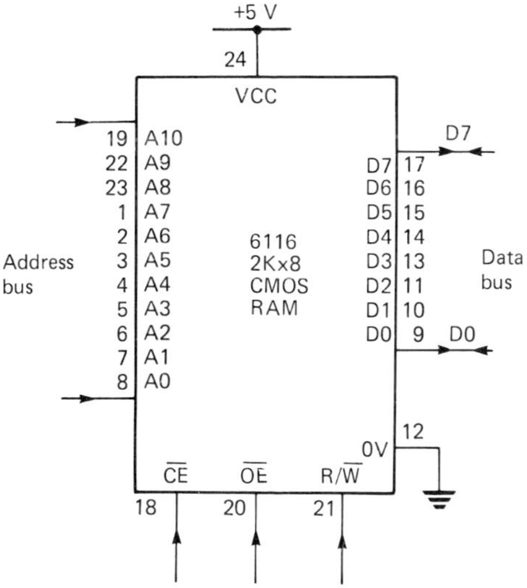

Fig. 5.2 A typical static RAM device (6116)

1s and 0s on their individual column (data) lines. However, all this data is ignored except for the one column which is enabled for reading or writing. When enabled, a given cell may be written to by taking one of the data lines high, and the other low. The cross-coupled transistors within the cell will retain these states when the cell is disabled, and the states may be read out from the data lines by other external logic at any time in the future. This describes the storage of a single bit, but many RAM chips have an internal organisation which is designed to store bytes from an eight-bit data bus. To achieve this, eight of these six-transistor cells are enabled at once, and each one applied to one of the eight data bus lines.

The essential point is that at least six transistors are required for each bit—a total of 48 devices for a byte of storage. Many different technologies (CMOS, TTL, etc.) are used for static RAM, but the principle of the flip-flop for this application is fairly universal.

As an example of a commonly available static RAM, Figure 5.2 shows the 6116 CMOS 2K bytes static RAM chip. It has 24 pins, an eight-bit bidirectional data bus, an 11-bit address bus, R/W line, chip-enable, output-enable, 0 V line and +5 V line. This chip is important as it introduces an industry-standard pin-out for memory devices of many kinds which is being accepted more and more by manufacturers. Any location on the chip may be written to by placing its address on the address lines, data on the data lines and pulsing R/W low while CE is held low (OE is irrelevant for writing). To read back from the location, the address is applied, the R/W line held high (read), and OE and CE both taken low. This causes the location's stored data to appear on the data bus. These sequences of operations can be achieved with a set of switches if required, though RAM chips are normally used in MPU systems where the MPU controls the lines as stated above. The essential point is that the 6116, as with any other static RAM, is very simple to use, and will retain its memory purely by ensuring that the power is retained. The 6116 is a CMOS device, and a few hundred microamps are required to keep it powered up while CE and OE are held high, i.e. when the chip is not selected. This is well within the capabilities of a small rechargeable battery. The 6116 can be connected directly to an MPU chip, as in Figure 1.1, to store 2K bytes of RAM in a simple MPU system. The enable shown in Figure 1.1 would be formed by joining OE and CE together, and connecting these to the address decoding.

The pin numbering for the data bus and address bus is the standard manufacturer's labelling for these lines. However, the lines of these buses may be permuted into any order, as this only affects the physical cell within the 6116 which is being contacted. For instance, if address 3AB contacts a set of eight cells in the 'bottom right-hand corner' of the silicon chip itself, permuting the address lines so that 3AB on the MPU address bus becomes 3BA on the 6116 will simply change the physical chip-location of the set of cells which are labelled '3AB' by the MPU. How the 6116 physically stores the data within its matrix is irrelevant to the MPU, as long as the data sent to any given location can be retrieved from that location at a later date. In a similar way, the lines of the 6116 data bus may be permuted with respect to the MPU's data bus. This just affects the order in which the data bits are stored within each eight-bit cell group. However, there are two advantages to using the standard pin-out numbers. First, it is generally easier for troubleshooting to stick to a standard, and secondly, the 6116 is pin-compatible with a family of ROMs, and these would always be programmed so that the standard numbering is adhered to. If the address and data bus were non-standard, the ROM data would be mixed up if placed in the 6116 slot.

The 6116 stores eight bits at a time, but it is possible to purchase static RAM chips which have less than eight-bit data buses. The internal organisation of such chips may have just four RAM cells enabled at any one time, or even just one. In the latter case, an eight-bit data bus would have to be constructed by connecting one RAM chip to each data bus line; all other signal lines of these chips would be connected in parallel. This type of system will be discussed again in the section on dynamic RAMs.

A popular format of static RAM chip has been the 2114 format,

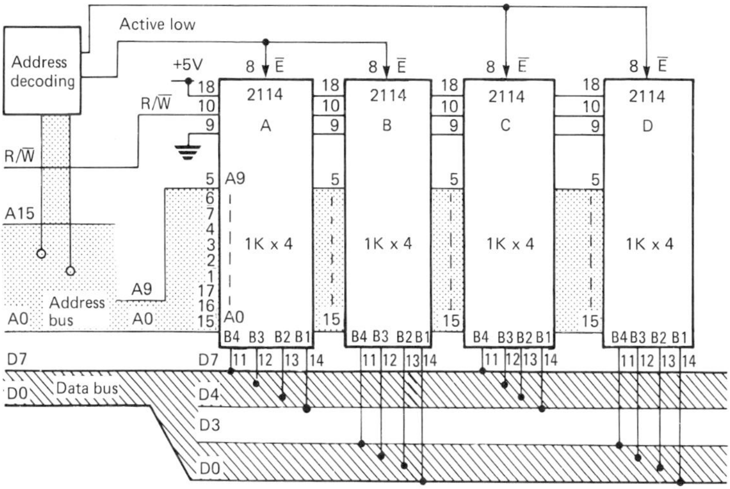

Fig. 5.3 2114 chips in a 2K RAM system

containing 1K of four-bit words. This is shown in Figure 5.3 to illustrate the method by which four-bit RAM chips are utilised. The 6116, however, has made this chip less economical to use as far as space and interconnection is concerned. Figure 5.3 shows a 2K bytes memory system using the 2114. Note that 1K of eight-bit memory is constructed from two 2114 chips, each contributing half of the byte to the data bus. Thus, chips A and B form the upper and lower 'nybbles' (see Appendix 1) of each byte written to or read from the memory by the MPU. As a consequence, their enable lines are connected together to ensure that they are enabled at the same time. Apart from their data lines, labelled B4–B1, all other pins on these two chips are connected in parallel. Chips C and D form 1K of RAM in a similar manner. Note how much interconnection and extra address decoding is needed to perform exactly the same function as a 6116 does in a single package. However, the principles shown apply to four-bit memory chips of any size, and indeed to all organisations other than four-bit.

Static RAM is easy to interface to MPU systems, but owing to its typically six-element cell it is very low in packing density. This is often not important in control applications where little RAM is needed, and where, therefore, the system may take advantage of the ease of use of static RAM devices. For larger memory systems, however, dynamic RAM, with its greater packing density, is necessary.

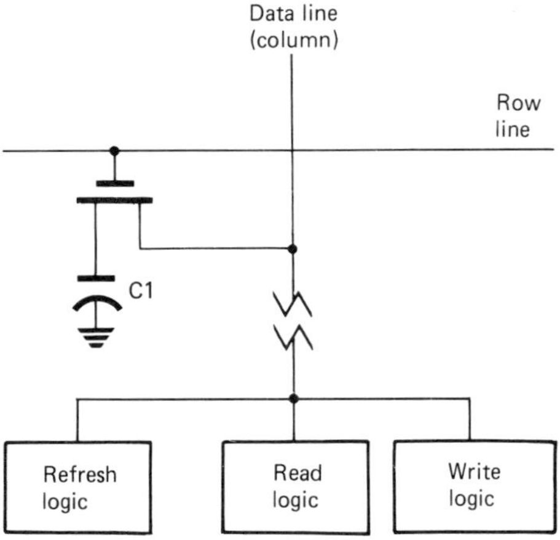

Fig. 5.4 One-transistor dynamic RAM cell

Dynamic RAM

Figure 5.4 shows a typical one-transistor dynamic RAM cell. The storage principle in this cell is that of charge storage on a capacitor. The major disadvantages of this highly compact memory cell are that the process of reading the state of the cell is destructive, and that the capacitor's charge naturally leaks away in a time of the order of 2–4 ms, depending upon the chip's design. As for static memory chips, the cells are arranged in a matrix of rows and columns. To read or write to the cell, the transistor shown is enabled, along with all the other cells on that row, and just one column is enabled. At the end of the column line, there are three blocks of logic—one for reading, one for writing, and one for refreshing. The reading logic block senses (destructively) and then restores the previous state of the cell by enabling the refresh logic. The writing block, on the other hand, simply changes the state of the cell when enabled.

To prevent the capacitor's charge from leaking away, the cell must be refreshed from time to time. A normal read will achieve this, as explained above. However, dynamic memory RAM chips are normally arranged so that the refresh blocks of all the columns are enabled at the same time. Thus, as all cells on the row containing the current element being accessed are enabled at the same time, and all the columns are refreshed, all the cells on that row are automatically refreshed simultaneously. However, it is not possible to rely on the normal reading and writing activities of the MPU for sufficient transactions to perform all the refreshing. Some method of pure refresh cycling is required. This is an activity which does not require the output of data from the memory chip to the data bus as for an actual read. Typical dynamic RAM chips allow just the refresh part of the read cycle to be activated, when required, for keeping the memory refreshed. This saves power and prevents data from being output at times when the bus is occupied with other activities. Special refresh logic is thus included on any dynamic memory system to perform this refresh cycling on a continuous basis. Such a system is described shortly. In addition, most dynamic memory chips on the market have an internal matrix organisation which allows just 128 or 256 refresh cycles to perform a complete refresh of the RAM chip.

It is easy to see why packing density makes dynamic RAM preferable to static RAM for mass storage. The present generation of dynamic RAM chips are available in 16-pin packages, and require just one power supply level. Previous generations of chips required three power supply levels, and consumed considerably more power. It is possible to purchase dynamic RAMs which supply more than one bit to the data bus at a time, but the more common devices are one-bit RAMs, and only these will be described here.

In order to pack a dynamic RAM chip onto a 16-pin package, the address bus must be multiplexed. This is similar to the way in which the 1802 processor produces a 16-bit address bus from just eight pins. The 64K dynamic RAM chip, for instance, requires 16 address lines, but only has room for eight on its package. This is one of the problems the user faces. The other is, of course, provision of suitable refresh circuitry. The solution to these problems is described next for the 4164 chip, which is a 64K by one-bit dynamic RAM chip, sourced by many manufacturers.

Addressing dynamic RAM

The 4164 (see Figure 5.5) has an eight-bit address bus, and contains latches to allow the upper and lower halves of the 16-bit MPU address bus to be latched in by special strobe pins on the 4164. When the RAS pin is taken low, the 4164 expects the lower (or row) byte of the address to be present on its address lines. This bit pattern is then latched internally. The CAS pin is used similarly to latch, within the 4164, the upper (column) byte of address. By this means the chip builds up a 16-bit address internally to allow it to contact the memory cell being addressed. The state of the R/W line then determines whether it feeds the state of that cell out onto its data-out line, or takes in a new state for that cell along data-in.

Figure 5.5 sketches this process. The address decoding initiates the read or write cycle in this diagram. The logic of such decoding will be given later for a Z80-based system. At the time that the address

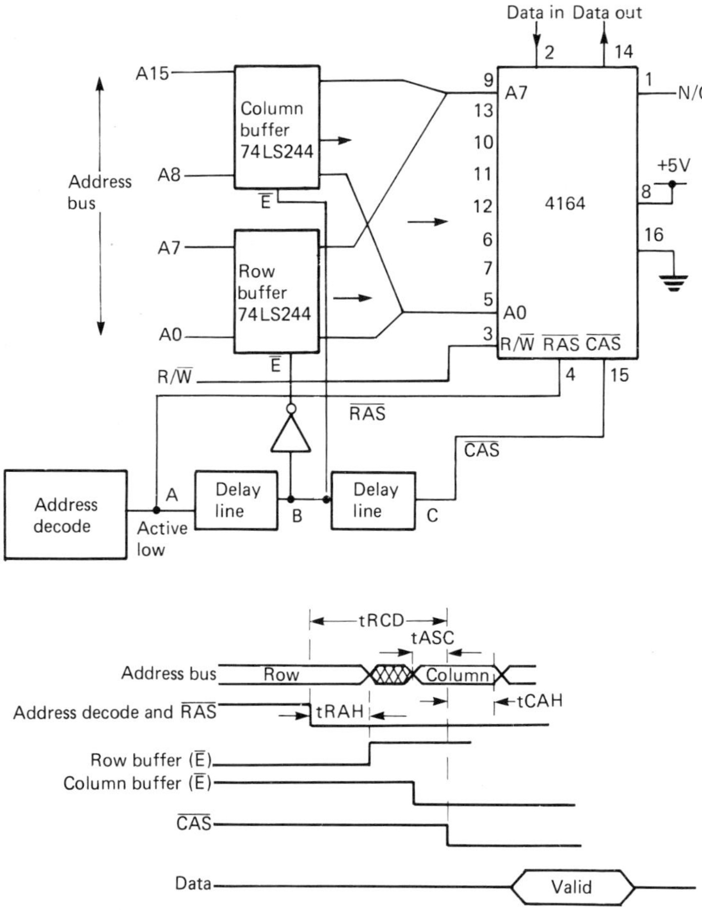

Fig. 5.5 Addressing dynamic RAM

decoding is active, there will be a valid 16-bit address on the address bus. This must be broken down into two eight-bit halves and fed to the 4164. Before the address decoding signal goes low, the points A, B and C are all high. This is inverted and applied to the tri-state row buffer. Thus, the normal (inactive) condition has the row addresses constantly applied to the 4164. When the address decoding signal goes low, point A falls and the consequent falling edge on RAS latches this row address in. A delay line then ensures that nothing else happens until the 4164 has fully strobed in the row address—this time is called 'tRAH' (row address hold time). It is typically a minimum of 25–50 ns from the falling edge of RAS. Then, the buffers are swopped over, and the column address is allowed through to the 4164. The time 'tASC' (column address set-up time) shown in the waveform diagram is the time between the column address being established, and CAS being active. A further delay is inserted to allow this pattern to settle fully before CAS is taken low to latch in the column address and fully enable the chip. The time 'tCAH' (CAS address hold time) is the time for which the column address must remain active with CAS low, to ensure that the address has been taken in by the memory. By this time, valid data will already have been placed on the data bus by the MPU if this is a write cycle. If a read cycle, the data will take of the order of 200 ns to be output from the memory from the falling edge of RAS, if the delays are correct. The access time of the memory depends upon the time 'tRCD' (RAS to CAS time). If this is too long, the access time will suffer.

This sequence of events is controlled by delay lines, the electronics of which can be implemented in a number of ways. There are specially manufactured delay lines for dynamic memory, and though comparatively expensive, they will ensure that the correct timing is established. Many designers use the gate delays inherent in TTL chips to produce the delay line. A single package of TTL inverters will give delays of the correct order. One disadvantage of this approach is a certain chip-dependency—different manufacturers' chips have varying delay-time spreads across a given batch, and different temperature characteristics. A further approach uses a high frequency crystal oscillator to clock a shift register. The address decoding signal is fed in at one end, and time-shifted versions of this signal are available at the shift register's outputs. A further effective, though more expensive, method of handling all the problems of dynamic memory, is by the use of a dynamic memory controller. Several companies make such devices, and these chips will handle all the address multiplexing and refreshing automatically. In addition, they will normally handle several banks of memory chips, in order to allow an MPU system to address larger amounts of memory than the address bus can handle on its own. Different 64K banks can be switched in using I/O commands to control a set of I/O lines to supply a further set of pseudo address lines.

Refresh is described next, with the use of discrete logic as opposed to the use of a dynamic memory controller.

Refresh

In order to refresh the 4164, a 'dummy read' must be performed to all the 256 row addresses, every 4 ms. This means that the lower address lines must be cycled through all 256 bit patterns while RAS is taken low and R/W is high. The 4164 does not actually enable its output buffers unless CAS is also low, and thus during a refresh, CAS is normally held high. This does not prevent the read from occurring internally, along with the restoration of data, but it does prevent any output from appearing on the data bus. The 4164 is constructed to use less power when CAS is high.

There are two styles of refresh: either the 256 bit-patterns can be cycled through in a fast burst of activity every 4 ms, or the 256 reads can be performed at spaced intervals over the 4 ms in between other memory activities. Either way, there is the danger of a clash between the MPU and the refresh logic requiring simultaneous memory access. Some processors have cycle types whereby there is always a period in each instruction cycle when no memory activity is taking place. Other MPUs will need to enter a wait state if they attempt to request a memory reference (a read or a write) while a refresh is being performed.

Figure 5.6 describes the principles of a method by which a complete dynamic memory system can be constructed. The actual logic to perform refresh is quite complex, and rather MPU-dependent. A simpler system for the Z80 will be given shortly. Figure 5.6 also shows how the complete eight-bit data bus is formed by using separate 4164's for each data line. Since the output of the chip is tri-state when CAS is high, the data-in and data-out lines can be connected together, and the correct data line selected by R/W and CAS. Apart from the data lines, all the other lines on the chips are connected together in parallel. Figure 5.6 is similar to Figure 5.5, but refresh logic has been added. Every few microseconds, the refresh controller tries to perform a dummy read. To prevent its clashing with the MPU, it requests a refresh period from the MPU. This could, for instance, be connected to the HALT line of a 6802. When the current instruction has finished, the BA line would go high, and this could be connected to the refresh acknowledge line of the refresh controller. When the current MPU instruction has finished, therefore, the refresh controller turns off both row and column buffers by setting the address disable line low. CAS and R/W are set high, and the refresh buffer enabled to pass the eight-bit counter onto the address lines of the memory. After a suitable delay to allow these conditions to settle, the controller pulses RAS low, to latch in this row address. By this method just the rows are cycled through continuously for the process of refreshing. Finally, the controller returns all the signals to their normal states, increments the eight-bit counter for the next refresh, and sets refresh acknowledge back to its inactive state. The MPU then continues as before until the next refresh.

This process of requesting and acknowledging a particular state

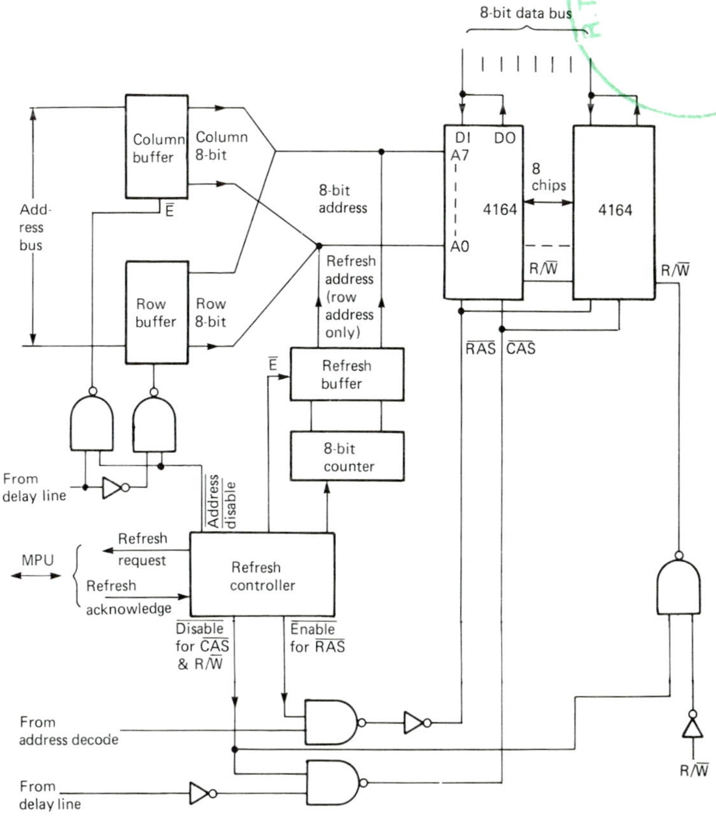

Fig. 5.6 Refreshing dynamic RAM

from the MPU is called 'handshaking'. It is a type of feedback loop which synchronises activities with the MPU's processing. Handshaking for refresh involves a certain slowing down of program execution. As the 256 refresh 'reads' must be performed in 4 ms or 4000 microseconds, the reads must be performed at less than 160-microsecond intervals. To be safe, these should be performed every 120 microseconds or less, and if any activities are performed with the processor which affect the handshaking lines being used, this could upset the refreshing. Note that a refresh cycle only takes approximately the time of a normal read, and thus takes up less than 1% of the total MPU time.

Referring to page 97, it would be possible to use the MR line of the 6802 to slow the processor down by one or two cycles using the

MR line each time a refresh was to be performed. There is no specific line to say that the MR 'stretch' has occurred, but the fact that E is high during that time could be utilised.

If the MPU cycle is such that at a certain time during the cycle it is possible to find a period when the MPU is not using the buses, it is a good idea to use this time for a refresh. This type of refresh regime is called 'cycle-stealing', and it does not place any overhead on the processor's time at all.

There are several special controllers on the market for the purpose of allowing dynamic memory to be used almost as easily as static RAM. They normally have special pins for causing the MPU to enter a wait state while the refresh is proceeding. Thus, if it is easy to force the MPU being used into a wait, the controllers are easy to use. Two such controllers are the Motorola MC3480, and the Intel 8203—an updated version of the 8202 used for the now obsolescent 4116 16K dynamic RAMs. Both the 8203 and the 3480 are suitable for 64K RAMs. However, the 3480 requires external monostables or other delay elements to attain its timing. The 8203 uses an external crystal, typically of the order of 20 MHz, to obtain all its timing. In addition, the 8203 can handle up to 128K of dynamic memory. Both devices slow the MPU's processing down in order to accommodate refresh. To use these devices, the manufacturers' data must be obtained and studied carefully.

An advance on the refresh regime introduced above is the so-called 'pin 1 refresh'. Most dynamic RAMs have pin 1 unconnected internally, to allow for future compatibility with 128K bit versions, which will require an extra address bit. However, some manufacturers take advantage of this by using pin 1 to allow an easier refresh method. Motorola, for instance, with their MC6664 device allow refresh pulses to be applied to pin 1, which update an internal refresh address counter automatically. This saves the necessity of producing an external counter for this purpose. In addition, if pin 1 is held low for a certain length of time, an automatic refresh system takes over, whereby the actual refresh pulses are produced internally too. This allows the memory to be placed in a low power standby state, while retaining the contents. The RAMs also allow the usual refresh method to be implemented, but only require a seven-bit refresh address instead of the full eight bits of the lower part of the address bus.

Z80 dynamic RAM interface

As was shown in Chapter 4, the Z80 has taken the idea of cycle-stealing to its logical end. Not only does it have a period in every M1 cycle when a refresh can be performed, but the Z80 also actually sends a seven-bit refresh address along its lower address lines during this time, and, further, has a special refresh pin to signal that a refresh may now be performed. It is thus not necessary to employ a counter, handshaking logic, or even the refresh buffer shown in Figure 5.6 to effect a refresh in a Z80 system. One or two problems remain, however. One concerns the delay line. Such components are not always fully reliable as to repeatability. A shift register, controlled by a crystal clock, may be found to be more reliable. In addition, the 4164 dynamic RAM requires an eight-bit refresh address, and the Z80 only supplies seven bits. Thus some form of counter is essential to toggle A7 on the memory chip's address bus every 127 refreshes. However, some RAM chip manufacturers have arranged their designs to allow seven-bit refresh—this solves the problem of toggling A7.

Figure 5.7 shows a dynamic memory interface suitable for a Z80 system. The memory chips most suited to the Z80 are the seven-bit refresh type, and these are used here. Many manufacturers make these devices, and they all have their own numbering for the chips. They will be referred to here by the Intel number '2164', and the 200 ns version will be assumed for all timing constraints below. These chips are fully pin-compatible with the 4164s shown in Figure 5.5. Figures 4.1, 4.2 and 4.3 should be consulted for the meanings and timings of the Z80 control lines mentioned here, along with the Z80 data in Appendix 4. The 4 MHz (Z80A) version of the Z80 will be assumed here, though the circuit functions with a Z80B at 6 MHz, with the correct choice of memory and logic chips. Figure 5.7 shows how a few simple logic chips can provide the signals for refreshing and address multiplexing of dynamic RAM. The Z80 itself acts as the dynamic memory controller. The weak point of the design is the necessity for a TTL-gate delay line. This component can, of course, be replaced by a standard LC delay line or a shift register. The Zilog Applications book (see the Bibliography) describes an example of a clocked design based around an 8 MHz clock. However, the circuit shown in Figure 5.7 gives good results with, essentially, just 12 chips if A, B and C are within one 74LS10 package. The address decoding, gate F, would normally be available from the rest of the system, but must be active high.

The circuit of Figure 5.7 uses MREQ to clock the memory access cycle. To understand the circuit, Figure 4.1 and the corresponding Z80 data in Appendix 4 should be consulted—the opcode fetch cycle is the most time-conscious for the Z80.

MREQ controls RAS, while CAS only goes active if the address decoding (gate F) and either RD or WR are active. WR must be active before CAS to allow data-in and data-out lines to be connected together without contention.

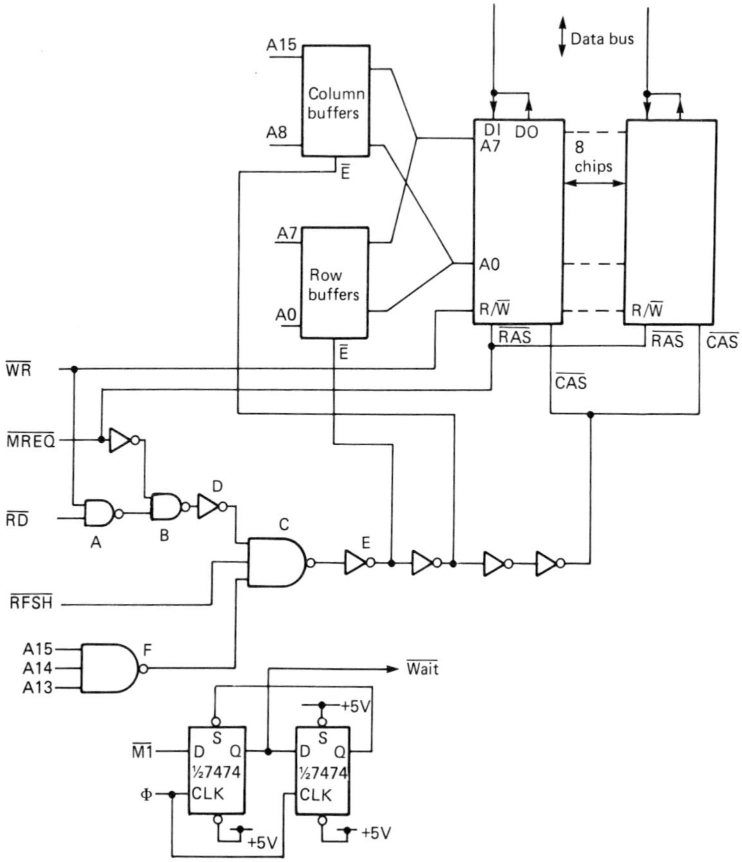

Fig. 5.7 Z80 dynamic memory system

There are two main timing constraints to be satisfied by the circuit—see Figure 5.5. First, the row buffers must not be disabled too soon after RAS has fallen to a 0—this allows the RAM time to take in the row address (tRAH), 30 ns is a typical minimum value. Second, the access time of the memory system must ensure that data is presented to the data bus of the Z80 at least 35 ns before the rising edge of T3. The second of these is dependent upon the first, among other things. The other timing constraints on the 2164 are easily satisfied by this circuit, and only these two critical parameters need to be considered.

In order to ensure the correct access time of the circuit, for any batch of ICs, a wait state generator should be used to lengthen the opcode fetch cycle by one wait state. M1 signals an opcode fetch, and examination of Figure 4.1 will show that the 7474 circuit at the foot of Figure 5.7 inserts just one wait state for each of these cycles. This makes the normal read cycle more time-conscious than the opcode fetch with its extra wait state.

As to the timing constraint on RAS, the circuit shown is very dependent upon the chips used. The delay between RAS going low and the enable to the row buffers going high is produced by the gates B, D, C and E. In general, these could be Schmitt triggers where possible, as they have a greater delay than standard gates. Further gates can, of course, be inserted between D and C to ensure the delay. A typical delay quoted for a TTL gate is 10 ns, with a maximum of 15 ns. It is good engineering practice to allow a minimum figure of half that of the typical figure, which implies that a delay of between 5 ns and 15 ns can be expected. Schmitt trigger gates have a typical delay of 16 ns, and a maximum of 22 ns. It is this skew in the figures, between minimum and maximum, which gives rise to the majority of problems in using gates in this way. It is a useful exercise for the reader to work out the minimum and maximum values for the critical timing parameters, using the timing diagrams in Appendix 4. Assume that only the inverters in Figure 5.7 are Schmitts. Assume, also, that the data is given out by the memory chips 200 ns after CAS falls. The exercise should be performed with and without assuming the extra wait, and then repeated for a Z80B running at 6 MHz, and finally at 8 MHz. For 6 and 8 MHz, assume the figures given in the appendix for a Z80A, but simply reduce the clock cycle time accordingly—a conservative assumption. What speeds of logic and memory chips are required for a successful system in the latter cases? Full Z80 and 2164 data sheets should then be obtained to allow an accurate calculation of the system's performance at the different frequencies.

Figure 4.1 shows how the WR line occurs considerably later than MREQ, and hence write cycles are quite safe, as to the delay between RAS and row buffer disabling. A further constraint, which affects the access time from RAS's falling edge, is the RAS to CAS delay (tRCD), which should be between 30 ns and 100 ns. If tRCD is within this figure, the data is supplied by the memory 200 ns from RAS's active edge, otherwise it is taken from CAS's active edge.

As can be seen from Figure 4.1, the address bus contains the current address some time before MREQ is active. This means that the address decoding of F is active at C—quite early enough to be discounted as a source of problems. The decoding shown here is presented purely as an example of a very simple decoding system. Any address below E000 will cause a 0 to appear on at least one of the inputs to F, therefore the output will be 1, enabling the gate C. This effectively removes 8K of the 64K available on the 2164s for other purposes if required.

The RFSH line from the Z80 is used purely to disable CAS, and hence the data output lines during a refresh. This is not necessary, but saves power. The actual refresh itself is performed during the T3 and T4 cycles shown in Figure 4.1, and is clocked by MREQ, just as for a normal memory cycle.

Finally, when using the Z80 for dynamic memory control it is important that such activities as the reset are not allowed to interfere with the process of refresh. If the reset is pressed by hand at any time, it is inevitable that the processor will be held in the reset condition for too long to ensure a proper refresh. Thus, if memory is to be preserved during reset, a special reset circuit must be employed which just pulses the reset line for long enough to effect a reset, but does not hold the reset line low for long enough to stop the refresh. In addition, the Z80 has the characteristic of giving an indeterminate MREQ signal 10 T-states after a reset if that reset has occurred during T3 of an M1 cycle. This peculiar state could destroy data in a dynamic RAM cell. To prevent this from happening, the falling edge on the reset line should be synchronised with M1 using a D-type flip-flop. This may then be fed to a monostable to give one short pulse to the reset line, however long the reset line is held low.

ROM

Read-only memory would normally be used for programs, which must be immediately resident within the machine upon power-up. There are many different forms of ROM, both fixed and programmable; they are generally known by their initials, some of which are presented below.

PROM—programmable ROM. This is often used, in the literature, to mean a type of bipolar read-only memory which is composed of memory cells, the states of which are determined by the presence or absence of fusible links on the chip. The chip comes with all the fusible links in place, and the user blows selected links out to form the required pattern of bits on the chip. Naturally, this type of memory cannot be erased and reprogrammed. The name 'PROM' is also used in some places simply to mean any form of ROM which is capable of being programmed.

EPROM—erasable programmable ROM. As its name suggests, this type of memory may be programmed, erased, and reprogrammed by the user with special equipment. The most common type of EPROM in use at present is the next type of ROM.

UVEPROM—ultra-violet erasable PROM. The contents of this ROM may be erased by exposure to UV light—there is a quartz window in the top of the chip's package through which the chip itself may be thus exposed.

EAROM (or EEROM)—electrically alterable (or erasable) ROM. These devices may be reprogrammed electronically, thereby saving the normal removal from the PCB and 20 or 30 minute exposure to UV light between programming cycles. EAROMs take of the order of one second to alter. These devices have not yet been manufactured to the same reliability or memory density as the UVEPROM, but will, no doubt, gain wide and grateful acceptance when they are up to the standard of the present EPROMs.

ROMs are also capable of being manufactured with a given bit pattern already resident within the memory matrix. These are called 'mask-programmed ROMs'. The bit pattern is formed in the photographic mask which is used to define whether or not there is a transistor at any given row-column intersection within the memory matrix. Such devices are expensive in small quantities. Normally a quantity in excess of 1000 provides the cost cross-over point, depending upon the type and manufacturer of the ROMs involved, otherwise EPROMs are cheaper. For an MPU-controlled device which is to be manufactured in volume, mask-programmed ROM is a very cost-effective alternative—unless the program is to be altered at any time. The option normally taken by companies is to use a type of ROM which is directly pin-compatible with EPROM chips. This allows prototyping and small quantity production to be entered using EPROMs, with the possibility of replacement by ROMs for mass production.

The technology of the UVEPROM (just called an EPROM from now on) is interesting, and one example is shown in Figure 5.8. As with all memory devices, the elements are arranged in a matrix to allow address decoding to be straightforward. The memory elements, as for the dynamic RAM cell, are arranged at the 'crossing' points of the rows and the columns. A MOSFET is used in lieu of the load resistor for the EPROM cell itself while reading. The EPROM cell illustrated consists of a stack of three layers which are insulated from each other by a very thin dielectric—typically 1000 Ångstrom units thick. The object is to trap charge on the middle layer, called the floating gate, by application of a high voltage (typically 20–30 volts) across the cell. A process called 'avalanche injection' causes electrons to cross the thin dielectric layer, and some of these become trapped on the floating gate. There is no electrical path for these electrons to leak away when the high voltage is removed, and it is claimed that the gate

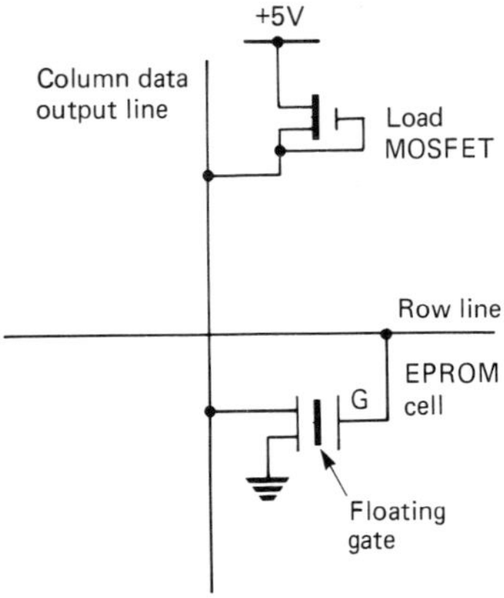

Fig. 5.8 EPROM cell

will retain its state for seven years at a temperature of 125°C. Much longer times are possible at normal temperatures due to the lower mobility of the electrons trapped in their potential well. The technology of the cell ensures that the presence of a charge on the floating gate causes the cell to be in its conducting (on) state. The amount of charge which is held is enough to ensure that no matter what the state of the gate G, the cell continues to conduct. When the cell is read, by applying a 0 to the row line and observing the state of the column, the presence of a charge will turn the cell on, and thus show a 0 by connecting the column data output line to ground. When no charge is present, the cell is off when the row line is low, and the load MOSFET pulls the column line high. The chip is supplied by the manufacturer with no charge on any of its floating gates, and hence is supplied full of 1s, which is the normal erased state.

To erase the cells, UV light is directed through the window in the top of the chip. If it is of the correct frequency, the photons are energetic enough to give the electrons the energy to jump the dielectric barrier, and the resulting photoelectric current leaks the charge away to the substrate.

The common characteristic of all memory devices is the organisation into rows and columns. Given such a matrix, any type of memory cell may be connected between row and column at the intersection points. The mask-programmed ROM, for instance, simply places normal transistors at those cells which must show a 0 when read. That is, the EPROM cell in Figure 5.8 is replaced by a transistor with gate connected to the row line. When the cell is read, the presence of a transistor produces a 0 on the column. The absence of a transistor causes a 1 to be read. This is a very compact cell, and requires only the simplest of extra decoding. The packing density of such devices is, therefore, very high. The bit pattern required is easily converted into a photographic mask, and for large quantity may be most cost-effective.

Other types of cell which may be placed at the intersection of the matrix lines are the EAROM device and the fusible-link cell, which have been mentioned above.

EPROM programming

An 'EPROM programmer' allows the user to store programs in machine-code form within the computer. Such programs, therefore, will be resident in the address map when the computer is first switched on. An EPROM or ROM would be required within a microcomputer system designed to form a small controller. This avoids the necessity for loading the program up each time the controller is switched on.

In order to use the device described in this section a certain amount of programming is necessary. The reader who has access to a system with a resident assembler to allow him to write machine-code programs will find this programmer most useful. A further facility required for the programmer is a set of parallel I/O lines, preferably from a special I/O chip. Such chips are described in detail in Chapter 7.

As explained above, there are several forms of programmable ROM. The type referred to here is the popular and ubiquitous UVEPROM, or EPROM chip. When these devices were first introduced, they conformed to no particular pin-out standard, and often required three levels of power supply. Modern chips now conform to an upward-compatible pin-out which is generally agreed in the industry, and which includes compatible pin-outs for other types of memory such as RAM. In addition, the EPROMs generally available now require just one level of power supply (+5 volts) for reading, and consume considerably less power than originally. The avalanche injection of charge to the floating gate is achieved by applying of the order of 20–30 volts to a special programming pin on the package. The exact programming voltage depends upon the design of the chip involved.

The EPROMs described here are of the '27XX' series whereby the XX is the number of K bits stored within the chip. The chips are organised to store and supply bytes, and hence a 2716, for instance, is capable of storing 16K bits, or 2K bytes. The MPU user is more interested in the number of bytes which any device can store, and one is thus led to wonder whether the manufacturers' description in terms of the number of bits held in the device stems from a desire to make the chip appear much larger than reality! The 2716 is now obsolete for new designs, and the EPROM programmer described here will be for the 2732 and 2764 devices, with 4K and 8K bytes respectively. In general, it is a sound idea to design for 2764s, as they follow the 28-pin standard into which the 24-pin 2732 will fit comfortably, as will the 27128 etc. Figure 5.9 shows the pin-out of the 2732 and the 2764 on a single socket. Compare the pin-out with Figure 5.2 for an illustration of the standards mentioned above—note, however, that 2 must be added to each pin number on the 6116 to equal those of Figure 5.9.

Figure 5.9 is drawn to show the standard socket required to take a 2732 or 2764. The pins where a difference exists are shown in the tables headed with the appropriate device name. Pins 1, 2, 27 and 28 are not present on the 2732. The 2732, therefore, only occupies part of the socket, and care should be taken to insert the 2732 into the lower part of the socket as shown. The only pins which require setting differently for the two different devices are ones which are used during programming. For reading a 2764, pins 1, 27 and 28 are connected to +5 volts, 2 is connected to A12, and 22 is connected to 0 volts. The chip is enabled using pin 20. Pin 26 of the socket is connected to +5 volts to ensure that when a 2732 is plugged into the 28 pin socket, its pin 24 is at VCC, as it occupies pin 26 of the socket.

Figure 5.9 shows the timing diagram for programming a 2732. The programming voltage (VPP) is applied to socket pin 22, and the address of the location and its data are set up on the buses. A time tS elapses and then the CE line is pulsed low for approximately 45 milliseconds. The next byte to be programmed, with its address, may then be set up and the process repeated. It is important that CE is only taken low for the specified time (45 ms) while VPP is present, or the device will be destroyed. To read a 2732, it is treated as any other type of static memory, with CE and OE taken low for it to be enabled. The set-up time, tS, is of the order of 2 microseconds.

The only difference for a 2764 is that CE is held low continuously during programming, and it is the PGM pin (27) which is pulsed low for 45 ms. The same caution applies for PGM as it does for the CE of the 2732. Different devices from different manufacturers have different VPP levels. For instance, the Intel 2764 and 2732A require 21 volts. The Intel 2732, however, in common with most other manufacturers' 2732s requires 24–25 volts, and exceeding either of these requirements will damage the device. Data sheets should be consulted where possible. The most thoughtful manufacturers actually print the programming voltage on the chip. Some manufacturers produce chips called 2532s, or 2564s, which are slightly different in pin-out from the 27 series.

A Programmer for 2732/64s should be capable of both program-

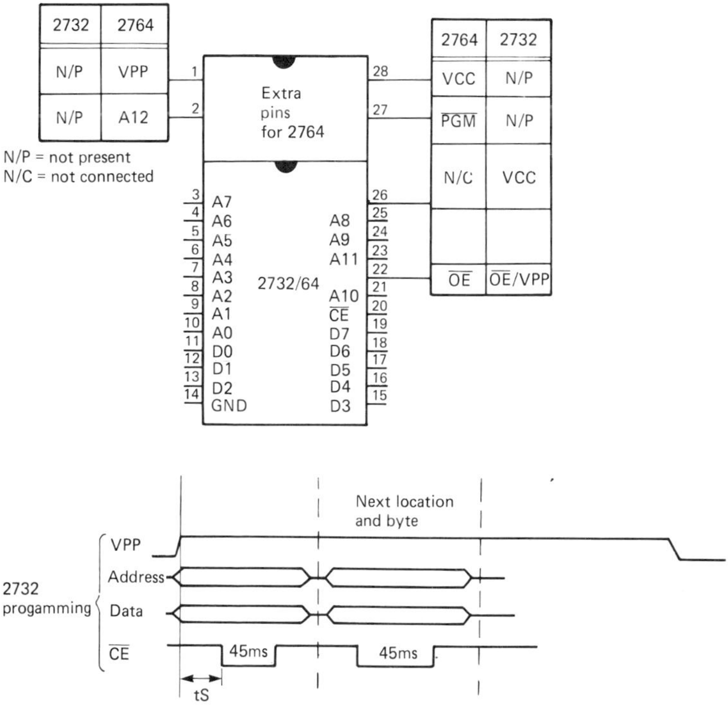

Fig. 5.9 2732/64 EPROM chip

ming and verifying the pattern 'blown' onto the chip. Most users will want to store a program which they have written in a development system, and now wish to plug into another, perhaps smaller, system. The programmer described here assumes that a source of around +16 volts is available, along with +5 volts. In addition, three eight-bit I/O ports are required along with some programming. The hardware is described first, followed by an outline of the software. These particular hardware requirements would be available, for instance, on the average S100 system. Some companies supply stand-alone EPROM programmers, whereby the data is loaded in via a special I/O port from a computer system. Such programmers store the data in RAM, and use counters to apply the necessary address and timing pulses to the chip while the data is retrieved from the RAM and fed to the chip. It is also possible to purchase S100 cards containing EPROM programmers, and the software is normally supplied to run them. Such cards would normally be able to burn the EPROM from a given block of data stored in the RAM of the computer.

The programmer described here is illustrated in Figure 5.10. The 16-volt line supplies a very common oscillator chip called a '555'. This oscillator is used to feed a classical voltage doubler consisting of diodes and capacitors. The 30 volts or so which this produces is then applied to a resistor and Zener diode of value equal to the appropriate VPP value. This is smoothed and used to program the EPROM. The doubler cannot supply very much current, but the author has found

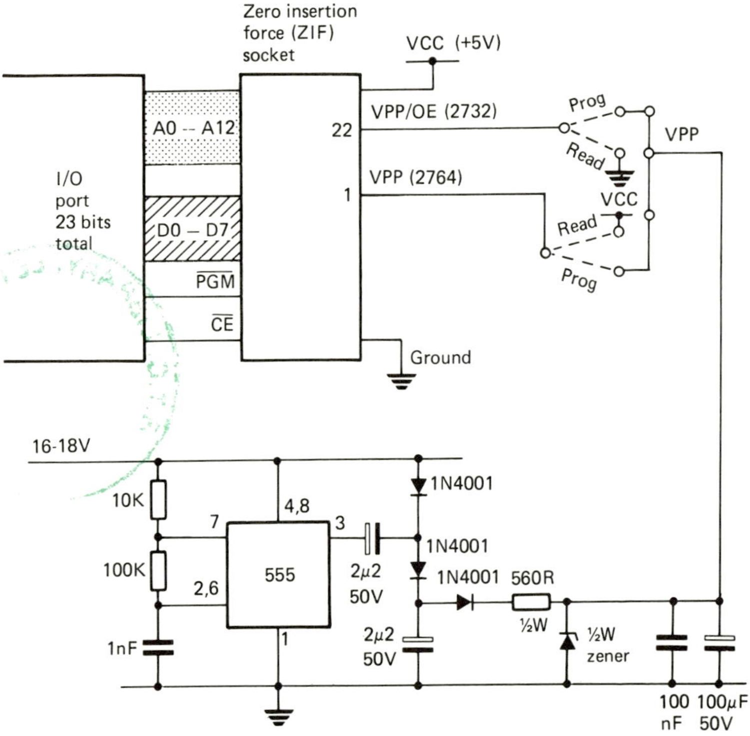

Fig. 5.10 2732/64 EPROM programmer

this to be quite sufficient for the purpose, where it is in constant use plugged into an S100 system. The diagram shows a zero insertion force socket (ZIF) which has a lever by the side to allow the EPROM to be dropped in the socket, and held firmly by applying the lever.

The patches and switches allow a 2732 or 2764 to be programmed, and the software applies CE or PGM pulses respectively. For a 2732, socket pin 22 must be held low when reading, and at VPP when programming. For a 2764, pin 1 is held high during reading, and at

VPP for programming. A different Zener diode will be needed for different devices.

Figure 5.11 suggests an appropriate software flowchart which simply relies on the timing diagram of Figure 5.9. It is assumed that the block to be programmed is resident in the computer's RAM, and that the switch is in the read position. Before the operator switches to program, the PGM (for a 2764) or the CE (for a 2732) is taken to the high state. This prevents damage to the chip. The operator is then

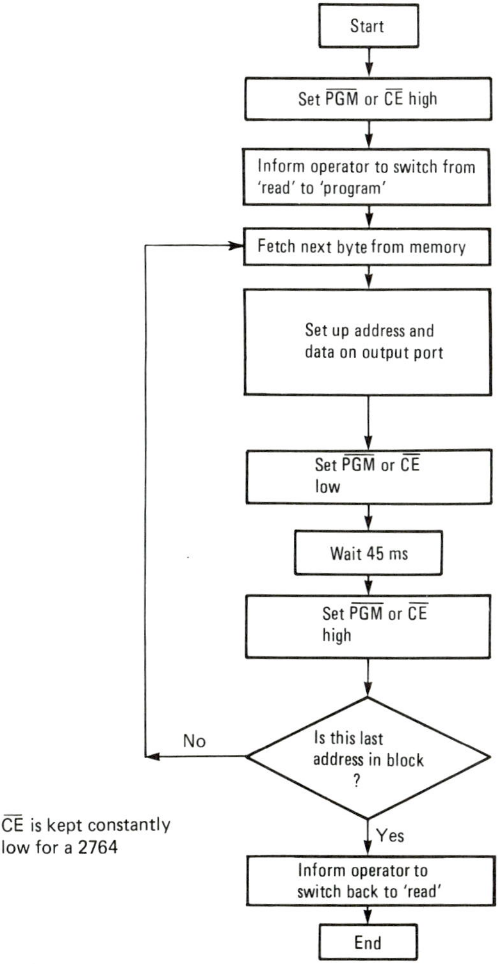

Fig. 5.11 EPROM programming software

asked to switch on VPP—for a 2764, the CE line can simply be taken low at this point, and held low throughout the programming. The first byte is fetched from memory, and address 0 set up on the I/O port, along with the byte to be programmed. PGM or CE is then pulsed low for 45 ms; the program can be counting up to a high number which may be found by experimentation. The process is then repeated for successive data bytes stored in memory. After the last location has been programmed, the program should prompt the user to switch back to read mode. The next program to be run should successively read the EPROM locations and compare them to the original as a verification. It should be clear from the process described above that any set of locations may be selectively programmed if required. It is not necessary to program every location of such an EPROM; it is not even necessary to program the locations in any particular order.

Some uses of ROM devices

Some examples of the use of ROMs of various different types have been given above. For instance, the most widespread use is as a means of storing programs. Another use given above was that of the fast bipolar PROMs for address decoding. ROMs are used in a variety of different places where a transform function on a set of data must be performed in a static manner—that is, a bit pattern is simply transformed into another without the need for any intelligence or decision making. Other applications which will be met later in this book will be for ROMs used as character generators for visual display units, and as keyboard encoders. Character generators store the actual pattern of dots which must be presented to a cathode ray tube in order to 'draw' patterns such as letters and numbers on the screen. Keyboard encoders store the bit patterns which correspond to the pressing of different keys on a keyboard.

Another use for ROMs is in the control of state-sequencing. This type of circuit is the solid-state version of the cam switch, which contains a motor to rotate a cam containing pins for switching sets of mechanical switches on and off with each rotational step. These are used extensively in washing machines for providing a program of tasks. The same effect may be produced by counting through the addresses in a ROM containing a sequence of tasks stored as bits in successive locations. Each data bit could be fed from the ROM's data bus to a transistor, and perhaps a relay, to control one element of a machine. Figure 5.12 sketches a state-sequencer, with a total of 20 outputs. As the clock oscillates, the binary counter sequences through the locations of the ROM. Each location is regarded as a state of the machine, and simply contains a bit pattern which, when output to the relay drivers, turns on the required functions at that instant. For a washing machine, the clock would be quite slow. For a high-speed application, the clock may be any frequency which will not prevent the ROM from having time to supply the data. Figure 5.12 also shows

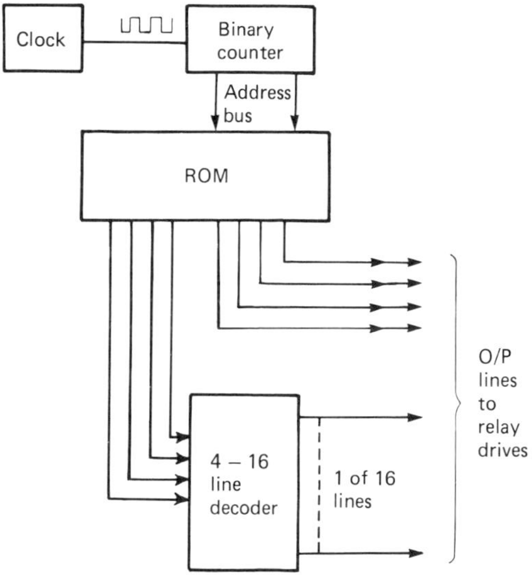

Fig. 5.12 ROM as a state sequencer

how an eight-bit ROM can control many more outputs. Four of the data lines are fed to a 16-way decoder, to allow the 1 of 16 different outputs to be turned on. The disadvantage is that only one of these 16 outputs can be turned on at once in this simple picture. By adding more and sophisticated logic, with flip-flops and latches, it is possible to produce remarkably complex operations. However, it soon becomes cumbersome, hence the widespread use of MPU systems.

Summary of memory systems for different MPUs

Chapter 4 has outlined the different methods by which our three sample processors interface to memory in general. These MPUs provide a very full range of interface methods, and they are reviewed here. Figure 4.4 shows a sketch of the interface required by the Z80. As usual, an eight-bit bidirectional data bus and a 16-bit address bus are fed to the memory devices. In addition, a certain amount of control is required. This takes the form, in the Z80, of an IORQ line to distinguish between memory and I/O, and RD and WR lines to determine the direction of data flow along the data bus. Most memory devices require just a single R/W line, and the WR line alone can be used for this purpose. A refresh line may also be used, and perhaps a WAIT line as described earlier in the present chapter, for dynamic memory. Figure 5.7 shows the MREQ line in use, as this line has a special purpose for dynamic memories, as shown in Figure 4.1, whereby MREQ goes low during a refresh cycle.

The 6800 is similar in its treatment of memory—see Figure 4.9. The difference is that the control lines required are just VMA and R/W, and perhaps an equivalent of the WAIT line, the MR line on the 6802, for dynamic memory. There is no I/O map to be confused with memory, and there is no refresh line or separate RD and WR lines.

The 1802 is different in that it requires its 16-bit address to be demultiplexed from eight lines. Figure 4.16 shows the hardware required for the process. Figure 4.15 shows the exact timing of the 1802's handling of memory. The falling edge of TPA is the safe place to latch the high-order byte of address, and not until the end of cycle number 4 is any writing performed. The separate MWR and MRD lines may be used for determining the direction of data flow, but for most memory chips, MWR is sufficient when used as the R/W line. The only confusion arises with reading. It is only when the full 16 bits are established at the end of cycle number 2 that the address at the address decoding, as well as at the chip's internal decoding, are demanding a valid location from the memory chip. Until that time, the chip may be outputting indeterminate data from random address locations. However, this is irrelevant as the MPU is only looking for data in the middle of cycle number 7, and it simply discards any data-bus states until that time, when the address has been stable for long enough to ensure that the memory chip is replying with the correct pattern.

The differences between the processors, therefore, show that the 6800 is the simplest to use, the Z80 the most sophisticated, and the 1802 the most hardware-intensive. One important note to add is that not all the control lines offered by an MPU need be used; their use depends upon the application. For the case of a simple controller, the 6800 and the Z80 would involve about the same amount of hardware, and several of the control lines would be redundant. The 1802, however, would almost certainly need the demultiplexing from 8- to 16-bit addresses, as 256 bytes is a very small amount of memory indeed. However, the 1802 may not require any I/O chips, as explained in Chapter 4.

Magnetic peripheral memory

So far, only internal memory to the MPU system has been described. Each location within such memory may be accessed by the MPU at maximum speed simply by placing the PC register on the internal address bus. However, until very large semiconductor memories can be manufactured which will not lose data when switched off, there will always be a necessity for external storage of data in a form which may be loaded into internal RAM for operation upon by the MPU. Of course, if high-density internal memory storage were possible, 16-bit address buses would be too small to address it. However, such memory can be arranged in banks and switched in and out as required, perhaps using I/O lines.

The most commonly available external memory devices utilise magnetic tapes or the much faster disks, which store the bits as magnetic patterns. Typical disk units available for micros will store from 90K bytes to tens of megabytes on a single unit, with minimum average retrieval times for a random byte in the order of tens of miliseconds, depending upon disk type, and the data organisation on the disk surface. Tapes are used either at the lower end of the market, for cheap external memory, or for the back-up of data from large fixed-disk systems which cannot be removed and stored in a library. This, in fact, is the greatest advantage of the tape. Even though removable disk packs are available with large capacities, they are expensive, and the storage of 'archive' information is most cost-effectively achieved using tapes. In addition, tapes are still cost-effective in data logging, where large amounts of information must be gathered over long periods in an industrial or scientific process.

In general, serious industrial applications for tapes will use special-purpose data cassettes. However, many small microcomputers still use the audio cassette as a cheap method of storing programs for later retrieval. This is one of the most important facilities offered by any MPU system. There are many different types of tape and disk system; the following sections will introduce the reader to some of them, along with the type of system which is necessary for their support. In order to use a microcomputer in any industrial setting, apart from simple control applications, it is generally agreed that some form of disk storage is essential. Within the near future it is predicted that other non-mechanical methods of peripheral non-volatile storage will be available. One of these, bubble memory, is mentioned below.

Types of tape and disk

The simplest microcomputers provide direct output to an audio cassette, and encode the data bits into electrical signals suitable for recording on the tape. The bits themselves are not recordable directly, as tape machines are designed to store and reproduce sine waves of audio frequencies. In order to record a block of memory, therefore, it is necessary to convert the block of bytes into a serial stream of bits, and convert these into sine wave packets. A common method is to convert a 1 into one tone, or frequency, and a 0 into another. This method is called frequency shift keying (FSK); some standards have been agreed, whereby a 1200 Hz tone is used for a 0 and a 2400 Hz tone for a 1. This protocol is sometimes called the Kansas City method, after a symposium held in November 1975 in that city where this tape-storage standard originated. There are many other ways to store data on a cassette; depending upon the sophistication of the electronics, different maximum speeds of transfer may be achieved. For the hobbyist, typical maximum speeds of 1200 bits per second may be expected by interfaces which generate their data clocks from the retrieved data, thereby cancelling the common effects of 'wow and flutter' from which any small tape system will suffer. Figure 5.13

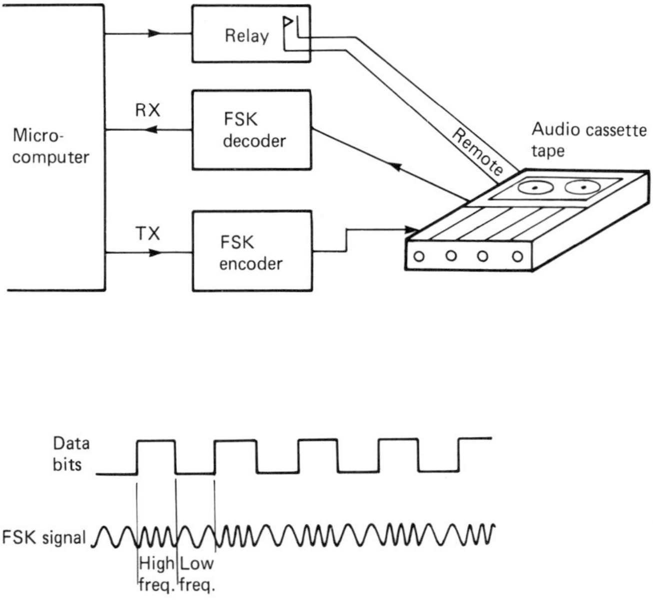

Fig. 5.13 Simple tape storage

sketches a small tape system where the computer controls the starting and stopping of the tape by a relay plugged into the remote socket of the cassette machine, and sends and receives data bits to and from the tape via special I/O ports which serialise data—these are described in the next chapter. The stream of bits is recorded onto the tape in a form shown in the waveform diagram as a sequence of high and low tones.

There are many published circuits for the electronics of tape interfaces, and communicating with them is a very simple matter. It is only necessary for the MPU system to have a method of serialising blocks of memory out of a serial I/O port, and of loading memory from the same port. Such activities are described in Chapter 6. Most small MPU systems offer storage on audio cassettes as a standard function, and require nothing more than the use of a normal audio cassette recorder.

There are two major classes of disk, floppy (or flexible) and hard

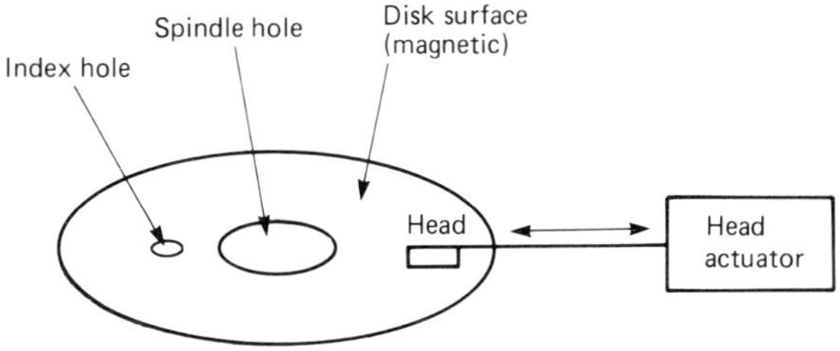

Fig. 5.14 Magnetic disk storage

(or rigid). Floppy disks are flexible discs of plastic (Mylar, normally) supplied within a protective jacket and coated with a ferromagnetic material. The jacket contains a number of cutouts for various purposes, such as allowing a magnetic head to contact the disk. The disk itself contains at least two holes—see Figure 5.14. One of these is at the centre to allow a cone-shaped spindle to clamp the centre of the disk accurately, and spin it. Other holes are placed off-centre to allow a photo sensor to locate the exact point in time at which the disk reaches a given angular position as it rotates. These are broadly called index holes, and there are two different methods of organising data on the disk surface which require different numbers of such holes. These two methods are called 'hard sectoring' and 'soft sectoring'. Hard-sectored disks require one hole for each sector, e.g. 16, while soft-sectored disks require just one index hole. Figure 5.15 shows a sketch of the magnetic zones on a typical soft-sectored disk surface. Bits are stored on the surface in a manner very similar to that of tape, though the method of actually transforming the bits to magnetic patterns is

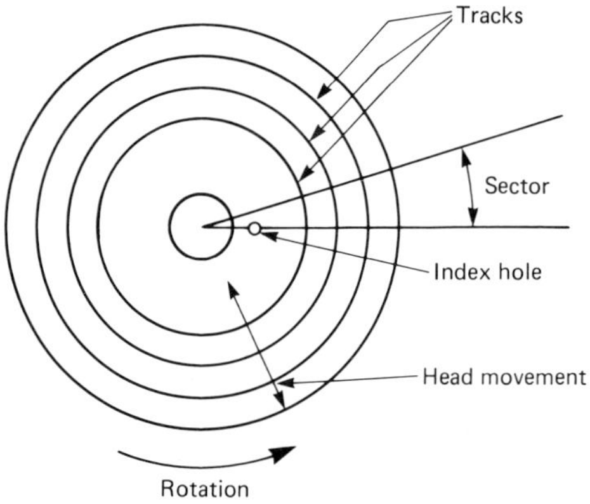

Fig. 5.15 Magnetic patterns on disks

more sophisticated than the Kansas City method mentioned above.

Zones within which the data is stored are organised on the disk surface as circles and angular regions. As the disk rotates, a complete circle of magnetic surface appears beneath the magnetic head. Such circles are called 'tracks'. Each track is further divided into equiangular regions called 'sectors'. The index hole shown identifies the first sector each time it passes over a photocell. The subsequent sectors on the disk are identified by the information stored on the surface itself. For this to happen, the MPU would have to have stored a 'formating' pattern on the surface. This formating allows feedback to the electronics to ensure that a piece of data is stored to or retrieved from the required disk sector accurately. This method of identifying sectors is called 'soft sectoring'. 'Hard sectoring' is performed by using disks with sector holes punched in a circle around the disk. Each hole corresponds with the start of a sector. Each subsequent sector is thus identified by its own index hole.

In order to accurately store and retrieve data, the radial position of the head must be controlled accurately. Floppy disk drives do not, in general, employ a feedback loop for this positioning, and accuracy of positioning is derived, normally, from a stepper motor. Steppers are described in a subsequent chapter, but suffice it to say that a stepper is a motor whose spindle may be rotated through an accurately reproducible 'step' angle by a digital system. Such angular steps are transformed into linear steps by a mechanical system and used to move the magnetic head along a radius. As the head moves radially it spans across the disk surface, and may thus contact any required track. Thus, by a combination of the spindle's constant rotation and control of head movement, all the tracks and sectors may be made to pass beneath the head. In floppy disks, the head is actually in contact with the disk surface. This does, of course, eventually, wear out the disk and head, as well as limiting the maximum speed at which the disk can be practically rotated. A typical speed is 360 rev/min. There are several advantages of head contact. First, the mechanics are more straightforward than for 'flying heads'. The effects of dust contamination are less pronounced, as the head normally pushes detritus aside as it wipes the surface. Also, the 'gap' in the head does not need to be as narrow as for 'flying heads' to achieve high densities of magnetisation.

In many aspects of the history of the magnetic disk, IBM has been a major force. It was IBM that originated the standard form of floppy disk (or 'diskette'), which has a diameter of 8 inches. This disk, still a standard today, is soft sectored, and has 77 tracks and 26 sectors per track. The density of tracks is 48 tracks per inch (TPI), and the recording density on a track is either 3268 bits per inch (BPI) (called 'single density') or 6536 BPI for 'double density'. The average access time to any given bit is of the order of 250 ms. Total capacities of the 8 inch disk are 250K bytes (single density) and 500K bytes (double) on a single side. These parameters will be compared with rigid disks shortly.

A later, and now very popular, type of disk is the so-called 'mini-floppy'. These disks are 5.25 inches in diameter, and hence are handled by much smaller and neater disk drives. 'Mini-diskettes', as the 5.25 inch disks are called, are taking over the field of floppy disk storage, and it is in this field that the greatest advances are taking place. 5.25 inch disks are now commonly used which can store one megabyte by using both sides of the disk, and whose drives will fit into a space approximately $8 \times 6 \times 1.75$ inches. Power requirements are typically +5 volts and +12 volts at less than one amp each.

The other main class of disk (hard) is the same in principle, but has a number of different aspects. The most important differences are that hard disks are more expensive, much faster, higher in capacity, and less amenable to cheap archive storage.

There are two main types of hard disk—fixed and removable. Fixed disks are used for fast access to large amounts of data, and the information on their surfaces must be backed up (copied), for safety, by other magnetic storage means, such as tape or floppy disk. Removable disks allow the rigid disk to be removed from the drive in a special rigid cartridge, and stored in a library. This is an expensive method of storage for large data banks, but is ideal otherwise, as backing up may be confined simply to using several removable disk packs, only one of which is resident in the computer at any time. The others may store the recent state of the system to prevent total loss of data if, for instance, the disk drive fails and destroys a disk.

The head on a hard disk is normally very light, and actually flies above the rotating disk surface. This allows the disk to rotate at ten times the speed of the floppy disks without damage to the head or the disk. However, such a system is highly susceptible to particle contamination. If a piece of grit should lodge in the air gap beneath the head while the disk is rotating at 3600 rev/min a tail of swarf is instantly raised from the magnetic coating of the surface. This will normally catch beneath the head and cause a fast progressive breakdown of the surface, and a condition called 'head crash'. To obviate this condition, head gaps are kept large unless the disk is completely sealed within a chamber. Either way, rigid standards of air filtration are adhered to during the operation of the unit.

The disk itself is normally aluminium for low inertia, and coated with a lubricated magnetic oxide. When the disk is at rest, the head actually rests in contact with the surface. As the disk spins up from rest, the head gradually rises until it is above the surface, held in that position by the air flow dragged around by the disk's rotation. The head will normally be 'parked' over a track which contains no data so that as the speed increases or decreases, the head does not damage a part of the disk surface where there is likely to be data.

The most common type of hard disk found on microcomputers is the so-called 'Winchester' disk, a name originated by IBM to describe a type of read/write head. The unique characteristic of the Winchester system is that the head flies just 19 microns above the disk surface—much nearer than previous designs. The object is to allow high densities of magnetisation, and hence of data recording within a small space for small systems. The inevitable consequence of the Winchester head was to require a sealed unit around the disk with continuous internal air filtration to remove any particles of contamination left within the cavity, or produced from the disk surface during speed-up and -down. At such small surface-head gaps, abrasive dust particles are the biggest threat to reliability.

Winchester technology disks are available in various sizes and capacities, but the 8 inch and 5·25 inch versions are typical physical sizes in common use. The first 8 inch Winchesters to be announced appear to have been the IMI model 7710 in 1978. This is a 10 megabyte drive with a fast access time which is still in use, appearing in the Corvus disk system, and used as the centre of a very popular networking system for Apple microcomputers. The 7720 is the 20 megabyte version. This disk typifies many of the characteristics of the physically larger type of Winchester. It has an average access time of 50 ms—one-fifth of that of the floppy mentioned above. Much of its speed comes from the technology of its head movement. The head actuator is a voice-coil, a type of linear motor, and works by a closed-loop feedback system to position the head accurately. Feedback is supplied by servo information stored on one of the disk surfaces. The drive contains two disks (or platters) on the same spindle, and four heads on the same actuator, providing four surfaces for data. One complete surface is devoted to this servo information. Hence feedback is used for both track and sector positioning, which further aids high-density storage in smaller spaces. The disk stores data at a density of 6000 bits per inch on each track (about the same as the double-density floppy), and at 300 tracks per inch (over six times that of the floppy). Thus track width and track spacing are of the order of 2 to 3 thousandths of an inch—hence the need for accurate head positioning.

The IMI 7710/20 devices are upper-end-of-the-market Winchesters. At the other end is a range of drives which are considerably cheaper, about half the speed and density, and whose head is positioned by such means as a capstan, stepper and band. In this configuration, as the stepper rotates, a steel band wraps or unwraps from a capstan to move the head linearly. No closed loop is used, and the disks are often 5.25 inches in diameter. They are designed to fit into the space of a standard floppy, but are about twice as thick as the floppy drive whose dimensions are given above. In all other respects they are manufactured to the same standards and philosophy as the more expensive Winchesters, but provide fast-access, high-density storage at a very low price.

To further increase capacity, Winchesters are often manufactured with several disks (or platters) on the same rotating spindle, in a stack. Each platter can have its own pair of heads for double-sided storage, and to increase speed of access multiple heads are sometimes used. Such heads are arranged along a radius, so that each head has its own track continuously presented to it, and thus the whole system has immediate access to as many tracks at any time as there are heads. In addition, the head assembly has to be moved a shorter distance to allow at least one head to read or write to any bit. Average access times can be reduced by a factor of three by this method.

The next advance in technology is the use of thin-film heads to achieve lower inertia and hence faster head movement. In addition, plated disks allow a more uniform surface, which will allow the head to fly closer to the disk, and increase the density of surface magnetisation. Other goals are higher capacities and even higher reliability—the Winchester is already well known for its reliability, due to the sealing of the disk and head within a cavity. Some progress is also expected towards a removable type of Winchester, where the whole disk and head assembly is sealed but removable.

System requirements for disks

A disk system allows the computer user to construct large programs and store large files of data. There is little point in providing a disk system with a memory of less than the maximum addressing capability of the MPU—i.e. 64K. Any serious use of the system will soon require this, and probably more. In addition, large quantities of data require some method of printing the programs and their results. A sophisticated computer system would normally have a full typewriter keyboard and a visual display unit (VDU) using a cathode ray tube (CRT). It is very uncommon for a simple control system to have all these facilities, unless there is some necessity for collection and analysis of data from the process.

Typical minimum hardware for a disk-based system, therefore, would be 64K of memory, a printer, a VDU and a full keyboard. These may reside in a single unit, or be spread over a number of enclosures. Chapter 1 gave a typical memory map of such a system, and the components are described in various chapters of this book.

To run a system of any size, there are normally several different levels of program which the machine will be executing at different times. Different machines approach the system software in different

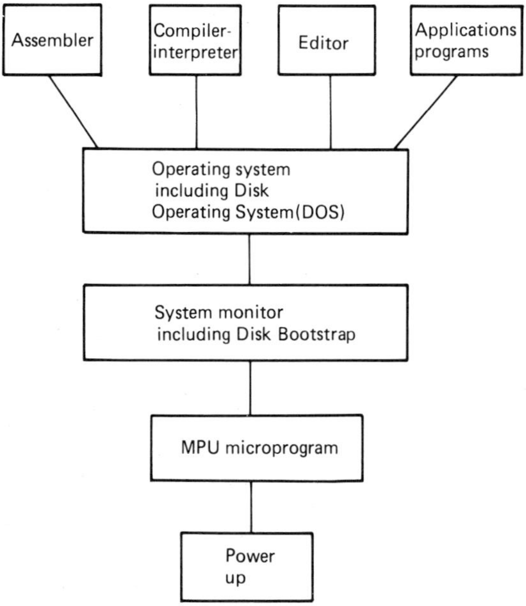

Fig. 5.16 Typical system software hierarchy

ways; one such method is illustrated in Figure 5.16. Here, power-up causes two programs to execute after the reset line goes high. The MPU microprogram is in constant action while the power is switched on; and as soon as power comes up, the ROM-based system monitor starts executing. This monitor is normally complex enough to allow the machine to be used for simple functional checking, and has routines for handling the keyboard and VDU and for starting up the disk function. While in the monitor, it is often possible to program and view memory locations, communicate with external devices such as printers, test the RAM, etc., depending upon the particular machine in question. By pressing different keys on the keyboard, all these different functions are available. One important such function is the loading of a program from the disk. It is normal to include a program called a 'disk bootstrap' for this purpose. The appropriate key is pressed on the keyboard, and a block of program instructions called a 'loader' is brought in from the disk by the bootstrap, and executed. This loader then loads in the much larger and more complex program called the 'operating system', which proceeds to control the machine from then on. Operating systems offer highly intelligent facilities, such as a 'disk operating system' (DOS) for organising data on the disk storage. Most programs on a computer run via or 'under' an operating system.

A very widespread microcomputer operating system is 'CPM'. This program was originated by a company called Digital Research for the Intel 8080 MPU, and will also run on a Z80, which is downward compatible, in machine-code, with the 8080. In order to run CPM on a given machine it must be adjusted for the specific requirements of the hardware of that system. The memory map of the system, for instance, will normally be unique in some way, and the method of communicating with the operator will certainly be so. These various changes are confined to a set of modules which CPM contains and which the user may configure for himself if he wishes. The vast bulk of CPM, however, is a block of machine code which Digital Research supplies, and which is common to any machine running this operating system.

CPM is a disk-oriented operating system. It allows fast copying, recalling and storing of disk-organised data and programs. The great advantage of a 'standard' operating system is that it is possible to buy software from a number of different sources to run on the computer under the operating system. CPM has one of the largest sets of generally available software packages of any operating system. Many software houses sell their products to run under CPM.

Important programs which any machine should be able to offer its users include the ability to write software in a variety of languages.

The user is able to write, test and run programs with the power of the computer to aid him continuously. Machine-code programs can normally be written using just the system monitor, but the task is made infinitely easier if the mnemonics for the code can be typed in, and simply converted or 'assembled' by the computer automatically. Such a program is called an assembler, and all computers offer this facility—normally to run under an operating system. There are many Z80 and 8080 assemblers available to run under CPM. Most programs are written as a set of statements into a disk-file using an 'editor'. The assembler then simply acts on the edited file and produces machine code for the MPU to execute in another file.

High-level languages are available which allow a user to write almost English statements for the computer to execute. Just as for assembly languages, the statements may be written into a file using an editor, and then presented to a program called a compiler for conversion into machine code. Another popular program to aid in this task is an 'interpreter'. The drawback of the compiler and assembler is that mistakes of syntax (the language's grammar) are not recognised by the machine until the conversion process begins. Any number of mistakes may be written into the file using the editor, which does not view the written statements intelligently. However, an interpreter, as its name suggests, interprets the statements as they are typed in. Each line is carefully checked by the machine as it is written, and any simple mistakes can be corrected as they are made. Interpreters are very slow at running the program, however, as they do not produce a complete machine-code version of the program at any time. Each line is read in and temporarily converted to run on the MPU on a line-by-line basis. This allows very easy testing and editing. When the program is complete and tested in this manner, a compiler may be set to work producing a complete machine-code version of the program which will then run at maximum speed. The original program is called 'source-code' and the machine code version is called 'object-code'. Programs produced on a computer for any task are generally termed 'applications programs'. For instance, a company may write or buy a set of applications programs for the company's payroll or ledgers.

The main point of this section is to bring home the fact that complex and sophisticated tasks on a computer require a disk system. To perform the above tasks without peripheral memory would be almost impossible, and to perform them with any slower magnetic memory than a disk very quickly becomes too cumbersome. The approximately 10:1 speed advantage of hard disks also provides a remarkable advantage when dealing with a disk-based operating system, or disk-based applications programs.

Bubble memory

Disk memory is not the only type of fast random-access peripheral memory which exists. To date, it is still the most cost-effective, especially with the great price reductions which have come from mass production. However, the hope for the future is to find ways of storing large densities of data in a non-volatile form without the use of moving parts. To this end, ways of using magnetism other than by the storing of magnetic patterns on a continuously moving magnetic surface are being sought.

To store digital information, the presence or absence of an area of magnetisation at a given position in a material can be used to imply 1 or 0 states respectively. A number of materials exist which are able to trap areas or 'domains' of magnetic polarisation within their surfaces, and one very efficient material for this purpose is the class of the 'rare-earth garnets'. These materials are compounds of iron oxide with the rare-earth elements. The material is chosen to ensure that the domains are all unidirectional in magnetisation. Figure 5.17(a) shows a typical picture of the magnetic domains in such a material which has been grown as a thin layer, usually on a non-magnetic garnet. To harness the magnetisation domains, they must be formed into controllable pieces, or 'bubbles'. These magnetic bubbles are formed from the domains when a magnetic field is applied. The effect

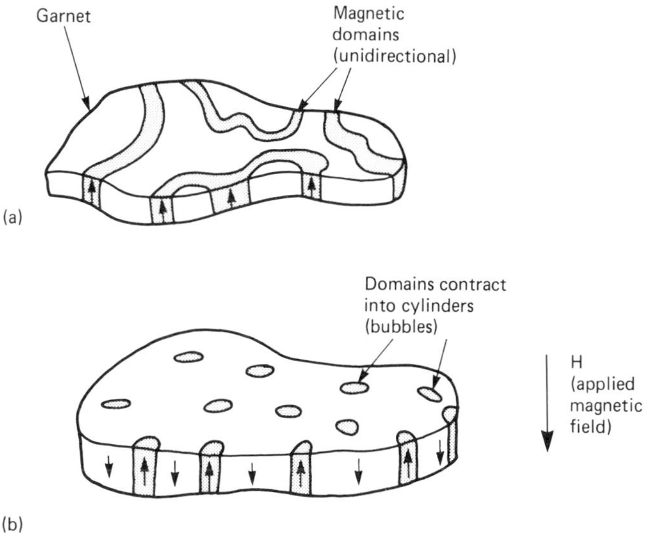

Fig. 5.17 Magnetic bubble formation

is to shrink the domains into circular cross-section regions. In the garnets used for bubble memories, the bubbles are very mobile and quite small—1 to 5 micrometres in diameter—and are attainable at relatively low magnetic fluxes. It should now be clear that if the bubbles can be controlled and sensed, the presence of a bubble could be taken as a 1, and the absence as a 0. In order to use this system, bubbles must be capable of being moved in continuous trains past a 'read/write head' of some kind. The object is to provide this movement purely electronically, and not resort to mechanical means.

To move the bubbles around the material, a pattern of magnetic islands of various shapes may be formed on the surface of the garnet, but the shapes shown in Figure 5.18(a) are the easiest to understand.

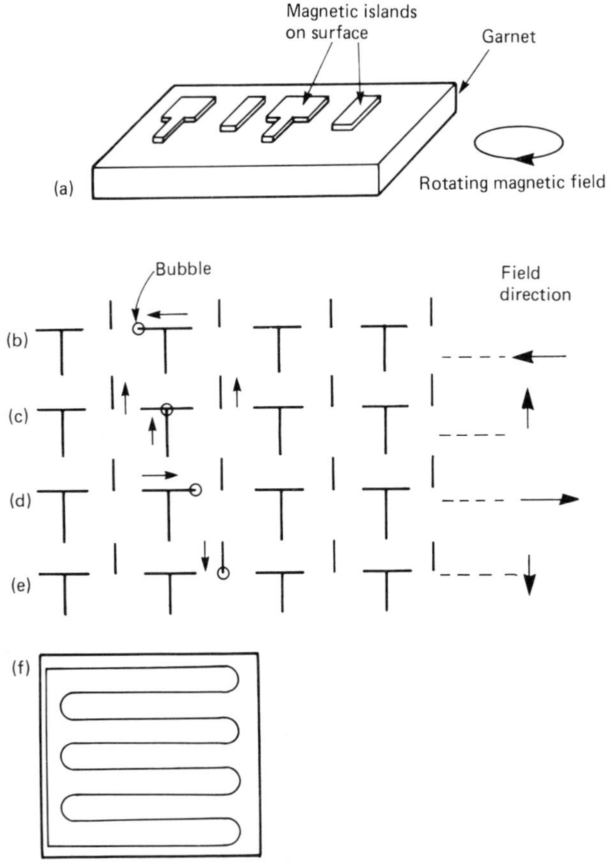

Fig. 5.18 Bubble transport

The 'T's and 'I's form a long continuous track on the surface of the garnet, as shown in (f). In addition to the constant magnetic field necessary to maintain the bubbles, a rotating magnetic field is applied; as the field rotates, the bubbles are transported along the train as shown in (b) to (e) of Figure 5.18.

Imagine the situation with the field direction from right to left at some instant, as shown in (b). The magnetic islands are magnetised by the field so that the tops of the Ts are magnetised strongly in the direction of the field, while the Is are only lightly magnetised across, as this is a difficult direction for magnetisation. Any bubbles which are freely available will tend to stick to the ends of the tops of the Ts. As all the bubbles are unidirectional, they will all tend to stick to the same end of the Ts, and will be transported in the same direction. Note that the bubbles are little cylinders, or bar magnets, formed in the surface of the garnet, while the islands are formed on the surface. This means that the islands attract just the tops of the bubbles, and the bubbles will be transported within the garnet in a direction normal to their axes. As the field rotates, the Is become magnetised as shown, with the T-tops becoming less and less magnetised. In addition, the stem of the T becomes highly magnetised in the direction of the field, and attracts the bubble-top, which drags the bubble along to the middle of the T as shown. The next step, in (d), shows the tops of the Ts magnetised again to move the bubble along to the end of the T. Finally, the bubble jumps to the adjacent I, and the process repeats.

By this means, a continuous train of 1s and 0s can be transported very much as are the bits on the surface of a disk. There are special patterns which may be formed on the garnet surface for creating bubbles, removing bubbles and reading the bubble-train. The speed of the memory depends upon the speed with which the field may be rotated before the transport ceases—this depends, among other things, upon the mobility of the bubbles themselves.

To produce the rotating field, orthogonal solenoids are wound around the bubble memory device, as shown in Figure 5.19, and sine-waves are fed to the coils 90 degrees out of phase. The resulting field rotates as required. Bias magnets are packed above and below the coils to give the constant field. Frequencies of oscillation of the fields are of the order of 300 kHz, and the trains of magnetic islands may be formed on the garnet surface in S-bends as shown in Figure 5.18(f). Hence the speed of access of a single bit may be calculated from a knowledge of the number of bits which the device is capable of storing in the train. To further speed up the access time, the train may be split into several parallel lines, and electronics used to read and write several bits in parallel.

The engineering required for the production of bubble memories is very exacting, and the technology is making great strides. For further information it is advisable to contact manufacturers such as Plessey, and request their data sheets.

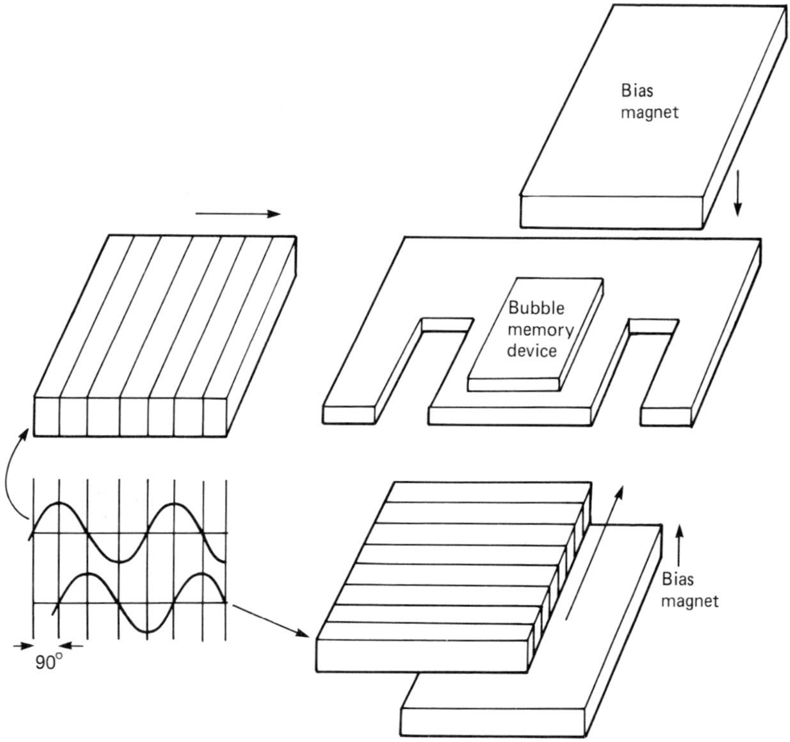

Fig. 5.19 Rotating fields in bubble memory devices

6

General I/O devices and standards

Input/output provides one of the most diverse fields in electronic engineering. In the field of control, for instance, almost any physical parameter can be sensed and controlled by electronic devices, and each has its own distinctive characteristics. In addition, the use of I/O in the transfer of data to and from computer systems is one of its most important applications. Data transfer is considered in detail with examples. This chapter presents some representative I/O concepts, along with examples of I/O chips and devices. The reader will find it easy to grasp most other I/O devices and principles in common use from the basic ones presented here. Once again, emphasis is placed on providing the foundations upon which the reader may further build his own knowledge by reading manufacturers' data on new devices. The concept of I/O has already been introduced in the previous chapters, and this chapter begins with some further examples of parallel I/O. Serial I/O is then considered in detail, with some examples of LSI chips, and transmission media such as fibre optics.

Parallel I/O

The type of I/O described so far is generally called 'parallel' as it provides the MPU with, typically, eight bits of 'outside world' data simultaneously. Figure 2.3 gave an example of a case where up to eight bits of I/O could be set or read by a simple read or write instruction. The blocks labelled 'IN1' and 'OUT1' are chips which ensure that MPU data bus states are transmitted to and from the external lines at just the right time. The data bus is used for a number of things in any given time interval, and these bit patterns must be given to or taken from the data bus 'on the fly' as it were. As the MPU 'knows' exactly when to perform this process, it enables the chips by its address and control buses, via the address decoding. The key to an appreciation of this concept is Figure 1.6, which gives the memory map of the MPU system containing the I/O chips. This system is capable of inputting the state of 16 parallel lines, in two separate bytes, and of controlling the states of a further 16 lines, again in two separate bytes.

These data channels may either be used, as indicated, to control physical processes, or to transmit information. For instance, suppose it is desired to transmit the contents of a written letter. This consists of a string of characters making up English words. Appendix 1 on hex and binary notation introduces a method of coding letters, numbers, etc. as single bytes. This code is called the ASCII set. The word BOOK, for instance, can be written as

BOOK = 42 4F 4F 4B

Here each letter has been encoded in a standard manner, and anyone who knows the ASCII set can take the above four bytes and reconstitute the word BOOK from them.

In order to transmit text, therefore, eight-way parallel highways could be set up to send one byte at a time, and hence communicate the contents of the letter. This method of communication will be described in a standard manner shortly.

A later section describes the other method of communcation and control which relies on single-bit-at-a-time transfer, and which is termed 'serial I/O'.

Figure 6.1 shows two TTL chips which may be used for parallel I/O. Almost any type and complexity of parallel I/O can be achieved using simple chips of this nature. The 74LS244 is an example of an input chip. It contains eight gates, which may therefore transmit a complete byte, and its outputs are tri-state as required for direct connection to a data bus. It is split into two halves, each with its own active low enable, and when these enables are connected together the chip may be used directly as block IN1 or IN2 of Figures 1.6 and 2.3. The fact that it is Schmitt triggered simply ensures that fast-edged signals are applied to the data bus. These chips have high-power outputs, and may also be used to boost the drive of an MPU's bus lines, to prevent the MPU itself from having to drive all the devices on its buses. Such an application uses the 74LS244 as a line-driver or buffer.

The 74LS377 complements the 74LS244 in that it may be used to capture MPU data from the data bus and present this data to external devices. The blocks labelled 'OUT1' and 'OUT2' may be produced using this chip, with a little interfacing. Figure 2.3 shows an enable line going to OUT1. This would in fact be the clock line on the 74LS377. The 74LS377 acts as follows. If the enable line is high, then the output states of the device (Qs) remain frozen no matter what the clock line or the inputs (Ds) are doing. When enable is held low, a rising *edge* on the clock line will transfer the input states to the output lines. Holding the clock at a constant level prevents changes on the inputs from affecting the outputs. This will become clearer from an example which is presented next.

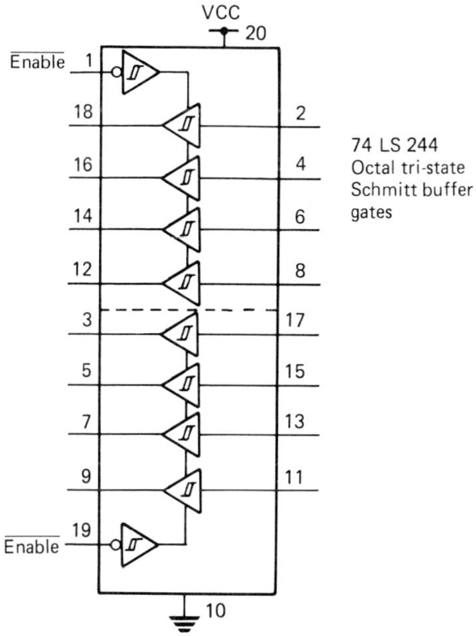

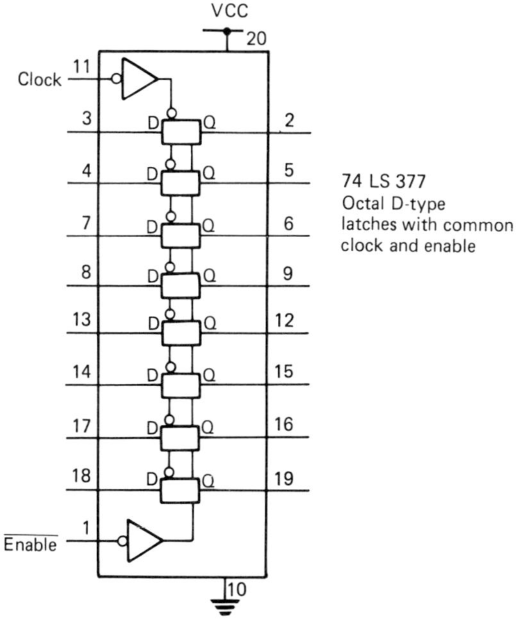

Fig. 6.1 Simple I/O chips

Driving a parallel printer

Chapter 2 contained an example of the control of a few lines for driving switches and solenoids. In contrast, this section concentrates on the problem of transmitting human-oriented information. In this case, a standard method of communicating with a printer is described. This gives examples of a number of things of great importance to the micro designer. One of these is the feedback-related concept of 'handshaking' which has been mentioned before. A printer is slow compared to the working of a computer, but ideally should be driven at the maximum speed it can handle. However, it is no use simply sending bytes to a printer at normal MPU speeds, as the printer would lose most of this data while it was performing the mechanical task of printing. The printer must be allowed to signal to the MPU when it is ready for the next character—this is 'handshaking'.

Figure 6.2 shows a possible hardware set-up for the interfacing of a printer. The printer prints letters, numbers etc., and the codes for these characters will be assumed to follow the ASCII set. The printer requires two 'handshaking' or control lines. These are BUSY and STROBE, both of which are active low. The sequence of operations is illustrated in the timing diagram of Figure 6.2. When the printer is busy printing and cannot accept another character, it holds its BUSY line low to signal this fact to the MPU. When the MPU sees that the printer is no longer busy (i.e. BUSY is high), it sends a new valid code (ASCII code) to the printer. When the MPU is sure that this data is settled and valid, it signals this fact to the printer by pulsing STROBE low, which starts the printer's operation. A short time (t) later, when the printer has taken in this new byte, it sets BUSY low again to prevent further codes from being presented, and starts to print. When printing is complete, the process is repeated. A significant feature of these activities is their sequentiality. They follow on from each other —no part proceeds until the previous one is complete. In general, the more successful I/O activities that the reader will encounter exhibit this type of sequential behaviour.

From the MPU side, only the most significant bit needs to be monitored to sense the state of BUSY. Figure 6.2 shows an outline flowchart of the MPU's activity. The MPU sits in a loop constantly reading from the 74LS244, which keeps the 74LS377 inactive. This loop checks the BUSY line—i.e. most significant bit of the byte fetched—until it changes to 1. When the bit is found to be high, a byte is written to the 74LS377 (74LS244 inactive) with the seven-bit ASCII code in the lower seven bits and a 1 in the most significant bit (strobe bit). This supplies the next ASCII code of a character to be printed, to the printer, with the stobe bit high. The operation is then repeated,

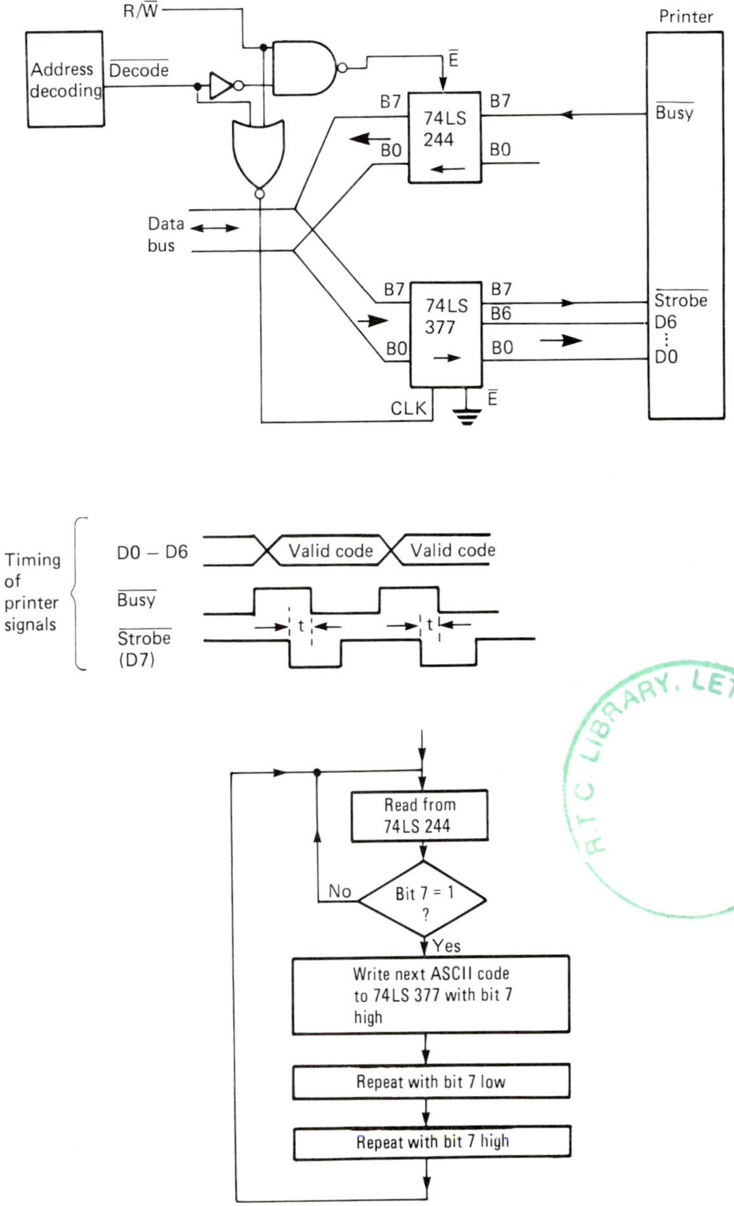

Fig. 6.2 Driving a parallel printer

but with a byte consisting of the ASCII code in the lower seven bits, and a 0 in the upper bit. This has the effect of maintaining the seven data bits to the printer, while setting STROBE low, to signal to the printer the presence of a valid code. The whole is then repeated with bit 7 high again to bring STROBE back to its inactive level. This sequence ensures that the bits presented to the printer have fully settled before the STROBE is activated. At typical MPU speeds, there will be a few microseconds between operations to ensure this settling. The clock pin of the 74LS377 is active on the rising edge only. Thus, when R/W goes low, with the address decode active, the byte currently on the data bus is transferred to the output lines of the chip, and there is no possibility of this changing until the point in time when these conditions are set up again.

The description above is completley independent of the particular MPU chosen. However, it is a worthwhile exercise to examine the timing diagrams of the three MPUs detailed in Chapter 4 to see exactly where, in normal operation, the conditions stated above are valid. In addition, it is useful to review the way in which the three MPUs would perform the control part shown in the flowchart. For instance, the Z80 is able to test an individual bit directly by a single instruction. The 1802, however, could dispense with the 74LS244, and simply use one of its EF lines, along with the associated branch instructions.

The above broadly describes what is known as the Centronics standard of parallel data transfer. This was initiated by the company of that name, and its economical nature has caused it to be adopted as an industry standard. Modern printers often use this standard, but usually employ a method of 'buffering' whereby a whole line, or more, of ASCII codes may be transmitted to the printer, which then goes away and prints this large amount of data in its own time, leaving the computer to continue with its tasks for a time before returning to supply more data in a burst to the printer. This saves the computer from being continuously tied up with printing. It should be clear that, in the example of Figure 6.2, the MPU probably spends greater than 99% of its valuable time sitting in a loop looking at the BUSY line. To prevent this sort of time-wasting, and to give various sophisticated options, printers normally contain their own complete MPU systems.

The method of communication detailed here can be applied to any transmission of data between stations. Between two computers, the speeds of transfer can be very high. However, there are disadvantages with parallel communications, mostly concerned with the number of wires which are required. This form of transmission could not be employed, for instance, over the telephone network.

LSI parallel I/O chips

Although the TTL chips described above provide a straightforward method of supplying parallel I/O to a system, there are several advantages in the use of special dedicated LSI I/O chips. These chips normally belong to one MPU family of devices, but are generally adaptable to other MPUs. The advantages are that the address, data and control buses may be connected directly to the chips, along with an address decoding signal, and they will often supply two or more bidirectional eight-bit I/O ports, the lines of which may be configured either as inputs or outputs. Indeed, it is usually possible to swop lines between input and output from one fraction of a second to the next at microprocessor speeds. In addition, as will be seen in an example shortly, LSI I/O chips often allow a sophisticated form of handshaking and control of data transfers between the micro and external intelligent devices. As will be seen, an internal control register normally allows a program to configure the necessary parameters at will. These chips will also handle interrupts in a sophisticated manner to allow priorities to be implemented for different devices.

An example of such a chip is the well known PIA (peripheral interface adapter) chip, or 6820, originally manufactured by Motorola for its 6800 family. The actual 6820 version of this chip has now been uprated to the 6821 version, whose outputs have higher current drive than the original. This is the version to be described here. There are many other chips on the market, but an understanding of the PIA will transfer easily to an understanding of the others. Figure 6.3 illustrates the PIA along with its internal registers.

The PIA

The PIA supplies two eight-bit bidirectional ports (I/O lines), along with four bits of control, which may be used to control data transfers over the eight-bit ports, or control interrupts in a comparatively intelligent manner. The port lines are labelled PA0 to PA7 and PB0 to PB7, and when defined as outputs they automatically latch just as the 74LS377 described above.

In order to contact the port on one side of the PIA, the MPU reads or writes to an internal register called the peripheral register A side (PRA), or B side (PRB). To define the direction of the I/O lines, an internal eight-bit register called the data direction register, for the A side and the B side separately (DDRA or DDRB), is programmed with 1s and 0s. A 1 in a given bit defines the corresponding line to be an input, and a 0 an output. The PIA connects directly to the data

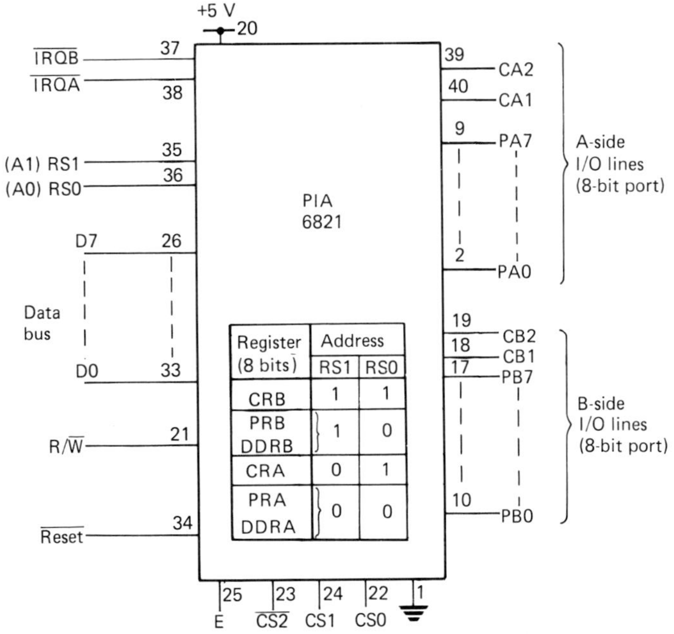

Register selection (X=don't care)

(A1) RS1	(A0) RS0	Control register bits CRA-2	CRB-2	PIA location
0	0	1	X	Peripheral reg. A (PRA)
0	0	0	X	Data dir. reg. A (DDRA)
0	1	X	X	Control reg A (CRA)
1	0	X	1	Peripheral reg B (PRB)
1	0	X	0	Data dir. reg. B (DDRB)
1	1	X	X	Control reg. B (CRB)

Control register A (CRA):

7	6	5	4	3	2	1	0
IRQA1	IRQA2	CA2 control			DDRA access	CA1 control	

Fig. 6.3 The PIA

bus, the R/W line, and the lower two lines of the address bus — RS0 and RS1 to A0 and A1 respectively. The chip automatically decodes the states of all these lines to allow reading and writing, and selection of the appropriate internal register. However, there are six internal registers, and only two address lines. The solution to this problem lies in one of the bits of the control register. At the foot of Figure 6.3, the control register (CRA) for the A side is illustrated. Bit 2 is effectively used as an address line to select between PRA and DDRA. The CRA is contacted by an address having A1 = 0 and A0 = 1—see the register selection table in Figure 6.3. Bit 2 of this register, labelled CRA-2 in the register selection table, must be set according to the table to allow access to PRA or DDRA. For instance, if CRA-2 were set to 1, address 00 (A0 = A1 = 0) would contact PRA. In this manner, addresses 00 and 10 in the PIA have double usages, and allow just two address bus lines to contact all the registers. The control register is also used to control the interrupt and control structure of the extra four control lines illustrated (CA1, CA2, CB1 and CB2). For instance, it is possible for the PIA to cause an interrupt to occur depending upon the state of an external device. Having caused an interrupt along one of the IRQ lines, the control register may then be read to determine from which side of the PIA the interrupt originated. This is also useful when several PIAs are resident in a system—the PIAs may all be interrogated to determine the source of an interrupt. In addition, the two IRQ lines are 'open-drain' lines and hence may be connected together (and held up to +5 volts with a pull-up resistor). Thus a zero on either will cause an interrupt if connected to the interrupt line of the MPU.

It is quite possible to have a mixture of input and output lines on a port—the DDR determines which lines are in and which are out on a bit-by-bit basis. Reading from the PRA will allow the input bits through to the MPU data bus, while the output bits from the PIA remain unaffected. Writing to the PRA will only set the output bits, leaving input lines unaffected. In addition, for an application where an external bidirectional MPU-type data bus is required, the DDR can be adjusted dynamically 'in real time' to change the direction of the lines as the process proceeds.

The two sides of the PIA are functionally similar (though not identical), and have differing electrical characteristics. The A side has internal pull-up resistors when programmed as inputs, while the B side will act as if it were tri-state (high impedance) when in the input condition. In addition, in the output condition, the B side can source up to 1.5 mA to drive transistor switches directly.

As can be seen, the PIA collects enough intelligence together in one chip to perform the same amount of control as two 74LS244s and two 74LS377s. The PIA has three enable lines to help simplify the address decoding logic required. In a minimal system, these enable lines would provide all the address decoding logic necessary, though there would be many repeats of the PIA in the system's memory map. For instance, consider A15 and A14 connected to CS1 and CS0, and A13 to CS2. As the pin-out diagram of Figure 6.3 suggests, A15 and A14 would have to be 1 and A13 0 for the PIA to be enabled. Thus any adress from C000 to DFFF would contain one of the PIA's registers. In a minimal system this waste of addresses would be irrelevant. Several PIAs could be co-resident in the system simply by permuting the pins to which A15–A13 are connected.

Note that pin 25 is labelled 'E'. This is a common line of 6800 family chips, and is connected to the external clock (E) of the 6802, sometimes ANDed with VMA. For other systems, E may be connected to one of the active high enables—it must never be left floating. It is from the transitions of the E line, for instance, that all interrupt timing is taken, and this assumes that a 6800-type MPU is connected to the PIA. If the PIA is to be used for its full control potential with non-6800 MPUs, the manufacturer's data sheets will be found useful for the necessary design work.

To describe the more sophisticated modes of the PIA, the control register for the A side (CRA) is considered in detail. The B side is almost identical to the A side, but the places where differences exist will be mentioned specifically below.

If external devices are to interrupt the processor for attention, the lines CA1 and CA2 may be used to direct the interrupting pulse through to the interrupt line of the MPU in a controlled manner, assuming that the IRQA line is connected to the MPU. Bits 0, 1, 3, 4 and 5 of the control register (CRA) control this operation, with the IRQA1 and IRQA2 bits acting as MPU-readable flags giving the source of the interrupt which has occurred. The MPU simply reads and writes to these locations in its memory or I/O map, depending upon the address decoding in the system, and thus controls the process. The different modes of the PIA's control lines will now be itemised according to the way in which the control register bits are programmed by the MPU. Note that the terms 'set' and 'reset' will be used to mean that a line or bit is programmed to a 1 or 0 respectively.

The following headings refer to bits in the CRA; the CRB bits are assumed to act identically for the control lines CB1 and CB2 unless otherwise stated.

Bit 1

The control line CA1 is used purely for interrupts. An external device connected to this line causes the IRQA1 flag in CRA to be set when a transition occurs on CA1. The active direction of the transition is defined by bit 1 if the CRA. If bit 1 = 1, a low-to-high transition sets IRQA1; if bit 1 = 0, high to low achieves the result.

Bit 0

The setting of the flag IRQA1 only sets the IRQA line low to interrupt the MPU if bit 0 is at a 1. If, however, bit 0 is at a 0, the IRQA line does not respond to the external interrupt request. Bit 0 therefore acts as an interrupt mask. However, when bit 0 rises to a 1 an impending interrupt is allowed through immediately.

Bit 5 = 0

If bit 5 is at a 0, bits 3 and 4 act exactly as bits 0 and 1 respectively but for CA2 and IRQA2 instead.

The interrupt flags IRQA1 and IRQA2 are read-only bits, and the PIA must supply some method of resetting them to allow the next interrupt to set them again. This is not done automatically when they are read, as this would prevent the MPU from reading them more than once without losing their state. The flags are reset by one of two methods. They are automatically reset by a 0 on the reset pin, or by a *read* from the peripheral register (PRA) — which is a condition specially decoded within the chip for this purpose.

The interrupt structure of the PIA, therefore, allows software masking without losing interrupts, and allows the program to determine which of up to four devices has caused an interrupt, and upon which PIA the interrupt has occurred. In addition, the polarity of the interrupting signal itself is flexible.

Under some circumstances, the control lines CA2 and CB2 can act as outputs in one of three different modes. This is described next.

Bit 5 = 1 and bit 4 = 1

In this condition, CA2 and CB2 simply follow bit 3. That is, the MPU may alter CA2 and CB2 simply by altering BIT 3 of the control register A or B respectively. In this manner, the PIA is able to offer two more output bits, perhaps useful as an 'on/off' control for the peripheral device.

Bit 5 = 1 and bit 4 = 0

In this condition, the A side and B side act slightly differently from each other, and the control lines may be used for handshaking, or pulse strobing, depending upon the state of bit 3:

Bit 3 = 0 (Handshaking)

In this mode, reading or writing to the external device via one of the I/O ports causes the CA2 or CB2 output to go low, indicating to the external device that a read or write has taken place. To ensure that the data has settled on the outputs, the actual low transition on CA2 or CB2 occurs on the next falling edge of the E line following the read or write. Thus E may be connected to an address-decoded active-high CS line (pin 22 or 24), as such a line will *rise* to enable the chip, remain high while the read or write proceeds, and then fall. The restriction on the PIA is that CA2 is only set low for a *read* operation, while CB2 is only set low for a write.

To complete the feedback loop for proper handshaking, the external device may indirectly reset the state of CA2 and CB2 back to high, to signal its acceptance of the read or write and readiness for a further transaction. It does this by sending an active transition to the input CA1 or CB1 respectively—'active' here simply means one which sets the relevant IRQ flag, depending upon the state of bit 1 (see above). Note that the interrupt request lines CA1 and CB1 still act exactly as defined before; if their active transitions are not meant to cause an interrupt, the PIA mask must be set as described above.

This type of handshaking can be used, for instance, to write to a printer. For this application the B side of a PIA could be used exactly as described on page 166, with no further logic devices. The reader should examine the above carefully, and work out just how the printer would be connected to the PIA, and how the flowchart of Figure 6.2 could be adapted accordingly.

Bit 3 = 1 (Pulse-strobing)

Here, the output lines CA2 and CB2 act similarly, but their states are reset not by CA1 and CB1, but by the next low-to-high transition of the E line. Thus a read from the A side would set CA2 low, and a further read to the PIA (either side) would reset CA2. Similarly for a write to the B side. These reads and writes may simply be dummy reads or writes, inserted into the program purely for the purpose of performing the resetting of CA2 and CB2.

This mode allows for fast transfer of data to and from a fast peripheral device, without feedback to slow the operation down. In this mode, the receiving device cannot signal that it is not ready for the next byte. This implies that the receiver must be fast enough to be ready for the next byte almost instantaneously after receiving the previous one—there is no chance to tell the transmitter to hold on for a time while the receiver makes itself ready for the next transmission. However, if the external device is fast enough for this mode, data may be transferred at very high speeds.

The PIA has been described in detail as an example of the type of LSI parallel I/O chip which is available. There are many others, and some of these are referred to below. The next section, however, deals with the important parameter of speed in transmission of data.

Speed of parallel data transmission

A common activity in computer systems is the transmission of data blocks from one system to another. This may be performed in a number of ways, but will broadly fall into one of two main classes of transmission type. These are parallel and serial. The former is the transmission of data one byte at a time, as described using the PIA above. The other class refers to the transmission of one bit at one time in a continuous serial stream. The latter is dealt with later. To allow a comparison between the speeds of these two methods, some simple calculations are presented now for the parallel case.

The PIA handshake mode is a common one for the transmission of data, and though slower than pulse strobing, gives a more typical picture of the activity. Since two computers cannot be regarded as being synchronous, it is normal to use handshaking to ensure that each communicates its readiness for the next byte of communication to the other during the transmission. To handshake, a certain amount of software is required, and is sketched in broad outline for speed considerations in Figure 6.4.

Two computers A and B are assumed to contain PIAs. Communication in one direction only will be considered to simplify the issue; this is shown in the figure. To aid the handshaking, the PIAs are connected together as shown. For considerations of speed of transmission, only the routines which actually perform the transmission from A and receiving by B will be considered. Thus, the initialisation routines referred to contain all the setting up of the PIAs, as well as any necessary communication of data such as the size of the memory block to be transmitted, to allow the receiver to set up an address counter of the correct size. In addition, for the following to proceed, the two PIAs must be set up so that CA1 and CB1 are active low. That is, a negative-going transition on either of them sets the relevant IRQ flag in the control register to a high state. The output CB2 of computer A may be considered as a write line (active low), and the CA2 output of computer B may be considered as a read line (active low). The main loops consist of the following.

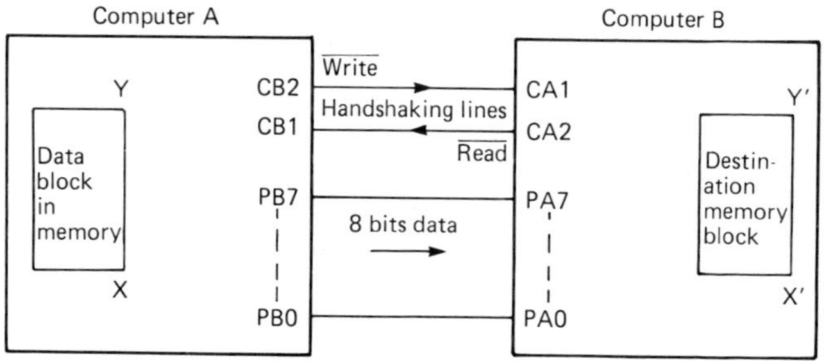

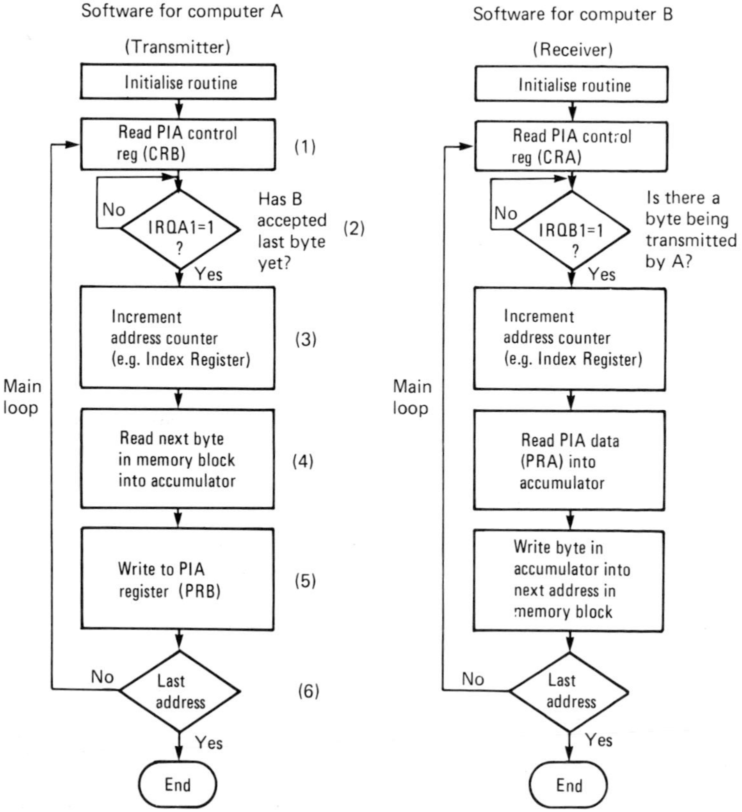

Fig. 6.4 Flowchart for parallel data transmission

A checks its PIA's control register to see whether B has read the last byte which A put out. If it has, the PIA in B will have reset its CA2 line to a low state which will have set computer A's CB2 line high automatically—see the section on PIAs above. This signals to computer A that it may place the next byte on its PIA's ouput lines. To do this, A increments an address counter to keep account of its position in the memory block being transmitted, fetches the next byte in the block according to the address counter, and places this on the PIA's output lines. This automatically resets CB2 to a low state, which connects to CA1 of computer B, and thus automatically sets its CA2 output high until computer B has a chance to read the byte. If this is the last address in the sequence, computer A ends its routine at this point. Otherwise, it returns to the start and waits for B to accept the byte. Meanwhile, B is checking the state of CA1, looking for the signal from A that a new byte is present. When it sees CA1 fall, via its control register flag IRQA1, it increments its address counter, reads the PIA data into the accumulator, and stores the byte at the next position in its memory block. This automatically sets its handshake line CA2 low, and computer A starts the process again.

Note that this entire process is sequential; at no time does any part depend upon one of the systems reacting in a given time interval. One of the computers could stop for an indefinite time, or be considerably slower than the other, and no loss of data would occur.

To estimate the speed of data transfer, the speed of processing is the major consideration. The charts in Figure 6.4 will execute at similar speeds, and only computer A will be considered. There are six (numbered) 'boxes' in the main loop of the flowchart; most contain commands requiring just one machine-code instruction on MPUs similar to the Z80 or 6800. Let us consider the 6800. In chapters 3 and 4 the 6800 was described in some detail. It will be recalled that the exact time taken by an instruction depends upon the addressing mode chosen for its execution. For instance, if the PIA were confined to the zero page of the memory map, writing and reading to and from the PIAs could be achieved by direct memory addressing, requiring just two bytes per instruction. This keeps the time required for fetching the instruction to a minimum. We will assume here, however, that all instructions are extended-mode instructions, but it should be clear to the reader that a certain amount of saving may be made on the times by careful design of the system.

The box labelled (1) is a simple load A instruction which will take four clock cycles. Box (2) contains a check on the most significant bit of the byte in the A register to see if it is high. This would be done by a bit-test instruction on the Z80, but on the 6800 it must be done by XORing the A register with 80; see Appendix 1 if this is unclear. A branch if not zero instruction will then have to be performed if the check fails. If it succeeds, IRQB1 must be reset by a (dummy) read to the peripheral register of the PIA, i.e. PRB. This all takes 10 clock cycles. If the address counter is the X register, the increment in box (3) takes four clock cycles. Box (4) takes four cycles, and box (5) takes five. Box (6) consists of a compare X register instruction, and a relative branch instruction, a total of nine cycles. This adds up to thirty-six cycles.

The actual speed of transfer depends upon two considerations. These are the frequency of the MPU clocks, and the number of times that box (2) is executed on average. This latter consideration determines the amount of waiting around that computer A finds itself performing while waiting for computer B to accept the data just sent. If we assume that computer B is faster than A by a factor which eliminates any waiting on A's part, and we assume that computer A has a clock frequency of 2MHz, then the speed of transmission will be approximately 54K bytes per second. This is nearly the complete addressing capability of the MPU in one second. The disadvantages of this type of transfer are that many lines must be connected between the computers; this is rather difficult over very long distances, which may include the telephone network, for instance. However, the speeds of transfer are very high, and will be compared to that of serial transmission shortly.

Other parallel I/O chips

There are many other I/O chips—all MPU families have one or more. Popular examples are the Z80-P10, the Intel PPI (8255) and the 6502 family chip called the VIA (6522).

The PIO is heavily Z80-oriented. It connects directly to the M1, IORQ, INT, RD and clock lines of the Z80 MPU. If it is to be used to its full extent with any other MPU, these control lines must be simulated with external logic. This is not recommended, however, as there are many other less specific I/O chips in existence. Like the PIA, the PIO has two eight-bit ports, and four handshake control lines. The handshake lines perform broadly similar activities to those of the PIA. The greatest strength of the PIO for Z80 systems lies in its sophisticated interrupt handling. The PIO, for instance, is capable of supplying the interrupt vector automatically for mode 2 interrupts. In addition, a special register within the PIO allows any number of the I/O lines to cause interrupts, and hence allows a number of different external devices to call attention in this way. Two lines are also provided for connecting several PIOs together in a system to allow a 'daisy chain' of interrupt priorities to be implemented. PIOs of higher priorities may thus prevent lower-priority PIOs from interrupting while the higher ones are being serviced.

The PPI is noteworthy in that it provides up to three eight-bit I/O ports (A, B and C), with a number of modes of control. For the straight forward control of up to 24 lines, this is one of the most efficient chips to consider. In addition, the PPI has no special MPU-family-orientated control lines to be connected, and may thus be used easily with any type of MPU. One disadvantage of this apparent simplicity is that the PPI has none of the sophisticated interrupt handling of the previous chips. However, interrupts may be caused by the PPI in a rudimentary manner for data transfer under interrupt control.

The PPI has four eight-bit internal registers, one each for ports A, B and C, and a control register. There is no data direction register, for instance, and the I/O lines cannot be defined separately as 'in' and 'out' on the same port, except for port C—half of which may be in and half out at any time. There are three modes of operation for this chip. Mode 0 allows each of the three ports to be defined as a simple input or output port, with port C half and half if required. Mode 1 allows port A to act as input or output, with the upper half of port C as handshake lines for data transfer. Port B is the same but uses port C lower half. Again, the handshaking is broadly similar to that of the PIA. One of the output control lines on Port C may be connected to the interrupt line, and is capable of being used to interrupt the MPU during data transfers, thus providing a simple form of interrupt-driven data transfer. Mode 2 allows port A to act as a bi-directional port, using port C for handshake control. Port B, meanwhile, may be in another mode, as it is not capable of being used in Mode 2.

The PPI is an excellent source of 24 bits of straightforward I/O (in mode 0) on a 40-pin package. However, the PPI must be used with care if port C is half defined as in and half as ouput, or if modes 1 and 2 are used—see Osborne Volume 3, mentioned in the bibliography.

The VIA (6522) is almost downward-compatible with the PIA upon which it is heavily modelled, but contains, in addition, two 16-bit programmable timers, and an eight-bit shift register for serial I/O. Each of these extra features is able to interrupt the MPU via the IRQ pin, and set internal flags within the VIA to signal to the MPU the interrupting section. The VIA is almost pin-compatible with the PIA. The only differences are that the VIA has four register select lines (RS0–RS3) on pins 38–35 respectively, R/W is on pin 22, and pin 21 is a single IRQ line, replacing the two of the PIA. The increased number of register select lines allows 16 different registers to be decoded by the MPU, without the necessity for using a bit in an internal register as an extra address—this is a welcome advance over the PIA architecture.

The CA and CB control lines act as for the PIA, but CB1 and CB2 may be used to communicate serial data. The VIA's eight-bit shift register may be written to and read from by the MPU, and the bits shifted in and out of CB2. The frequency of the shift register may be determined by several different methods, including an external clock connected to CB1.

The two 16-bit timers are contactable as internal registers within the VIA, and operate in a number of modes including the counting of a predetermined number of pulses from one of the PB lines.

The VIA contains two registers devoted to interrupts. These are the interrupt flag register (IFR) and the interrupt enable register (IER). The IFR allows the MPU to determine whether an interruptable condition from the control lines, the timers or the shift register has occurred, and the IER allows each given condition to actually set IRQ low. An interrupt can be caused when one of the timers times out, and when the shift register has completed an eight-bit shift.

There are many other I/O devices in existence, and each MPU family has at least one. Sometimes, as for the 1802 family, an I/O chip also contains ROM or RAM to allow the designer to design a minimal system with as few chips as possible. The 1802 family also has a PIA type of parallel I/O chip called the 1851. A great advantage of this chip is its CMOS power requirement. The 1851 typically requires 1.5mA of operational current at 5 volts, plus whatever current it is supplying through its ouput lines. This makes the 1851 very attractive for use in low-power or battery applications. The designer studying this chip will find an understanding of the PIA, above, very useful. Indeed, the chips described above are representative of most of the devices on the market.

IEEE 488 parallel protocol

This protocol is one of the most widely used general-purpose bus standards, and is much in evidence in the field of scientific instrumentation. The IEEE 488 bus is also known as the GPIB (general-purpose interface bus), and gives a method of communicating along a parallel bus. The standard bus was originated by Hewlett Packard, for communicating data to and from bench test-instrumentation. The GPIB was adopted as an ANSI standard and an IEEE standard in 1975.

The IEEE bus consists of 16 signal lines—eight for data, three for handshaking, and five for general control; the signals sent along these lines are at TTL levels. Up to 15 devices may be placed on the bus, communications may proceed at speeds of up to one megabit/second, and bus lengths may be up to 65 metres. Any design which is undertaken with the GPIB must be done with reference to the standard; this section introduces the GPIB for the reader's interest, but does not give enough detail for design of actual equipment.

Figure 6.5 sketches the details of the GPIB. There are three types of device which may be connected to the bus. They are 'controllers', 'talkers' and 'listeners', whose function within the system is broadly defined by these labels. It is perfectly acceptable for any given device to contain the electronic logic for a combination of these activities. Each device is connected to the GPIB through tri-state or open collector buffers to prevent electronic clashes from occurring.

On the GPIB, all signals are active low—that is, a level below 0·8 volt is regarded as a 'true' state, and one above 2·0 volts as 'false'. Thus when a line is said to have been asserted, it will be at a level below 0·8 volt. This situation will be a familiar one to the reader from

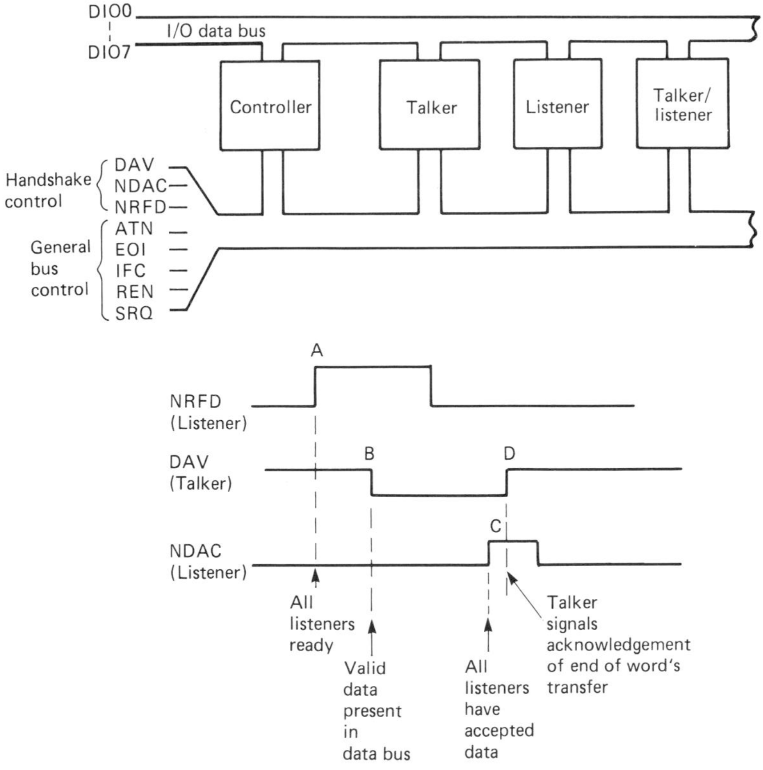

Fig. 6.5 IEEE 488 (GPIB) interface bus

the preceding work in this book. However, the literature on the IEEE 488 bus can be confusing in that it uses 'negative true logic' labelling. That is, an electronic level of less than 0·8 volt is labelled as a logic 1, and one above 2·0 volts is labelled as a 0. The importance of the low electronic level comes from the fact that a TTL gate is capable of sinking a line to ground more strongly than it can to a high electronic level. In particular, open collector gates pull to ground when they are in the 'on' state, and allow a line to float in the 'off' state. In order to ensure that each line on the bus adopts a GPIB 0 state, pull-up resistors may be attached to the lines. In practice, however, a pull-up and pull-down resistor is normally used on each line, with the values adjusted to ensure that each line floats above the 2·0 volts level when no device is outputting a 'true' state on that line.

The three handshake lines, DAV, NDAC and NRFD, are used to control the transfer of bytes along the data bus. These bytes may contain seven-bit GPIB standard device commands, addresses of individual devices, or eight-bit data words. The actual method by which a word is transferred over the bus is illustrated in the timing diagram of Figure 6.5. NRFD stands for 'not ready for data', DAV for 'data valid' and NDAC for 'not data accepted'. The transfer occurs in four stages labelled A to D in the diagram. When a talker wishes to place a word on the data bus, it must first wait for all the listeners to be ready for data. The NRFD line, which is connected to each listener, is held low by any listener which is not yet ready for a data transfer. When all listeners are ready, the line floats up to its inactive state. This takes the process to A in the figure. When a talker has placed the data on the data bus, it holds its DAV line active, and DAV goes low —at the point labelled B. When all the listeners have finished accepting the data, their NDAC lines will all be high, and C is reached. Finally, to complete the feedback for the handshaking, the talker acknowledges that the listeners have finished accepting data at point D.

The significance of the word transferred is signalled by the ATN (attention) line. This line is used to distinguish between an eight-bit data byte and a seven-bit command or address. The control of who should be speaking to whom is decided and controlled by the controller. It is the controller which begins by alerting one or more listeners to wait for a talker to give some information. The controller then addresses the talker and commands it to give the data to the listeners.

The EOI line (end or identify) is used to signal the last data byte in a sequence of eight-bit transfers. The other control lines perform tasks such as reset and a form of interrupt.

The use of the IEEE 488 bus is fairly complex, and in addition the use of the bus in proprietary devices has to be licensed by Hewlett Packard.

Probably the most efficient method of implementing a GPIB system is by employing a dedicated LSI chip for the purpose. There are several such chips in existence; the Motorola 68488 is an example.

Serial communications

The term 'serial' in this context means bit-serial, though it could be argued that the parallel data transfer of the previous sections communicates a serial stream of bytes, and is therefore serial communications. However, the term 'serial' is rarely used in this way. At the present time, for a number of reasons, serial data communications is probably the most generally used method of communicating between separated devices. One major reason for this is the extreme simplicity of the hardware of such a communicating medium; as will be seen, two wires, or other single-line data channels, plus perhaps a ground are adequate. Because of the simplicity of the communicating medium, it is one of the most successful of all the universal standards for connecting different devices together. There are several standards for serial communication protocols, but by far the most popular is a standard known as 'RS232'. This serial protocol, described in detail below, does not require synchronisation of the two devices which wish to communicate. Such a system is termed 'asynchronous'. A number of synchronous systems also exist, which will be seen by their very nature to be capable of faster data transfer, but RS232 is an accepted standard for microcomputers and their peripherals.

Serial communications may also be used in a number of places to make a system more ergonomic or easier to manufacture. An example of this would be for the design of an ASCII (or typewriter-type) keyboard (described in the next chapter). If the keyboard is to be detached from the computer for comfort and easy use, the wires connecting the keyboard to the computer would have to send seven-bits of ASCII, a power supply and a strobe line to inform the computer that a new key-pressing has been made. This would require 10 lines minimum — not very easy to contain satisfactorily within the light coiled cable which would be the neatest type of connection to the computer. In addition, a cumbersome 10-way connector would be needed for the attachment. These problems may be considerably alleviated by collapsing the eight-bits of ASCII, plus strobe, into a one-way serial line. The number of wires required would be just three: power supply, ground, and data. This produces a pleasant, economical and ergonomically satisfying design.

The concept of serial communications brings with it the full gamut of communication media such as telephone links, the use of satellites, communications by microwave link, and so on. These possibilities would cease to be economic if parallel communications were contemplated. It is true to say, however, that it is always possible to communicate faster in parallel, and the hardware can turn out to be cheaper and simpler in some circumstances.

The ease of defining a simple hardware protocol for serial communications has led to its being offered as standard on many devices, though parallel (such as Centronics) continues to be used, for instance, as an alternative for printers.

RS232 serial communications

The EIA RS232C standard, to give its full title, contains specifications as to the connection between two devices to allow them to communicate serially over maximum distances of the order of 20 metres, at up to 20K bits per second. It does not concern itself with whether the communications are synchronous or asynchronous, or with the format of the way in which a data word should be serialised, but it does specify the electrical levels which should be used in the process, and a number of control lines which may be used. We shall deal, here, with the most common format found on microcomputers for serial communications, and broadly refer to this as RS232, as is common in the industry. The Control structure of the standard will not be described in detail.

The top diagram of Figure 6.6 shows a common activity on an RS232 line while transmitting a data word. In order to combat the effects of electrical noise, the RS232 standard demands (nominally) +12 and −12 volt levels. These levels are normally inverted and converted to TTL levels before being used by the computer. A quiescent level ('mark') is defined as being below −3 volts, and an active level ('space') above +3 volts. Typical common level conversion devices are the 1488 and 1489 gates shown in the figure. These are manufactured by a number of semiconductor companies, and several different device numbers may be encountered. The 1488 contains three NAND gates, to allow extra control if required, plus a single inverter; it is fed with RS232 levels of supply, and converts the TTL signals into RS232C. The 1489 only requires a power supply equal to the voltage to which it is converting the RS232C levels. The 1489 also allows the designer to tailor the threshold level of the incoming signals by a pull-up resistor on the response pins, and allows a certain amount of filtering of noise by a capacitor to ground from the response pins.

A typical non-critical system, shown in Figure 6.6, would simply leave the response pins unconnected. Serial data may have to be sent

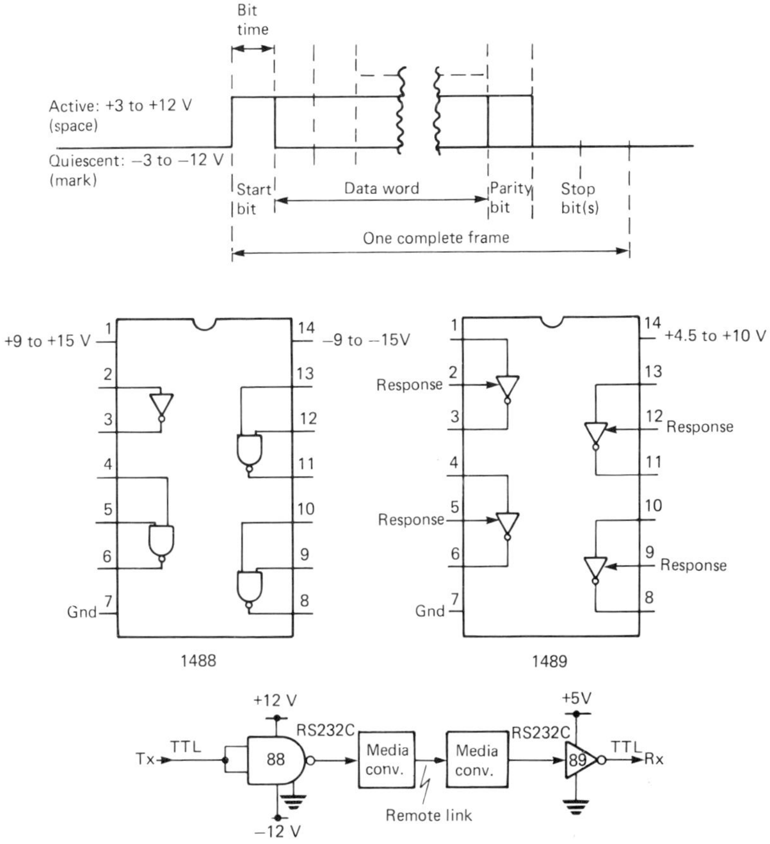

Fig. 6.6 RS232 communications

over a medium other than electrical wire, or perhaps converted to frequency-shift-keying form for some types of transmission; this may be performed by media converters — examples of such systems will be introduced later. Figure 6.6 only shows communication in one direction, whereas normally bidirectional communications would be required. It is possible to communicate bidirectionally along a single wire, depending upon the media conversion, but the computers at each end of the line have separate Tx and Rx lines. If the Tx line of each is connected to the Rx line of the other, then it is possible for each to be transmitting and receiving simultaneously. This is termed 'full duplex'. Whether this is possible or not depends upon the hardware and software of the computer systems involved.

The secret of the type of 'asynchronous' communications shown in

Figure 6.6 is that each data packet, or frame, which is sent starts with a start bit (at +12 volts), and ends with one or two stop bits (at −12 volts). The rising edge of the start bit may occur at any time, and hence the receiver is not able to predict when the word to be received will be coming—the receiver uses the rising edge of the start bit to synchronise its decoding activities for that frame. This 'time-local' synchronisation only lasts for the time of the frame itself; thus each new data word causes the receiver to resynchronise. This will be seen to allow considerable leeway in the timing constraints on the receiver and transmitter devices.

The packet of bits sent along the line consists of the high-level start bit(s) followed by a number of data bits (+12 volts for a logical 0 and −12 volts for a 1), possibly an error-checking bit (e.g. parity), and a number of stop bits which are always low. The last ensure that the line is in a quiescent condition for at least one bit-time before the next transmission can occur. Each bit in the sequence takes up the same amount of time—called the 'bit-time'.

Normal communications found on microcomputers use one start bit, seven or eight bits in the data word, possibly parity, and one or two stop bits. These options are normally selectable by the user, either using a bank of switches or via the operating system of the machine.

To send a block of alphanumeric text from one machine to another, the most common code in use is ASCII. Only seven bits are required in the data word for ASCII transmissions. If the information to be sent is a block of binary data, then the bytes are sent exactly as they are, with eight bits per word. The parity bit has nothing to do with the data; it is a purely hardware aspect of the communications method.

The speed of communications depends upon the bit time. The speed of an RS232 link is normally quoted in baud. One baud is defined as a frequency of one bit per second. If communications are occurring at 110 baud, for instance, with one start bit, seven data bits, one parity bit, and two stop bits, then this 11-bit frame would take one-tenth of a second to be transmitted. That is, 110 baud, for this type of frame, transmits 10 characters per second. Typical baud rates range from 110 baud to 19200 baud. The baud rate is dependent upon the hardware involved, particularly the medium over which the link is to be established. If the national telephone network is to be used, the RS232C levels are normally converted into FSK data (see Figure 5.13) by a media-conversion device called a 'modem' (modulator–demodulator). This is necessary as only audio-type data can be carried by the network. The bandwidth of the medium will only allow up to about 1200 baud unless a special telephone link is installed.

110 baud was a common speed of transmission for the old type of mechanical teletype, and is now largely out of use. The most common

baud rates encountered range from 300 to 9600 baud by doubling (300, 600, etc.), and many devices allow the next step above this at 19200 baud. At this latter speed, with eight bits of data, parity, and one start and one stop bit, nearly 2K bytes of data can be transmitted per second. This speed is at the limit of the standard, but there is no absolute limit at this point, and successful communications will be found to be possible up to speeds of several hundred kilobaud, depending, of course, upon the hardware involved.

Error checking

There are several different approaches to the problem of detecting a fault on a serial link. Such faults, unless catastrophic, will normally involve just a few bits of error from time to time. It is clearly of the utmost importance to ensure that such a transient loss is at least signalled by the receiver, and if possible corrected. *Full* correction by the receiver is not possible, and it is normally up to the receiver to flag that an error has occurred, and allow the transmitter to try again—perhaps after any faults have been cured. Error detection falls into two categories: those which act on each byte, and those which act on a block of data. Some examples are given below.

The most common form of byte error detection is parity. A parity bit, if used, is set according to whether the data word contains an even or an odd number of 1s. If the parity bit is set to a 1 when the word contains an odd number of 1s, the transmission is said to be using 'odd parity'. If parity is set to 1 for an even number of 1s, it is 'even parity'. Thus the transmitter calculates and transmits the state of the parity bit for each data word. The receiver also calculates the parity of the incoming signal, and compares this with the actual parity bit sent. If they agree, the receiver assumes that no corruption of data has taken place. It should be clear, however, that if the byte has suffered an even number of bit-inversions parity will be conserved, and the error will remain undetected.

A further type of byte error detection, common in serial communications, is that of 'framing'. If the receiver finds that a stop bit is in fact at a +12 volt level, the receiver signals that the word is incorrectly framed. This is most successful in detecting errors of clock-frequency drift between the receiver and transmitter.

The examples above are simple types of error correction, and the more complex types will normally demand that a set of data to be transmitted is split into equal-sized blocks, and a complex calculation performed on the contents of the block in order to produce a single error code. This error code is then transmitted at the end of the block, and the receiver compares its own calculation of the code with the one it receives. If they differ, the receiver normally demands a retransmission of the block, or 'retry', up to some maximum number of times before an error signal is produced, thereby allowing automatic error correction. This type of error handling is largely a software exercise. The program controlling the communications will be responsible for calculating the check data, and adding these to the end of the transmission, or checking them on receipt, and asking for a retransmission if required. This sort of sytem assumes a handshaking method of some sort, and will be described shortly.

There are several common examples of calculations which are performed on the data block to be sent. For instance, a simple eight-bit binary addition (with carry) of the bytes in the block can be performed, transmitted and checked at the other end. This is called a 'checksum', and though it is only the lower eight bits of the *actual* sum of the bytes, there is a good chance that this will differ before and after transmission if there has been a fault on the line. This can be made more effective by simply increasing the precision of the sum to more than eight bits. Another form of check may be made, for instance, by XORing all the bytes together. The more checksum-type information sent, the greater the chance of detecting an error.

Another form of error detection is the CRC (cyclic redundancy check). Under this system, CRC byte(s) are added to the transmitted block in order to make it divisible by a given quantity. If, upon receipt, the data is not divisible by this quantity, an error is assumed to have been detected. This method of error checking is used by disk drives for error-checking data as it comes off the disk surface. CRC detection is normally carried out by hardware, and single chips exist to allow this to be performed economically. This type of detection is also well suited to very fast transmission hardware, where high-speed logic families may be utilised for a continuous checking of the data in a manner which is transparent to the user, until an error occurs.

Finally, a cumbersome but interesting form of error detection and correction on a bit-by-bit basis is by the use of Hamming codes. A full description of this method is beyond the scope of this book, but broadly it is a method of extending the byte itself by a number of bits to allow the receiver to run a continuous check, byte by byte. If a bit has been altered in the byte, this check actually allows the receiver to identify the incorrect bit and hence correct the fault. The more Hamming code bits are added to each byte, the more incorrect bits may be actually corrected by this method.

Hardware and handshaking for serial data

So far, no detail has been given of the hardware of the receiver or the transmitter. It was mentioned in an earlier section that, essentially, shift registers may be used to transmit data serially. This is quite true, but it should now be clear that a certain amount of intelligence is required by both receiver and transmitter for such activities as ap-

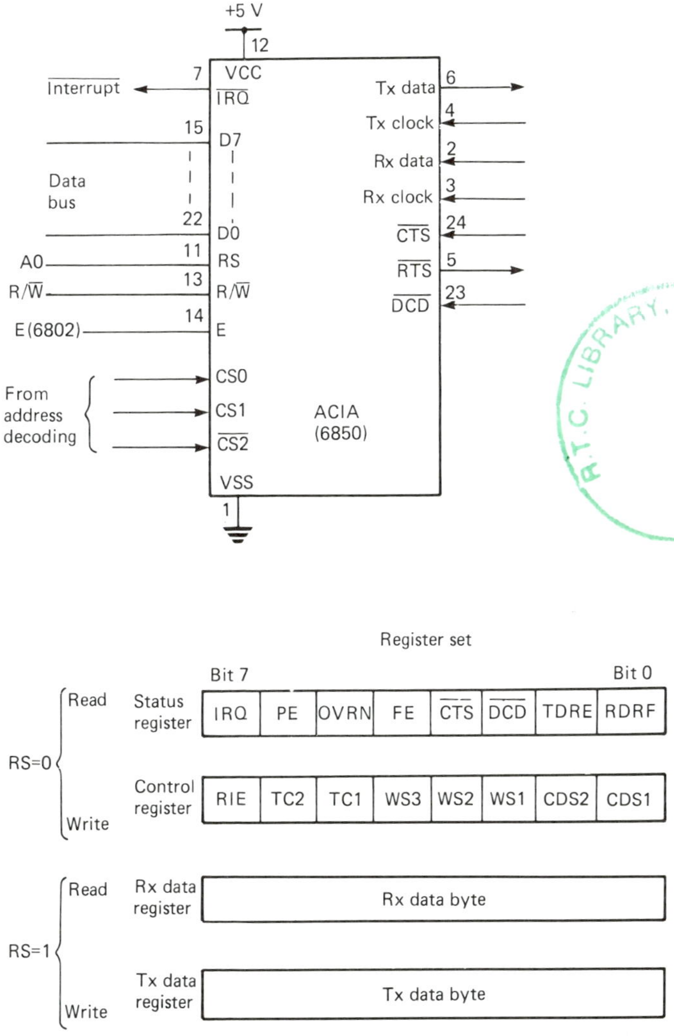

Fig. 6.7 The ACIA UAR/T

pending and observing start and stop bits, handling byte errors, and communicating with an MPU.

LSI chips, within an MPU system used for the control of asynchronous serial communications, are generally called 'universal asynchronous receiver/transmitters' (UAR/Ts). They are devices in the same general class as the parallel I/O devices in that they usually have internal registers, connect directly to the data bus, and take in control lines externally and internally. An example of a UAR/T is the 6850 Asynchronous Communications Interface Adaptor (ACIA), originated by Motorola and shown in Figure 6.7. This chip offers a typical selection of features for a UAR/T, and is useful for comparison with other devices which will be introduced later, and which the reader will meet from time to time.

The ACIA has the normal data bus lines, along with a number of chip select lines—two active high, and one low. In addition, it has an R/W line, an RS line for internal register selection, and an E line as for the PIA. The E line will connect directly to the E of a 6802, or to an active-high chip select. It is used particularly for the correct timing of interrupts. The open-drain IRQ line may be wire-ORed with other such lines and connected to the MPU interrupt, but a pull-up resistor will be required.

The ACIA has four internal registers, but appears to the MPU as two memory locations. The reason for this is that the R/W line is used to distinguish between the different registers. The RS line is used to select either the status and control registers (RS = 0), or the receive/transmit data pair (RS = 1). Each register is either read only or write only. RS is connected to A0 in a typical system, so that when the address decoding section selects the ACIA, A0 may be used to select the register pair itself. Thus reading from the lower address, for instance, selects the status register. Data to be transmitted is written to the upper register, and data received is read from that register.

The ACIA also controls three external control and handshaking lines; CTS, RTS and DCD. These are standard RS232 control lines, and they allow hardware control of media conversion devices, such as modems, or allow hardware handshaking between receivers and transmitters, if the extra lines can be connected. In fact CTS, RTS and DCD are members of a larger set of standard RS232 control lines which are not introduced here, but which allow a large amount of quite sophisticated control of media converters.

The transmitter is a simple shift register, which shifts data out of the Tx data line according to a division of the Tx clock. The CDS1 and CDS2 bits of the control register decide whether the Tx clock is divided by 1, 16 or 64 before being used to shift the data out. This will be explained when the receiver is examined. If the ACIA is not actually in the process of transmitting, the actual shifting out of the data written into the Tx data register starts to occur automatically one bit-time from the end of the MPU write operation, and a new bit is shifted out on each negative transition of the (divided-down) Tx clock. The ACIA is double-buffered, and hence a new piece of data may be written in as the last piece is being transmitted. This new data will automatically be transferred into the shift register when it is ready. However, the ACIA can only hold one extra piece of data, and it is possible for the MPU to overwrite the last byte sent to the ACIA before it can be shifted out. To prevent this, a bit in the status register is devoted to informing the MPU of the current status of the transmitter. Bit 1 is termed TDRE—transmit data register empty—and is a 1 when a new byte may be transferred into the ACIA. It is up to the controlling program to note the state of this bit before writing new Tx data to the ACIA. In addition, the ACIA may interrupt the MPU when TDRE is at a 1, to inform the MPU that a new byte may be sent to the Tx data register. This facility allows the MPU to be processing a program while the ACIA is transmitting data.

The receiver is more complex than the transmitter. It must at least be capable of detecting the leading edge of a start bit, and sampling the incoming data, bit-time by bit-time, as it assembles the final byte for reading by the MPU. In fact, the ACIA receiver is capable of rather more than this.

In order for the receiver to sample the incoming waveform, it must be capable of referring to a clock for the actual bit-time which is involved. An incoming byte may be all 1s, for instance, except for the start bit, and the resulting waveform will be at a 1 level for most of the time. It is up to the receiver to split this up into separate bits, and store the result in its Rx data register. This is done in the following manner, when the Rx clock line is divided internally by 16 or 64—a

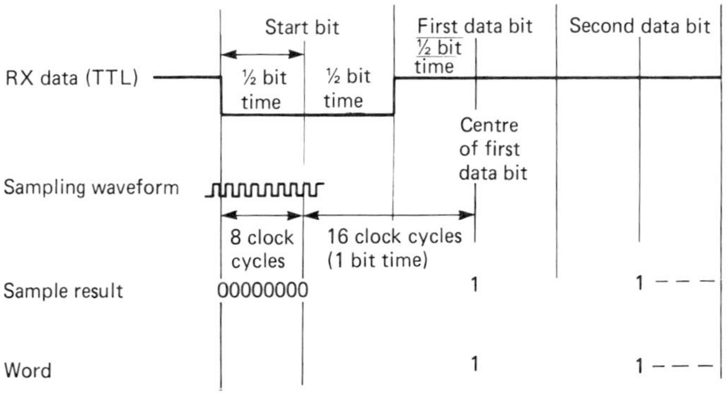

Fig. 6.8 ACIA operation

parameter which is controlled by the control register. Figure 6.8 sketches the operation of the receiver, with TTL logic signals as opposed to the (inverted) RS232C levels. In this picture, a high level is the quiescent (and stop-bit) condition.

When the leading edge of the start bit is detected, the receiver samples the Rx data line for 8 (or 32) cycles of the Rx clock line, if the division selected is by 16 (or 64). If the Rx data line is low for each of these samples, the ACIA assumes that it has reached the centre of a start bit. It then samples once every 16 (or 64) cycles until the stop bits have been received. This ensures that it is looking at the centre of each bit of transmission. If the first 8 (or 32) cycles do not all yield 0s, the ACIA discards the start bit as being false. This facility is called 'false start bit deletion'. The sampling of the incoming data at the centre of a bit allows a certain amount of leeway between the frequencies of receiver and transmitter. Such differences in frequency have a cumulative effect on how accurately the ACIA samples the centre of the bit's time. In order for the sampling pulse to overrun the frame by the time the stop bit is encountered, the frequencies would have to be sufficiently different for there to be a discrepancy of over half a bit-time within the frame. If the frame is 10 bits long, this requires a 5% difference. Thus, as long as the transmitter and receiver have their clock frequencies within $\pm 5\%$ of each other, the transfer of data will succeed. Larger frames require more accuracy of similarity between clocks at each end of the line.

In addition to assembling the data in this manner, the ACIA is checking parity, looking for framing errors (stop bits not equal to 1) and checking for overrun errors whereby a new byte has been received before the MPU has read the current one — this causes the old byte to be discarded. The overrun does not occur until the end of the next frame, thereby allowing nearly one complete frame-time for the MPU to read the received byte. The MPU should be fast enough to perform this function with time to spare, as it is working in a time frame considerably faster than that of the ACIA. The presence of any of these error conditions will affect a flag in the status register, and hence may be noted by the MPU.

The control register is used to control the working of the ACIA. By writing to it, the MPU may alter the division ratio of the clock, perform a special master reset function, alter the application of parity, etc.

The status register bits are as follows (see Figure 6.7):

IRQ This bit is set to 1 if an interrupt condition (IRQ = 0) has been caused, and is thus available for the MPU to determine which device has caused the interrupt. The bit is reset by a read or write to the Rx/Tx data registers.

PE This bit is set to 1 if a parity error has occurred in the received data. It is reset when the next correct word is transferred into the Rx data register.

OVRN Overrun is set to 1 when a new word is placed in the Rx data register without the MPU having read its previous contents. It is reset on the falling edge of the E line following a read of the Rx data register. Thus, in a non-6800 system, the E line must be connected to an active-high chip select line, or to an inverted active-low CS line.

FE Framing error is set to 1 when the first stop bit is absent. This is reset when a byte is transferred into the Rx data register after the correct receipt of a frame.

CTS This equals the state of the CTS (clear to send) input line, and may be used by the MPU to handshake with the system with which it is communicating.

DCD This bit (data carrier detect) is a standard RS232 control line for controlling a modem.

TDRE This signal (Tx data register empty) is taken low on the falling edge of E after a write to the Tx data register, and is set back to a high when this word is transferred to the shift register for transmission. Thus when the MPU wishes to transfer a byte to the ACIA it must first read this bit to ensure that the Tx data register is empty. As mentioned above, TDRE going high may initiate an interrupt, depending upon TC2 and TC1 in the control register. This can be used to save the MPU from wasting its time by continually reading TDRE and waiting for the Tx data register to become empty. In addition, when the CTS input is high, TDRE is set to 0. This allows an external system to inhibit transmission.

RDRF This bit (receive data register full) goes high to indicate that a byte has been received and transferred into the Rx data register, and that the appropriate states may be noted on PE, OVRN and FE. This bit is used to prevent the MPU from reading the same byte several times. RDRF is reset by a master reset, or on the high-to-low transition of E after the Rx data register has been read. The empty condition (RDRF = 0) is also caused by the DCD line going high—if input from a modem, the DCD line going high indicates that the modem transmission link has been broken.

The CTS and RTS signals may be used by the communicating devices for handshake control. In these circumstances, the transmitter's CTS line would be connected to the RTS line of the receiver. If the receiver has to perform some slow activity on the received data, e.g. printing, it could output a high on its RTS line, until ready, which would hold the transmitter's CTS high, and inhibit transmission.

An important facility of the ACIA, and UAR/Ts in general, is the 'divide by one' state of the Rx and Tx clocks. In this state, each transmit data bit is shifted out following a falling edge of the Tx clock, and normal sampling of the received bits does not occur. The UAR/T expects the bits received to be synchronised with the same clock, and samples the data on the rising edge of the Rx clock. This implies that the ACIA can be run at a maximum bit rate equal to the maximum clock rate which it can accept, instead of one-sixteenth or one-sixty-fourth. The B version of the ACIA can be run at 1 megabit. However, two problems occur. First, the processor has to be fast enough to accept the data from the Rx data register, and second an extra line has to be run from transmitter to receiver to carry the clock signal which synchronises the two devices. This mode is called 'isosynchronous' or 'isochronous', to imply that the clocks are physically synchronised, and to distinguish it from 'synchronous' communications which will be introduced shortly. The problem of the speed of the processor is a real one, and limits the maximum speed of communication to less than a third of a megabit on most systems. However, this problem can be solved by the concept of DMA, which has been introduced for the 1802, p.107. This will not be pursued here, other than to add that LSI chips exist to allow certain UAR/Ts to transact directly with memory without using the MPU. This is particularly true for the Z80 family of chips. The second problem is more straightforward to address. In general, it is possible to encode the data in such a manner that the actual clock itself effectively forms part of the encoded data. There are several methods in general use, and the example of 'Manchester encoding' will be mentioned later. The use of isosynchronous communications is that it offers communication speeds of the order of synchronous communications, but is more straightforward to implement.

This concludes the description of the essential elements of the ACIA. Though not complete, the essential functions of the chip which the reader will encounter in most UAR/Ts have been introduced. Serious design using the ACIA will require the manufacturer's data on the chip.

Other serial chips

Examples of other serial chips include the Z80 family chip called an SIO, and an Intel chip called the 8251. These chips also have internal registers, and a number of functions in common with those of the

ACIA. The SIO is interesting in that it offers two independent serial ports, as well as the facility of isosynchronous and synchronous communications, described below. It occupies a 40-pin package, and as with most Z80 chips, has Z80-specific control lines which must be simulated if it is to be used with other MPUs. As the SIO offers synchronous communications, it is called a 'USAR/T' or universal synchronous and asynchronous receiver/transmitter. This chip is one of the most complex serial I/O chips on the market, and should be considered for any serious design. The 8251 is also a USAR/T, but offers no advantage over the SIO. It occupies a 28-pin package, but only has one serial channel.

As an example of another class of UAR/T, the General Instruments AY-3-1015 will be described below. There are various different forms of this chip, including the AY-3-1013 which requires a further supply level in addition to the normal +5 volts. RCA make a CMOS version, the 1854, for their 1802 family which is identical to the AY-3-1015 when its 'mode' pin is held low. It may be made compatible with the 1802 MPU and its control structure by holding the mode pin high. The power consumption of the 1854 is, of course, very low.

A disadvantage of the ACIA, SIO and 8251 is that none of them will operate without some software for their set-up. It would not be easy to use an SIO, for instance, within a non-MPU based peripheral to capture a serial byte, and present it on a set of parallel lines. It is simple to transmit data serially; a shift register will accomplish this, as will be seen in the next chapter. It is the receiving of data, with the attendant functions of stripping off the start bit and checking the parity and stop bits, which requires a certain intelligence. An excellent application for the AY-3-1015 is in the addition of an extra serial port to a computer system which has plenty of parallel I/O. This UAR/T is suited to interfacing directly with the I/O lines of a PIA or PPI, if an external clock is available. The software required would be minimal, as this UAR/T can be set up simply by applying permanent logic levels to its control pins. There are no internal registers; all its functions can be set up by hardware. Communication with the chip is simple and requires no lengthy software routines, which can slow a processor down considerably when communicating to I/O devices.

The AY-3-1015 is illustrated in Figure 6.9. Each control line in the diagram is active at the level denoted by the presence or absence of the 'bar' above its label. For instance, pin 39 is an input which determines the state of the parity bit. It is called EPS (even parity strobe), without a bar, implying that 1 gives even parity.

The pin-out in Figure 6.9 shows a bewildering number of control lines, as well as 16 data bits. The reason for all these lines is shown in the block diagram of the UAR/T at the bottom of the figure. This

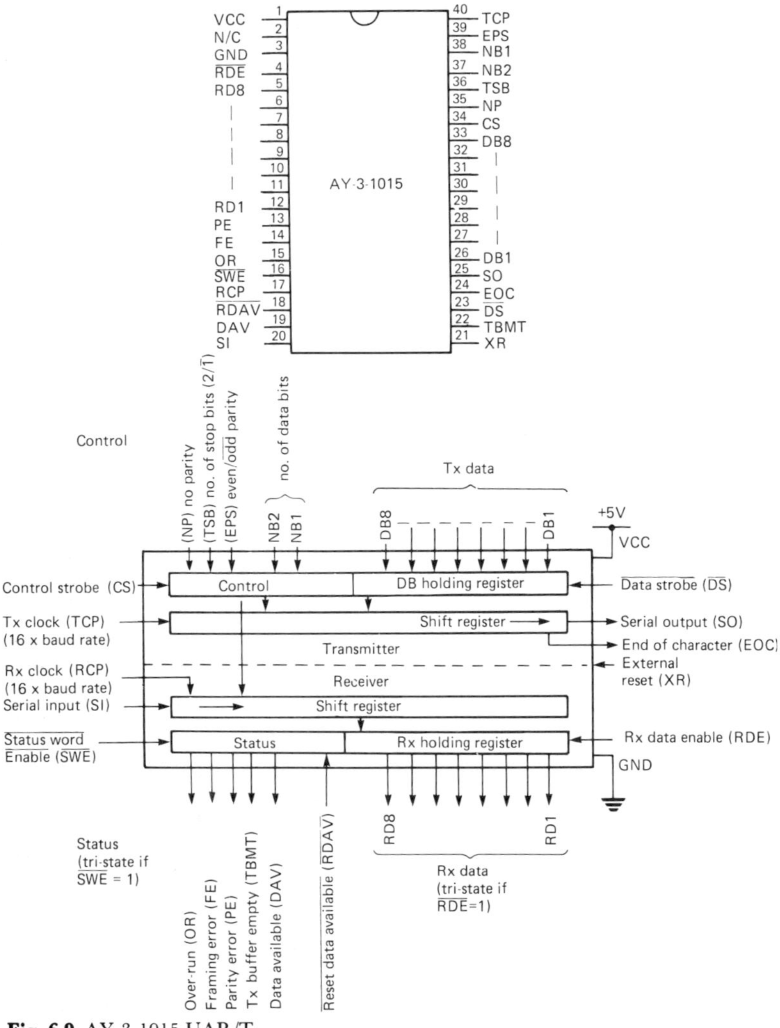

Fig. 6.9 AY-3-1015 UAR/T

chip is effectively split into two almost independent parts—transmitter and receiver. The only link between them is the five control lines which act on both.

Most of the lines on the UAR/T fall into one of four classes. These are control, status, receive (Rx) data and transmit (Tx) data. Other lines, shown on the left and right of the block diagram, include the serial data lines, an external reset line, clock inputs, power supply and four strobe/enable lines. Note that there is no R/W line, and no overall chip-select lines. Also, since there are no internal memory-mapped registers, there are none of the usual address lines of the previous I/O chips. The lack of special MPU-orientated control lines makes this chip equally compatible with any MPU. In addition, all outputs but one are tri-state, to allow the UAR/T to be included in the memory map of an MPU system if required.

Control lines. The five control lines control the parity, the number of stop bits (1 or 2), and the number of bits in the data word of the frame from 5 (NB2 = NB1 = 0) to 8 (NB2 = NB1 = 1). These control lines affect Rx and Tx alike, and may be set up by constant logic levels. If they are to be under software control, the control strobe (CS) must be raised to a 1 to strobe the current states of the control lines into the UAR/T. If not, CS can be tied constantly high.

Rx and Tx Data. When the data to be transmitted has been presented to the DB lines, the data strobe (DS) line must be taken to a low state to strobe this data into the DB holding register for later transmission along the serial-out (SO) line. Similarly, when a frame has been fully received through the serial-in (SI) line, and transferred to the Rx holding register, this data may be output to the Rx data lines by taking the Rx data enable line (RDE) low. Otherwise, the RD lines are tri-state, to allow them to be connected to the data bus of an MPU. In order to connect the chip to an MPU system, the MPU R/W line and some address decoding would have to be gated together to signal the DS and RDE lines to read and write data to the UAR/T. In a non-MPU application, RDE could be held low permanently.

Status. There are five status lines. Three of these are used to signal over-run, framing and parity error on receive. TBMT signals that the transmitter holding register is empty and may be loaded with the next frame of data. DAV signals that a complete frame has been received and may be read, along with any error signals. DAV must be reset externally, when the data has been accepted. This gives the UAR/T a positive assurance that the last character has been read from the UAR/T. The OR line signals an over-run if the next character is received before DAV is reset. DAV is reset by applying a low level to the reset data available (RDAV) line, which could be generated automatically by the logic which reads the Rx data. These status lines are tri-state, and are enabled when status word enable (SWE) is taken low. Again, R/W and address decoding logic would be used to enable SWE and hence present the status lines to an MPU data bus as required. Otherwise, SWE could be held permanently low.

To interface this UAR/T to an MPU, therefore, all the Rx data lines, Tx data lines, status and control lines would be connected to the MPU data bus. Some of the data bus's lines would therefore contain four of the UAR/T's lines at once, unless some of the error states were to be disregarded and/or some of the control lines set by permanent logic levels. Distinction between the use of the data bus lines would rely upon address and R/W decoding to enable that part of the UAR/T with which the MPU wishes to communicate at any time. The only non-tri-state line from the UAR/T is the end of character (EOC) line, and this is not strictly necessary for MPU communications. The EOC line is useful for calling attention to the need for a new character, perhaps via the interrupt line in an MPU system, or via the logic of a non-MPU system.

The reader should be aware of the essential similarities between this UAR/T and the ACIA as to control and interfacing. A useful exercise would be to compare the software requirements of each in normal use.

Apart from its uses in a non-MPU system, or as an addition via a parallel port, the AY-3-1015 is important as it is available in a CMOS version. There are very few such UAR/Ts which are applicable to hand-held battery applications. A disadvantage of this UAR/T is that it occupies a 40-pin package for just one serial I/O port, whereas the SIO, for instance, offers two very sophisticated ports within the same sized package.

So far, the problem of two unsynchronised systems which wish to communicate has been examined. For most UAR/Ts, however, the divide-by-1 mode requires a separate clock line to be fed between the systems to allow them to be synchronised for a form of synchronous communications. However, start and stop bits are still required. A fully synchronous system allows the transmitted data to keep the two ends of the line synchronised continuously, thereby obviating the need for start and stop bits for synchronisation within a frame. This cuts down the number of bits which have to be sent, and allows faster communications to be effected. In an asynchronous eight-bit, single start and stop bit frame which includes parity, two bits out of the 11 are devoted to synchronisation—approximately 18%.

The method adopted for synchronisation in synchronous communications consists of sending synchronisation characters from time to time during transmission, as well as during the times that the link is not in use for data transfer. During data transfer, approximately 1% of the information is devoted to synchronisation, giving a significant decrease in the non-data part of the transmission.

As has been mentioned, the RS232 standard applies to maximum data rates of the order of 20K baud. The maximum asynchronous baud rate offered on most systems is 9600 or 19200. However, the SIO is capable of communicating serial data at speeds up to one-fifth of its system clock. When used in a Z80A system (clock frequency of 4MHz) therefore, the maximum clock rate attainable is 800 kHz. Using an asynchronous protocol, sampling of the incoming data depends upon dividing this clock by at least 16. This gives 800/16 = 50K baud. For an 11-bit frame, 50/11 = 4·5K bytes would be transmitted per second.

If a synchronous protocol is employed, neither division of the clock nor start and stop bits are necessary, as the sampling and synchronisation is achieved by other methods. The baud rate rises to that of the clock, i.e. 800K baud. The transfer of data, by nine-bit frames if parity is still used, rises to almost 90K bytes per second. If the Z80B version is used, at an MPU clock rate of 6MHz, the speeds of transfer rise to over 130K bytes per second. Hence the maximum transfer speed of serial data can be considerably higher than that of standard RS232, if the transmission medium can take it. The next section examines some examples of different media, and their maximum frequencies of transfer.

As a final note, it should be added that the use of UAR/T type chips to unload the chores of data transfer has its own disadvantages. A disadvantage of LSI chips in general is that they are normally fashioned using such technologies as NMOS (N-channel metal-oxide semiconductor). This is inherently slower than TTL or ECL bipolar-type technologies. If discrete bipolar gates can be used for data-transfer tasks, the speed of transfer can be increased by one or two orders of 10, assuming that the MPU system can keep up. One standard protocol becoming more and more important in the field of networks of computers is known as Ethernet. This will be referred to in Chapter 8. The transmission of data in an Ethernet system is serial, and proceeds at 10 megabits per second. This gives around one megabyte of data along the line per second, and uses ECL logic for its final transmission stages, along with (base-band) coaxial cable as the medium.

Examples of transmission media and interfacing

The previous sections have all dealt with communication of data, whether by parallel or serial protocols. This section is oriented towards serial data transmission, but similar principles will hold for the many lines of a parallel system.

The most common form of link is, of course, simple wire. For short links—of the order of 20 metres—ordinary two-or three-core wire is adequate. This is particularly true if RS232 levels are being employed, as such levels are less prone to noise pickup. However, for truly remote links, more thought must be given to the actual medium along which the data travels. In addition, thought must be given to the impedances of the Rx and Tx devices at each end of the link. High-impedance, voltage-dependent systems will suffer from noise pickup more easily than low-impedance systems. This is illustrated most strikingly by simply placing a finger on the end of an oscilloscope probe—it is not uncommon for 50 volts at the prevailing mains frequency to be registered by the 'scope. The reason for this is that we are constantly subjected to electrical pickup from surrounding equipment, through the air. However, this medium of connection is of a very high impedance indeed—air is a good insulator. Thus it is not easy to draw much current from the air. A 'scope has a very high input impedance, and does not take much current when it is measuring voltage, which is one of its greatest advantages as a measuring device. It is therefore able to give a more accurate representation of the actual voltages which appear at your finger when you are near to mains equipment. It is this pickup from the air that the wires of a data link can be very efficient at registering. If the end of the 'scope probe is now connected to earth through a 330 ohm resistor, the resulting voltage at one's fingertip will be scarcely discernible, thus illustrating the need for low-impedance ends to any wired data link.

An alternative approach is to change to a different medium entirely, with media converters at each end of the line. One of the most commonly used conversions is via a modem. The FSK data which is transferred will easily pass through wires, radio link, microwave link, fibre optics, etc. The RS232 standard recognises the importance of modem transmission by providing a number of special control lines to allow a serial link to join computers over this type of link. The data is less prone to noise pickup as more complex electronic information is being sent than simply 1s and 0s. For instance, an FM radio link is highly noise-rejective.

Within a given site, a large computer network which is to communicate efficiently between terminals separated by distances of the order of 500 metres or more will benefit from non-electrical media. This is especially true of sites where there is a significant number of large machines in use. The obvious technology is that of fibre optics. In addition, the non-conductive nature of the fibres allows their installation in any convenient ducting which may be to hand. For instance, the author has experience of the installation of a fibre-optic network where a proportion of the material passes along convenient high voltage ducting around the site—a practice prohibited by health and safety considerations with a normal conductive medium.

A fibre-optic link may consist of a pair of glass fibres within a single plastic sheath. One is used for transmission, while the other is used for receiving at any given station. The plastic sheath is flexible but robust, and designed to prevent the cable from kinking or otherwise subjecting the fibres to small-radius bends. A high-power LED is mounted in a connector for transmission down the line, and a light-sensitive diode is mounted at the other end for receiving. The spectrum in common use is near the red end of the visible range. The actual medium of transmission may be glass-coated silica. The coating is important, as the refractive index change at the interface aids total internal reflection of the light within the fibre, to ensure that none escapes. By this means, the light from the LED is guided along the fibre to the receiver. Data may be sent as light pulses following the 1s and 0s, as FSK data modulating the light beam, or using Manchester encoding, as described in the section on Ethernet in Chapter 8. The advantages of Manchester encoding include the fact that synchronous or isosynchronous data may be sent along with a synchronising clock within a single fibre.

As there are only two lines between the link ends, handshaking to ensure that the receiver is ready for data is done by sending characters back and forth along the line. For instance, if the transmitter wishes to send data, it could start by sending a control code to ask the receiver if it is ready. If the receiver replies in the affirmative, with another control code, the transmitter sends a fixed block of data. The transmitter could also be looking at its receive line at the same time as it is transmitting. If the receiver finds an error, it could send down a control code to ask the transmitter to repeat the block. This type of handshaking is called software handshaking, and many different versions exist.

The bandwidth of fibre optics is only limited by the maximum frequency response of the transmitter and receiver electronics. It is fairly straightforward to achieve one-megabit data communication with commonly available, cost-effective components. The majority of the design problems which the author has encountered are in the building of stable high-gain amplifiers which will work effectively in industrial environments. This area of design is outside the scope of the present work. However, it should be mentioned that, once again, Manchester encoding has an advantage, in that it requires a comparatively narrow bandwidth of amplifier for its transmission and receipt, and may be fully AC-coupled throughout.

Another successful medium for serial data of all types, including analogue data for applications such as video communications, is the coaxial cable. A typical impedance of 50 ohms, along with the shielding nature of the cable, limits noise to very low levels indeed. As mentioned above, this is the medium specified for the Ethernet network standard at 10 megabits.

7

The human interface

This chapter uses the information of Chapters 1 to 6 to describe some of the peripheral devices and systems which are employed for the man–machine interface. The data flow is bidirectional, and it will be noted that technology for the transmission of data to the human is considerably more advanced than that for the other direction.

Simple displays and keyboards are introduced, followed by a description of the visual display unit (VDU) based around a cathode ray tube (CRT). Light-pen input from a CRT is an example of a method of inputting data from the human operator to the machine in a very efficient manner.

A full ASCII keyboard is described as the most common form of operator input device. Speech synthesis is also introduced as a state-of-the-art interface method. Other general interfaces are described, along with examples of their use.

Displays

There are many different types of display for the presentation of alphanumeric data to the human operator. Common examples use principles such as segmented light-emitting diode (LED) or fluorescent arrays, dot matrix arrays, and liquid crystal elements. One important type of array is the seven-segment display, and this is described below.

A simple type of display is one which is capable of showing the 10 decimal digits. The seven-segment display was originated for this application, and is illustrated in Figure 7.1. As can be seen, there is usually an eighth element to represent a decimal point. The segments may be LEDs, filament lamps, fluorescent discharge elements or any other method of indication. The decimal numbers are shown displayed in seven-segment format in Figure 7.1. As such displays are so widespread and cheap, the advent of microcomputing caused them to be utilised for an early attempt at showing hex numbers. Letters are displayed as shown with a mixture of upper and lower cases. This provides a very simple and cost-effective method of utilising the seven segments when hex numbers are required.

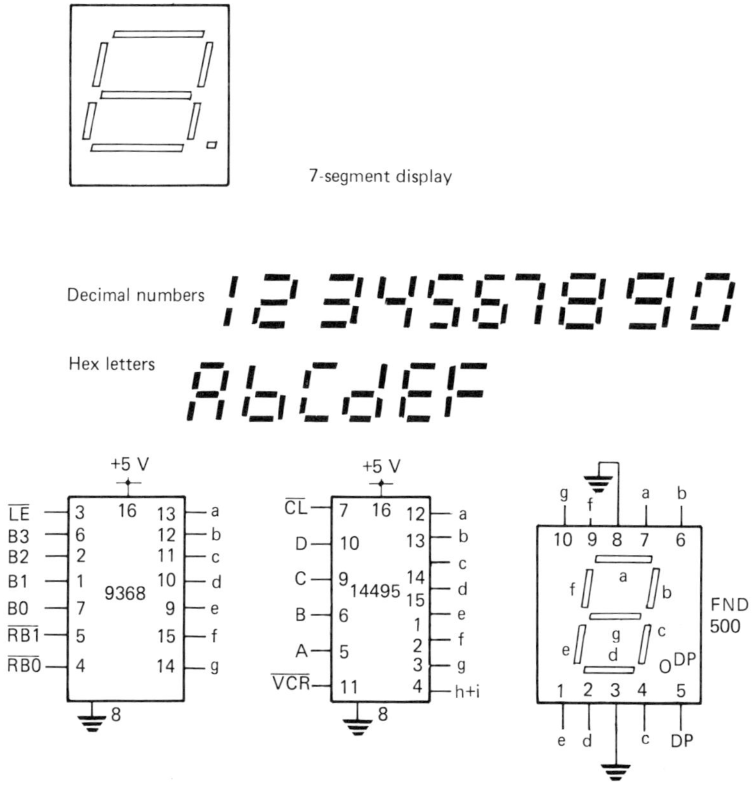

Fig. 7.1 Seven-segment displays and drivers

Fairchild produced a TTL chip, called the 9368, which would decode a four-bit binary code into seven-segment hex form. This is shown in Figure 7.1 with its compatible seven-segment LED device —the FND500. Motorola also produce this type of display decoder in a CMOS–bipolar hybrid called the MC14495. The MC14495, shown in Figure 7.1, has bipolar output transistors and internal limiting resistors, as does the 9368, to save the need for external resistors. The use of these display decoders illustrates several important points about display electronics in general, and the principles described below hold good for all such display devices.

The display decoders source 20mA per LED segment, and latch data presented to their input bits on the rising edge of the latch enable (LE or CL) lines. In the example of Figure 7.2, the 9368 (or 14495) is shown connected directly to the data bus of an MPU system; this is possible for both chips owing to their high-impedance input

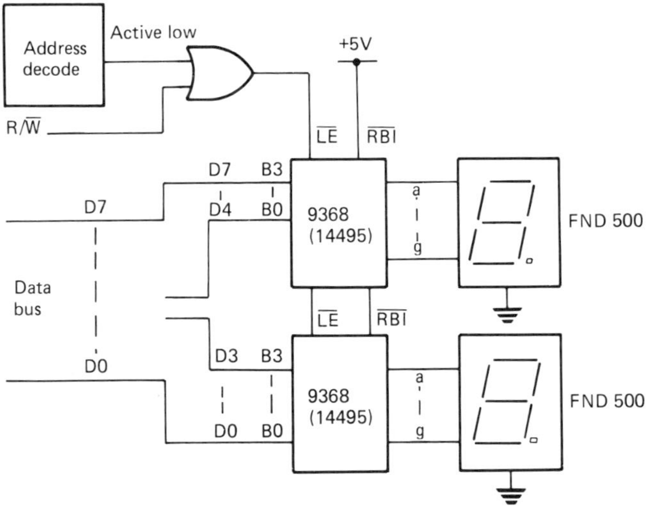

Fig. 7.2 Seven-segment display electronics

characteristics. Care should be taken when connecting chips directly to an MPU data bus, to ensure that the bus is not overloaded; if there is any doubt, it should be buffered with driver chips such as the 74LS244.

When the display is to be used for output, the address decoding and R/W line allow the MPU to write to the address occupied by the display components directly. The normal timing of MPUs presented earlier in this book shows that data is held valid to the 9368s (or 14495s) for the 'window' during which the decoding holds LE low. Thus the data is still valid when the LE line rises—this latches the data into the decoder chips. The FND500 is a common-cathode display, and thus all elements have one side (pins 3 and 8 on the package) connected to ground. No other power supply is required.

A further feature of the 9368 is that it allows automatic leading-zero suppression when each ripple blank input (RBI) is connected to the ripple blank output (RBO) of the next lower chip. The most significant chip's RBI must be grounded to ensure that the chain is complete. The least significant chip is normally left out of this chain as it is not normal to allow the whole display to blank when it should be displaying the number 0.

Such display circuits can be connected to parallel I/O devices if preferred, and if many digits are to be used, it is possible to multiplex the I/O lines. This is shown in Figure 7.3. Here, one eight-bit I/O port is used to control eight displays. The top four bits of the port contain

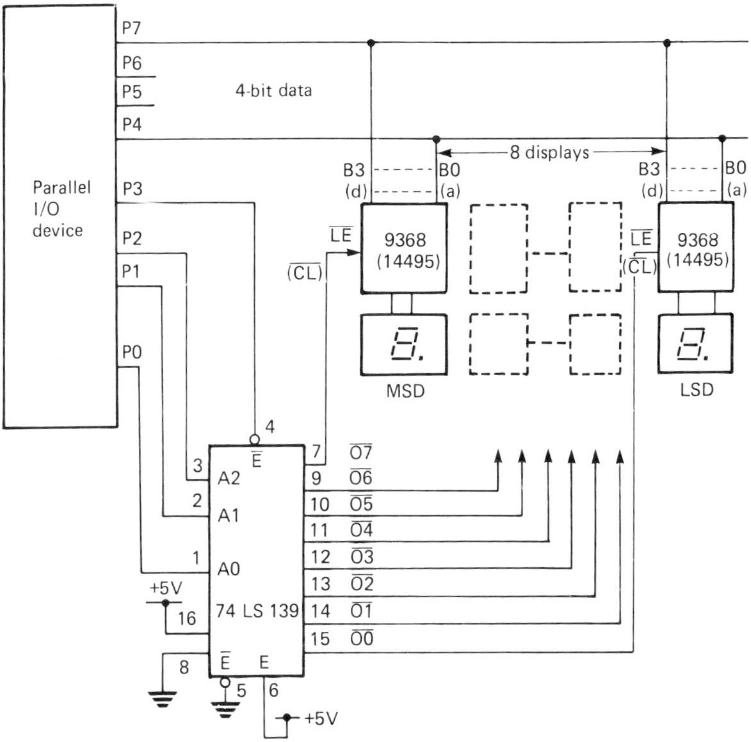

Fig. 7.3 Display multiplexing

a four-bit code to be displayed on a given display. The lowest three bits of the port hold the address of the digit which is to be written to, and P3 of the I/O chip is an enable line for the address decoder—a 74LS139 chip. The 74LS139 is a three-line to eight-line decoder which simply sets one output low corresponding to the bit pattern which is input along A0, A1 and A2, when its enable lines are all active. For this application, only one of the active low enables is required, and the other enables are held in their active states permanently.

To write a '5' to the third digit, for instance, the following sequence of operations may be performed.

(a) The byte 01011010 is written to the I/O chip. This byte has three fields:

0 1 0 1	1	0 1 0
4-bit code	enable	digit address

The most significant four bits are the binary code for '5'. The next bit, which appears on P3, ensures that the 74LS139 is disabled during the setting up of this byte. The lowest three bits contain the binary for '2' which is the address of the third digit whose display decoder is connected to 02 (not to 03!) on the 74LS139.

(b) Once the above conditions are set up, the enable line of the 74LS139 can be taken low to allow 02 to fall and enable the latch of the third display decoder chip. This is achieved by writing the following byte to the I/O chip:

0 1 0 1   0   0 1 0

This leaves the data and address stable, but sets 02 low.

(c) Finally, the first of the above bytes is written out again to close the latch of the display decoder, and freeze the number '5' on the display. This is repeated for the other displays as required.

Notice how a careful sequential procedure is used, with the various conditions being set up piece by piece. In this case, the system should work if step (a) is omitted. Step (b) can be used to place a 0 on the 74LS139's enable as the data and address are set up. Step (c) then returns the enable to 1, freezing the displayed data. This procedure is sufficient because it is the rising edge on P3 which latches the data into the 9368 and MC14495 chips. Such a procedure will also be faster. Great care must be exercised in such processes to ensure that no prohibited conditions can occur, and that data is always fully stabilised before it is used.

This type of multiplexing is useful in increasing the number of I/O lines which an eight-bit port can control. However, a latch is usually required, as shown here, to hold the state of any given line constant while others are being adjusted.

Different formats of display elements are illustrated in Figure 7.4. The star display gives the flexibility to display alphanumeric characters, but is more difficult to control than the seven-segment display, simply due to its increased number of elements. A full display of any type of ASCII character, along with graphics characters, can only satisfactorily be attained with a dot-matrix display.

Dot-matrix displays normally come as a module, containing a certain amount of control logic. The control of such a module is very similar to that of a cathode ray tube visual display unit, as will be seen in the next section. In order to use the display, some external devices are required. The number and complexity of such devices depend upon the intelligence of the display module. Figure 7.5 illustrates a typical system. The MPU system which is using the display for output is connected along the external bus lines. The characters to be displayed on the module are stored in the RAM as ASCII codes. The

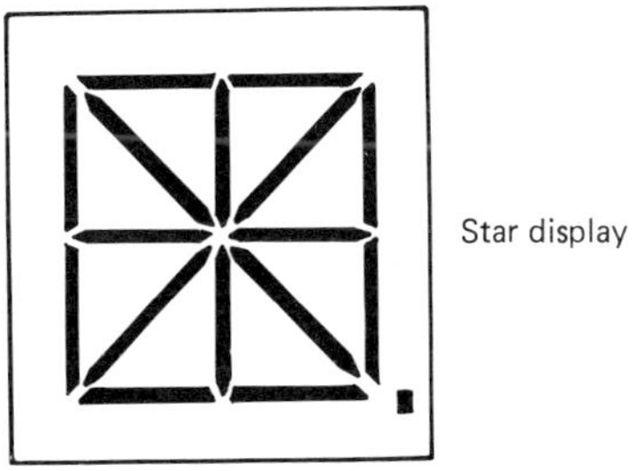

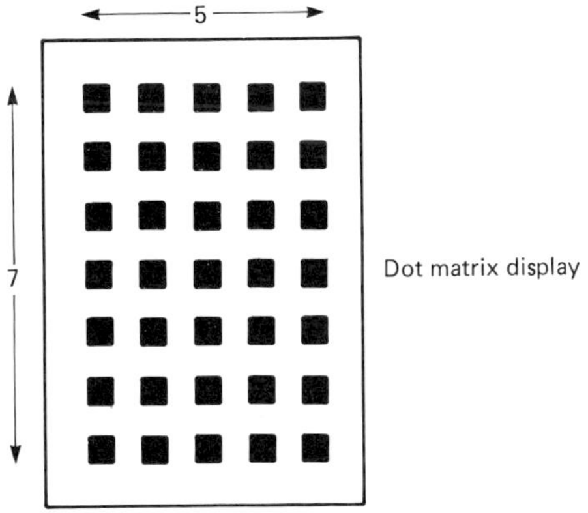

Fig. 7.4 Star and dot matrix displays

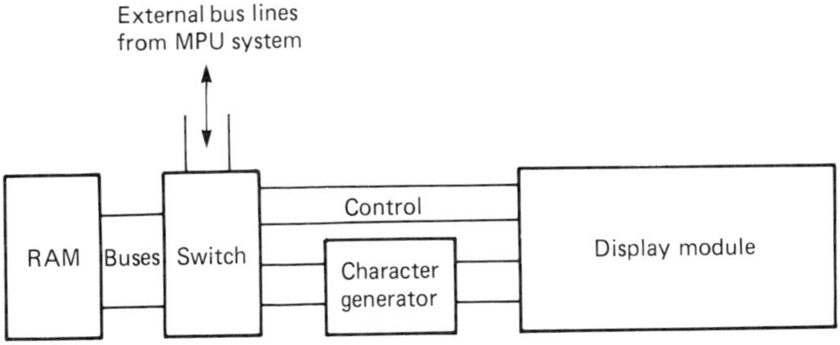

Fig. 7.5 Dot matrix display control

module fetches these codes through a character generator which converts the ASCII code into patterns of dots for use by the display matrix within the module. When the MPU wishes to change the display, it simply writes the codes of the characters to be displayed into the

RAM, as it would for any block of memory, and the module takes over the activity of displaying the information. This type of module may be found using LEDs, or the low-power liquid crystal displays (LCDs).

LCDs are available in seven-segment format, and there are special drivers for the purpose. However, driving LCDs is straightforward, and can be achieved using the same decoder chips as for LEDs. Figure 7.6 illustrates how a 9368 or 14495 ouput would be used to drive an LCD display segment. One side of each LCD segment receives an excitation signal in the form of a square wave continuously. To turn a segment on, an input to the other side must be made with a square wave which is 180° out of phase with this signal; thus each time the excitation rises, the input signal falls, thereby ensuring that a con-

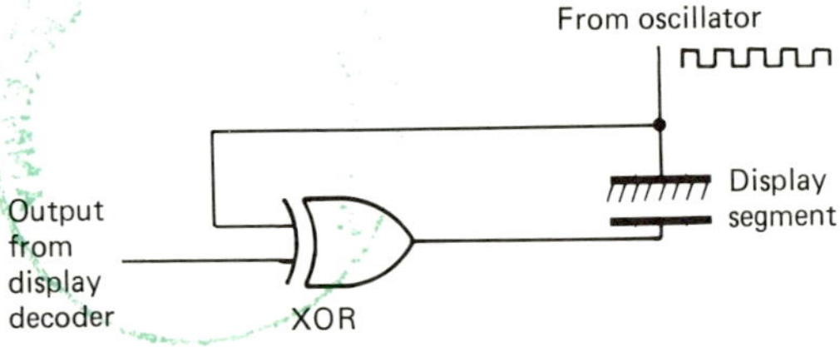

Fig. 7.6 Driving LCD displays

stantly reversing voltage is developed across the segment. To achieve this, the output from the decoder is passed through an Exclusive OR (XOR) gate. To see that this gives the correct effect, the reader should consider the XOR gate as a programmable inverter. When a 1 appears on one of its inputs, the *inverse* of the other input appears on its output. Otherwise, the true version of the other input is allowed through. If a 1 is input to the XOR gate from the decoder, the square wave on the other input is inverted, and the segment receives anti-phase wave forms across it. This causes the segment to turn on. Hence any standard driver can be converted for use with LCDs. The special LCD decoder-drivers simply incorporate the XOR gates within the chips themselves.

A simple keyboard

Communication from the human to the computer is largely restricted to the use of keyboards. Simple keyboards with numbers and a few dedicated keys may be sufficient in many control applications, but for programming and general data entry a full typewriter-type, or ASCII, keyboard will be needed. This section examines the simple type first, and then gives a design for an ASCII keyboard for a full computer system.

Keyboards may be generally considered as matrices of key switches. There are several different types of key-switch and detector circuit, ranging from straight switch closure to detection of a capacitive effect as the key is pressed. Key closure will be assumed for this section. Figure 7.7 shows a 16-key keyboard matrix. When a switch is closed,

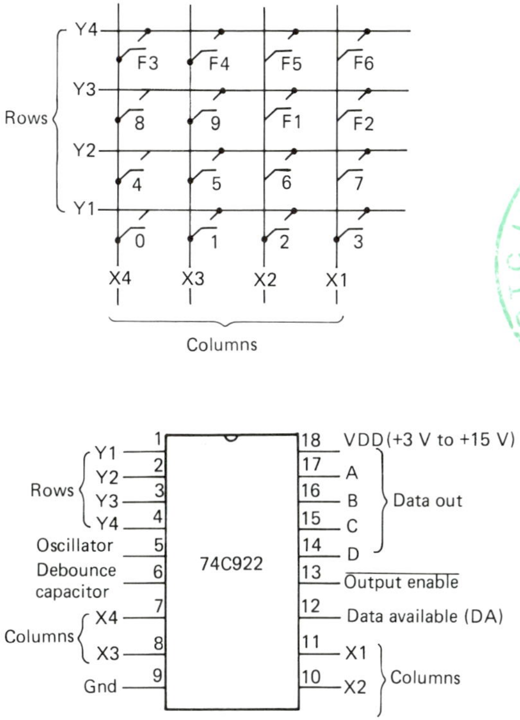

Fig. 7.7 A keyboard matrix

a unique row–column pair is connected together. If a signal is fed to that row, and the columns monitored, the column containing this key switch will pass the signal to the monitoring device. By this means any key press can be noted. A common method of performing this type of key-press monitoring is by sending 'walking bit' data to the rows and observing the columns. This is done as follows.

The MPU, or a special keyboard encoder chip, scans the rows by holding all but one row high. The 0 on just one row is moved from row to row and back again at a high enough frequency that any key press is bound to transmit at least one occurrence of this 0 to its associated column. The columns are monitored, and when the row 0 is observed on any column, the decoder knows the position of its walking 0 on the rows, and may thus tie down the particular key being pressed. The complexity of the keyboard encoder, or MPU program, determines what happens next. In a very simple system the scanning may be halted until the actual key press has been read by the computer, to prevent subsequent pressings from causing the current key press to be lost. This would 'lock up' the keyboard until read. Other more sophisticated systems allow several key pressings to be stored before the first one is lost. By using the MPU system to read the key press whenever it occurs, perhaps under interrupts, the process of reading the key press is so fast that a human operator would find it difficult to press the keys faster than the system can accept the data. In systems which cannot allow this type of speed, a simple 'handshaking' system could instruct the operator, via a display, when to press the next key. Any system of keyboard utilisation depends upon the application, as will be seen.

Even if an MPU system is used to read the key press, it is most wasteful to use the MPU to produce the walking-bit information itself. It is the job of special keyboard encoder chips to scan the key matrix, notice a key pressing, and convert this into a binary code for the MPU to read easily. The keyboard in Figure 7.7 could be decoded by a chip such as the 74C922.

The 74C922 shown in Figure 7.7 is typical of many simple keyboard decoders, but is also a CMOS device. By connecting an external capacitor (typically 100 nF) between pin 5 and ground, the 922's internal oscillator performs the scanning of rows and columns as described above. Alternatively, an external oscillator may be connected to pin 5 to synchronise the operation with other processes. Pin 6 is used to set up the switch debounce delay. A capacitor (typically 10 microfarads) between pin 6 and ground will cause the 922 to delay before accepting a key press, to allow any switch bounce which may occur to settle down. When a key press is detected, the data available (DA) pin goes high, after the debounce period, for as long as the key is pressed. If another key is pressed while the first is down, the DA line remains high until the first key is released. Then after the debounce period, DA goes high again to signal another key pressed. This is called 'two-key roll-over'. Some keyboards have n-key roll-over, whereby no key pressings are lost, no matter how many keys are pressed at once. For normal operations in most applications, a keyboard in correct use should never need more than two-key roll-over.

Whenever DA is high, an internal latch holds a four-bit code which may be read from the data-out lines to determine which key has been pressed. The data-out lines are tri-state to allow them to be used in an MPU system, and are enabled by the output-enable line. A restriction of the 922 is that the DA line is not tri-state, and if this is to be read by the MPU it must be passed in by an I/O line, or via a tri-state buffer.

An ASCII keyboard

An ASCII keyboard can be constructed using the same principle as for the simple keyboard. However, it is not uncommon to find that an ASCII keyboard for a computer system is controlled by a single-chip microprocessor. The major disadvantage of this approach is that the manufacture of a large number of keyboards must be contemplated in order to make the set-up charges cost-effective. If this can be attained, the unit cost can be very low indeed. Many manufacturers, however, take a middle approach whereby a simple controller is used, along with an EPROM holding the control program. This requires no expensive set-up charges, and allows the keyboard a little more flexibility, with the option of mass manufacture of the EPROM in masked ROM form at a later date.

However, an excellent and flexible keyboard can be manufactured using standard cheaply available parts, based around an ASCII keyboard encoder, and incorporating an EPROM code-converter for customisation of the keyboard as required. There are many keyboard encoders on the market; one of the most common is the 2376, manufactured by General Instruments (GI). The main disadvantage of this chip is its multi-supply requirement. However, the device gives an excellent example of the type of encoder in common use, and will be used for the design example which follows.

A typical example of an ASCII keyboard is shown in Figure 7.8. There are the usual typewriter keys, along with a SHIFT key to change to upper case. Other keys on the keyboard are specific to computer use. For instance, there is a row of function keys at the top of the keyboard, which may be customised to output certain special characters which a given applications program requires. There is a 'CAPS LOCK' key. This is used to change the keyboard to output capital letters. When this key is in the pressed condition, lower-case letters disappear from the keyboard, while all other keys remain the same. If SHIFT is pressed while CAPS LOCK is down, the letters remain capital, but the other keys change to their upper-case characters. This key is useful in programming, as most programming languages and operating systems use capital letters primarily. A further computer key is the CONTROL key, labelled 'CTRL'. While this is held down, certain of the keyboard keys output special control codes,

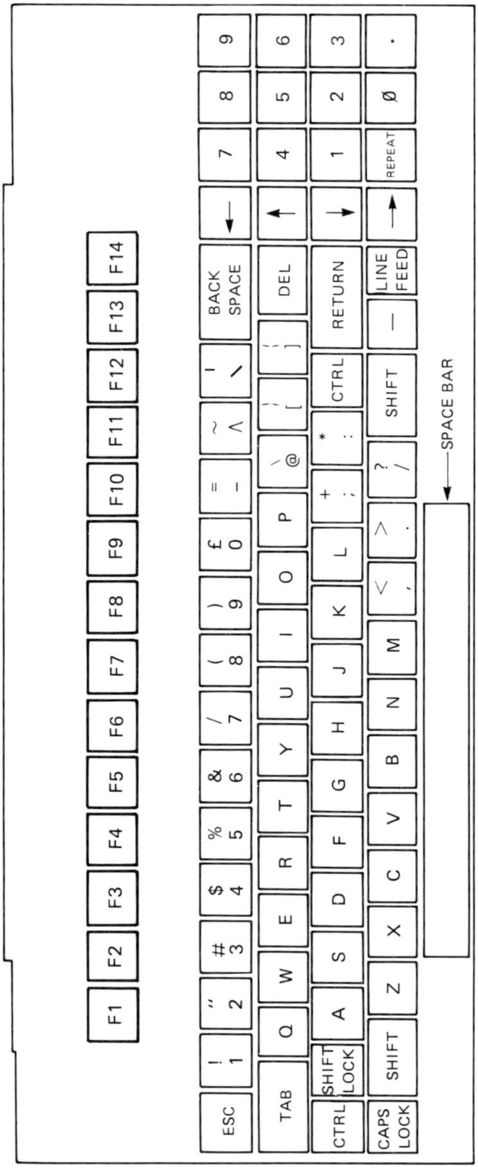

Fig. 7.8 An ASCII keyboard

which appear at the beginning of the ASCII set—see Appendix 2. These are standard codes for program use. Some of the control codes are used so often that they are available on dedicated keys on the keyboard. For instance, the carriage return code (0D in hex) is output by the keyboard when the RETURN key is pressed. Most computer systems will accept this code to mean that the current line which has been typed is to be accepted by the computer as a valid entry. The SHIFT, CAPS LOCK and CONTROL keys are not within the X-Y matrix in the example below; they are connected separately to the keyboard encoder.

The 2376, shown in Figure 7.9, is an 88-key keyboard encoder, with many of the characteristics of the 74C922, even including two-key roll-over. It is, effectively, an intelligent ROM. There are 11 row lines (Y0–Y10) and eight column lines (X0–X7), as well as inputs for SHIFT and CONTROL. There is no CAPS LOCK input, however. When the key switches of the ASCII keyboard of Figure 7.8 are arranged in a matrix according to the data on the 2376, the encoder will output the ASCII code of the key pressed, for reading by a computer system; the output is not tri-state, and will require buffering. In addition to the eight-bits of data, the 2376 produces a parity bit, the polarity of which is controlled by pin 6. The frequency of the scanning is normally set at about 50 kHz by external components on pins 2, 3 and 40, and the strobe delay is set by components on pin 19. Pin 20 may be used to invert the data and strobe pulse if required. With pin 20 held at 0, the strobe line, pin 16, goes high when a key is pressed, after the delay. The strobe line remains high until the key is released.

In order to use the 2376 for the ASCII keyboard of Figure 7.8, it is necessary to find a method of allowing the extra function keys to be encoded, and to allow for a CAPS LOCK function. In addition, it is a useful feature to allow the actual code which the keyboard sends out to be able to be changed for customisation. Finally, it is becoming increasingly clear that keyboards which are physically attached to the machine they feed are unergonomic and cumbersome. It is easier for the operator to be able to detach the keyboard from the machine, and place it in a position which is convenient. For reasons given earlier, this implies that a serial link is needed to send the keyboard data to a UAR/T in the host computer. For a 2376-based keyboard, this implies that a four-way cable is required: one way for the data, and three for ground and power supplies. This is not inconvenient, as standard microphone coiled cables supply the need perfectly. An alternative approach is to generate the necessary −12 volts on the keyboard itself, but this is not suggested here.

Figure 7.9 shows a circuit which fulfils the above requirements. It

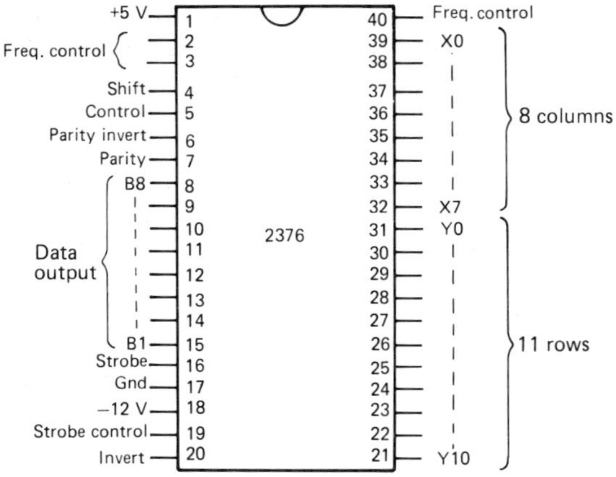

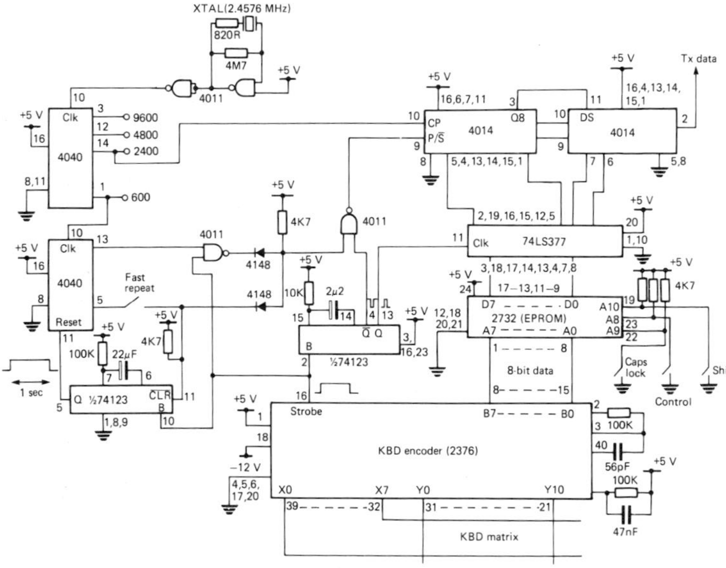

Fig. 7.9 Circuit for an ASCII keyboard

consists of a 2376 decoding a keyboard matrix, feeding the resulting code to a 2732 EPROM for code-conversion. This is then latched and presented for serialisation to a pair of CMOS shift registers fed with a clock whose frequency is equal to the baud rate at which the data is to be sent to the host system. The rest of the electronics is devoted to allowing two modes of auto-repeat of the key pressing. If a key is held down for more than one second, it automatically repeats at around

2 Hz. There is also fast-repeat key on the keyboard, which is connected as shown, to allow the last key pressed to be repeated at around 37 Hz. Note that the SHIFT and CONTROL inputs on the 2376 are discarded. These keys simply connect to address-bus lines of the EPROM, and thus shift the area being addressed within the EPROM. This allows complete flexibility of key code output in all modes. If a 2764 EPROM were to be used, two versions of the keyboard could be stored on the EPROM, and a switch incorporated on the keyboard to change from one to the other. One important note of caution should be added here. When the standard version of the 2376 is used in the manner described above, without using the shift and control lines, only 84 key-codes are available. The codes associated with matrix points (X4, Y4), (X4, Y8), (X2, Y9) and (X2, Y10) are repeated by other crossing points, and should thus be left unused by the key switch matrix.

To understand the following explanation of the circuit, the reader will have to be familiar with the chips described, or have access to the relevant data.

The two 4040 counters produce all the clock frequencies used on the keyboard. A patch area allows a user to select the baud rate at which data is sent, and 2400 baud has been found to be perfectly adequate. The 2·4576 MHz crystal used in the clock generator is a standard available frequency for this purpose. When a key is pressed, the strobe rises after the debounce period, and sets two monostables timing. The 74123 was found adequate for this purpose, providing delays of up to one second with ease. The code appearing at the output data lines of the 2376 is converted by the 2732 and latched by the monostable pulse into a 74LS377. This is the ASCII code which is required, and at this point may be used, along with the strobe, to provide parallel data to a system if required. The low-going pulse from the same monostable is used, via a NAND gate, to parallel load the 4014 shift registers. Up to this point, they have been shifting out a constant 1. When the monostable pulse ends, the final 4014 begins by sending the five 1s connected to pins 1, 15, 14, 13 and 4. Then a 0 is sent, which is present upon pin 5. This is treated as the start bit by the receiving UAR/T in the computer. The ASCII code, as an eight-bit frame, is then sent with no parity, though this could be added into the 4014 from a parity generator. Finally, two stop bits are sent, and the shift registers continue to send 1s until the next transmission. The bit-time is one cycle of the clock fed to pin 10 of the 4014s.

When a key is pressed, the other monostable begins timing one second. For the duration of this time, it holds the lower frequency 4040 in a reset condition, with its outputs low. This creates no effect on the rest of the circuit. After one second, this 4040 begins to count, and pulses from pin 13 are allowed through the NAND gates (the 2376 strobe is still high) and diode to the P/S pins of the 4014s. The result is that they send the current key-code over and over again until the key is released, and the 2376's strobe returns to zero, closing the NAND gate between pin 13 of the 4040 and the diode.

A fast repeat key is also incorporated on the keyboard, whose frequency of repeat must not exceed that at which the 4014s can shift out the data. When the fast-repeat key is pressed, pulses from pin 5 of the 4040 are allowed through the diode and NAND gate to the 4014 with the same effect as for holding a key pressed. In order to ensure that the one-second timer is not still timing, which would stop the 4040 from supplying these pulses, the fast-repeat key is also connected to the reset pin of the 74123. Diodes are used here purely to obviate the necessity of a further logic package. If there is any fear of interference due to the forward voltage drop of these components, a germanium diode such as the OA47 can be substituted. However, the author has experienced no such problem.

Other types of keyboard are becoming more and more widespread. An example is the 'membrane' keyboard. Instead of switch closures, key pads are printed on to plastic surfaces using a silver-based ink. The surfaces are kept slightly apart by the elastic resilience of the plastic material, and slight finger pressure brings the conductive ink surfaces in contact. The contact resistance is higher than gold-contact key switches, but most keyboard encoders are able to accept this type of input. This produces a very robust and flat keyboard surface well suited to industrial equipment. However, the majority of computer system users agree that a key-switch-type keyboard with a positive 'feel' is best suited to programming and other computer-intensive activities. It is unlikely that the membrane or 'touch' keyboards will displace the conventional units for this purpose.

Visual display

Simple visual displays have already been introduced. However, for a serious computer system which is to be used for program development or intensive high-level activities, the cathode ray tube (CRT) is still the most efficient and widespread form of visual display. The term visual display unit (VDU) will refer to this type of output in the following.

Originally, a VDU was a stand-alone unit with a keyboard which accepted display and command data from an external computer, usually via an RS232 line. Indeed, many of the control codes in the ASCII set, originally intended for teletypes, are orientated to this type of RS232-connected peripheral. The original concept of multi-tasking computers, which allows several users to be in apparent communication with the computer at the same time, was based around terminals connected to the computer by serial communication lines. This concept is still in widespread use, but more and more systems are being designed around the concept of spreading complete computers around the users' stations, and tying the whole group into a computer network. More will be said about this in Chapter 8. Suffice it to say that most microcomputers being designed and manufactured at present have their own internal VDU, which is simply part of the memory map of the machine. This concept is called 'memory mapping', and it is this type of display which will be described here.

Figure 1.8 showed a possible position within the memory map of a computer for a VDU. It illustrates that the VDU is not separate from the system; indeed, it is essential to look upon a VDU simply as a 'window' into a block of internal memory. As the MPU writes binary data to the VDU RAM, the electronics of the VDU interprets this data as ASCII codes, and throws upon the CRT screen their human equivalents—patterns forming letters, numbers, etc. It is the electronics involved in this process which will be examined below.

To control a CRT, the process by which it works must be understood. The screen at the front is bombarded by a single spot of electrons originating from a hot wire and accelerated towards the phosphor on the back of the front face. If a very fast snapshot could be taken of the screen, just one spot would be seen, perhaps with a certain persistence left over from the last few positions which the spot occupied. The spot traverses the front face from left to right, normally, and along constant lines from top to bottom. As this 'flying spot' moves, the brightness is varied continuously, and hence builds up a picture-frame on the screen. The eye is not fast enough to discern the actual movement, and it welds the whole conception into a single two-dimensional image. The speed with which the spot actually moves across the screen is fixed by the electronics associated with the CRT, and cannot normally be altered by the MPU system. However, the exact time at which the spot starts its left-to-right traverse can be altered to some extent to allow the VDU electronics to keep in synchronisation. As the spot moves across the screen line, the VDU logic modulates the brightness of the spot, and hence allows the computer to build up a complete image.

At the end of each line of the frame, the spot is darkened and flies back to the start of the next line. A 'horizontal sync' pulse is then fed to an input on the CRT electronics to cause the flying spot to start travelling from left to right again. Similarly, at the end of each complete frame, the spot is darkened and flies back to the start of the frame, where the VDU electronics again synchronises the exact time at which the spot begins its journey from top left of the screen to bottom right. A 'vertical sync' pulse is issued for this purpose. A character on the screen occupies several lines, and each time the flying spot traverses the region of that character, the VDU logic must modulate the spot to build up that row of dots of the character. Figure 7.10 shows this process in progress for a capital X displayed at the top

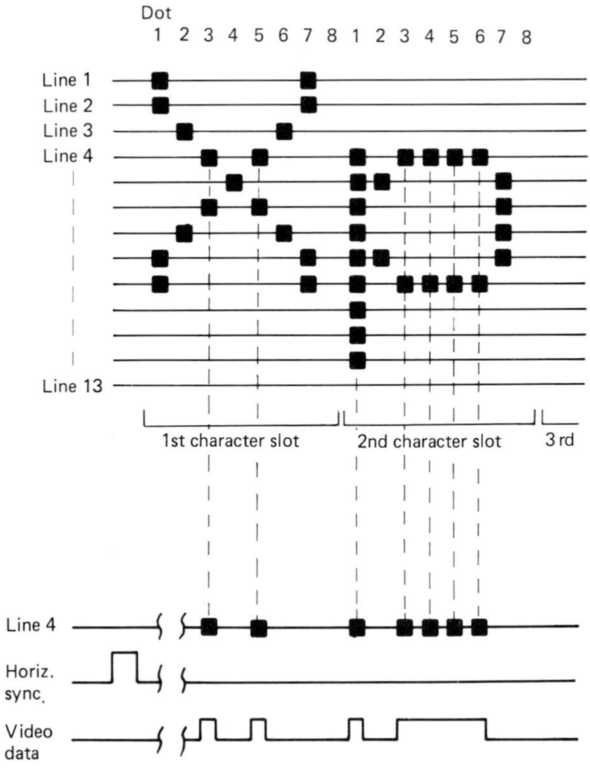

Fig. 7.10 Character imaging on a CRT

left character slot, and a lower-case p in the second slot. The actual character slot here is a matrix of 8 × 13 dots. In order to separate characters vertically, a blank line is left at the bottom of each character. Horizontal separation is effected by leaving the right-hand column of dots blank, i.e. dot 8.

The flying spot on the screen does not naturally split its display into the dots shown, and it is up to the VDU electronics to modulate the electron beam, as it moves, into these separate dots of black and white.

The spot is displayed on each screen line, as it moves across, for approximately 50 microseconds. This means that for an 80-column display, $80 \times 8 = 640$ dots will be displayed on a single line within 50 microseconds. In fact, in order to prevent the character display from overlapping the edge of the screen, the display is normally restricted to around 42 microseconds of the line. This implies that the clock which sequences the electronics from dot to dot with each cycle, known as the 'dot clock', has to oscillate at a frequency of approximately 15 MHz for this format. Fewer characters on the line would demand a slower dot clock, and more columns one of a higher frequency.

Figure 7.11 sketches a block diagram of a typical VDU system. The characters which are displayed on the screen are stored in the VDU RAM by the MPU. This block of RAM is continually scanned by the VDU, and the data within it is presented to the display electronics. When the MPU wishes to display a character at a given location on the screen, it simply writes its ASCII code to the appropriate location in the VDU RAM, and it is automatically diplayed. The method by which this display is produced is described in the following.

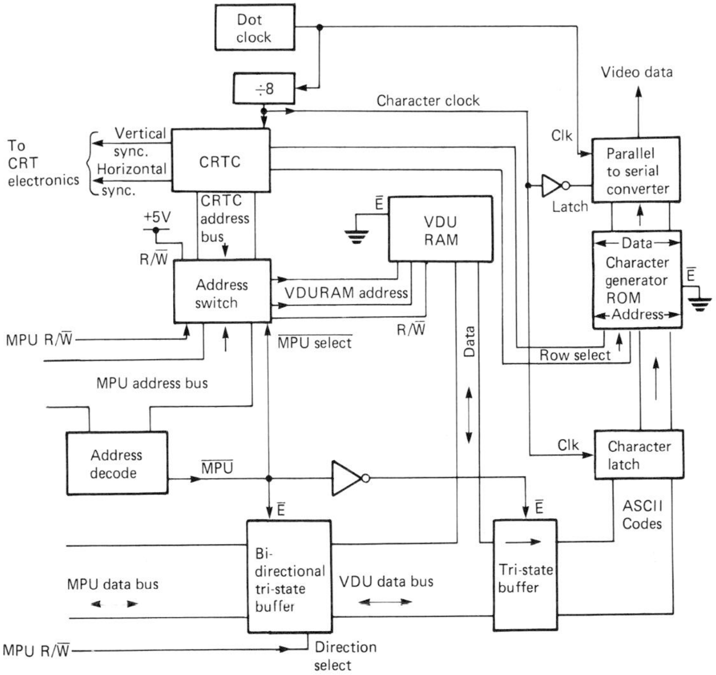

Fig. 7.11 Schematic of a VDU

At the heart of the VDU is a complex counter chip called a cathode ray tube controller (CRTC). This chip keeps track of the position of the electron beam at all times, and synchronises the activity of modulating the beam's intensity with its position on the screen's surface. Each time the flying spot flies back to the start of the line, the CRTC has a chance to resynchronise its activity with that of the CRT. The first few lines of the screen are not normally used by the display. Figure 7.10 shows the first 13 lines of actual display. The events described below start with the horizontal sync pulse of line 1 in Figure 7.10.

The CRTC is connected to the dot clock divided by the character width (eight dots), and all its timing is referenced to this oscillator, which is called the 'character clock'. One cycle of the character clock is the time it takes for the electron beam to cross the region of one of the displayed characters. The first character-time is often discarded, and the CRTC addresses the VDU RAM, via the address switch, for the first character which it is to display. At this time, the address switch is connecting the CRTC address bus through to the VDU RAM, which is in the read state. The ASCII code of the first character, an X (code 58), appears on the data bus, and is allowed through the tri-state buffer to the latch. This is latched, and appears at the address bus of the character-generator ROM. The CRTC sets the row select address of the character generator to complete the address of the byte containing the top row of the X character. This is simply a set of 1s and 0s which exactly corresponds to the light and dark dots of the top row of the letter X. Figure 7.10 shows that this is the binary pattern 10000010. That is, a bright dot at the start of the row, five dark dots, one bright and one dark. This pattern is sent to the parallel-to-serial converter, where it is latched and converted to a serial stream of dots at the speed of the dot clock. This stream is fed to the CRT, where it is amplified and used to modulate the flying spot's brightness as it passes across the region of the X. Meanwhile, the CRTC has fetched the next ASCII code: 70, for 'p'. The row select remains the same, thereby fetching the top row of the p. This corresponds to a set of 0s as the top row is dark. Each successive character clock cycle causes the CRTC to fetch the next ASCII code, with the row select address held constant. The top rows of each character are thus fetched and serialised to the CRT. To ensure that the access time of the RAM and ROM in the chain does not upset the system, it is up to the CRTC to time its activities correctly to ensure that the character latch is not clocked to store the ASCII code from the VDU RAM before this data is present. The falling edge of the character clock causes the CRTC to address the RAM, and a full half-cycle later the rising edge latches the RAM data into the character latch—this gives the RAM approximately half a microsecond to supply the data. Similarly, this data is fed to the character generator, where it causes data to be fed to the parallel-to-serial converter. This data is not latched into the converter until the next falling edge half a cycle later, when it then begins to be serialised. This sequence gives all the elements in the VDU a chance to settle, and once again gives an excellent example of the sequential 'clocked' nature of a successful electronic system.

At the end of the line of display, the spot is darkened and flies back to begin again. When the CRTC is ready, it issues the horizontal sync pulse, and selects the second row of each character. As an example, the waveforms associated with line 4 are shown in Figure 7.10. The separation of the dots is exaggerated in the figure. Thus when the four dots of the top of the 'p' are displayed, they appear to weld together, as shown in the video data waveform, to form a connected line. As can be seen, the space between characters on a line is actually stored within the character generator. If the characters were meant to join up, the character generator would simply contain 1s in that region instead of 0s. Similarly, the character generator stores the dark lines between characters vertically. This means that by manipulating the data within the character generator, graphics characters could be formed which would connect up and allow the computer to form general connected patterns such as histograms and geometric drawings.

This process continues repeatedly until a complete frame has been produced. The whole frame is then repeated at a rate of 50 frames per second. For a very high resolution picture two interlaced frames can be used, as for a television picture, and some CRTCs allow this format to be used.

By the above means, the CRTC is continually scanning the VDU RAM and throwing the picture of its contents upon the screen. This process only ceases when the MPU wishes to change the VDU RAM contents. When the address decoding block signals a write or read to the VDU RAM, the MPU data bus is switched onto the VDU RAM, as is the address bus, via the address switch. The transaction takes place, and the VDU then returns to normal. The MPU has precedence in this system. However, it is rather irritating for the user to have the picture on the screen interrupted while the MPU reads or writes, and it is usual to restrict the MPU access to the time during which the flyback is taking place. This is achieved by causing the MPU to wait between its attempt at access and the flyback itself. Such a system slows the MPU's screen activities by a large factor, as the flyback period is very short, and hence the MPU can find itself spending large amounts of time waiting.

There is a great variety of CRTCs on the market. One of the most sophisticated is the 6845, originally manufactured by Motorola for their 6800 series. This chip has 16 internal registers for setting suc parameters as character format, number of character lines and charac ters per line, sync pulse frequency and width, etc. The chip also has light-pen input which will be described in a later section.

VDU character attributes

The above gives a description of the method by which a norma character can be displayed on a CRT. If it is wished to allow th character to take on a number of different attributes such as revers video, flashing, low intensity, etc., these must be added by furthe logic on the video data.

Reverse video is a very common attribute, and may simply be achieved by inverting the video data. However, it is normal to require that normal and reverse video characters be displayed on the same screen. Thus each character must be treated differently by the inverter on the video data. In addition, some extra memory is needed to store the state of the attributes of each character. A common method is to use the fact that ASCII codes only need to be seven bits in length.

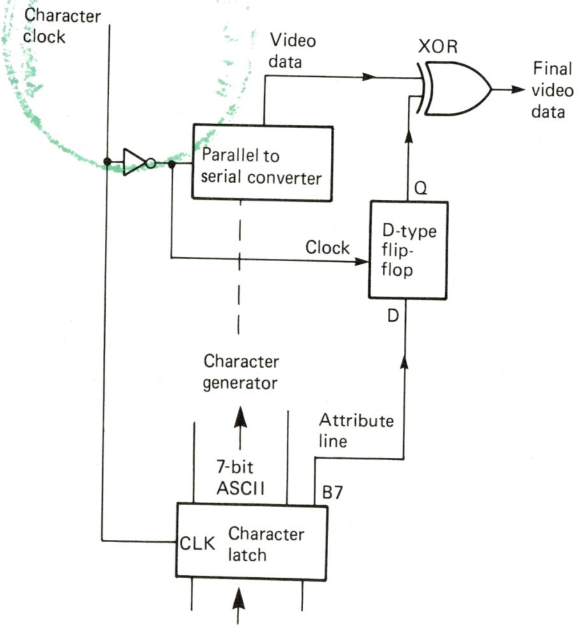

Fig. 7.12 Reverse video

Thus the eighth bit (B7) in the VDU RAM may be used to store the state of that character. For normal characters, the ASCII code is stored in the VDU RAM with most significant bit (B7) set to 0; for reverse video, it is set to 1. As this character is fetched by the CRTC, the top bit is also latched in the character latch, and then it is treated as in Figure 7.12. When a reverse video character is latched into the character latch, B7 is set to a 1. This appears as data to a D-type flip-flop. When the serial-to-parallel converter latches its data for serialisation, the flip-flop sets its Q output to a 1, and this causes the XOR gate to invert the resulting video data. The flip-flop is set back to normal the next time that a normal character is to be displayed, as such a character has B7 equal to 0.

This method of causing the characters to take on different attributes can be used for any character-oriented attribute. To allow more than just one such attribute, further RAM must be incorporated in parallel with the VDU RAM. This simply extends the number of bits which are fetched for each character. This may also be used to extend the size of character generator which may be used to allow several types of character to appear on the screen: normal, italic, script, etc.

Graphics characters

There are two main types of graphics: character-slot and high resolution. Character-slot graphics simply involve storing graphics characters in the character generator. High-resolution graphics require the ability to write to each 'pixel' (picture cell or dot) individually.

In the 128 ASCII characters, there is a set of 32 non-printing codes called control codes. This region of the character generator could hold some simple graphics characters. Figure 7.13 suggests a format for dividing the character slot into large picture cells each composed of a number of dots. A 3×2 format is suggested. Four of the possible graphics characters are shown in Figure 7.13. It is a simple matter to show that there will be 2^6 (64) possible characters, because there are $3 \times 2 = 6$ cells in each character and each cell can take on one of two states. However, there are only 32 control code locations available to store graphics characters in the character generator. The problem of storing 64 patterns is resolved by observing, as suggested in Figure 7.13, that half of the characters are simply the reverse of the others. This means that with 32 patterns and a reverse-video attribute, the full 64 graphics characters can be synthesised. This does not give a high-resolution display, but it provides a useful method of allowing simple patterns to be displayed such as histograms, forms and tables.

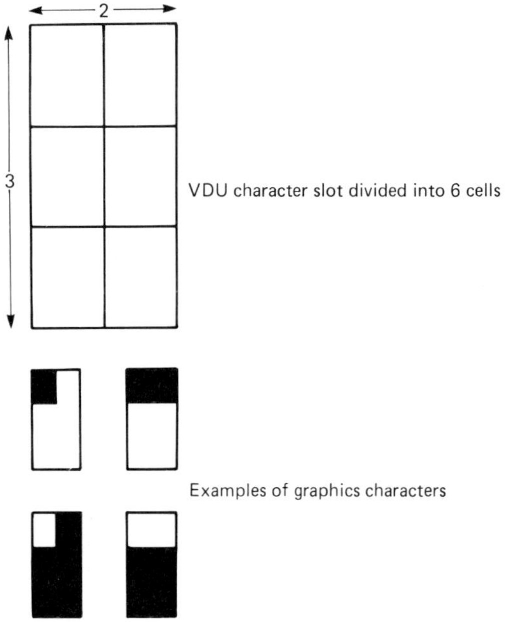

Fig. 7.13 Character-slot graphics

No 0s are left at the edges of the characters in the character generator, and hence these characters all join up with no gaps vertically or horizontally.

To achieve more resolution, as mentioned above, the character generator could be increased in size, and one of the character attributes could be an alternate character set of graphics characters. However, it would be most cumbsome to try to produce true high-resolution graphics in this manner.

True high-resolution graphics are produced by displaying the actual 1s and 0s stored in the VDU RAM. Broadly speaking, if the character generator is left out, this is the result. However, it is important to arrange the pixels in a logical manner in the VDU RAM in order to make the task of writing software for the display easier. Thus the CRTC is replaced by a counter which sequences through the VDU RAM in this logical sequence as it supplies data for serialisation. A further consideration is that previously just one byte was needed in the VDU RAM for a complete character of 13 rows. For high-resolution graphics, each row of dots takes up one complete byte. For an 80-column by 24-line display, it is normal to use a 2K RAM such as a 6116 for the VDU RAM, with a few locations wasted. An equivalent high-resolution graphics board would require 26K bytes of RAM. Clearly this cannot be simply included in the memory map of the MPU, as half of its usable addressing space would be used up. It is common to find that such VDUs are either contacted through I/O space, or via a 2K window which is moved around the VDU RAM for reading and writing to different parts of the screen.

Another approach to the production of graphics involves the character generator itself. In a non-graphics VDU, the patterns which appear on the screen are decided by the data in the character generator. If that could be changed at the program's will, any type of pattern could be created. This is achieved by replacing part or all of the character generator by RAM, which is addressable. By doing this, the programmer can create unique graphics characters as required.

Light-pen input

Several different methods of picking information from the screen of a VDU have been developed, including a system which senses the position of a stylus, or even a finger on the screen by a set of interlacing beams aimed across the screen surface. However, the most common and widespread method of communicating with the screen directly uses a light-pen with a photodiode or phototransistor in the tip. The light-pen is held up at a character on the screen, and as the flying spot passes across the tip, the pen picks up the light, converts to an electrical voltage, and transmits this to the VDU. Figure 7.14 shows the process. The timing diagram shows four character slots: two before, one under the light-pen and one after. When the video data of that character line reaches the pen, the dots of that character are amplified and may be used to clock an address latch on the VDU RAM address bus. This address may then be read by the MPU system, and used to determine the character at which the light-pen was pointing. Recall that the timing of the VDU system was such that the data at a given VDU RAM address was serialised out when the next character is being fetched by the CRTC. This implies that the address which will be latched by the appropriate circuitry will in fact be one character behind. In addition, it is not uncommon for light-pen circuitry to insert further delays in the pulse which does the latching, and the actual address which is stored may be several characters behind. However, these delays are all constant, and the software can therefore compensate.

Only the VDU RAM address in Figure 7.11 need be latched, the row-select information is irrelevant. This requires a latch on that address bus, and some means of reading the stored address by the

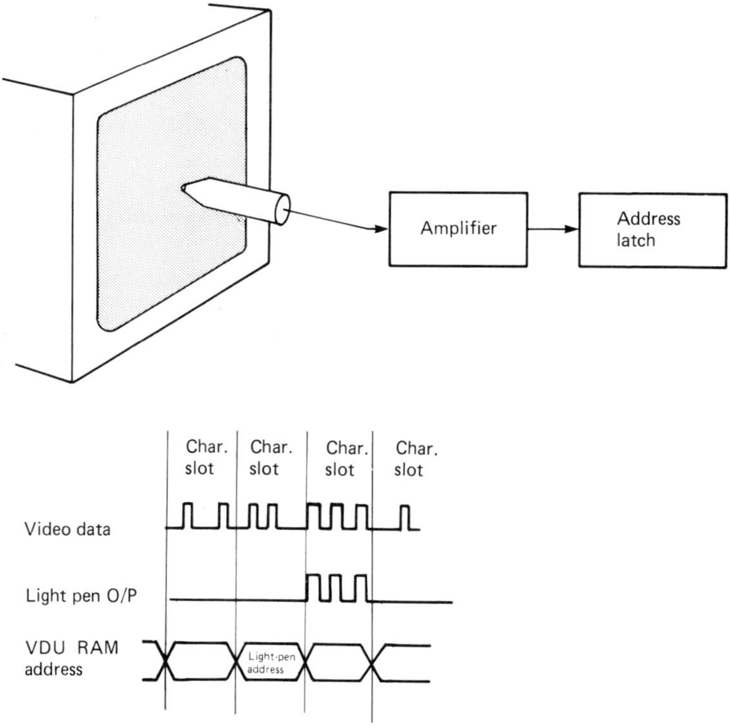

Fig. 7.14 Light-pen

MPU. Most CRTCs have internal circuitry for this purpose included. There is a light-pen input on the chip, which causes the CRTC to latch the VDU RAM address when the light-pen strobes the line. This address may then be read from an internal register by the MPU at will.

Speech synthesis

So far, I/O to and from a human has been based on sight and touch. The ultimate method of using the human senses to communicate with a computer is via voice. Unfortunately the most important direction, from human to machine, has not yet been perfected. There is, however, a well-understood technology for the reverse direction. Computers can now speak with almost complete naturalness by a number of different electronic methods. Before describing some of these, let us consider the application of voice synthesis.

First, the most widespread application is for the blind. The many uses to which such equipment can be put for those who cannot see is fairly obvious. The machine can be used to call out the state of domestic appliances, which would normally show a visual indication. Voice output could warn of danger, and in the ultimate machine a computer would convert the written word from a common paperback into speech, and literally read the book out loud. Attempts at this last have been made with some success in prototype form by Telesensory Systems Inc. of California.

The application of speech in the normal world has by no means been exploited; the surface has hardly been scratched. Examples of danger signals have been tried, including some within cars. Speech is used by the telecommunication services to replace the grooved-disc type of players in services such as the telephone clock. Almost any activity where an operator has his hands and eyes full, but requires constant advice of the state of some parameter, should provide a setting for voice output. However, experience so far has shown that such ideas are very slow to catch on. It is probably true to say that speech synthesis cannot catch on until speech recognition has been perfected. At that point, computer speech will begin to pervade our existence in a considerably more fundamental manner.

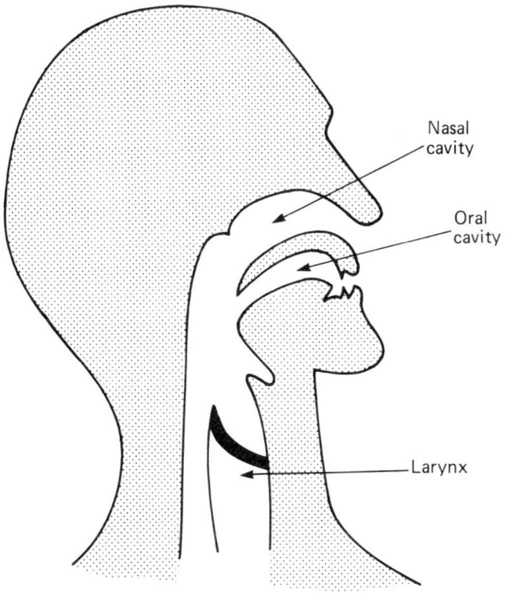

Fig. 7.15 The human voice

To understand the technology of speech synthesis, it is helpful to understand how the human voice works. Figure 7.15 shows the principal parts of the human voice system. The principles of speech production centre around the physics of audio filtering. The larynx is a comparatively wide-band noise source, which is filtered in real time by the brain's manipulation of a set of muscles in the head. This continuous adjustment changes the filtering characteristics of the nasal and oral cavities, and just those frequencies required from one fraction of a second to the next are allowed out. It is an electronic analogue of this system which gives the most successful synthesis of the human voice. Before describing this, it should be mentioned that a number of devices on the market used a system of digitising the actual sounds of the human words, and then 'playing these back' when called up. This turns out to be a very wasteful method of storing speech, as the waveforms of speech are highly redundant and may be considerably condensed with no loss of quality.

Two main methods of synthesising speech are in use at present. These are 'formant synthesis' and 'linear predictive encoding'. A full description of these two systems is beyond the scope of this book, but Figure 7.16 sketches their elements. The first of these is a system for taking an electronic noise source (voice source) and filtering it to allow the human sounds through. Human voice sounds are made up of a number of frequencies which are filtered out of the noise source. There are three main frequencies (called formants), a fixed nasal sound, and white noise which appears in sounds such as the 'zz' of 'jazz', or the 'ss' of 'hiss'. These are termed 'fricatives', the latter being an 'unvoiced' sound. If all the necessary components of a given vowel or consonant sound can be mixed together, the correct sound will result. This is the principle of the formant synthesis system. Just nine parameters are required to be adjusted in real time to achieve natural speech. There are four volumes and five frequencies. To store a word, a computer program takes in the sound through a microphone and breaks the sound up into its components. Typically, the program will take a frame of data every 20 milliseconds. Thus playing the word back entails feeding the nine parameters to the synthesiser and updating them 50 times per second. The more bits per parameter, the more real is the resulting speech.

Linear predictive encoding (LPC) performs a similar filtering process, but not on audio waveforms. The LPC module takes a stream of bits representing a noise source, either voiced or unvoiced, and performs a fast arithmetic transform on the data according to a set of parameters fed to it much as for the formant synthesiser. The arithmetic transform removes certain frequencies, and prepares the data for conversion from digital data to an analogue waveform in a

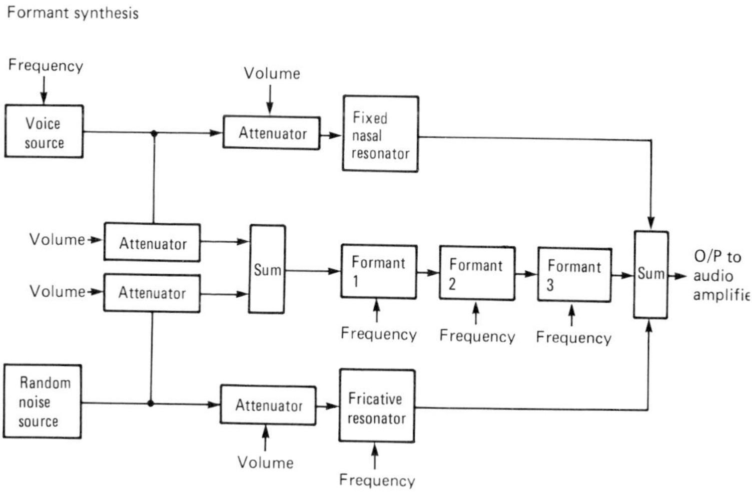

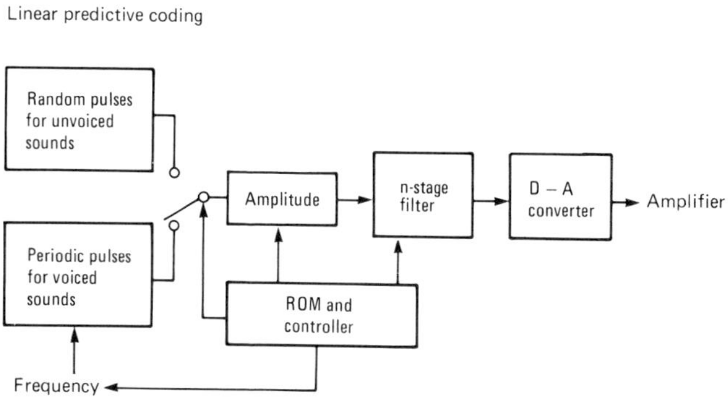

Fig. 7.16 Speech synthesis

digital-to-analogue converter (D/AC). The number of stages to the filter determines the clarity of the resulting speech. Ten stages is considered a minimum for acceptable speech, and twelve gives near perfection. The data for the synthesiser is produced as for formant synthesis.

The LPC module has a number of advantages over the formant synthesiser, the major one being that it may be formed entirely on a chip, with few extra passive components.

There are two main classes of machine which use a synthesiser as described above. They are the 'stored speech', and 'synthesis by rule' systems. Stored speech has been described above; it provides the user with the ability to customise his word requirements, store them on a ROM and call each word or phrase back at will to make up sentences. Synthesis by rule, however, is a method of producing unlimited speech. The computer simply sends a sentence to the device as a set of ASCII codes, and the words are synthesised according to the English (or any other) language rules. Of course there are many exceptions to these rules, and a number of fixed vocabulary words are held on the device and recognised when encountered. The synthesis-by-rule method is analogous to the way in which the human brain speaks by controlling the filtering cavities in the head as words are to be uttered.

The actual device chosen for speech synthesis depends heavily upon the application. Stored-speech devices with LPC encoders produce the cheapest and most realistic systems, but require expensive and memory-intensive storage of a limited vocabulary. However, good synthesis-by-rule devices are expensive, and the speech is more liquid and less real.

The problem of speech recognition is very different from that of the technology described above. The problem has only just been touched, and it is generally agreed that the solution will provide a remarkable leap towards the intelligent computer.

8

Systems and applications

This chapter brings together a number of sample applications which will use the foregoing data. The emphasis is on the practicalities of using MPUs. The examples are all case studies, and they start with a simple application for a single-board controller. A more complex example requiring an S100 system is then given, and some general principles for the solution of control problems are introduced. The next section deals with an application which bridges the gap between control and large computer systems—that is, data collection and production control. This leads the chapter onto the important concept of local area networks of computers. Comparisons of methods of achieving high-speed data communications are mentioned. The Ethernet standard is introduced as an example of a powerful networking system.

A simple control example

The preface suggested an ideal method of solving general problems using a single 'super design-aid'. The concept is equivalent to sitting in front of a VDU, typing in the problem, modifying the solution which evolves, and blowing the resulting program onto an EPROM. This is then plugged into a general machine, which is the final product. Let us consider the solution to a sample problem, and derive from it as many general concepts as possible.

The problem described below comes from a real situation. It is a hardware control problem: in later sections typical problems are considered which will require larger computer solutions.

A manufacturer of contact-lens turning machines has designed a completely electronically operated machine. It is small and compact, with a front panel, a few sensors and servos, and a keyboard. In order to recommend an approach to the control, the computer systems manufacturer must perform a complete systems analysis, with a flowchart for the machine's operation. Figure 8.1 shows a starting point for the systems analysis. The input and output lines are decided, along with their number and character, and the computer can be specified.

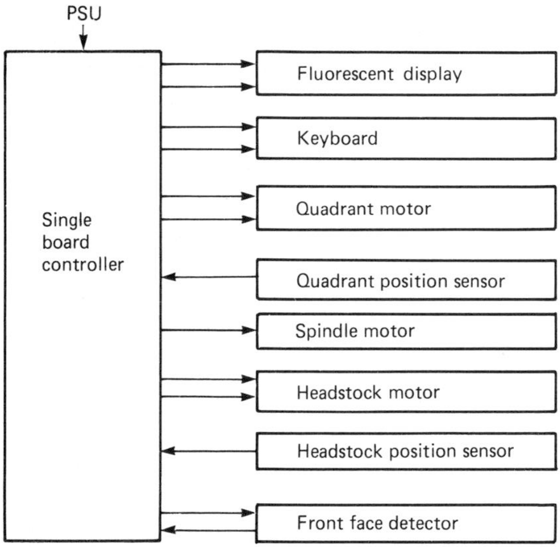

Fig. 8.1 Contact-lens cutting machine controller

Meanwhile, the machine's manufacturer must come up with a flow-chart or similar statement of the operational sequence of the machine. The computer manufacturer would normally be heavily involved in this process.

Figure 8.2 shows the keyboard and display. The membrane keyboard has between 16 and 32 keys, and the fluorescent display is of a standard 16-character type, which is interfaced by some parallel TTL level lines—it is a star display with a controller included. The 'button' of special acrylic, from which the contact lens is made, is mounted at the end of the spindle—just as for a lathe. The diamond tool, which cuts the acrylic, is held on a rotating quadrant, driven by a motor which is to be switched on and off by a TTL level signal. The quadrant's angular position is sensed and sent to the computer, as a voltage which varies with angle, from 0 to +5 volts. The spindle rotates, and its motor is turned on and off by a TTL signal. The spindle and its motor are mounted within the 'headstock', which is movable in and out by a stepper motor. The stepper is controlled by a few TTL lines which give its direction and speed. As the headstock moves, its position is sensed to a resolution of one micrometre. This is done by a sensor which pulses for each micrometre of movement of the headstock, and is also able to indicate direction of movement. An interface circuit on the machine contains an up–down counter which the computer may read along some TTL lines to determine headstock

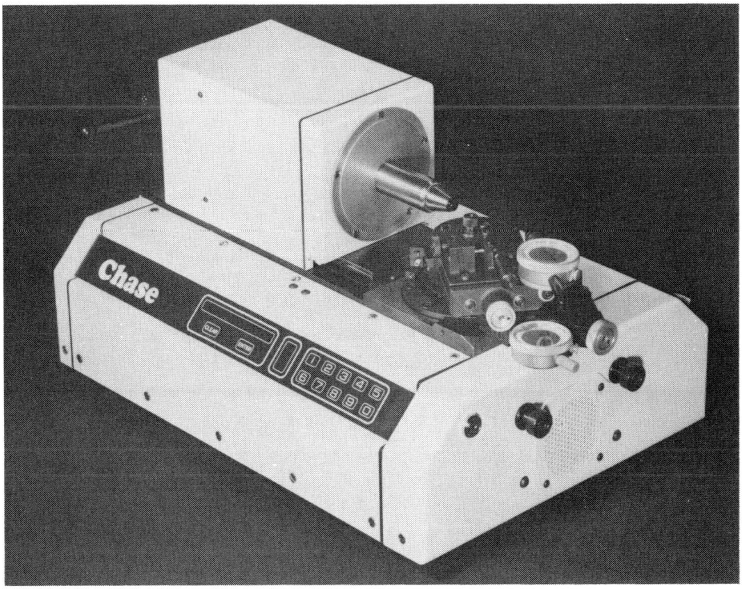

Fig. 8.2 Contact-lens cutting machine (courtesy Chase Precision International Ltd)

position. Finally, in order to control the machine to the required accuracy, it is necessary for the machine to be able to detect the front face of the button after it has been loaded. For this purpose, a detecting probe is moved into place via a TTL signal, the computer moves the headstock forward until the button presses against the probe, and a TTL signal tells the computer that the headstock is at the starting position from which all measurements of position are to be taken for that button.

The sequence of events is broadly as follows. A setter sets the machine up for production. Thereafter the process is mechanical and repetitive. An operator loads a button and presses the keyboard start switch. The machine advances the headstock and presents the front-face detector. When the front face has been detected, the spindle is started and the headstock moved forward. The quadrant holding the tool is then swung round as the spindle and button rotate. This cuts the first part of a concave cut into the button. The headstock then moves further forward, and the next deeper cut is taken with the quadrant moving the tool, once again, around and into the button's surface. This continues with varying speeds and fineness of cut until the concave face is fully fashioned. If the headstock is kept still during the cutting, a spherical face emerges. If the headstock is moved as the quadrant moves, an aspheric but radially symmetric face results. Finally, the headstock moves back, and the operator may remove the button and insert a new one. When the batch of concave surfaces is cut, the buttons are mounted on this face by an adhesive which does not affect the finish. As the next cut is to be a convex surface, the quadrant is adjusted to move the diamond tool along the necessary external curve as the lens is turned, and finally cut. It is also possible to produce an astigmatic lens by this process, by applying a controlled degree of distortion to the button during the convex cut.

As the machine manufacturer has taken care to interface TTL level signals throughout, a standard single-board controller (SBC), produced by the computer manufacturer, was used. The standard computer used is shown in diagrammatic form in Figure 8.3. The lens lathe uses a proportion of these facilities, and the decision to use this device can only be taken after the full systems analysis has been performed. If the decision is marginal, it may be useful to point out to the manufacturer that it is probably more cost-effective to reduce the required parameters slightly than to design a new computer controller. The alternative is to multiplex any further I/O signals required down onto the ones offered by the SBC. However, for this application, the SBC shown is well fitted to the problem, and even allows for some future expansion. Furthermore, being highly compact, it fits neatly behind a back-plate on the machine, and is easily accessible.

This application has been satisfied by a standard hardware product, which shifts the main part of the work to the software. For this purpose a development system is required with the same I/O structure as that of the SBC. The SBC manufacturer requires an emulator, which could take the form of an S100 board with all the SBC's I/O devices included, and mapped at the same locations. A standard S100 computer could then be used to develop the program, and test the sequence by plugging the actual machine into the emulator board. This allows all the powerful program development tools of a large system to be used. As mentioned before, the final stage is to blow the program onto EPROM, and plug it into the SBC in the machine itself.

This example shows how important it is for a computer company to have a range of compatible products. It allows continuous commonality of hardware and software. The next example is many times more complex, and is used to bring out some of the important hardware aspects of general control systems.

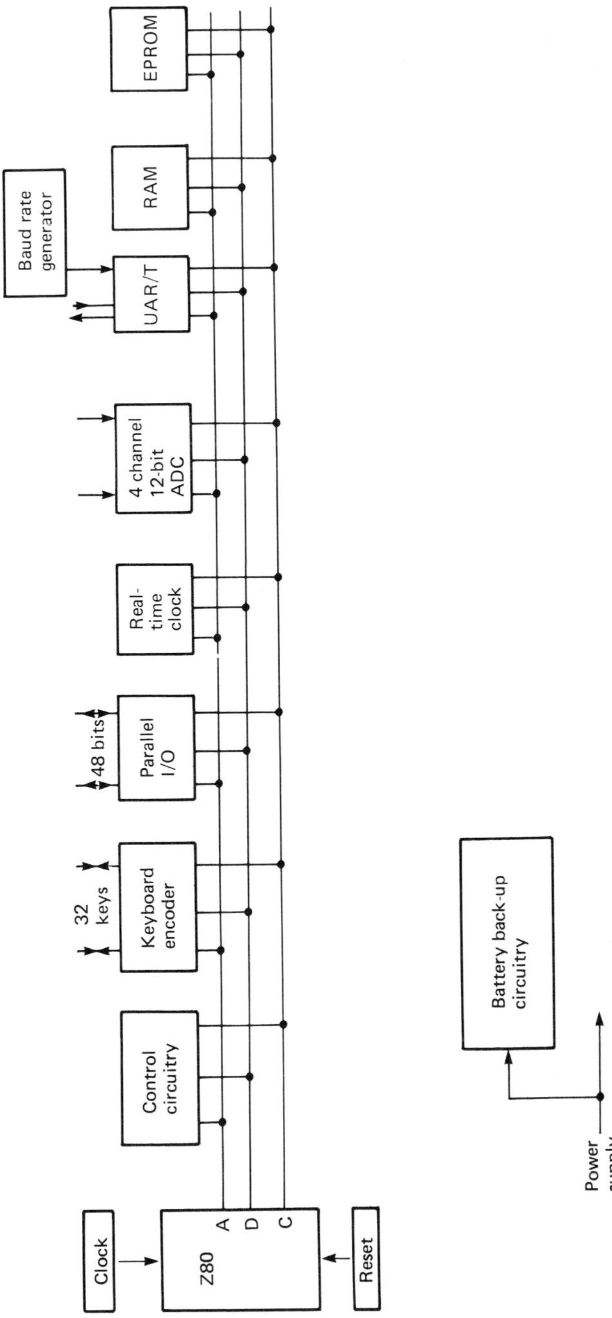

Fig. 8.3 Single-board controller (SBC)

Thermoformer controller

This example is one where completely standard products would not be cost-effective. The problem, as will be seen, has a number of unique factors, and a custom-made solution is the answer.

A company which produces large thermoforming machines has decided to replace its relay-based controllers with computer-controlled equipment. The need for this change comes from a number of sources. The relay-based controllers, though reliable, are difficult to modify, and provide a rather rudimentary type of control. Competitors are in the process of computerising with great benefit, and the market is becoming more alive to the advantages of computerisation.

The thermoforming machines are designed to take in sheets of plastic in one end, heat them under a bank of heaters, and mould them while hot into the shape of a bath-tub or plastic fridge-liner. The heater-bank is quite large, having up to 500 quartz-element heaters, and the temperature pattern on the heater-bank is critical. When the softened sheet meets the moulding station, the highly stretched parts of the sheet must be at a lower temperature than the portions which will only be slightly deformed during moulding. This prevents the sheet from thinning dangerously at the highly stretched parts, and preserves an acceptable distribution of material thickness.

Some of the advantages of computerisation are as follows:

(a) The front panel of a computer controller can give more complex and user-oriented information on the process.
(b) The setting of the numerous parameters of the machine can be changed more easily, and even stored on cassette tape.
(c) The controller is easier to adapt to the various different requirements on a custom basis.
(d) The machine can be more diagnostic of failures, and even allow the operator to keep production going by adjustments to the system until the machine can be repaired. The 'mean time to repair' (MTTR) is correspondingly smaller, and fewer production hours are lost.
(e) The mains supply may fluctuate from time to time, and the computer can sense these changes and automatically compensate.
(f) A more efficient method of heating the plastic can be utilised, which requires fast changes to the heater pattern, with feedback from the process as it proceeds. This allows production to proceed at an optimised speed.

Other advantages will be clear from the following. In order to decide upon the correct approach to the problem, these considerations are weighed up:

(a) The controller must be easy to modify to the customer's changing requirements.
(b) If the controller is more expensive than the relay-based controller, will it provide a correspondingly large number of advantages, making the final product considerably more saleable?
(c) The controller will be large and complex, and will be seen to be controlling a large number of inputs and outputs—is there a case for a multi-processor system?
(d) How accurately does the manufacturer of the machine know the advantages which it is possible to gain from a computer approach? Is there an accurate and full specification for the device?
(e) How varied is the full range of machines manufactured by the company, and can one controller be designed to fulfil the requirements of the complete range?

These are some of the points to be considered during a complete technical appraisal of the situation.

In almost all cases of control, the first technical step is to determine as accurately as possible the number of inputs and outputs required by the controller, and their electrical character. The next step is to hammer out a flowchart or timing diagram of all the activities which the machine must perform, as a basis for a program specification.

There are several types of I/O device on the machine; they are as follows.

Inputs

(a) Simple limit switches and contactors, the contacts of which can be wired to change over from ground to any other voltage. These switches are placed on the machine to signal the state and position of various mechanical actuators and devices. Water is also used on the machine, and a switch is used to detect the presence of water pressure, without which the machine should be forced to stop.
(b) Proximity switches are used instead of limit switches in some places, for positional detection of some parts of the machinery without the necessity for mechanical contact.
(c) A pyrometer, with a highly linear analogue output, is used to sense sheet temperature. It is desired to use a considerably cheaper non-linear device, with the computer performing the linearisation in software.
(d) The mains voltage is to be sensed continuously from step-down transformers. This will be used to allow the computer to adjust the heaters' output to keep the temperature constant and repeatable on the surface of the plastic.

(e) A number of switches are to be sensed for fault conditions.
(f) A complex front panel is to be scanned continuously for operator input.
(g) Cassette-based recall of parameters is required.

Outputs

(a) The sequential control of the thermoformer revolves around solenoid-operated valves (SOVs). The machine is actuated pneumatically, and solenoids operate air valves for the different functions. The SOV coils have 110-volt AC windings.
(b) The heaters are up to 1 kW, 240-volt AC elements in quartz tubes.
(c) The front panel has a large number of digital displays, as well as a bank of lights which must flash, individually, under program control.
(d) The state of the heater pattern must be continuously displayed on a two-dimensional array corresponding to the heater bank itself. The lamps used should follow the heaters exactly. If a heater burns out, the lamp must be extinguished.
(e) Cassette storage of parameters is required.

An analysis of the above system should include a complete count of the inputs and outputs, and a complete sequence diagram of the machine's activities. This is a complex affair, and requires a full interplay of ideas between the thermoformer manufacturer and the computer company. The mechanical design of the machine, in this case, was also new, in order to make full use of the computer's ability. This caused an immediate complication in that the new design was of an 'in-line' type. This means that all the stations within the machine are in use, and the thermoformer may be processing three sheets of plastic at various stages at any time. Plastic is fed in at one end, and finished product appears at the other on a conveyor belt. This implies that the computer has to keep control of all processes simultaneously. Add to this the fact that the operator may decide to change some of the machine's operating parameters during the process, and it becomes clear that a two-processor approach was considered with some seriousness.

The other area of control which needed careful attention was that of the heater banks. The sheet of plastic being heated up is, in fact, sandwiched between an upper and a lower heater bank. Each has its own particular pattern of heat to inject into the plastic sheet, and the pattern's design is a matter of operator skill and experience. In designing the pattern, it is necessary for the machine to provide the setter with continuous information as to the state of the heaters—hence the two-dimensional indicator panel. Having designed the pattern, and stored it in memory, the computer must set up the pattern, and adjust the power fed to the heaters continuously if the mains supply voltage varies. In addition, the thermoformer manufacturer had recently discovered a new method of injecting heat at a higher rate into the plastic surface, which could be used to speed the production process by a very desirable factor. This heater control was found to be impossible using conventional controllers, and hence provided a further argument for computerisation. However, the complexity of this heater control finally required the two-processor approach to become a necessity.

An analysis of the total problem led to the conviction that two processors would be sufficient for the whole machine—one for the sequencer and the majority of front-panel transactions, and one for the heaters.

The next decision which had to be made was whether to follow a single-board or a multi-board and motherboard approach. In the final analysis, this depends upon the number of I/O bits which must be accommodated. If the number is high, a multi-board approach will allow easy maintenance, and easy expansion or contraction depending upon the job in hand. In this case, there was the added consideration of a range of machines to accommodate, and it was felt that the diversity of size from top to bottom militated towards a multi-board approach. It is also easier for a non-computer company to provide its own front-line maintenance and trouble-shooting in a modular system, and less has to be changed when a board is damaged than in a system which has just one very large board. Again, none of these arguments hold for a system which has very few I/O bits, as has been seen. Here, however, with a number of the order of 150 inputs, and the same number of outputs, the multi-board approach was a near-necessity.

There are many standardised buses in use industrially, and if a standard bus approach is adopted it is easier to obtain the necessary hardware components for its production. Accordingly the S100 bus was adopted, and all hardware and software development was performed on an S100-based computer system. This allowed prototypes and final boards to be plugged into the development system for testing on the final mechanics before storing the program onto EPROM. In addition, maintenance and troubleshooting of the components of the system could be performed using the same development system, with specially written test programs. In this manner, machines used for research and development become the field service engineer's tool when the development is complete.

Some of the techniques for the control of the thermoformer will now be described for their hardware attributes.

The sequencer

Figure 8.4 shows a sketch of the computer system and interfacing for the control of the sequence of events in the machine. Figure 4.20 should be consulted for a general sketch of the type of computer system used in the sequencer—an S100 computer. The term 'sequencer' is generally used for a system which controls the sequence of events which a machine must perform. The proximity and limit switches require their outputs to be converted to TTL levels for sensing by the computer. The SOVs are 110-volt devices, and are controlled here by

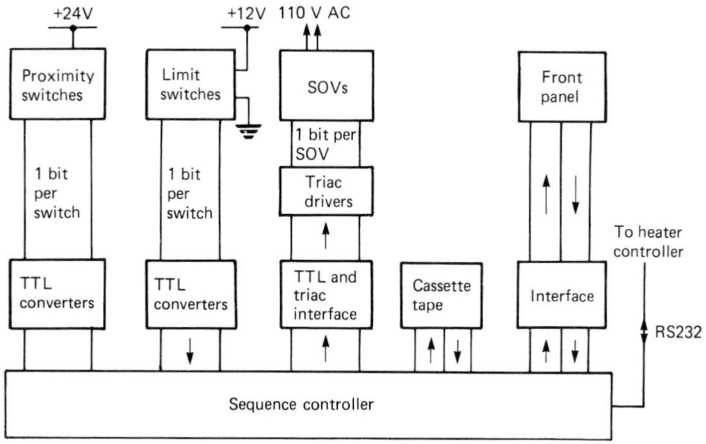

Fig. 8.4 Block diagram of thermoformer sequence controller

triac drivers from a TTL interface. The front panel is composed of buttons, switches, lamps and intelligent digital displays, and requires interfacing with the computer. The cassette storage facility is connected to the sequencer, and all parameters, including those from the heater controller are stored here. The interface for the cassette contains an LSI chip as a controller, with internal registers mapped into memory space. Finally, the whole system is tied together by an RS232 line which allows the sequencer to communicate with the heater controller. Figure 8.5 shows the complete machine, with the control panel in the foreground containing the computer equipment.

Figure 8.6 shows some of the I/O circuits which are used. Proximity

Fig. 8.5 Plastic thermoforming machine (courtesy Shelley Thermoformers International Ltd)

switches and change-over limit switches send +24 volts or +12 volts respectively, and these are converted into TTL levels by the simple circuit shown at the top of Figure 8.6. R2 is used to drop the voltage to ensure that the Zener diode can limit the voltage to +5 volts for the input device in the computer. R1 is a pull-down resistor, which was found to be necessary for the proximity switch used, to ensure a good ground signal when signalling the 0 state. The circuit's characteristic impedance can be adjusted to give excellent noise-rejection, and has been found to be faultless in practice. Boards of 34 such conversion circuits are manufactured to provide high-density input interfaces for the I/O boards in the computer. Output to the SOVs from the computer is fed via a transistor to an opto-isolator. This device is simply an LED and phototransistor in the same package. The TTL output drives the transistor and turns on the LED, and the phototransistor grounds the base of another transistor which is used to control the triac. The need for an opto-isolator comes from the fact that the ground of the triac circuitry must be connected to the neutral of the 110-volt supply. This circuit provides isolation between the computer equipment and the 110 volts AC. In order to preserve the isolation, two power supplies are required. One, V1 and G1, has a

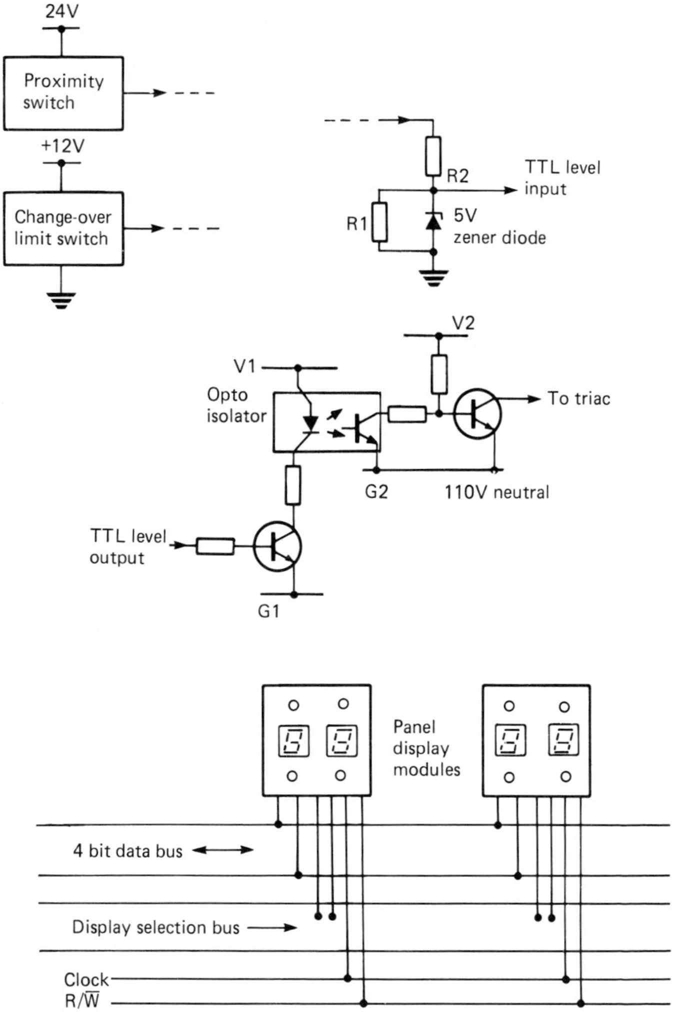

Fig. 8.6 I/O interfaces for the sequencer

common ground (G1) with the computer, the other, V2 and G2, common with the 110 volts. The inputs and outputs from the computer were provided by S100 boards having 80 separate inputs and outputs. The chips and circuit used are shown in Figures 6.1 and 6.2.

The front panel has change-over switches which interface to the computer as in the top diagram of Figure 8.6. In addition, the front panel includes lamps which are turned on and off by transistor interfaces similar to the ones shown turning opto-isolators on and off. However, the machine also needed a number of digital displays. This caused an immediate problem, as it was essential for both the operator and the computer to read and write to the displays. This was solved by the system shown at the foot of Figure 8.6. A common four-bit data bus is used to read and write data to the displays. Each display has its own select line from a special interface board, and an R/W line decides the data direction. The basic circuit is similar to Figure 7.3, except that the state of the displays can be read from the module. The display modules have up-down counters on board which are used to allow the operator to change the display. He presses a button above any display to increase the current number displayed, and presses the one below to reduce the number. A clock is fed to each display to control the speed with which this up or down counting occurs, and allows the computer to disallow any changes when required, by turning the clock off. The whole array simply plugs into part of an 80-way I/O board.

An important aspect of the front panel is that it represents the main method of supervision during the operation of setting up the machine. As this is a finely controlled process, the computer is used as an aid as far as possible. The principle is to store the complex data shown on the front panel onto cassette tape, so that the whole machine can be reset after power-up with the minimum of effort. This is particularly true for the heater controller described later. The computer must also allow the setter to experiment with the settings continuously during set-up. A full description of the extent to which this is allowed is beyond the scope of this book. However, broadly speaking, the computer allows a mode whereby the setter can adjust as many of the working parameters as he wishes while the cycle is continuing. By this means, he effectively builds up a complete set of front-panel values on the digital displays. This is then stored for future use. Needless to say, the set-up can be altered at any time, and the tape image retained at will. When the machine is to be put into operation, a key switch is turned, the key removed, and the machine's values are frozen to prevent any change to the settings. As the machine sequences, the various parameters on the panel change to inform the operator of the machine's status continuously.

As can be seen, the machine is quite large, weighing some 15 tons, and has a number of dangerous aspects. It was therefore necessary to include as many interlocks as possible to prevent a dangerous condition from occurring. However, it should be borne in mind that a serious spike along the mains, or a failure in the computer cabinet, may render its full control impossible at some instant. Such analogous occurrences are well known in relay circuitry, where a relay might stick on, or fail to act. To this end, it is absolutely necessary to interlock the pneumatic circuitry within any such machine. It should be self-protected from being able to enter a condition whereby large metal components can come into contact with others if the controller fails. This is a general principle which should always be considered.

The heater controller

Figure 8.7 shows the heater controller. The philosophy adopted for the control of the heaters was to write a calculated heater pattern into a block of RAM on a dedicated S100 board. This dedicated heater controller board continuously scans the RAM block, very much as a VDU does, and sends this data serially to serial-to-parallel converters. The outputs of these converters then switch the triacs connected directly to the heaters themselves. This philosophy has two major

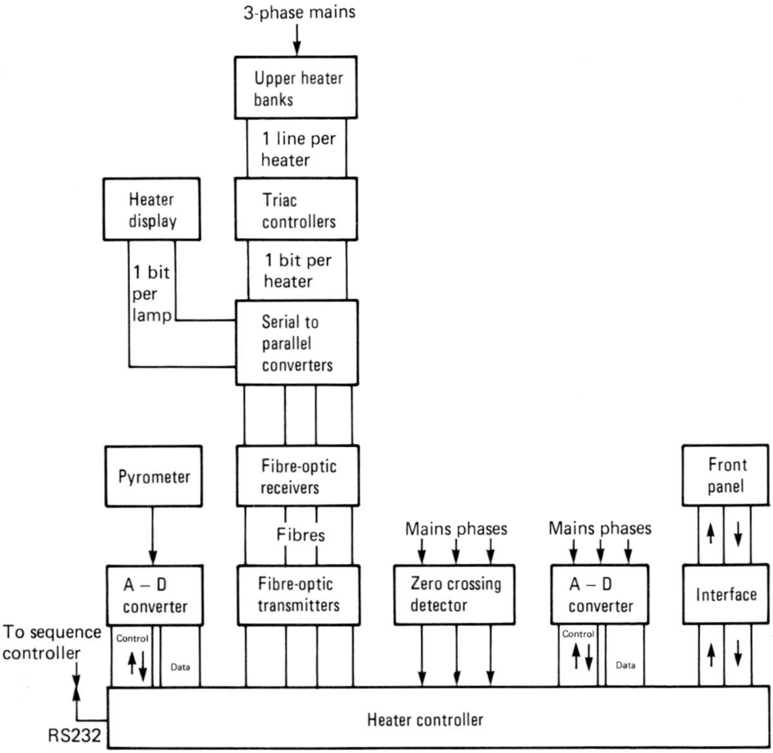

Fig. 8.7 Block diagram of thermoformer heater controller

advantages. First, the computer does not need one output bit per heater, with the attendant saving of wiring, output boards, power supply requirement, etc. Secondly, the software is only ever communicating with a block of internal memory, and may use all the fast and sophisticated machine-code instructions which that implies. Transformations may then be performed on the RAM data for such calculations as mains-voltage compensation. In addition, the new method of injecting heat into the plastic sheets involved superheating by applying an extra high-temperature time-dependent heater pattern. This required continual changes to the pattern on a fast time-scale.

It was decided to send the serial data along low-cost plastic fibre-optic cables, as this gives excellent noise-immunity, and total mains isolation. Four cables are required, one for the data, and one each for the clocks used to clock data into the serial-to-parallel converters. There are three clocks, as the whole system is divided into the three mains phases used for power. Each clock feeds to one line of serial-to-parallel converters, and controls the heaters connected to one mains phase. Figure 8.8 shows this process. Note that each heater has a corresponding display lamp, which may be seen in Figure 8.5 to be part of a mimic panel for the heater banks, on the side of the machine.

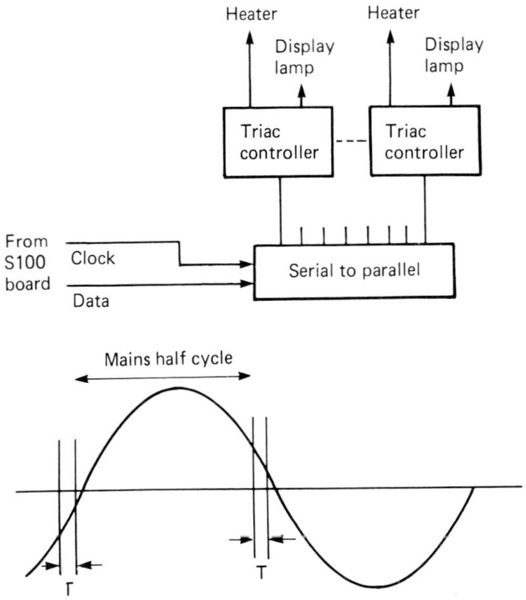

Fig. 8.8 Heater control

In addition to displaying the heating pattern, if a heater goes open-circuit its lamp remains extinguished as a signal.

The S100 board controlling the heaters takes in the three phase waveforms of the mains, and detects the zero-crossing point. This is used to synchronise the communication of data to the heaters. An accurate timer circuit creates a delay from the zero-crossing point until near the end of the current half-cycle. The data is then clocked into the serial-to-parallel converters in a high-speed burst before the half-cycle ends, within a time T, as shown. The converters are connected directly to the heaters through triac controllers similar to that shown in Figure 8.3. As the data is clocked through the converters, this changing data appears on the outputs, and triacs are switched on in a random pattern. However, the required pattern establishes itself just before the zero-crossing point, when all the triacs switch off. This period of random switch-on is kept very short, and causes no problems. As the next half-cycle begins, the turn-on pattern is stable, and just the triacs required turn on their heaters. This establishes the heater pattern. This process occurs 100 times per second, and a one-second frame is chosen for heater control, to match the thermal inertia of the quartz-clad elements. If, for instance, a given heater is switched on for just 63 of the 100 half-cycles within this frame, its effect is that of 63% on. In order to even out the on and off periods of the heaters, the calculation to produce the RAM data includes a routine which distributes the on and off periods as equally as possible over the full one-second frame. This prevents the heaters from pulsing on and off unacceptably. If the heater pattern is to remain constant, the RAM data does not change from second to second. If the mains voltage of one phase changes, it is necessary to recompute the complete set of data for all the heaters on that phase, and store it in the RAM. The same is true for the special superheating of the sheet, whereby the heater levels are taken high, and then progressively lowered to more normal values.

Figure 8.7 shows how the heater controller connects to a number of external devices. The mains phases are input for zero-crossing and for their voltages. A non-contact infra-red pyrometer is aimed at a representative spot on the sheet, to detect when the heating process is complete—a fact which is transmitted to the sequence controller along the RS232 line. The heater settings, both normal and for the superheating of the sheet, are sent along the RS232 line for storage on cassette tape when complete. Finally, the front panel has some heater-controller displays as described for the sequencer, along with a keyboard for entering heater settings. The heater controller is an S100 computer, and also has at least one 80-way I/O board.

This completes the overview of the thermoformer controller, and though there are several improvements possible to the basic system, a prime consideration is to ensure that a cost-effective system results.

Data collection and production control

The preceding examples were both of a hardware control nature, and can be considered to be placed within the class of robotic computers. Here we shall consider an application involving a broader class of controller, and interfacing to a more classical type of computer system for the purposes of data collection and production control. Such systems are found within manufacturing industry, for providing instantaneous information on the production process and allowing control of that process by properly constructed plans.

The problems of manufacture, apart from those associated with the specific process involved, are those of planning, and testing the plan. In an ideal world, a manufacturer would know how much cash there is locked up in 'work in progress', the production yield of each part of the factory instantaneously, the amount of raw material being wasted, and so on. It is well known that manufacturing company failure is often associated simply with a lack of knowledge of the basic parameters of the activity. Even in a small factory, a few simple packages to aid the directing of resources and ordering of stock can save quantities of money quite out of proportion to the price of a computer and software. This lesson is one which Japanese and American companies, in particular, have been very quick to learn.

In order for a company of any size to derive the full benefit of this type of system, it is essential to distribute data-collection units throughout the factory. These can be hand-operated systems, whereby work-observation personnel observe the process at key points, collect pieces of paper, and return to a central point to calculate yields and production-line down-times etc. by hand. By this means, the production planner, who knows, for instance, how much has been ordered and how much spare cash he has for raw material, can direct the operation. He can direct parts of the process to produce certain amounts, perhaps delay others, and generally plan the best use of his resources. It needs very little foresight to realise that a company of any size will find it extremely difficult to collect and collate data sufficiently quickly by hand, to allow a real-time analysis of the situation to be contemplated. It is quite possible, within a reasonable budget, to present figures on production yield, say, three days after the event. However, any problems which have occurred will only be rectifiable then. If problems can be detected quickly, their solutions can be applied in the same time-scale.

The other problem which hand-operated systems suffer from is inherent human inaccuracies. It is not easy for a human being to concentrate on a repetitive mechanical job for a full day—it is no reflection on any of us that we prefer interesting, creative work. The lack of accuracy in such systems can range from irritating to disastrous.

The solution is a computerised data-collection and planning-aid system which provides immediate access to data, in a ready-digested form, to allow production planning staff to appraise the situation and produce accurate plans. This section will not deal with the software aspects of the subject, but only describe the type of hardware required.

Once again, a case study is presented. A large food manufacturer, who has a hand-operated data-collection and production-planning system, wishes to automate the system. The factory is divided into a number of halls. As food is handled, the hardware of the system must conform to health standards, and any equipment on the shop-floor must be contained in stainless-steel boxes, which are capable of being wiped down.

Broadly speaking, raw material enters the hall through one door, it is processed, and exits through others. There are several production lines within each hall, and the raw material must be directed from the entry door to a line, and the exact amount of processed product must be collected, along with the amount of waste. By this means, a weekly and daily plan can be constructed, and the actual production figures compared with the intended figures. Any remedial action can be taken very quickly, as the computer system produces reports instantly. In addition, surprise orders, or the need to change the production plan, can be incorporated instantly.

In order to collect the data, a number of data-collection and production-control nodes are constructed and distributed about the production halls. One level of computer system spends its time collecting data from these nodes on a regular basis; another computer system, on a higher level, is used as a planning and reporting computer, taking its raw data from the level below as to the state of the shop-floor. This is illustrated in Figure 8.9. There are three levels of computer activity. Level 1 is situated in the production planning office, and consists of a number of computer systems connected together by a shared-resource network, or local area network (LAN). Such systems will be described later. This network has a large quantity of disk storage, and acts as the production controller for the entire factory. The next level consists of a number of computers which provide supervisory staff with continuous direct information on the state of the shop-floor at any time, as well as concentrating data from the nodes on the shop-floor. Level 3 consists of the actual hardware performing the data collection and control. Approximately 20 nodes

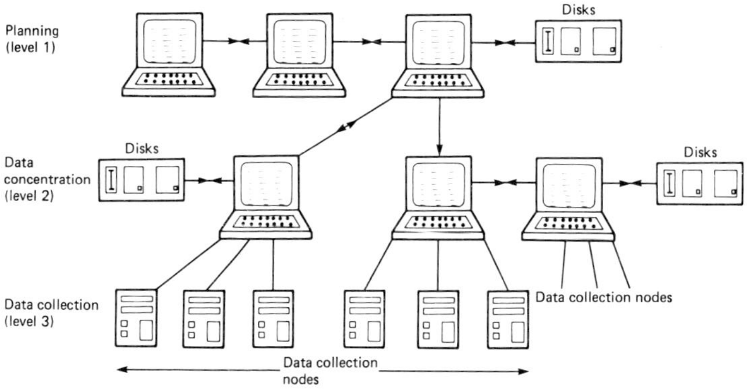

Fig. 8.9 Data-collection system

are used continuously to direct and monitor the activities of production, according to the current plan as constructed by the planners using level 1. We shall examine the nodes now in detail.

The process involved in this factory requires the operatives to wheel product in trolleys from areas and preparation rooms, out onto a set of scales and on to one of the production lines. The ideal place to control this part of the process is at the scales. Thus the nodes communicate with the scales used to weigh the product. The scales used here have RS232 outputs, as well as digital displays, and lend themselves well to interfacing with computer equipment. In addition to weight, it is up to the operator to input various parameters such as tare weight of the trolley, type of product, his own operator number etc. Thus a keyboard and display are required. An important parameter for the process is time, and hence the computer equipment must have a real-time clock included. This particular application also required a printer, to accumulate all transactions on a tally roll, within the node, for later checking if required, or to recreate all transactions in the event of a system failure. The data which the node accumulates is stored internally and sent to the computers in level 2 on demand. If the power fails the node retains its memory, and the clock continues to run, for many hours. If the main system should fail at level 2, the node is capable of accumulating data for a normal eight-hour shift without overflowing. If it does overflow, the complete memory can be printed out on the tally roll, and hence no transactions are lost. The factory is slowly going over to bar-codes, and it is important that the nodes can be connected to bar-code wands if required. Finally, the entire system within the factory is tied together by high-quality glass-fibre-optic lines, and communications between the computers proceed by a synchronous serial protocol. The nodes must contain fibre-optic transceivers.

The above constraints, along with various environmental ones, led to a design based around a six-slot S100 computer system. This would allow any type of data-collection situation and interface, in any part of the factory, to be included within the basic design. Figure 8.10

Fig. 8.10 Stainless-steel-clad data-collection node (courtesy Modus Systems Ltd)

shows one of the nodes, and Figure 8.11 shows a sketch of the hardware design. There is enough commonality with the computer systems to allow program development and emulation with ease. In addition, the food manufacturer is able to hold some spares in common with both the computers and the nodes. The only non-TTL devices here are the scales, fibre-optics and bar-code wand. The scales require RS232 level converters, the fibre-optics have their own transceiver boards which interface to TTL, and the bar-code wand just needs a TTL level Schmitt trigger such as the 74LS14 in order to supply its data. The power distribution within the node is a little involved, and care is taken to ensure that no hot-spots arise, and that the system

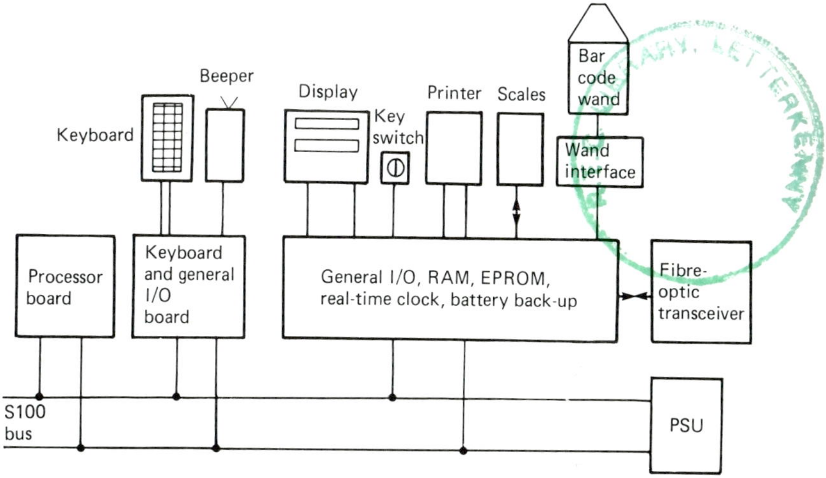

Fig. 8.11 Data-collection node

components are all decoupled from each other and any external noise which may occur. The keyboard chosen is a membrane type to allow the outside of the node to be wiped with a damp rag without damage. Such keyboards are normally manufactured to a British Standard which even demands that they be able to resist wiping down with a petrol-soaked rag.

Nodes of the type described above should be regarded as the 'eyes and ears' of the system. The system is only capable of 'seeing' the data which a node collects. It is of the utmost importance, therefore, that all parameters possible be included within the nodes' sight. The nodes are loaded with the production plan either via their RS232 lines from the computer systems or, in the event of system failure, manually by the supervisors. These data are used to direct production, and to correct mistakes by the operatives during the process. Nodes are also placed at points where the final product leaves the shop-floor, and at points where waste product collects. In this manner the loop is finally closed. The collection of data from the entire network of nodes gives the planners and directors exact information on the process of production, and allows them to correct shortfalls instantly.

Industry is sometimes slow in taking up the automation of its production processes. This is almost certainly due, in part, to the difficulty of proving cost-effectiveness before the fact. The savings appear intangible. However, these savings can be immense, and it is generally observed that the equipment rapidly becomes second nature to the users. It is often difficult for anyone to imagine the system before automation, let alone consider a return to hand-produced reporting. The success of any manufacturing system depends upon the systems analysis which is done before the equipment is specified and manufactured. It cannot be emphasised enough that the specification of the system must be constructed with great care before any design is contemplated. In many ways it was the rash and muddled organisation of many companies in the 1960s which gave computerisation a bad name for a number of years. Thankfully, it is the introduction of cheaper, flexible, and more accessible computer machinery which is at present leading industry to a new appraisal of automation and computer introduction. It is by no means a difficult matter to predict that, remarkable though the rise of the personal and small business computer has been, the most radical changes, yet to come, will be in the field of manufacturing industry. It is manufacture which is at the base of our prosperity, and it is certain that this is the market which provides the largest, almost untapped, potential for the use of computers in the future. One concept, which is rapidly finding its way to the very heart of the computer industry, is the subject of the next section.

Local area networks

Definitions of LANs abound in the literature. Common to most of them is the exclusion of the classical mainframe situation, where a large centralised computer system shuffles data to and from unintelligent VDUs. The disadvantages of this type of computer include extreme expense, the need for specially controlled environments, and the bottlenecking of a system where every keypress on every VDU keyboard must be attended to by the central computer itself.

LANs are simply collections of computers—and often their peripherals—connected to (usually serial) communication systems which allow the resources of the network to be shared. Thus, as for the centralised processor case, there may well be a central magnetic store, with files accessible by everyone. This file-sharing is one of the most valuable aspects of LANs. In the simplest case, a LAN may provide internal postal and communication systems, with the advantages of processing power at each terminal. The fact that each terminal is a computer system in its own right means that the total system is a collection of processors. The result is that, in terms of processing power, a system considerably more powerful than a mainframe can quickly be constructed. This concept is called 'distributed processing', and is a form of 'parallel processing'. In a mainframe installation, a program is normally running which 'time-shares'. This means that every user is given a certain proportion of the processor's processing time. Time-sharing is performed in a number of ways. One method is simply to allow a given time-period for each user, and at the end of that time-period the memory image of the data and program being used by that user is stored away to disk, and the next user's current memory image is fetched and executed for its time-period. This is complex, and means that each user must await his turn. The system is considerably refined on this crude description, but nevertheless there is only one processor in the system.

A LAN works by allowing each user to hold his own program and data continuously. The only time he must contend for time on the network is when he requires disk access, or the use of a communal printer. If the user cannot tolerate this wait, he may even have his own local disks upon which he works and, say, loads the completed files down to the main store at the end of the day. By this means, many users can be processing their own applications, with a minimum load on the system and minimum waiting time. It is not possible, of course, to apply these principles in all cases, and in a system where many users are using the central resources continuously the network will slow down appreciably.

There are many types of hardware set-up for networks, and a few will be described below. In general, the word 'topology' is used to describe the different ways in which the users' computers connect together to form the network. In addition, the users' computers are called 'nodes', as are any devices connected directly to the network communications link itself. There are three main topologies. They are 'star', 'closed ring' and 'open loop bus'. These are broad names at present, and some systems use combinations of topologies. Figure 8.12 illustrates some of the characteristics of the different topologies.

The star network has a central hub, which controls the entire system and where it is natural to hold the shared resources, though this is by no means necessary. If the hub should fail, the outlying processors cannot share the resources, but should be able to continue processing,

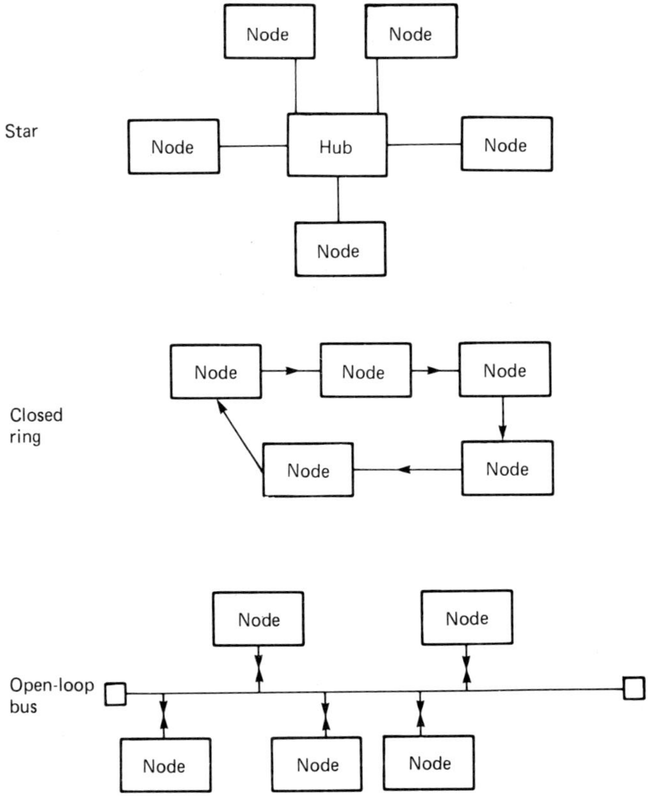

Fig. 8.12 Network topologies

particularly if they have their own local disks. A star network may well be connected to its outlying processors by RS232 links, of a synchronous or asynchronous nature.

The ring comes in many forms, but it is normal for data to proceed around the ring in one direction only, and to be passed on by each node until one of them recognises its own address. This node then removes the packet of data from the communications line, and replies to the sender that it has received it. If a node should fail, it is normal for a shorting link to come into play to allow it to be removed without bringing the whole system down. In addition, one of the other nodes should be capable of noticing a lack of communications on the network, and reporting the fault. Again, if one node computer is devoted to a given resource, the vulnerability of the resource is that of the node's vulnerability.

Bus topologies are among the fastest and most sophisticated forms of LAN. A length of cable, often a single coaxial cable, is normally used, and any node wishing to communicate with any other has to gain control of the network bus-line. If the line is busy, this node will detect a carrier waveform on the line, back off, and try again later. Once in control, a data packet is fed to the bus, and the address portion is recognised by the recipient. While the bus is in use, other nodes may try to gain control, but will be forced to wait when they sense the carrier of the node on the line. The type of problem encountered with such a system occurs when multiple nodes try to take control of the bus simultaneously. If they all back off and then immediately try again, they will never succeed. If they simply back off for the same given time, they will all try simultaneously, and their message packets will 'collide'. It is not possible to give each node its own unique back-off time, as new nodes would then have to be specially configured in some way, and the organisation of such a system would soon become cumbersome. The problem is solved by causing any collision to force each node to back off for a randomly selected time—each of them should eventually succeed. Much academic literature exists on the complex subject of back-off algorithms.

The application of this system has a general technical name—CSMA/CD. It stands for 'carrier sense multiple access with collision detect'. The system was invented by Xerox, in 1973, and forms the basis of a networking system of the bus type called 'Ethernet'. Any company employing this technique must purchase a license from Xerox for the product. This system has been adopted by Intel, and they are heavily committed to providing hardware and software as support. Any designer wishing to use the Ethernet standard should contact an Intel distributor for the specification manual. Ethernet is fast becoming a standard for the type of engineering which should be employed in networks, and the next section describes some of its attributes.

Ethernet

Ethernet is a local area network which was originally developed by Xerox, and later fully researched and specified by a collaboration between Xerox, Intel and DEC. As such, it has the backing of three of the most important names in the electronic computer field. The original specification will no doubt suffer change before being fully accepted, but must clearly be taken seriously as a future international standard. It is already a subject of debate, however, as to whether the designers should have used a medium other than base-band coax for the line. The advantage of a wider-band system would be the possible incorporation of all types of data transmission. Voice, video data and various other simple data links could all have been included within the Ethernet line, hence saving the necessity of stringing many different cables around the site. However, the argument against the more complex problem of allowing for general communications is that any given site will always have a large number of services such as mains electricity, water and gas, and adding more is a simple matter.

The Ethernet system is a bus topology networking system employing 10 MHz serial communications over a single base-band coaxial wire. It employs CSMA/CD techniques to resolve bus contention, and allows up to 1024 nodes, with a maximum node separation of 2·5 km.

Data is sent along the cable by an encoding method called 'Manchester encoding' which is illustrated in Figure 8.13. Each bit-time has a transition in the centre, and the bit's value is equal to the state of the line during the first half of the bit-time. The sequence 0010011 is shown being transmitted. As indicated previously, this type of

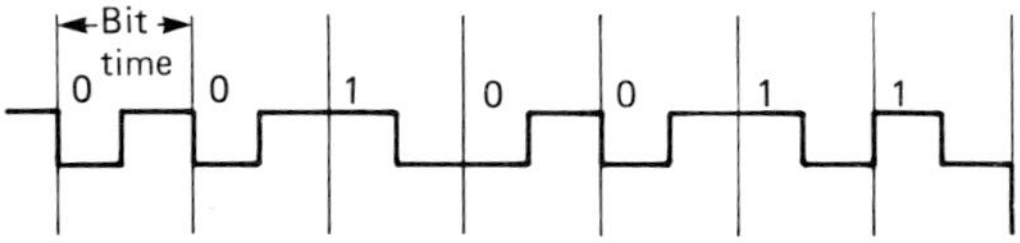

Fig. 8.13 Manchester encoding

transmission encoding is in general use in serial communications; apart from allowing high speed, it has two major advantages over asynchronous bit-for-bit transfer as used, for instance, between UAR/Ts. First, its simple AC nature allows the use of straightforward narrow-band AC-coupled amplifiers, along with excellent isolation components such as pulse transformers. Second, the clock used for transmission timing can be recovered from the transmitted waveform at the receiver. This allows full synchronisation of receiver and transmitter, without the need for a special clock line to be connected between them.

In order to employ the full potential of Ethernet, a set of repeaters would need to be placed along the cable. This keeps the cable segments down to the specified 500 metres, while allowing a tree structure to be incorporated. Figure 8.14 shows a typical large-scale implementation system. This shows the maximum of two repeaters and 1500 metres of coax which are allowed between any two stations. In addition, two remote repeaters are allowed with a maximum of 1000 metres point-to-point between. By this means, the 2500 metres maximum separation is attained. As can be seen, a moderately large site can be cabled

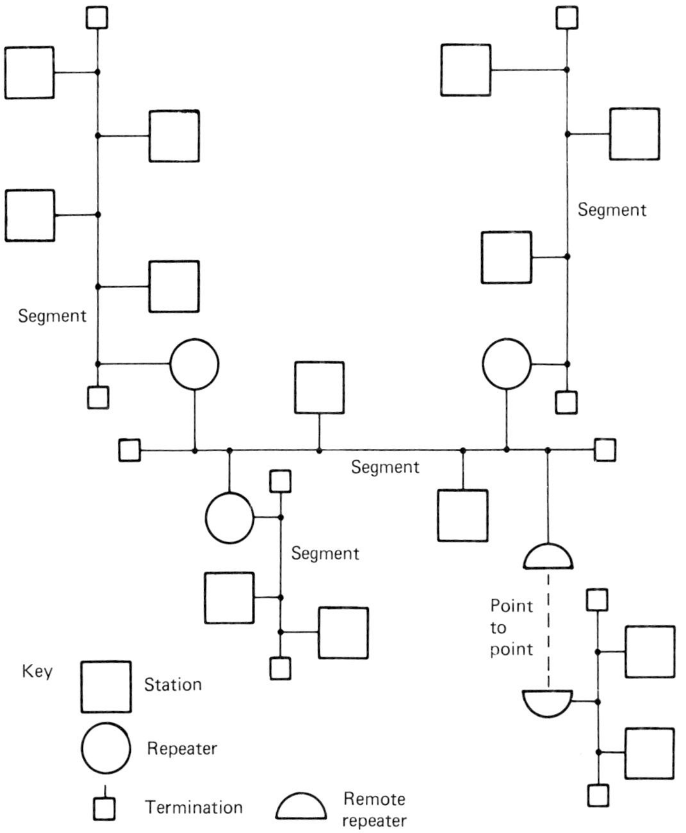

Fig. 8.14 Large-scale Ethernet system

throughout to provide a shared resource network with many different types of device tied together for any purpose required. A large data-collection and production-planning application would be an excellent example of its use.

The Ethernet specification includes statements about two 'layers'. The lowest layer, or 'physical layer', details the manner in which serial data is communicated along the coax. This includes electronic specifications, such as logic levels, actual waveforms and impedances, as well as methods for collision detection. The next layer above is called the 'data link layer' and specifies the manner in which data is collected into packets, error checking, addressing, framing of data, and collision management. The data link layer is media-independent.

A network which has a single link threading its way between all the nodes is termed a 'broadcast network'. A study of the Ethernet specification provides the network designer with an excellent set of design criteria for any type of broadcast network. Even if Ethernet itself is too sophisticated for a given application, there are several possible 'sub-Ethernet' designs which can be implemented to great effect.

Computer systems in general

Much of this book has been concerned with the concept of control, with the proviso that most of the design ideas incorporated within this area carry over to the design of systems. For full utilisation of the network philosophy, it is important to have well-designed computers to use as controlling stations, even if the majority of nodes are dedicated to data collection and production control. The types of system on the market for this purpose are manifold, and should be viewed with a number of criteria in mind. This section details some of the main characteristics of computers which are to be used in an industrial environment.

It is by no means of primary importance to consider the environmental shielding of a computer which is confined to the dry, clean offices where production plans are made and checked over the network. However, it is the author's experience that a customer who requires his system to perform to the utmost will very soon need computer terminals to be mounted next to the production process itself. Thus it would be doubling the work of design to confine one's efforts to the office environment. It is important that, besides being acceptable from a cosmetic point of view, the machinery be robust, protected, and easy to use by non-office staff. This leads the design along certain paths. First, it is an advantage to have a large screen to allow people to see the information displayed, even if they are not actually sitting down in front of the computer. Second, ease of maintenance is a must for machinery confined to a dusty dirty environment where there may be a certain amount of vibration, and where the users are heavy-handed. An important part of this is the need for a detachable, or easily removable and replaceable, keyboard, as this clearly takes the most wear. Detachability also allows the keyboard to be positioned at will—a desirable feature in the non-office environment.

As part of a network having disks as a shared resource, there is no advantage in incorporating disks within the case of the machine. The node computers are more like intelligent VDUs, and can benefit from the use of a maximum-sized CRT, by dispensing with the need to take up front-panel space with magnetic media slots. It is essential, however, to allow for the addition of magnetic media, if required, in a separate purpose-built case.

The question arises whether to use a single-board computer or a motherboard-based design. The major point to consider is flexibility. There is a great advantage in being able to plug in special boards, as required, for a variety of I/O functions. However, there are also advantages in the single-board approach. Single-board computers are cheaper to produce, and less dependent upon connectors holding the system together—they can be made very robust with ease. In fact the requirements of expansion and flexibility for the production environment are undoubtedly best served by a system which is a mix of the two concepts. A single-board computer will fit comfortably on a standard bus-system board such as S100, and can be constructed to run the bus at the same time. This gives the essential feature of expandability, while giving a compact and robust centre to the system. Certainly, for the reasons mentioned above, a single-board approach incorporating everything, including keyboard, is not recommended.

A useful system-level diagram is illustrated in Figure 8.15 to show the items which, in the author's experience, are incorporated in a single-board-based S100 system. The single-board computer contains all the elements needed for a computer system, except VDU and disk or network controller. The elements shown on the computer board will just fit on a single S100 board. The other boards on the bus depend upon the application.

If the computer is to be a node, a network controller will be required if the system is a broadcast network. Alternatively, if used in a star network, the spare serial data channel on the computer board may suffice. A VDU board will also be required. However, this may be considered unnecessary if one of the computer board's serial lines is used to communicate with a standard RS232 VDU with keyboard. By this means a low-cost but highly sophisticated system could be constructed, with the single-board computer not plugged into an S100 bus, but communicating to the user via the simple RS232 VDU.

If the computer is to be a node, with local disks and a dedicated applications use, all the boards shown in Figure 8.15 will be required.

The single-board approach described here has a further advantage as a consequence of its compact nature. It is not difficult to use these devices for a different kind of network from that described in the preceding work. Several of these boards may be plugged into the same S100 bus, and multiprocess to provide a network of computers over the S100 bus itself. This provides a restricted but fast method of tying several users together to share the resources plugged into the same S100 bus—such as disks. The users are connected into the system by using RS232 VDUs, each one connected to a serial line on one of the

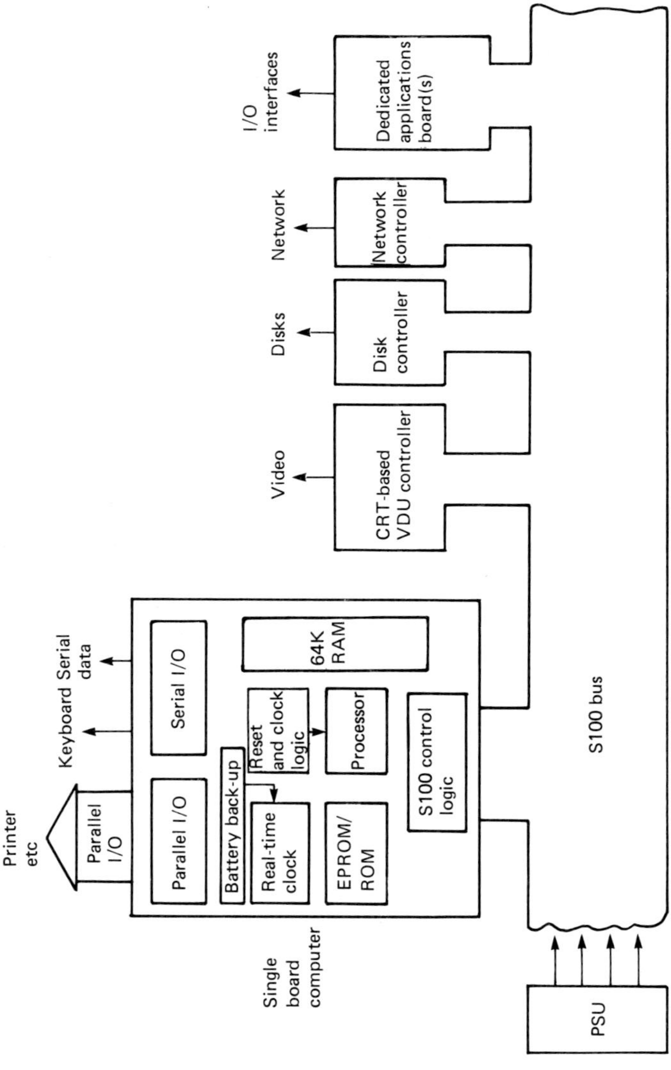

Fig. 8.15 Single-board-based S100 system

Fig. 8.16 Networking computer station with disk system containing up to 120 megabytes of storage (courtesy Modus Systems Ltd)

single-board computers. The system software is quite complex to ensure that there is no contention for the shared resources and the bus. Each user has a 64K RAM-based computer at its disposal for processing at any time, and can access the disks as required. Also, the VDUs communicating to the users can be connected by slow links, as the high-speed communications required to keep the system response fast are those over the S100 bus between the computer boards and the disk controllers.

A further approach for the single-board computer is to provide two or more completely separate processors within the same case, perhaps joined by fast parallel links. Each of these may be dedicated to a given task, such as printing reports or collecting data from a number of collection nodes, without causing the usual overhead on the main processing requirement being performed by another in the set. This can be a simple and effective method of multiprocessing where many simple mechanical tasks must be performed continuously.

The ideas described here are meant to provide some motivation for the type of design philosophy which has been adopted throughout the book. The majority of designs have focused on systems aimed at industrial uses of the microprocessor.

Appendix 1

Binary and hexadecimal number systems

This appendix provides material necessary for an understanding of the number systems employed in the study of MPUs. Very little binary arithmetic is required for this book, but the notation described below is vital.

Binary numbers

The 'base' (namely 10) of the number system we employ in our everyday life is certainly derived from the number of fingers and thumbs on our hands. The word digit, for instance, is used interchangeably to mean 'finger' or 'positive integer less than ten'. The actual numbers themselves, however, do not depend upon man's labelling. For instance, the number of eyes we have is labelled with the word 'two' or the sign '2'. That number, the second positive integer, may as well be labelled by any other squiggle on a piece of paper, and according to any other base, as long as we all agree to accept that new labelling. Computers use devices which have just two active states—'on' and 'off' or '1' and '0'. This means that a succession of 1s and 0s must be employed to encode or label every piece of information which a computer wishes to hold or communicate. In principle, this labelling may be achieved in any way we may choose. For instance, suppose we were all to agree to represent a 2 by 11001, a 3 by 0011, etc. in any random manner, the computer could still hold and communicate all its data. However, imagine trying to perform arithmetic with such an illogical and random method of coding the numbers. The problem would be of the same order as that encountered by the Romans with their number-labelling system! It is necessary to find a logical and arithmetically straightforward labelling of the numbers using just 1s and 0s. This is done by examining the familiar decimal system of our normal life, and generalising to a binary system dependent upon digits having just two states instead of ten.

Consider the number:

1578

This number is composed of 1 'thousand', 5 'hundreds', 7 'tens' and 8 'ones'. The essential point is that this number has been broken down into single digits multiplied by powers of 10. For instance, the most significant digit (MSD) is 1—this implies that the number contains 1 times a thousand, or 1 times 10 raised to the third power. The number 1578, therefore, should really be written as:

$$1 \times 10^3 \quad + \quad 5 \times 10^2 \quad + \quad 7 \times 10^1 \quad + \quad 8 \times 10^0$$

Notice that 10 raised to the power 0 is equal to 1. If we were to write all our numbers in this long-winded form, our arithmetic would be cumbersome, but still possible.

For numbers expressed in other bases we can similarly split the numbers into digits multiplied by powers of the base. The number of digits available in any base is equal to the base itself—starting at zero. Thus, in decimal, ten digits are employed from 0 to 9. If we were to employ 2 as the base, numbers would be expressed in the following type of form:

11000101010

using just two digits—0 and 1. To work out the decimal representation of this number, the number should be written out in the long-winded form:

$$1 \times 2^{10} + 1 \times 2^9 + 0 \times 2^8 + 0 \times 2^7 + 0 \times 2^6 + 1 \times 2^5 + 0 \times 2^4 + 1 \times 2^3 + 0 \times 2^2 + 1 \times 2^1 + 0 \times 2^0$$

Just as before, every power of the base is represented up to the largest power required for this number. Any larger powers would all be multiplied by zero, as they are not required to be added in. This number can be reduced to:

$$1024 + 512 + 32 + 8 + 2 = 1578$$

leaving out the zero components. Hence the two representations above, one in decimal and one in binary, are equal—they are exactly the same number, with different labelling. A common notation to emphasise the base being used would be:

$$(11000101010)_2 = (1578)_{10}$$

The subscripts denote the bases.

If a numbering system has just two digits at its disposal, therefore, it is wise to stick to the above system of coding the numbers. The rules of arithmetic are exactly the same as for decimal, but restricted to fewer digits. It is clear from the above that the binary representation of numbers is cumbersome in terms of the quantity of actual digits required to represent any number. For this reason, it is helpful to the humans using computers for the binary digits, or bits, to be grouped together in threes or fours. Consider a grouping of the above number into threes, shown below. Any group of three bits can have one of eight bit patterns, and it is useful to represent these different bit patterns by the digits 0 to 7. That is, (000) is represented by 0, (001) is represented by 1 etc., to (111) which is represented by 7. Therefore only the eight digits from 0 to 7 are required to represent the above binary number into a more manageable form as follows:

011	000	101	010
3	0	5	2

The binary number 11000101010 has been split into groups of three bits, with a zero added at the left-hand side to make up the numbers. Beneath each group is the representation, using numbers between 0 and 7. This representation is called *octal*, as it uses eight digits. Thus the number above may be expressed as:

$$(11000101010)_2 = (3052)_8 = (1578)_{10}$$

The octal system is a representation to the base 8. However, MPUs normally group their bits in 8s or 4s, and so another system is more appropriate. Groups of four are normally chosen, and these groups therefore require enough digits to be able to represent the numbers 0000 to 1111—a total of 16 patterns. These numbers are 0 to 15, in decimal. The labels chosen for the 16 digits are the normal 10 (0–9) of the decimal system plus the letters A–F. Thus this *hexadecimal* ('hex' for short) or base 16 system has the following digits, with their binary and decimal equivalents:

Hex	*Decimal*	*Binary*	*Hex*	*Decimal*	*Binary*
0	0	0000	8	8	1000
1	1	0001	9	9	1001
2	2	0010	A	10	1010
3	3	0011	B	11	1011
4	4	0100	C	12	1100
5	5	0101	D	13	1101
6	6	0110	E	14	1110
7	7	0111	F	15	1111

This table should be borne in mind for all the chapters of this book, and indeed for any other works on MPUs.

The number 1578, therefore, is represented in hex as:

0110 0010 1010
6 2 A

The representation 62A is even more compact than the decimal representation of this number, and thus computer coding of even quite large numbers can easily be grasped and remembered by the human user. In addition, by the method of grouping above, hex and binary can be interchanged with great ease.

The hex system may be converted to decimal in just the same way, by powers of 16, as for the binary system (or any other system). For instance, using the table above, 62A (hex) can be written as:

$$6 \times 16^2 + 2 \times 16^1 + A \times 16^0 = 6 \times 256 + 2 \times 16 + 10 \times 1 = 1578_{10}$$

As usual, the powers start on the right with 0 (any number to the power 0 equals 1).

Binary states

It is important to realise that the state of any group of lines within a computer can be represented by a binary number. For instance, a group of eight pins on an MPU chip which may serve some special purpose can be arranged in order, and the 1s and 0s on these lines at any instant can be written as a binary number. The decimal number associated with such a state would be between 0 and 255. The reason for this is that eight lines can have states between 00000000 and 11111111. The first of these numbers is, of course, 0. The second can be understood by the method of grouping:

$$1111\ 1111 = FF = 15 \times 16^1 + 15 \times 16^0 = 255$$

Thus there are 256 different states on eight lines, which may be labelled by the hex numbers from 0 (or 00) to FF. It should be borne in mind constantly that objects are normally to be numbered from zero.

The MPUs described in this book have two major groups of lines. One is an eight-way 'bus' called the data bus, and the other a 16-way bus called the address bus. From the above, there are 256 different states for the data bus; you can work out for yourself that the address bus may take a total of 65 536 different states.

The K notation

To represent large numbers, we normally think in terms of hundreds, thousands, etc. This is inappropriate for computers, which are based on the binary system, and a more convenient form of numbering consists of units of 1024 or 2^{10}. This is conveniently near to 1000, and computer language has grown up to use the notation 'K' to mean units of 1024. (This should not be confused with the SI prefix 'k' (kilo-) which means one thousand.) Thus 1K = 1024, 2K = 2048, etc. The address bus, therefore, may take 64K different states, and the data bus, one-quarter of a K. It will be seen that the different states of the address bus are simply different 'addresses' or labels for the memory locations which may be resident within the MPUs described in this book. Thus the MPUs here may take up to 64K of memory locations. The data bus, however, is used to transfer the data stored in those locations, and hence only numbers from 0 to 255 may be stored at any location.

Bits and bytes

The 0 and 1 digits are called binary digits or *bits* for short. As can be seen, 4, 8 and 16 are important quantities in MPUs, and the first two of these numbers are given special names. Four bits are referred to as a *nybble*, which may be written using one hex digit, and eight bits as a *byte*, requiring two hex digits. The 'memory word length' (data stored in a memory location) of the MPUs described here is therefore a single byte. An address takes up two bytes and requires four hex digits, so it is not possible to store an address (16 bits) in a memory location. If an address has to be stored in memory, it must be stored as two bytes.

Binary arithmetic

Addition, subtraction, etc., may be performed in the binary, and hex number systems in exactly the same way as we normally perform such operations on decimal numbers. To see this, consider the decimal addition:

```
   5619
 + 7102
 ------
 1 2721
 ------
 1   1
```

The numbers underneath the answer are the usual 'carries' which are necessary during the addition. A carry is said to occur when the addition of the two digits in a given column gives an answer greater than the base—i.e. 10. Note, also, that despite the fact that the operands were four digits in length, the answer has overflowed to a fifth digit.

Now consider the addition of two bits. If 0 and 0 are added, the answer is, of course, 0. If 0 and 1 are added, the answer is 1. If, however, 1 and 1 are added together, the answer is in fact 2 (in decimal), which in binary (see the table above) is written '10'—an overflow to the next digital place has occurred. Addition of binary numbers is performed by stringing together one-bit additions. For instance:

```
  10
+ 01
 ---
  11
 ---
```

In this case, no carry from column to column is needed. Consider, however, the following:

```
  10
+ 10
 ---
 100
 ---
 1
```

In this case, the first column was $0+0=0$, the second was $1+1=10$, and a carry was performed.

As mentioned above, the word length of the MPUs here is eight bits or one byte. The MPU data, therefore, is often stored as complete bytes, and these bytes have to participate in arithmetic operations. Here is an example of an eight-bit addition:

```
  11100101
+ 10110101
 ---------
 110011010
 ---------
 111  1 1
```

The result of this addition is nine bits in length, and cannot therefore be stored in a single location in memory. The MPU has a special provision for this common type of problem. The lower (i.e. right hand) eight-bits are stored as a single byte, and the most significant bit (MSB) is stored in a special one-bit location within the MPU, called the 'carry flag'. In this manner, additions of many more than eight-bits precision may be performed in eight-bit segments, with the carry flag forming the link to take carries from byte to byte. Similar techniques are used for the other arithmetic operations.

Finally, hex arithmetic is performed in exactly the same way. Each pair of digits in a column may be added and a carry performed if the addition overflows above 15. Verify the following examples for yourself, using the hex to decimal equivalents given above:

$$A+3=D, \quad E+A=18, \quad A13E+BC5E=15D9C$$

It is also worthwhile converting both operands and answers into decimal and checking the results.

BCD number coding

To store decimal numbers in a computer, it is helpful for the process of conversion to and from binary to encode the decimal digit by digit. However, it would be a waste of memory space to encode each digit by a whole byte in memory. It is possible to pack two decimal digits in a byte. The table above shows that any of the ten decimal digits can be represented by just four bits. The binary coded decimal (BCD) system sets aside four bits for each decimal digit, and thus gives the following coding:

Decimal	*BCD*	*Decimal*	*BCD*
0	0000	5	0101
1	0001	6	0110
2	0010	7	0111
3	0011	8	1000
4	0100	9	1001

Coding each digit in this manner would mean that the number 1578 would be stored in two bytes as 00010101 and 01111000 using BCD. This is a total of 16 bits, and is quite different from the binary representation of this number given above. This coding for numbers should not be confused with binary itself. Arithmetic can be performed on these numbers quite easily, but most importantly, the conversion to and from decimal is straightforward.

Logical operations

There are four main logical operations which are required for an understanding of MPUs. These are NOT (or 1's complement), AND, OR and XOR. They follow the usual meanings of these terms applied to digital logic gates. The NOT function simply complements a bit, or a byte by turning all 1s to 0s and vice versa. AND follows the following truth table, where bits labelled A and B are shown 'ANDed' for each possible combination of states:

A	B	A AND B
0	0	0
0	1	0
1	0	0
1	1	1

If this is applied to bytes, the AND function is applied to each pair of bits in each position within the bytes. For example, 3F AND A5 gives:

	00111111	(3F)
AND	10100101	(A5)
	00100101	(25)

The OR function has the following truth table:

A	B	A OR B
0	0	0
0	1	1
1	0	1
1	1	1

Again, bytes are treated bit by bit. Thus 3F OR A5 is as follows:

	00111111	(3F)
OR	10100101	(A5)
	10111111	(BF)

Exclusive OR or XOR is as follows:

A	B	A XOR B
0	0	0
0	1	1
1	0	1
1	1	0

This is similar to OR, but if both bits are the same the answer is 0. This can be regarded, for instance, as a method of determining whether two bits are equal. 3F XOR A5 is shown below:

	00111111	(3F)
XOR	10100101	(A5)
	10011010	(9A)

Applications of these logical operations are manifold. Some examples are given below. On the Z80, a given bit in the accumulator may be examined to determine whether it is 1 or 0 by a machine-code instruction. Very few other MPUs have this facility. However, this is hardly a disadvantage as the XOR instruction may be used to perform the same function. For instance, if it is required to test bit 3 of the accumulator, XOR with 08 will yield 08 if the bit is set to 0, and 00 otherwise, which may be used directly by a branch instruction. The logic is shown in the following:

	xxxx0xxx	(Accumulator)
XOR	00001000	(08)
	00001000	(08)

	xxxx1xxx	(Accumulator)
XOR	00001000	(08)
	00000000	(00)

where 'x' is any bit state.

Another use for these operations would be for separating a byte into two halves and storing them in separate locations. If the byte AD, for instance, is resident in the accumulator, it should first be stored in a temporary storage location, as the operations on the accumulator destroy its contents. The accumulator is first ANDed with F0. This places 0 in the lower half, without affecting the upper half, and the result may be stored where required. The temporary location is then used to restore the accumulator which is ANDed with 0F to separate the other half. The logic is shown below:

Accumulator	10101101	(AD)		10101101	(AD)
AND	00001111	(0F)	AND	11110000	(F0)
	00001101	(0D)		10100000	(A0)

Hence, the accumulator contents have been separated into two halves, with 0000 in the other halves. This type of operation will be referred to in the next section.

ASCII code

The need continually arises for a method of storing all the symbols of human language, such as letters, punctuation marks, special characters, etc. There is no need for these codes to conform to arithmetic laws as they do not participate in arithmetic operations. Therefore, an international code for the labelling of these objects has been agreed to ensure that everyone communicates in a similar manner. The ASCII code is the most universal such code for microcomputers. ASCII stands for American Standard Code for Information Interchange. The basic code contains 128 seven-bit codes for all the upper- and lower-case letters, the numbers, the punctuation marks and a group of command codes which are standard codes used for signalling the state of a computer system, or for commanding a peripheral to perform some action. For instance, there is a standard delete character called 'DEL' and having the code 7F. This is meant to be interpreted by the peripheral to rub out the previous character sent. This ASCII code is the final code in the set. Note that it is written as a two-hex-digit number, and that the top bit of the number is 0. The ASCII codes occupy the numbers from 00 to 7F. These codes are given in Appendix 2.

To write the contents of the accumulator as two ASCII codes, perhaps for printing, the contents must first be separated into two hex digits in two separate locations. A routine may then be performed to turn each half into an eight-bit code, the lower seven bits of which contain the ASCII for each hex digit in the original accumulator contents. This routine would contain a number of logical operations, and is left as an exercise for the reader.

Summary

(a) The states of groups of lines in an MPU system may be represented by binary numbers.
(b) Binary numbers are composed of bits (1s and 0s), which may be conveniently grouped into fours (nybbles) and eights (bytes).
(c) Four bits can be represented by one hex digit.
(d) A byte is represented by two hex digits.
(e) Memory locations are addressed by 16 bits (represented by four hex digits), and they contain eight bits (represented by two hex digits).
(f) Decimal numbers may be represented in BCD by representing each digit by four bits.
(g) ASCII codes from 00 to 7F are used to store or communicate any character in a standard manner.

Appendix 2
The ASCII codes

The table given here contains hexadecimal and decimal codes for the ASCII set. This set may be split into the following areas.

00 to 1F (hex) These are the control codes which a VDU or printer would not normally print out, but which are used in some systems to mean commands or signals of various types. A standard ASCII keyboard would produce these codes using the 'control' key. The notation 'ctrl D', for instance, implies that the D key is depressed while the control key is pressed.

20 to 2F Some special characters, from SPACE (20) to / (2F).

30 to 39 Decimal digits 0 to 9.

3A to 40 More special characters, from : to @.

41 to 5A Upper-case letters A to Z.

5B to 60 More special characters, from [to '.

61 to 7A Lower-case letters a to z.

7B to 7F Some special characters, from { to DEL.

Note that the upper hex digit is always below 7. This means that the ASCII codes all have their most significant bit equal to 0.

Character		*Hex*	*Decimal*
NUL	(crtl @)	00	0
SOH	(ctrl A)	01	1
STX	(ctrl B)	02	2
ETX	(ctrl C)	03	3
EOT	(ctrl D)	04	4
ENQ	(ctrl E)	05	5
ACK	(ctrl F)	06	6
BEL	(ctrl G)	07	7
BS	(ctrl H)	08	8
TAB	(ctrl I)	09	9
LF	(ctrl J)	0A	10
VT	(ctrl K)	0B	11
FF	(ctrl L)	0C	12
CR	(ctrl M)	0D	13
SO	(ctrl N)	0E	14
SI	(ctrl O)	0F	15
DLE	(ctrl P)	10	16
DC1	(ctrl Q)	11	17
DC2	(ctrl R)	12	18
DC3	(ctrl S)	13	19
DC4	(ctrl T)	14	20
NAK	(ctrl U)	15	21

Appendix 2

Character	*Hex*	*Decimal*
SYN (ctrl V)	16	22
ETB (ctrl W)	17	23
CAN (ctrl X)	18	24
EM (ctrl Y)	19	25
SUB (ctrl Z)	1A	26
ESC (ctrl [)	1B	27
FS (ctrl \)	1C	28
GS (ctrl])	1D	29
RS (ctrl∧)	1E	30
US (ctrl _)	1F	31
SPACE	20	32
!	21	33
"	22	34
£	23	35
$	24	36
%	25	37
&	26	38
’	27	39
(	28	40
)	29	41
*	2A	42
+	2B	43
,	2C	44
–	2D	45
.	2E	46
/	2F	47
0	30	48
1	31	49
2	32	50
3	33	51
4	34	52
5	35	53
6	36	54
7	37	55
8	38	56
9	39	57
:	3A	58
;	3B	59
<	3C	60
=	3D	61
>	3E	62
?	3F	63
@	40	64
A	41	65
B	42	66
C	43	67
D	44	68
E	45	69
F	46	70
G	47	71
H	48	72
I	49	73
J	4A	74
K	4B	75
L	4C	76
M	4D	77
N	4E	78
O	4F	79
P	50	80
Q	51	81
R	52	82
S	53	83
T	54	84
U	55	85
V	56	86
W	57	87
X	58	88
Y	59	89
Z	5A	90
[	5B	91
\	5C	92
]	5D	93
∧	5E	94
_	5F	95
‘	60	96
a	61	97
b	62	98
c	63	99
d	64	100
e	65	101
f	66	102
g	67	103
h	68	104
i	69	105
j	6A	106
k	6B	107
l	6C	108
m	6D	109
n	6E	110
o	6F	111
p	70	112
q	71	113
r	72	114
s	73	115
t	74	116
u	75	117
v	76	118
w	77	119
x	78	120
y	79	121
z	7A	122
{	7B	123
|	7C	124
}	7D	125
~	7E	126
DEL	7F	127

Appendix 3

S100 bus lines

This appendix gives the pin assignments of the S100 bus in tabular form for quick reference.

Symbols. A ‘P’ prefix denotes a processor command/control signal. ‘S’ denotes a processor status signal.

Loading. All inputs to a card are loaded with a maximum of one TTL low-power load.

Level. All bus signals except those for the power supply are TTL compatible. Signals whose names are barred ($\overline{\text{DO DSBL}}$, for example) are active low (0 volts). All others are active high (+5 volts).

Number	*Symbol*	*Name*	*Function*
1	+8V	+8 volts	Unregulated input to 5 volt regulators.
2	+18V	+18 volts	Positive unregulated voltage.
3	XRDY	External ready	For special applications: pulling this line low causes the processor to enter a wait state and allows the status of the normal ready line (PRDY) to be examined.
4	VI 0	Vectored interrupt	Line 0
5	VI 1	Vectored interrupt	Line 1
6	VI 2	Vectored interrupt	Line 2
7	VI 3	Vectored interrupt	Line 3
8	VI 4	Vectored interrupt	Line 4
9	VI 5	Vectored interrupt	Line 5
10	VI 6	Vectored interrupt	Line 6
11	VI 7	Vectored interrupt	Line 7
12	XRDY2	Extra ready line	For special applications.
13 to 17			To be assigned.
18	$\overline{\text{STA DSB}}$	$\overline{\text{STATUS DISABLE}}$	Puts buffers for the eight status lines in their high-impedance third state. In this state, no information can be transferred.
19	$\overline{\text{C/C DSB}}$	$\overline{\text{COMMAND/}}$ $\overline{\text{CONTROL}}$ $\overline{\text{DISABLE}}$	Puts the buffers for the six command/control lines in their high-impedance third state.
20			

Number	*Symbol*	*Name*	*Function*
20			
21	SS	SINGLE STEP	Indicates that the computer is in the process of performing a single step.
22	$\overline{\text{ADD DSB}}$	$\overline{\text{ADDRESS DISABLE}}$	Puts the buffers for the 16 address lines in their high-impedance third state.
23	$\overline{\text{DO DSBL}}$	$\overline{\text{DATA OUT DISABLE}}$	Puts the buffers for the eight data-out lines in their high-impedance third state.
24	$\Phi 2$	Phase 2 clock	
25	$\Phi 1$	Phase 1 clock	
26	PHLDA	Hold acknowledge	Processor output signal which appears in response to the HOLD signal indicates that the data and address buffers will go to the high-impedance third state.
27	PWAIT	WAIT	Processor output indicates that the processor is in the WAIT state.
28	PINTE	Interrupt enable	Indicates interrupts are enabled; displays contents of the CPU interrupt flip-flop. This flip-flop may be set or reset by the EI or DI instructions. When reset, it prevents the CPU from acknowledging interrupt requests.
29	A5	Address line 5	
30	A4	Address line 4	
31	A3	Address line 3	
32	A15	Address line 15	
33	A12	Address line 12	
34	A9	Address line 9	
35	DO1	Data-out line 1	
36	DO0	Data-out line 0	
37	A10	Address line 10	
38	DO4	Data-out line 4	
39	DO5	Data-out line 5	
40	DO6	Data-out line 6	
41	D12	Data-in line 2	
42	D13	Data-in line 3	
43	DI7	Data-in line 7	
44	SM1	M1	Status output that indicates that the processor is in the fetch cycle for the first byte of an instruction.
45	SOUT	OUT	Indicates that the address bus contains the address of an output device and the data bus will contain the output data when PWR is active.
46	SINP	INP	Indicates that the address bus contains the address of an input device.
47	SMEMR	MEMR	Indicates that the data bus will carry memory read data.
48	SHLTA	HLTA	Acknowledges a HALT instruction.

Number	*Symbol*	*Name*	*Function*
49	$\overline{\text{CLOCK}}$	$\overline{\text{Clock}}$	Inverted output of the 2 MHz oscillator that drives the clock.
50	GND	Ground	
51	+8V	+8 volts	
52	−18V	−18 volts	
53			
54	$\overline{\text{EXT CLR}}$	$\overline{\text{EXTERNAL CLEAR}}$	Clear signal for I/O devices.
55 to 67			To be assigned.
68	MWRT	MEMORY WRITE	Indicates that the current data on the data-out bus is to be written into the memory location currently on the address bus.
69			
70			
71	RUN	RUN	Indicates that the RUN/STOP flip-flop is reset.
72	PRDY	READY	Input that controls the run state of the processor. If the line is pulled low the processor will enter a WAIT state until it is released.
73	$\overline{\text{PINT}}$	$\overline{\text{INTERRUPT REQUEST}}$	The processor recognises a request on this line at the end of the current instruction or while halted. If the processor is in the HOLD state or the interrupt-enable flip-flop is reset it will not honour the request.
74	$\overline{\text{PHOLD}}$	$\overline{\text{HOLD}}$	Requests the processor to enter the HOLD state. This allows an external device to gain control of the bus as soon as the processor has completed its current machine cycle.
75	$\overline{\text{PRESET}}$	$\overline{\text{RESET}}$	May be connected to a RESET button.
76	PSYNC	SYNC	Provides a signal to indicate the beginning of each machine cycle.
77	$\overline{\text{PWR}}$	$\overline{\text{WRITE}}$	Used for memory write or I/O control. Data on the data bus are stable while PWR is active.
78	PDBIN	DATA BUS IN	Indicates to external devices that the data bus is in input mode.
79	A0	Address line 0	
80	A1	Address line 1	
81	A2	Address line 2	
82	A6	Address line 6	
83	A7	Address line 7	
84	A8	Address line 8	
85	A13	Address line 13	
86	A14	Address line 14	
87	A11	Address line 11	
88	DO2	Data-out line 2	
89	DO3	Data-out line 3	

Number	*Symbol*	*Name*	*Function*
90	DO7	Data-out line 7	
91	DI4	Data-in line 4	
92	DI5	Data-in line 5	
93	DI6	Data-in line 6	
94	DI1	Data-in line 1	
95	DI0	Data-in line 0	
96	SINTA	INTA	Acknowledges signal for interrupt request.
97	$\overline{\text{SWO}}$	$\overline{\text{WRITE OUT}}$	Indicates that the operation in the current machine cycle is a WRITE memory or output function.
98	SSTACK	STACK	Indicates that the address bus holds the push down stack address from the stack pointer.
99	$\overline{\text{POC}}$	$\overline{\text{Power-on-clear}}$	
100	GND	Ground	

Appendix 4

Data on three typical microprocessors

This appendix gives the pin assignments and a brief description of the Z80, 6800 and 1802 microprocessors.

The Z80 microprocessor

A0–A15 (address bus) Tri-state output, active high. A0–A15 constitute a 16-bit address bus. The address bus provides the address for memory (up to 64K bytes) data exchanges and for I/O device data exchanges. I/O addressing uses the eight lower address bits to allow the user to directly select up to 256 input or 256 output ports.

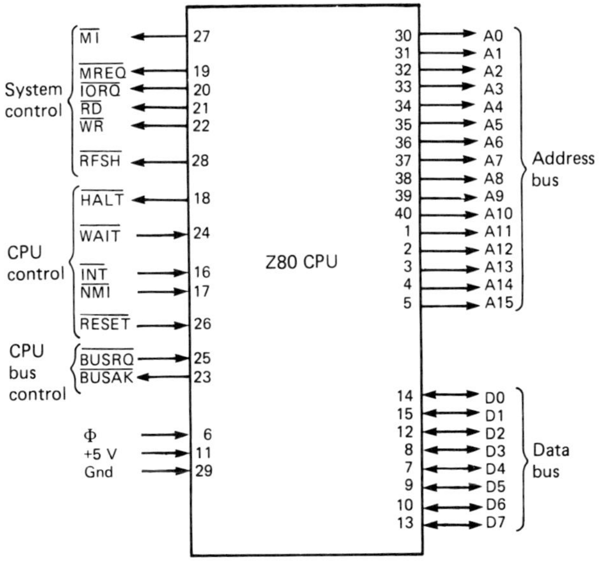

Fig. A4.1 Z80 pin configuration

A0 is the least significant address bit. During refresh time, the lower seven bits contain a valid refresh address.

D0–D7 (data bus) Tri-state input/output, active high. D0–D7 constitute an eight-bit bidirectional data bus. The data bus is used for data exchanges with memory and I/O devices.

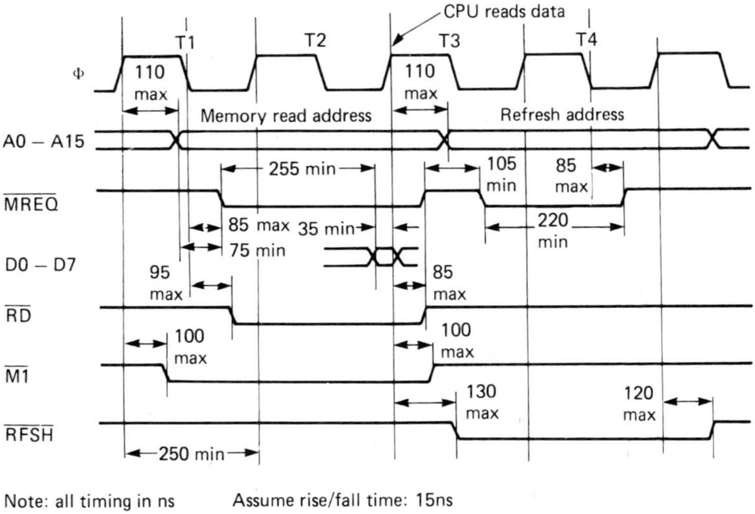

Fig. A4.2 Z80A CPU opcode fetch cycle timing at 4 MHz clock

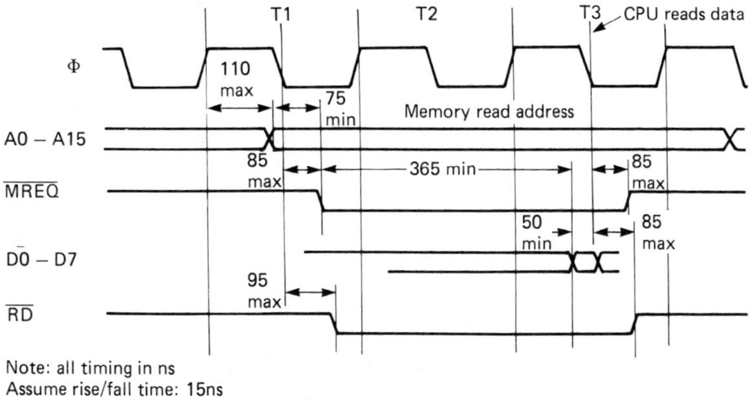

Fig. A4.3 Z80A CPU read cycle timing at 4 MHz clock

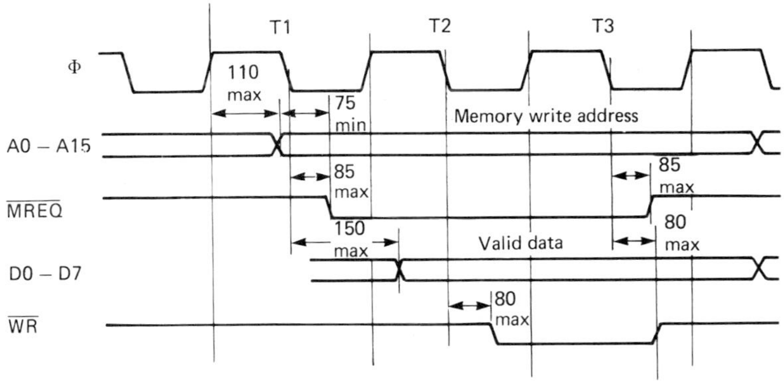

Note: all timing in ns   Assume rise/fall time: 15ns

Fig. A4.4 Z80A CPU write cycle timing at 4 MHz clock

$\overline{\mathrm{M1}}$ (machine cycle one) Output, active low. $\overline{\mathrm{M1}}$ indicates that the current machine cycle is the opcode fetch cycle of an instruction execution. Note that during execution of two-byte opcodes, $\overline{\mathrm{M1}}$ is generated as each opcode byte is fetched. These two-byte opcodes always begin with CBH, DDH, EDH, or FDH. $\overline{\mathrm{M1}}$ also occurs with $\overline{\mathrm{IORQ}}$ to indicate an interrupt acknowledge cycle.

$\overline{\mathrm{MREQ}}$ (memory request) Tri-state output, active low. The memory request signal indicates that the address bus holds a valid address for a memory read or memory write operation.

$\overline{\mathrm{IORQ}}$ (input/output request) Tri-state output, active low. The $\overline{\mathrm{IORQ}}$ signal indicates that the lower half of the address bus holds a valid I/O address for an I/O read or write operation. An $\overline{\mathrm{IORQ}}$ signal is also generated with an $\overline{\mathrm{M1}}$ signal when an interrupt is being acknowledged to indicate that an interrupt response vector can be placed on the data bus. Interrupt acknowledge operations occur during M1 time; I/O operations never occur during M1 time.

$\overline{\mathrm{RD}}$ (memory read) Tri-state output, active low. $\overline{\mathrm{RD}}$ indicates that the CPU wants to read data from memory or an I/O device. The addressed I/O device or memory should use this signal to gate data onto the CPU data bus.

$\overline{\mathrm{WR}}$ (memory write) Tri-state output, active low. $\overline{\mathrm{WR}}$ indicates that the CPU data bus holds valid data to be stored in the addressed memory or I/O device.

$\overline{\mathrm{RFSH}}$ (refresh) Output, active low. $\overline{\mathrm{RFSH}}$ indicates that the lower seven bits of the address bus contain a refresh address for dynamic memories and current $\overline{\mathrm{MREQ}}$ signal should be used to do a refresh read to all dynamic memories. A7 is a logic zero and the upper eight bits of the address bus contains the I Register.

HALT (halt state) Output, active low. HALT indicates that the CPU has executed a HALT software instruction and is awaiting either a non-maskable or a maskable interrupt (with the mask enabled) before operation can resume. While halted, the CPU executes NOPs to maintain memory-refresh activity.

WAIT* (wait) Input, active low. WAIT indicates to the Z80 CPU that the addressed memory or I/O devices are not ready for a data transfer. The CPU continues to enter wait states for as long as this signal is active. This signal allows memory or I/O devices of any speed to be synchronised to the CPU.

INT (interrupt request) Input, active low. The interrupt request signal is generated by I/O devices. A request will be honoured at the end of the current instruction if the internal software-controlled interrupt enable flip-flop (IFF) is enabled and if the BUSRQ signal is not active. When the CPU accepts the interrupt, an acknowledge signal (IORQ during M1 time) is sent out at the beginning of the next instruction cycle. The CPU can respond to an interrupt in three different modes.

NMI Input, negative edge triggered. The non-maskable interrupt request line has a higher priority than INT and is always recognised at the end of the current instruction, independent of the status of the interrupt-enable flip-flop. NMI automatically forces the Z80 CPU to restart to location 0066H. The program counter is automatically saved in the external stack so that the user can return to the program that was interrupted. Note that continuous WAIT cycles can prevent the current instruction from ending, and that a BUSRQ will override an NMI.

RESET Input, active low. RESET forces the program counter to zero and initialises the CPU. The CPU initialisation includes:

(1) Disable the interrupt enable flip-flop
(2) Set Register I = 00H
(3) Set Register R = 00H
(4) Set Interrupt Mode 0

During reset time, the address bus and data bus go to a high-impedance state and all control output signals go to the inactive state. No refresh occurs.

BUSRQ (bus request) Input, active low. The bus request signal is used to request the CPU address bus, data bus and tri-state output control signals to go to a high-impedance state so that other devices can control these buses. When BUSRQ is activated, the CPU will set these buses to a high-impedance state as soon as the current CPU machine cycle is terminated.

BUSAK* (bus acknowledge) Output, active low. Bus acknowledge is used to indicate to the requesting device that the CPU address bus, data bus and tri-state control bus signals have been set to their high-impedance state and the external device can now control these signals.

Φ Single-phase system clock.

* While the Z80 CPU is in either a WAIT state or a bus acknowledge condition, dynamic memory refresh will not occur.

The 6802/8 microprocessor

A0–A15 (address bus—outputs) These lines constitute a typical 16-way MPU address bus, used by the MPU to address memory and I/O devices.

D0–D7 (data bus—bidirectional) These eight lines are two-way data highways through which the MPU reads in and writes out data from and to memory and I/O devices. These lines are capable of going into the tri-state mode to allow other devices to control the bus.

HALT (input) This level-sensitive input halts all MPU activity at the end of the current instruction, when taken to the low state. The BA line goes high, VMA goes low, and the address bus holds the

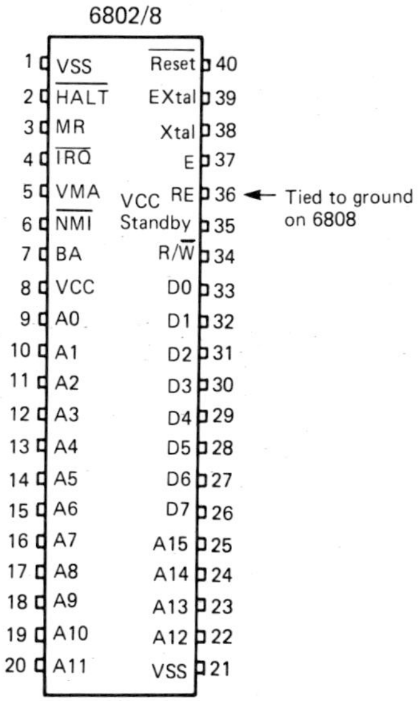

Fig. A4.5 6802/8 pin assignment

address of the next instruction. This line should be tied high when not in use.

R/W (output) This line signals the direction of travel of data along the data bus.

VMA (valid memory address—output) This indicates to external devices the presence of a valid address on the address bus. VMA allows the activities of external devices to achieve synchronisation with the working of the MPU.

BA (bus available—output) This line signals to external circuitry that the MPU has entered a state whereby the bus lines are available for control by the external devices.

IRQ (interrupt request—input) This line allows the MPU to be interrupted by external devices, if the MPU's internal interrupt-mask bit is not set.

RESET (input) This line is used to restart the MPU, from a power-down or runaway condition, in a predictable and controlled manner.

NMI (non-maskable interrupt—input) This is similar to IRQ, but is unconditional—it cannot be masked.

EXTAL and XTAL (inputs) These pins allow an external clock to be attached to the MPU. Alternatively, the internal clock generator may be utilised by attaching a crystal to these pins.

Memory ready (input) This input allows external devices to stop the MPU without losing any data for an integral number of clock cycles. This is similar to the Z80 'WAIT' line, and may be used, for instance, to give slow memory devices or peripherals time to respond.

E (enable—output) This is the clock for the MPU and the whole system. The E line is a common 6800-family chip signal.

VCC standby (6802 only—input) This is a separate power-supply pin for the internal RAM of the 6802, and may be used to retain the memory contents when the MPU is powered down.

The 1802 microprocessor

BUS 0 to BUS 7 (data bus) Eight-bit directional data-bus lines. These lines are used for transferring data between the memory, the microprocessor, and I/O devices.

N0 to N2 (I/O lines) Activated by an I/O instruction to signal the I/O control logic of a data transfer between memory and I/O interface.

EF1 to EF4 (flags) These inputs enable the I/O controllers to transfer status information to the processor. The levels can be tested by the conditional branch instructions.

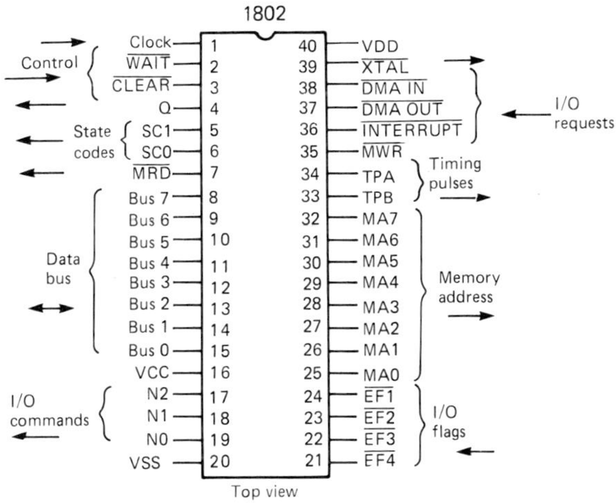

Fig. A4.6 1802 terminal assignment

INTERRUPT, DMA-IN, DMA-OUT (I/O requests) These inputs are sampled by the CDP 1802 during the interval between the leading edge of TPB and the leading edge of TPA.

Interrupt action: X and P are stored in T after executing current instruction; designator X is set to 2; designator P is set to 1; interrupt enable is reset to 0 (inhibit); and instruction execution is resumed. The interrupt action requires one machine cycle (S3).

DMA action: finish executing current instruction; R(0) points to memory area for data transfer; data is loaded into or read out of memory; and increment R(0).

Note: in the event of concurrent DMA and INTERRUPT requests, DMA-IN has priority followed by DMA-OUT and then INTERRUPT

SCO, SC1 (state code lines) These outputs indicate that the CPU is: (1) fetching an instruction, or (2) executing an instruction, or (3) processing a DMA request, or (4) acknowledging an interrupt request. The levels of state code are tabulated below. All states are valid at TPA. H = VCC, L = VSS.

	State code lines	
State type	SC1	SC0
S0 (fetch)	L	L
S1 (execute)	L	H
S2 (DMA)	H	L
S3 (interrupt)	H	H

TPA, TPB (timing pulses) Positive pulses that occur once in each machine cycle (TPB follows TPA). They are used by I/O controllers to interpret codes and to time interaction with the data bus. The trailing edge of TPA is used by the memory system to latch the higher-order byte of the 16-bit memory address. TPA is suppressed in IDLE when the CPU is in the load mode.

MA0 to MA7 (memory address lines) In each cycle, the higher-order byte of a 16-bit memory address appears on the memory address lines MA0–7 first. Those bits required by the memory system can be strobed into external address latches by timing pulse TPA. The low-order byte of the 16-bit address appears on the address lines after the termination of TPA. Latching of all eight higher-order address bits would permit a memory system of 64K bytes.

$\overline{\text{MWR}}$ (write pulse) A negative pulse appearing in a memory-write cycle, after the address lines have stabilised.

$\overline{\text{MRD}}$ (read level) A low level on $\overline{\text{MRD}}$ indicates a memory-read cycle. It can be used to control tri-state outputs from the addressed memory which may have a common data input and output bus. If a memory does not have a tri-state high-impedance output, $\overline{\text{MRD}}$ is useful for driving memory/bus separator gates. It is also used to indicate the direction of data transfer during an I/O instruction.

Q Single-bit output from the CPU which can be set or reset under program control. During SEQ or REQ instruction execution. Q is set or reset between the trailing edge of TPA and the leading edge of TPB.

CLOCK Input for externally generated single-phase clock. A typical clock frequency is 6.4 MHz at VCC = VDD = 10 volts. The clock is counted down internally to eight clock pulses per machine cycle.

$\overline{\text{XTAL}}$ Connection to be used with clock input terminal, for an external crystal, if the on-chip oscillator is utilised. The crystal is connected between terminals 1 and 39 (CLOCK and $\overline{\text{XTAL}}$) in parallel with a resistance (10 megohms typically). Frequency-trimming capacitors may be required at terminals 1 and 39.

$\overline{\text{WAIT}}$, $\overline{\text{CLEAR}}$ (control lines) Provide four control modes as listed in the following truth table.

$\overline{\text{CLEAR}}$	$\overline{\text{WAIT}}$	Mode
L	L	Load
L	H	Reset
H	L	Pause
H	H	Run

The functions of the modes are defined in the text.

Pause Stops the internal CPU timing generator on the first negative high-to-low transition of the input clock. The oscillator continues to operate, but subsequent clock transitions are ignored.

Run May be initiated from the pause or reset mode functions. If initiated from pause, the CPU resumes operation on the first negative high-to-low transition of the input clock. When initiated from the reset operation, the first machine cycle following reset is always the initialisation cycle. The initialisation cycle is then followed by a DMA (S2) cycle or fetch (S0) from location 0000 in memory.

VDD, VSS, VCC (power levels) The internal voltage supply VDD is isolated from the input/output voltage supply VCC so that the processor may operate at maximum speed while interfacing with various external circuit technologies, including TTL at 5 volts. VCC must be less than or equal to VDD. All outputs swing from VSS to VCC. The recommended input voltage swing is VSS to VCC.

Bibliography

The list of books given here is of a very general nature, and not just concerned with the topics discussed in this book. They are works which have been found useful or interesting in the past. In order to purchase the semiconductor companies' data manuals mentioned below, it will be necessary to find a distributor of the ICs involved. The best sources of information on distributors are undoubtedly the electronic engineering and computing magazines.

Aspinall, D. (ed.), *The Microprocessor and its Application* (Cambridge University Press)
This book is very expensive and highly academic in its approach. It cannot be regarded as a practical book, and is not recommended. However, it is interesting for its first chapter which is written by Wesley A. Clark on the subject of the technology of integrated circuit techniques. If the reader is interested in this aspect of the subject, it is one of the most readable accounts of the technology from semiconductors to LSI chips which can be found.

Burskey, Dave, *The S-100 Bus Handbook*
This book takes the reader through a number of topics in MPUs, and ends by giving a very large number of circuit diagrams for S100 boards manufactured in the USA. It provides a certain amount of useful source-data for design, though it is rather out of date.

Fairchild F6800 Programming Manual
Fairchild second-sources the 6800, and their programming manual is well set out and very useful for reference while programming the 6800 from any source.

Garland, Harry, *Introduction to Microprocessor System Design* (McGraw-Hill)
Useful for background material on MPUs.

Lancaster, Don, *TTL Cook Book* and *CMOS Cook Book* (Howard W. Sams and Co. Inc.)

These books describe, in a readable form, the theory and use of logic chips of the TTL and CMOS families. They are excellent both for learning from scratch, and for constant reference. They are easy to find in technical bookshops and IC suppliers.

Lesea, A., and Zaks, R., *Microprocessor Interfacing Techniques* (Sybex)
This book is an excellent reference work on MPUs and their interfacing to the outside world. In places the authors attempt to explain some very complex concepts in too small a space, but in general this is one of the most highly recommended books of its kind.

Millman, Jacob, *Microelectronics: Digital and Analogue Circuits and Systems* (McGraw-Hill)
This book provides an excellent and very complete reference work on modern electronics. It contains a large amount of excellent design and explanatory data for the practising electronic engineer. Its use to the MPU system designer is in providing the essential background material for peripherals and the general electronics required in such fields as I/O peripherals. However, it does not cover MPUs themselves.

Mostek Memory Data Book & Designer's Guide
This book should be available from Mostek distributors and is continually updated.

Mostek Z80 Microcomputer Devices Technical Manuals
This range comes as grey A4-sized soft-covered books. They are some of the best works yet discovered covering the Z80. The one entitled *MK 3880 Central Processing Unit* covers the Z80 itself, and is highly recommended. Mostek second-source the Z80 family, and their data in general is excellent and highly readable. Again, these books are available from Mostek distributors.

Motorola 6800 Applications Manual
This is an early but complete manual on the 6800, including information on how to use the 6800 and its early peripherals in applications. Such applications as bar-code wand interfacing, with software, are described. The book is partly out-of-date as it does not include the latest devices, and is not very well set out.

Motorola Microprocessors Data Manual
This book is updated from time to time, and contains, primarily, data sheets on all their MPU products and peripheral chips. The 6800 family, including the 6809, features prominently. The book also contains data on the 3870 and the 68000.

National Semiconductors Data Books
Same comments as for Texas Instruments.

Osborne Books
This range of books is published in the USA, and provides a full, if rather expensive, reference work which is continually being updated by the addition of full data sheets for new products. These books try to form a readable roundup of all the knowledge on MPUs and related peripherals. They are often more readable than the data sheets from manufacturers, but should not be used to replace them in critical design situations. They are acknowledged to form an important addition to any library on MPUs, and certainly form an excellent complement to manufacturers' data sheets. They are published by Osborne and Associates Inc., Berkeley, California, and are very widely available at computer shops and MPU distributors.

RCA User Manual for the CDP1802 Cosmac Microprocessor
This manual is a very good example of an MPU manual. It is very well set out, and explains the 1802's working in an easily read and logical form.

RCA 1802 Data Sheets, File no. 1023
This is a shortened version of the above.

Texas Instruments Data Books
Texas Instruments publish a very large number of excellent data books on integrated circuits—the TTL book is particularly well set out. These are available from distributors of Texas chips.

Zilog Microprocessor Applications Reference Book Vol. 1
Published in July 1981, this book should be available through Zilog distributors. It covers a wide range of applications, including the 16-bit Z8000 devices. The section on dynamic RAM interfacing deals only with 4K and 16K devices, but the timing is the same as for 64K RAMs.

Index

Index

Index